CRIP AUTHORSHIP

Crip Authorship

Disability as Method

Edited by

Mara Mills *and* Rebecca Sanchez

NEW YORK UNIVERSITY PRESS

New York

NEW YORK UNIVERSITY PRESS
New York
www.nyupress.org

Frontispiece: *Two Spirit Yarning* (2017), Paul Constable Calcott, Australian First Peoples Wiradjuri Nation, artist living with disability. Hotpinkgoanna.com. *Two Spirit Yarning* talks about the intersectionality of disabled First Nations People who identify as LGBTIQ+, and how the introduction of Western religion and values have impacted traditional cultural perspectives. Yarning is sharing stories, having a conversation. *Image description*: The artwork is predominantly in pink hues using the traditional dotting-style artwork of Australian Aboriginal culture. There is a rainbow path running through the center of the art work with Aboriginal symbols that represent people and community groups.

Please contact the Library of Congress for Cataloging-in-Publication data.
ISBN: 9781479819355 (hardback)
ISBN: 9781479819362 (paperback)
ISBN: 9781479819386 (library ebook)
ISBN: 9781479819379 (consumer ebook)

New York University Press books are printed on acid-free paper, and their binding materials are chosen for strength and durability. We strive to use environmentally responsible suppliers and materials to the greatest extent possible in publishing our books.

Manufactured in the United States of America

10 9 8 7 6 5 4 3 2 1

Also available as an ebook

CONTENTS

CRIP AUTHORSHIP

Introduction: On Crip Authorship and Disability as Method

MARA MILLS AND REBECCA SANCHEZ

We kept two books nearby while writing this introduction. Two blue books: hospital blue, code blue, wheelchair symbol blue. Blue like the benches installed in galleries and inhospitable public spaces by disability artist Finnegan Shannon, *Do You Want Us Here or Not?* (2018–present) (figure I.1). Two blue softcover books with queer trim sizes. If "blue books" are traditionally almanacs and manuals, we took ours to be guides to crip authorship.

The Clearing by JJJJJerome Ellis is 10" × 13". Big for a paperback and hard to hold in one hand. The book is a transcription of an experimental album: jazz, electronics, and spoken word. Each page equals sixty seconds of playback. The music and other sounds on the album are described in the book with italicized text. When Ellis speaks it is also transcribed, and his stutters are "rendered in real time on the page" (Ellis 2021, xi). Ellis plays with typography to represent stuttering and to design the time of reading. There are two shades of type, dark and light; irregular capitalization and spacing; and repeated letters and words. What happens when we read (with) a stutter?

Ellis says that stuttering and other dysfluencies are ways to pause, expand, and break up time, to resist temporal standardization and regulation. "Dysfluencies are gifts of ellipsis," he writes. "Lacuna. Caesura. Aporia. Opacity" (Ellis 2020, 226). A stutter's "interval of silence" is filled with possibility. Ellis theorizes dysfluency alongside Blackness and music, as forces that "open time." In a context of "temporal subjection"—a defining feature of capitalist society, more or less severely administered among social groups—these forces offer "temporal refusal, temporal escape, temporal dissent" (Ellis 2020, 216). Ellis's typography suggests, but does not dictate, temporality for the reader. We do what we will with the words and the pages, but we meet him in the clearing his voice and typography create.

In the page reproduced in figure I.2, Ellis cites (recites) the eighteenth-century German philosopher Novalis: "Jede Krankheit is ein musikalisches Problem" (Every illness is a musical problem). There is a strand of theory that understands disability to be a creative force, a spur, a method of production. The mismatch between disabled bodyminds and built and social environments leads to particular crip ways of thinking, being, representing, and making. Tobin Siebers explains the connection between disability and method like this: "The disabled

Figure I.1. Finnegan Shannon, *Do You Want Us Here or Not (MMK)*, 2021. Production by Jack Brennon, Julia Eichler, Finnegan Shannon, Mikael Fransson, Patrick Keaveney, Zabotka S. Palm, and Daniel Sarvari. Photo by Axel Schneider for Museum MMK für Moderne Kunst, Frankfurt am Main.

Image description: A cushioned bench with big text running across it that reads, "It was hard to get here. Rest here if you agree." The text is hand-painted and a little uneven. White letters in a field of vibrant blue.

body changes the process of representation itself. Blind hands envision faces of old acquaintances. Deaf eyes listen to public television. Tongues touch-type letters home to Mom and Dad. Feet wash the breakfast dishes. Mouths sign autographs. Different bodies require and create new modes of representation" (Siebers 2008, 54).

In "Crip Technoscience Manifesto," Aimi Hamraie and Kelly Fritsch more strongly urge a crip approach to making and unmaking, *crip* referring to "the noncompliant, anti-assimilationist position that disability is a desirable part of the world." In the realm of technical creation, they emphasize "practices of critique, alteration, and reinvention of our material-discursive world" (Hamraie and Fritsch 2019, 2). We start along a similar desire path to consider crip *authorship* as an aesthetic, felt, and performed phenomenon, as well as a media-technical one. *How does disability shape authorship?* This question takes individuals and collectives into account, bodyminds and communities of discourse. Crip authorship, in one register, transgresses the rules of authorship. In another, it refers to crip forms and composition practices. It can be "unpublishable" or it can alter conventions. As important as outcomes and products are disability experiences, the temporalities and affects of authorship.[1]

Is crip authorship always agential, successful? Is it necessarily *creative*—can it accommodate destruction and loss? Our second blue book does not let us forget that there is no crip standard time and no universalizing when it comes to disability. Shulamith Firestone's *Airless Spaces* is almost a pocket book. It was almost

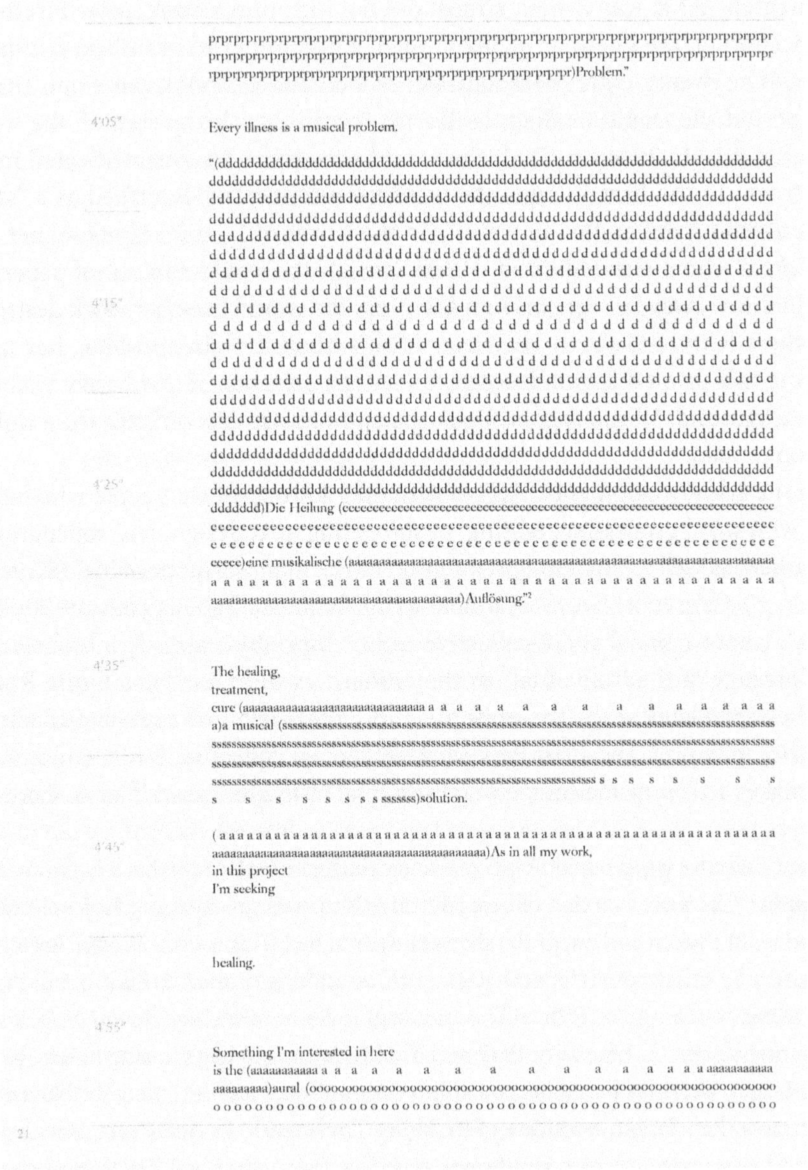

prprprprprprprprprprprprprprprprprprprprprprprprprprprprprprprprprprprprprprprprprprprprprpr
prprprprprprprprprprprprprprprprprprprprprprprprprprprprprprprprprprprprprprprprprprprprprpr
rprprprprprprprprprprprprprprprprprprprprprprprprprpr)Problem."

4'05"

Every illness is a musical problem.

"(ddddddddddddddddddddddddddddddddddddddddddddddddddddddddddddddddddddddddddddddddddddddddddd
ddddddddddddddddddddddddddddddddddddddddddddddddddddddddddddddddddddddddddddddddddddddddddddd
ddddddddddddddddddddddddddddddddddddddddddddddddddddddddddddddddddddddddddddddddddddddddddddd
dddddddddddddddddddddddddddddddddddddddddddddddddddddddddddddddddddddddddddddddddddddddddddd
ddddddddddddddddddddddddddddddddddddddddddddddddddddddddddddddddddddddddddddddddddddddddddd
dddddddddddddddddddddddddddddddddddddddddddddddddddddddddddddddddddddddddddddddddddddddddd
dddddddddddddddddddddddddddddddddddddddddddddddddddddddddddddddddddddddddddddddddddddddd
ddddddddddddddddddddddddddddddddddddddddddddddddddddddddddddddddddddddddddddddddddddd
ddddddddddddddddddddddddddddddddddddddddddddddddddddddddddddddddddddddddddddddddddd
dddddddddddddddddddddddddddddddddddddddddddddddddddddddddddddddddddddddddddddddd
dddddddddddddddddddddddddddddddddddddddddddddddddddddddddddddddddddddddddddddd
ddddddddddddddddddddddddddddddddddddddddddddddddddddddddddddddddddddddddddddd
dddddddddddddddddddddddddddddddddddddddddddddddddddddddddddddddddddddddddddddd
ddddddddddddddddddddddddddddddddddddddddddddddddddddddddddddddddddddddddddddddddd
dddddddddddddddddddddddddddddddddddddddddddddddddddddddddddddddddddddddddddddddddd
ddddddddddddddddddddddddddddddddddddddddddddddddddddddddddddddddddddddddddddddddddd
ddddddddddddddddddddddddddddddddddddddddddddddddddddddddddddddddddddddddddddddddddddd
ddddddd)Die Heilung (eeeeeeeeeeeeeeeeeeeeeeeeeeeeeeeeeeeeeeeeeeeeeeeeeeeeeeeeeeeeeeeeeeeeeeeeee
eeeeeeeeeeeeeeeeeeeeeeeeeeeeeeeeeeeeeeeeeeeeeeeeeeeeeeeeeeeeeeeeeeeeeeeeeeeeeeeeeeeeeeeeeeeeee
e e e e e e e e e e e e e e e e e e e e e e e e e e e e e e e e e e e e e e e e e e e e e e e e
eeeee)eine musikalische (aaaaaaaaaaaaaaaaaaaaaaaaaaaaaaaaaaaaaaaaaaaaaaaaaaaaaaaaaaaaaaaaaaaa
a a a a a a a a a a a a a a a a a a a a a a a a a a a a a a a a a a a a a a a a a a a a a a
aaaaaaaaaaaaaaaaaaaaaaaaaaaaaaaaaaaaaaaaaaaa)Auflösung."

4'35"

The healing,
treatment,
cure (aaaaaaaaaaaaaaaaaaaaaaaaaaaaaa a a a a a a a a a a a a a a a a a a
a)a musical (sssssssssssssssssssssssssssssssssssssssssssssssssssssssssssssssssssssssssssssssssssssssss
sssssssssssssssssssssssssssssssssssssssssssssssssssssssssssssssssssssssssssssssssssssssssssssss
sssssssssssssssssssssssssssssssssssssssssssssssssssssssssssssssssssssssssssssssssssssssssssssss
ssssssssssssssssssssssssssssssssssssssssssssssssssss s s s s s s s s
s s s s s s s sssssss)solution.

(a a a a a a a a a a a a a a a a a a a a a a a a a a a a a a a a a a a a a a a a a a a a a a a a a a
aaaaaaaaaaaaaaaaaaaaaaaaaaaaaaaaaaaaaaaaaaaaaaaa)As in all my work,
in this project
I'm seeking

healing.

4'55"

Something I'm interested in here
is the (aaaaaaaaaa a a a a a a a a a a a a a a a a a a a a a a a aaaaaaaaaa
aaaaaaaaa)aural (oooooooooooooooooooooooooooooooooooooooooooooooooooooooooooooooooooooooooooo
o o o o o o o o o o o o o o o o o o o o o o o o o o o o o o o o o o o o o o o o o o o o o o o

Figure I.2. JJJJJerome Ellis, page from *The Clearing* (Wendy's Subway, 2021). Courtesy of the artist and Wendy's Subway.

Image description: A page from *The Clearing* transcribing Ellis saying, "Every illness is a musical problem. 'Die Heilung eine musikalische Auflösung.' The healing, treatment, cure, a musical solution. As in all my work, in this project I'm seeking healing." When Ellis stutters, it is represented by a letter (*d, e, a*) repeating with various spacings across and down the page.

their copyright over to a publisher, as some of us have done in this book, but otherwise they control the reproduction, display, and distribution of the work. Through copyright, the work can become a commodity from which an author and a publisher profit.

Although we had been using *author* and *authorship* in a colloquial way as we began planning this collection—to refer to writing or composition across many fields and formats, along with the publishing process—we quickly ran up against the blockades of the western legal definition. We learned the hard way that copyright is ableist. In the legal sense, crip authorship can seem like an impossibility or, at best, a contradiction in terms. Who is allowed to be an author? To own intellectual property? Who has the right to copyright? When French philosopher Michel Foucault asked, "What is an author?" in 1969, he urged scholars to consider the contexts and "modes of existence" (Foucault 1998, 205) of authorship rather than the psychology or standpoints of individual authors. Ruminating on "the author function," he asked, "Who can appropriate it for himself?" (222). Few (if any) subsequent critics have reckoned with the foundational exclusion of many disabled people from legal authorship.

People with mental and cognitive disabilities who are subject to guardianship—a phenomenon recently brought to widespread attention by pop star Britney Spears—are "stripped of legal personhood," often including property rights (Kohn and Koss 2016). To publish *Crip Authorship*, all of the writers were required to sign standard contracts with New York University Press granting the publisher copyright, among other things. Yet some of our participants did not have the legal right to do this, or even to choose without guardian consent whether to be named as the authors of their own words. We were reminded that some people are permanently excluded, and do not have the choice to oppose assimilation. Other participants could not accept the stipends we offered for their work, and would not have been able to receive royalties, because of Supplemental Security Income restrictions. Some of us are, and are not, *authors*.

Foucault, citing Beckett, also asked in his critique of the author function, "What difference does it make who is speaking?" (1998, 222). Many of the chapters in this collection do not take this question to be rhetorical. They attend to the personal and to particular social and linguistic worlds, if not the "new modes of representation" manifested by disabled bodyminds. Yet we also hold space here for crip anonymity. Not the anonymity imposed by ableist societies that render disabled people invisible, nor the disability anonymity required for passing and assimilation (which are often survival skills), but a desired giving-away of the author function, a calling-in of networks, collectives, crip pseudonyms, fluctuating selves, and impersonality (Cox 2013; see also Hickman, this volume, on nondisclosure).

We further learned that for a work to be copyrighted—for legal authorship to be granted—it must be "fixed in a tangible medium of expression" (US

Copyright Office, n.d.). It must take a form that can be copied: a page, an audio-tape, a digital format. Not all crip composition can be accommodated within the commodity version of authorship. When, for instance, does a Protactile work become copyrightable? In other words, *what is a Protactile author?* John Lee Clark, in his chapter, models the translation and description of this DeafBlind language as it moves between media. Protactile can be filmed or transcribed—copyrightable formats—but it cannot truly be "fixed" by a visual medium. Clark's chapter describes a Protactile composition that is *tangible* in a way conventional media are not.

Copyright and the legal definition of authorship have also barred disabled readers. When copyright holders control publication, alteration, and distribution under a for-profit model, formats such as Braille (i.e., for small "markets") are not often produced. The lack of accessible publications is often described as "a book famine," language that marshals development and charity rhetoric to call attention to what should simply be a compliance, if not justice, issue (National Library Service for the Blind and Print Disabled 2020). The American Library Association (n.d.) points to a "disconnect between the accessibility mandates in federal law and the limits imposed by the copyright law." Even the fair use exception to copyright law only allows a fraction (usually 10 percent) of a book or other work to be adapted and copied without permission from the author or owner of copyright.

In the U.S., the 1997 Chafee Amendment was meant to resolve this disconnect by providing a "disability exception" to copyright, but the American Library Association underscores the amendment's continued inadequacies: "The Chafee Amendment only permits printed books to be translated into certain named specialized formats: Braille, digital text, and audio. Large print, for example, is notably absent from the list of specialized formats. . . . Additionally, the Chafee Amendment provides only for a literal translation of the book, so additional supports that would likely be used for students with learning disabilities (such as abridged versions, prompts, definitions, etc.) would not be permitted" (American Library Association, n.d.). "Certification" of print disability is required for someone to request electronic files or translated or adapted materials from a library, school, or publisher, yet this category is not clearly defined and an ever-growing number of disability groups have petitioned to be included. (Mills, 2012, has called formats that require such certification "prescription media.") Significant delays in obtaining reformatted books and other copyrighted materials also result from strictures on who is allowed to adapt them—namely, a handful of government and nonprofit groups.

Given the topic of *Crip Authorship* and the many reading modes of our own authors, we asked the Press to make an open access (OA) version available along with the print book and eBook. Each digital platform for the paid electronic version, from JSTOR to Kindle, has its own accessibility issues, and certain steps like

Braille Ready file formatting for text-to-Braille translators are often overlooked. It can also take publishers weeks to respond to requests for accessible scans, electronic files, or html alternatives that can be used with Braille or speech output screen readers. Although OA versions aren't instantaneously accessible if web content accessibility guidelines aren't followed, they are immediately free and available online. More than one press quoted $10,000–$15,000 to us as the industry standard for simultaneous OA and commercial editions; hence an additional step or two of grant writing, for OA and Braille Ready publication subventions, is often a feature of crip authorship.[2]

It's no wonder that disability piracy is on the rise. Crip piracy ranges from digital text and sound recordings to assistive technology software itself. Screen readers like JAWS, Priyank Chandra has shown, are themselves proprietary rather than open source, and they are prohibitively expensive for most users, especially in the Global South. From Peru to India, assistive software piracy is "an act of self-making" and a necessary reclamation of control from accessibility tech corporations that in fact erect new barriers for disabled people around the world (Chandra 2020, 1–2). As Kavita Philip argues, the author function is always attended by the pirate function: "At the very historical moment that technological authorship seems to become widely accessible, the law marks off certain authorial spaces as transgressive" (2005, 207).

Unlike *authorship* (and, for that matter, *disability*), *crip* does not have a legal definition; it is not a term under which people make legal or rights-based claims. *Crip* signals community affiliation and political resistance. Although *crip* can indicate disability, as Robert McRuer notes in this volume, crip theory "is also always particularly interested in that which is in *excess* of an able-bodied/disabled binary." In use since the early twentieth century as a shortening of the offensive term *cripple*, *crip* (sometimes spelled with a *k*, as Leroy F. Moore Jr. and Keith Jones discuss in their chapter) has more recently been reclaimed by disability activist and justice communities to indicate people, relationships, and behaviors existing outside bodymind norms within a given society, and connected by those experiences.

As a term gesturing toward a large collective, and sometimes a more deliberate coalition, *crip* does not necessarily index a particular disabled person's (or disabled group's) experiences. In recognition of the vitality of particulars, the authors in this book use many words in addition to *crip* and *authorship* as they discuss the processes of making and communicating, including *blind*, *deaf*, *autistic*, *contingent*, *chronically ill*, and *mad*. They discuss lived experiences including caste (Islam and Jana), gender and gender identity (Awkward-Rich), and violence and injury (Ralph) that have ambivalent relations to disability. Each of these terms is its own internally diverse constellation. Authors in this collection also reckon with translation (McRuer on *disca*); critique English-language imperialism (Nguyen on the transnationalization of western discourse via the

United Nations); and consider Indigenous, Black feminist, and other genealogies for the field of disability studies and its concepts (Deerinwater; Bowen, Kuo, and Mills). They write about writing, but disabled composition has always exceeded writing, and disabled people are sometimes excluded from conventional reading and writing techniques.

Although we alternately use the terms *crip* and *disability* in our introduction, depending on context, we take Aimi Hamraie's counsel that "*crip* is not a synonym for *disability*, nor is it simply a political orientation. Rather, it is a specific commitment to shifting material arrangements" (this volume). The shifting of material arrangements, through being and doing, is directly tied to unjust, inaccessible conditions that need to be understood as part of its context. As Patty Berne, cofounder of Sins Invalid, writes, "Crip life invites us into fierce creativity. Because the world continues to treat us as worthless, creating new worlds is a matter of survival for us. Dreaming is a matter of survival" (Berne 2021, 9).

Crip Authorship is about avenues of that fierce creativity, dreamed and enacted. In some contexts, this work involves celebrating people, experiences, and methods that have been obscured; in others it involves protest and dismantling. It can mean innovating around accessibility and crip worldmaking, or attending to the false starts, dead ends, and failures resulting from misfit and oppression. Often it is all of these / and. We've taken the tensions inherent in the phrase "crip authorship" as provocations to explore the shaping of authorship by disability, whether that has to do with modality, access, language, organization, collaboration, funding, translation, or dissemination. In other words, we take disability as method, beyond content and author function.

Disability scholars began using the phrase "disability as method" across several disciplines in the 2010s, although similar ideas had previously circulated in academic and activist spaces using different language. We convene those theories here. In a 2014 collection published in Slovenia, Arseli Dokumaci asked "whether there could be ways of approaching disability as a methodology; modes of considering the disabled body as something to think with rather than to think about" (108). She followed up in 2018 with an article in *Disability Studies Quarterly* titled "Disability as Method," demonstrating "the new possibilities of media-making informed by blindness gain." In literary and cultural studies, *Lateral* published a conversation in 2016–2017 between Julie Avril Minich, Jina B. Kim, and Sami Schalk in which Minich (2016) asked that scholars reframe disability studies as a methodology rather than a subject, and Kim (2017) replied that disability itself should be shifted "from *noun*—an identity one can occupy—to *verb*: a critical methodology." Also in 2017, Jonathan Sterne and Mara Mills published a coda ("Dismediation") for the anthology *Disability Media Studies* in which they considered the ways "disability as method" was sometimes a formula appropriated by industry: "Dismediation takes disability as method, not simply as content for media studies. . . . We scrutinize the ways disability has been deployed as a routine, program, or resource in the history of technology. We work toward digital justice, which may take the forms of cripped or minor media or of mainstream access" (368). In other words, disability and disabled people may be enrolled in a wide range of methodological and political pursuits, underscoring the need for the related term, *crip*. Mills first presented this discussion of "disability as method" at the Queer Method conference held at the University of Pennsylvania, a set of conversations grounded in queer theory and transgender studies that influenced her and Sterne's thinking on the topic (Queer Method, 2013).

An understanding of disability as method has recently animated a range of other conversations, including Moya Bailey and Izetta Autumn Mobley's analysis of Black Feminist methodology (2018); Jess Waggoner and Ashley Mog's special issue of the *Journal of Feminist Scholarship*, "Visionary Politics and Methods in Feminist Disability Studies" (2020); a special issue of *Curriculum Inquiry* titled "Disability as Meta Curriculum," edited by Nirmala Erevelles, Elizabeth J. Grace, and Gillian Parekh (2019); and a special issue of the *South Atlantic Quarterly* titled "Disorienting Disability," edited by Michele Friedner and Karen Weingarten (2019). In their introduction to that issue, Friedner and Weingarten note that "disability as method helps to avoid the sedimentation of disability as a category since it allows us to place disability in conversation with other concepts and worlds" (2019, 485). Disability can be a method in situations seemingly remote from disability, as in *Disability Aesthetics* (2010), when Tobin Siebers reads classic sculpture and modern art through a disability lens.

Disability as method is also related to "cripistemology," Merri Lisa Johnson and Robert McRuer's term for disabled ways of thinking, knowing, and telling. Cripistemology "extends *beyond* disability" and makes room for "negativity, failure, hopelessness, and passivity" (Johnson and McRuer 2014, 142, 127).[3] Crip authorship spans knowing, making, style, and media formats, but—keeping cripistemology in mind—it is not always about *making it*. Cripping is not a technical protocol and it does not always "work." Where crip authorship meets media and technology, or publishing and the commodity version of authorship, it encounters the foundation of those tools and industries in the "ideology of ability" (Siebers 2008, 7). Moreover, authorship is durational and has phases (a term we prefer to *stage*), sketched by the sections that follow, each with distinct affective and political registers.

Crip Authorship is organized into five sections that emerged in dialogue with the authors. Many of the chapters serve as expositions of methods for which the authors are known. The chapters have been created in a range of registers and styles reflecting the diversity of disability authorship. They are written by scholars, activists, journalists, artists, librarians, and archivists. Although most of the contributions were written for publication as chapters in this volume, we also include an edited group chat, song lyrics, a description of a Protactile poem, and examples of crip graphic design (immediately following this introduction). One author, Louise Hickman, theorizes transcription as a crip assemblage that challenges the "will" and visibility of authorship—different kinds of transcripts, from Communication Access Realtime Translation (CART) to a transcript of a podcast, appear throughout this volume. Our frontispiece, *Two Spirit Yarning* by Paul Constable-Calcott, is a rendition of an Indigenous Australian storytelling and information-sharing practice (yarning). Each section also contains a chapter previously published online that we preserve here in print (and ebook) form. We have produced a book, but we recognize how much crip authorship exists beyond the market, beyond exchange, as a gift, for a collective, or for an audience of one.

We open with writing, perhaps the most commonly understood sense of authorship, which we take to span numerous modes of composition. This section expands on disability rhetoric (Dolmage, 2014; Yergeau, 2017) to consider the temporality and affect of writing, as well as diction, performance, and labor. Many authors refer to the political economy of writing in K-12 classrooms and universities, from tracking and standardizing to what Travis Chi Wing Lau describes as the ableism of academic "hyper-productivity" (Lau, 2019). The ways we compose language are tied intimately to our bodyminds and cultural norms, from how we arrange words to the styles we choose or invent; from writing in more than one language to counterstorytelling (Padilla, this volume); from the ways we relate to writing partners or collectives to the networks of care, relation, finances, and access that surround us and enable (or don't) writing to take place.

Often it is "writ[ing] for/with each other" that facilitates crip composition, as Mel Y. Chen and Alison Kafer describe it, embedding a coauthored fragment within each other's chapters (see also Isolation Nation and Ginsburg and Rapp, this volume). The authors in this section highlight the logistics of what Leah Lakshmi Piepzna-Samarasinha describes as "time-honored crip creative practice" (2018, 17), the material components necessary for it to occur, and the ways those differ from person to person. They discuss racism, migration, ableism, and education or employment; standards of grammar and rationality (Bruce on "mad black rants," this volume); the power that a slip of writing from a teacher or psychologist can wield over our life chances. Crip writing practices also include practices of not writing, recognized by Mimi Khúc in the opening chapter.

The next section takes on research methods and politics, specifically the access tools and disability justice–informed methods that scaffold work in disability studies. Chapters examine topics ranging from reading methods to community-based participatory research, with some scholars taking up existing methods and others devising new ones.[4] The authors in this section are trained in literature, social work, history, education, anthropology, sociology, and science and technology studies, each field deserving its own disability methods handbook. With our focus on authorship, we don't promise to be comprehensive, but we tackle cross-cutting themes such as collaboration, access matters for disabled researchers, and methods informed by decolonial theory.

We are also interested in the politics of "the research subject" for disabled as well as nondisabled researchers. Who participates in authorship and makes it possible beyond the named author? What labor, knowledge, and collaboration are obscured by publishing norms? Who defines disability, and what power do those definitions hold—what happens when "subjects" have understandings of the concept that differ from those of researchers? Our thinking in this section is influenced by Margaret Price and Stephanie Kerschbaum's 2016 article "Stories of Methodology: Interviewing Sideways, Crooked and Crip," in which they combine principles of disability justice with grounded theory, narrative analysis, and critical discourse analysis. Arguing that "disability crips methodology" (20), they ground their qualitative interviewing practice in collective access, flexible timing, and affective presence for disabled researchers and subjects alike.

As *Crip Authorship* goes to press, we note a parallel upswing of attention to terminology and interpretation among historians, especially those working on "disability before disability" or disability in periods when disabled people had little opportunity for writing themselves. In a 2021 call for papers for an edited volume on "cripping the archive," Jenifer Barclay and Stefanie Hunt-Kennedy flag a series of critical issues for disability historiography, including "the paradox of disability as both hypervisible and invisible in the historical record," "the absence of disability in archival finding aids and indexes," "the challenges of locating disability in already contested archives (e.g. slavery, colonialism, etc.)," and "revisiting familiar archival sources through a disability lens" (Barclay and Hunt-Kennedy 2021). Surveying the capaciousness of the word *disability* before the nineteenth century, as well as the constellation of other terms that referred to what we now call disability, Sari Altschuler and Cristobal Silva take a different tack by suggesting that "literary approaches are particularly well suited to tracing intellectual and rhetorical genealogies of concepts like disability through close textual analysis across a range of genres and forms" (Altschuler and Silva 2017, 2). In *Crip Authorship*, concerns about cataloging, indexing, and library classification systems (past and present) are detailed in Stephanie S. Rosen's chapter "Disability in the Library and Librarianship," found in the publishing section. In this section on research, Helen Selsdon, a historian and former archivist at the American Foundation for the Blind, enumerates the steps taken to build an accessible digital archive, foregrounding disabled historians.

Regarding research access, Emily Lim Rogers details the benefits and drawbacks of virtual ethnography for disabled researchers and community members. She and Laura J. Wernick also discuss cross-disability research and collaboration (Rogers, Wernick). Interdependence between collaborators, or between interviewers and interviewees, is a common theme (Mauldin, Ginsburg and Rapp).

Yet other chapters consider friction, failed research, and revised or iterative research (Wool, Ralph). Xuan Thuy Nguyen offers decolonial methods for refusing "damage-centered research" (Tuck 2009) and other western models in disability ethnography, drawing on the example of participatory arts-based research in Vietnam. And some authors emphasize affect, including depression and trauma—neglected or even contested topics in disability research (Awkward-Rich, Mauldin).

The next section explores crip genres and forms. Genre and form are often linked in library catalogs—for instance, in search menus. The Folger Shakespeare Library explains, with reference to its own collection, "Genre/form terms in catalog records describe what an item *is* (or contains), not what it is about. *Genre* corresponds roughly to the intellectual content of what is being described: for example, almanacs, depositions, plays, and poems. *Form* corresponds with physical characteristics: for example, embroidered bindings, imposition errors, manicules, and sammelbands" (2019). *Genre* refers to the style or category of something; *form* references its shape. While form has some overlap with *medium*, the theme of the final section in this volume, it more often gestures at a smaller scale to "characteristics of works with a particular format and/or purpose" (Library of Congress, 2011).

The relationships between forms of making and the human body are entwined in genre's roots. According to the *Dictionary of Untranslatables*, genre derives "from the Greek *genos* [γένος] (from *gignesthai* [γίγνεσθαι], 'to be born, become') and its Latin calque *genus*. . . . The biological network is the starting point, as witnessed by the Homeric sense of *genos*: 'race, line'" (Cassin 2014, 384). To return to Patty Berne, there is a direct link between nonnormative bodymind experience and "fierce creativity"; the development of not only new content but new forms of content. The chapters in this section explore the relationships between disability and genre. Some styles or forms have been made different in their encounters with disability: life writing (Islam and Jana), academic writing, metaphor (Ito). Some have been newly developed: public disability scholarship (Virdi), Krip-Hop (Moore and Jones). Others owe an unacknowledged debt to disability: manifesto (Kafer), autotheory (Samuels).

An enormous amount of gatekeeping, which ultimately determines who is formally (and legally) considered an author, takes place in the publishing process. Prestige, authority, circulation, and financial benefits accrue to certain kinds of authors, certified by elite presses. Yet much disability theorizing takes place among disability activists on social media and in community spaces—and it is too often ignored or, worse, appropriated by channels of establishment authorship, as pointed out by Liz Jackson, Rua Williams, and others in their calls for "citational justice" (Williams 2021).

In the section on publishing, chapters examine structural exclusion as a result of ableism—including inaccessible publishing formats—as well as racism and bias within disability publishing itself (Bowen, Kuo, and Mills). Cynthia Wu outlines the practicalities of launching a disability series with an academic press, and the tacit knowledge as well as technical access required to make publishing more accessible. An often-forgotten yet essential component of disability justice in publishing is found in librarianship, starting with call numbers, metadata, and other classification practices. Stephanie S. Rosen brings this infrastructure to light and offers alternatives from a critical librarianship perspective. Others examine or enact expression, translation, and publication in visual and tactile languages (Burke, Clark). Robert McRuer considers the movement of ideas across languages, via the example of translating one of his own English-language books for republication in Spanish.

Disability also crips the media required for writing, research, and publishing. In our final section, activists and scholars address the spectrum of "media" from digital divides to accessibility tools to "crip making" (Hamraie). Some authors stress the rampant lack of access to internet infrastructure and mainstream media based on class, region, or Indigeneity in conjunction with disability (Deerinwater; Chidemo, Chindimba, and Hara). This lack of access to the fundamental tools of communication is a serious barrier to work, education, and creative authorship. Others examine access techniques like audio description that can be found across mainstream radio and disability podcasting (Kleege), an example of what Graham Pullin calls "resonant design" (2009, 93). At the same time, they highlight disability aesthetics (Kleege) and broader principles of collective access (Bri M). If the phrase "assistive technology" implies "a technological fix that is unconcerned with education, community support, or social change" (Mills 2015, 178), other authors theorize tools like augmentative and alternative communication (AAC) from the perspective of crip mentorship (McLeod), or automated captioning as part of the legacy of past communities of speakers (Hickman). What crip "technical cultures" make authorship possible (Haring 2006)? Aimi Hamraie surveys tactics and styles of crip making, from critical design to "crip technoscience" (Hamraie and Fritsch 2019).

Across each of these phases, this book is a collective exploration of some of the things *crip authorship* means and entails. Critical theory can sometimes seem to pin down definitions and assign ownership to terms, yet every word in the dictionary has multiple senses, arriving through use. We go beyond the dictionary in our openness to signification. We describe crip authorship inductively after thinking across the essays in this collection, and alongside the scholars and activists whom we first gathered for a works-in-progress conference in August 2021. In academic hierarchies and the publishing industry, edited collections are often denigrated (for various reasons, including profitability), but disabled writers like Alice Wong—among many activists—have lauded the essay form for its precision and impact (Wong 2022, xv). We appreciate short essays as an example of "disability minimalism" (Mills and Alexander, 2023), a necessary economy of energy or material, and we value the edited collection as a repository of disability thought.

Starting with the premise that disability shapes authorship—authorship taken to encompass composition and dissemination—we're interested in how the chapters build on one another and how they pull in different, sometimes productively contrary, directions. *Dissensus* is essential to disability politics, aesthetics, and community (Rancière 2010; Ojrzyńska and Wieczorek 2020). Crip authorship can be revolutionary, like a manifesto (Kafer), or inward and quiet. It can be complex or plain (Chen, Acton). It can be intentional or unintentional. Some set out to crip authorship through activities like hacking (Hamraie). Others enact crip authorship by being themselves and communicating with their communities in their everyday ways (McLeod).

The material intervention of cripping authorship ranges from the critique of digital divides (Deerinwater), to counterstorytelling (Padilla), to the elaboration of new or hybrid genres and styles (Moore and Jones). It can involve access (Acton, Kleege) or the development of new methods and media (Rogers, Burke). These new methods may be appropriated by nondisabled authors or otherwise overbrim the disability community (Samuels). Crip authorship takes place within and beyond the commodity version of authorship, in books and on social media (Bri M, Virdi) and in writing that will never be published. It is often collaborative, even across time and the automation of vast crowd-sourced archives (Hickman). It usually involves friction, including in-community friction such as the "crip refusal" Zoë H. Wool describes regarding the academic research process.

Crip authorship is also an affective relation to composition (Awkward-Rich) and a temporal one (Yergeau on perseveration, Chen on slowness, Bruce on rants). As Louise Hickman notes in her chapter, "Crip authorship is a necessarily incomplete project." Failure—crip failure—might serve the purposes of antiproductivity and rest (Khúc), or it might look like the sheer crip loss indicated by Shulamith Firestone in a passage of *Airless Spaces* where she cannot find any paper for writing: "I fished for my white letter writing pad and then I remembered I had used it up writing a will shortly before entering the hospital" (1998, 63). Loss is always a presence, a shaping force, and as we write this introduction we acknowledge the many absences from this book, the losses personal and in our communities that have stalled and animated our writing over the past three years.

It was hard to get here. Rest here if you agree.

NOTES

1 We think alongside the Sins Invalid statement on language justice (2021), which *describes* disabled modes of communication and also *commits to* a language justice approach in the group's own work: "There are languages created and used specifically by disabled and Deaf people, as our bodyminds inform our means of expression. We use Augmentative and Alternative Communication (AAC), American Sign Language (ASL), Lengua de Señas Mexicana (LSM), Black American Sign Language (BASL), ProTactile Communication, with

and through our trachs and our staccato breathing, through our brain fog and aphasia, through pain and pain meds, through masks and voice amplifiers, through text and videos, through our grunts and moans and sounding our worlds, through blinks and blowing through straws and more ways than we can outline . . . Language justice isn't just about access, we strive to flatten hierarchies by creating spaces where each person is respected and where power is shared amongst speakers of all languages."

2   The standard cost is also evidenced by the grants awarded by the Toward and Open Monograph Ecosystem (TOME) initiative, https://www.openmonographs.org/faq/.

3   See Liat Ben-Moshe on the related concept of dis-epistemology, which prompts her to inquire, "How does being disoriented lead one to new knowledge or/and to being humbled (tenderized) about not knowing? How can not knowing aid in liberatory struggles, in alleviating oppression, or even in being in community with like-minded people in an ethical manner?" (2018).

4   By "reading," we refer to *interpretation* in this section on research methods. Exciting work on reading as decoding and meaning-making across a range of symbol systems and media is also taking place in disability studies. For an argument that "reading is overrated," calling instead for more analysis of disabled literacies, see Logan Smilges, "Neuroqueer Literacies; or, Against Able-Reading" (2021).

BIBLIOGRAPHY

Altschuler, Sari, and Cristobal Silva. 2017. "Early American Disability Studies." *Early American Literature* 52 (1): 1–27.

American Library Association. n.d. "Access to Print Materials." ALA Accessibility Basics for Librarians Tutorial, Office for Information Technology Policy. Accessed July 26, 2022. https://www.ala.org/ala/washoff/contactwo/oitp/emailtutorials/accessibilitya/14.htm.

Bailey, Moya, and Izetta Autumn Mobley. 2018. "Work in the Intersections: A Black Feminist Disability Framework." *Gender and Society* 33, no. 1 (2018): 19–40.

Barclay, Jenifer, and Stefanie Hunt-Kennedy. 2021. "Call for Abstracts for Edited Volume— Cripping the Archive: Disability, Power, and History." H-Announce, April 2, 2021. https://networks.h-net.org/node/73374/announcements/7515044/call-abstracts-edited-volume -cripping-archive-disability-power.

Barthes, Roland. 1977. "The Death of the Author." In *Image, Music, Text*, 142–148. London: Fontana.

Ben-Moshe, Liat. 2018. "Dis-orientation, dis-epistemology and abolition." *Feminist Philosophy Quarterly* 4 (2): 1–9.

Berne, Patty. 2021. Foreword to *Crip Kinship: The Disability Justice and Art Activism of Sins Invalid*, by Shayda Kafai, 7–10. Vancouver, Canada: Arsenal Pulp.

Cassin, Barbara, ed. 2014. *Dictionary of Untranslatables: A Philosophical Lexicon*. Translated by Steven Rendall, Christian Hubert, Jeffrey Mehlman, Nathanael Stein, and Michael Syrotinski. Translation edited by Emily Apter, Jacques Lezra, and Michael Wood. Princeton, NJ: Princeton University Press.

Chandra, Priyank. 2020. "Piracy and the Impaired Cyborg: Assistive Technologies, Accessibility, and Access." *Proceedings of the ACM on Human-Computer Interaction* 4:1–21.

Cintron, Lourdes. 2021. "On Shulamith Firestone and the downtrodden." *Airless Spaces and Mental Illness* blog, 14 October 2021, https://airlessspacesandmentalillness.wordpress.com /2021/10/14/on-shulamith-firestone-and-the-downtrodden/.

Cox, Peta. 2013. "Passing as Sane, or How to Get People to Sit Next to You on the Bus." In *Disability and Passing*, edited by Jeffrey A. Brune and Daniel J. Wilson, 99–110. Philadelphia: Temple University Press.

Dokumaci, Arseli. 2014. "Misfires That Matter: Habitus of the Disabled Body." In *MISperformance: Essays in Shifting Perspectives*, edited by M. Blažević and L. C. Feldman, 91–108. Ljubljana: Maska.

Dokumaci, Arseli. 2018. "Disability as Method: Interventions in the Habitus of Ableism through Media-Creation." *Disability Studies Quarterly* 38 (3). https://dsq-sds.org/article/view/6491.

Dolmage, Jay. *Disability Rhetoric*. Syracuse: Syracuse University Press.

Ellis, JJJJJerome. 2020. "The Clearing: Music, Dysfluency, Blackness, and Time." *Journal of Interdisciplinary Voice Studies* 5 (2): 215–233.

Ellis, JJJJJerome. 2021. *The Clearing*. New York: Wendy's Subway.

Erevelles, Nirmala, Elizabeth J. Grace, and Gillian Parekh. 2019. "Disability as Meta Curriculum: Ontologies, Epistemologies, and Transformative Praxis." In "Disability as Meta Curriculum: Epistemologies, Ontologies, and Transformative Praxis," special issue, edited by Nirmala Erevelles, Elizabeth J. Grace, and Gillian Parekh. *Curriculum Inquiry* 49 (4): 357–372.

Firestone, Shulamith. 1998. *Airless Spaces*. Los Angeles: Semiotext(e).

Folger Shakespeare Library. 2019. "Genre and Form." *Folgerpedia*, April 4, 2019. https://folgerpedia.folger.edu/Genre_and_form.

Foucault, Michel. 1998. "What Is an Author?" In *Michel Foucault: Aesthetics, Method, and Epistemology*, edited by James D. Faubion, translated by Robert Hurley, 205–222. New York: The New Press. Originally published in 1969.

Friedner, Michele, and Karen Weingarten. 2019. "Introduction: Disorienting Disability." In "Disorienting Disability," special issue, edited by Michele Friedner and Karen Weingarten. *South Atlantic Quarterly* 118 (3): 483–490.

Hamraie, Aimi, and Kelly Fritsch. 2019. "Crip Technoscience Manifesto." *Catalyst* 5 (1). https://catalystjournal.org/index.php/catalyst/article/view/29607/.

Haring, Kristen. 2006. *Ham Radio's Technical Culture*. Cambridge, MA: MIT Press, 2006.

Johnson, Merri Lisa, and Robert McRuer. 2014. "Cripistemologies: Introduction." *Journal of Literary and Cultural Disability Studies* 8 (2): 127–147.

Kim, Jina B. 2017. "Toward a Crip-of-Color Critique: Thinking with Minich's 'Enabling Whom?'" *Lateral* 6 (1). https://csalateral.org/issue/6-1/forum-alt-humanities-critical-disability-studies-crip-of-color-critique-kim/.

Kohn, Nina, and Catheryn Koss. 2016. "Lawyers for Legal Ghosts: The Legality and Ethics of Representing Persons Subject to Guardianship." *Washington Law Review* 91 (2): 581–636.

Lau, Travis Chi Wing. 2019. "Slowness, Disability, and Academic Productivity: The Need to Rethink Academic Culture." In *Disability and the University: A Disabled Students' Manifesto*, edited by Christopher McMaster and Benjamin Whitburn, 11–19. New York: Peter Lang.

Library of Congress. 2011. "Frequently Asked Questions about Library of Congress Genre/Form Terms for Library and Archival Materials," *https://www.loc.gov/catdir/cpso/genre_form_faq .pdf*.

McArthur, Park, and Constantina Zavitsanos. 2013. "Other Forms of Conviviality." *Women and Performance: A Journal of Feminist Theory*, October 30, 2013. https://www.womenandperformance .org/ampersand/ampersand-articles/other-forms-of-conviviality.html.

McRuer, Robert. 2004. "Composing Bodies; or, De-Composition: Queer Theory, Disability Studies, and Alternative Corporealities." *JAC* 24 (1): 47–78.

Mills, Mara. 2012. "What Should We Call Reading?" *Flow*, 3 December 2012, *https://www.flow journal.org/2012/12/what-should-we-call-reading/*.

Mills, Mara. 2015. "Technology." In *Keywords for Disability Studies*, edited by Rachel Adams, Benjamin Reiss, and David Serlin, 176–179. New York: New York University Press.

Mills, Mara and Neta Alexander. 2023. "Scores: Carolyn Lazard's Crip Minimalism," *Film Quarterly* 76 (2): 39–47.

Mingus, Mia. 2017. "Access Intimacy, Interdependence, and Disability Justice." *Leaving Evidence* (blog), April 12, 2017. https://leavingevidence.wordpress.com/2017/04/12/access-intimacy -interdependence-and-disability-justice/.

Minich, Julie Avril. 2016. "Enabling Whom? Critical Disability Studies Now." *Lateral* 5 (1). https:// csalateral.org/issue/5-1/forum-alt-humanities-critical-disability-studies-now-minich/.

National Library Service for the Blind and Print Disabled. 2020. "Marrakesh Treaty." September 15, 2020. https://www.loc.gov/nls/about/organization/laws-regulations/marrakesh-treaty/.

Ojrzyńska, Katarzyna and Maciej Wieczorek. 2020. *Disability and Dissensus: Strategies of Disability Representation and Inclusion in Contemporary Culture*. Leiden: Brill.

Philip, Kavita. 2005. "What Is a Technological Author? The Pirate Function and Intellectual Property." *Postcolonial Studies* 8 (2): 199–218.

Piepzna-Samarasinha, Leah Lakshmi. 2018. *Care Work: Dreaming Disability Justice*. Vancouver, Canada: Arsenal Pulp.

Price, Margaret, and Stephanie Kerschbaum. 2016. "Stories of Methodology: Interviewing Sideways, Crooked and Crip." *Canadian Journal of Disability Studies* 5 (3): 19–56.

Pullin, Graham. 2009. *Design Meets Disability*. Cambridge, MA: MIT Press.

Queer Method (@QueerMethod). 2013. "Proposing disability as a method for new media." Twitter post, October 31, 2013. https://twitter.com/QueerMethod/status/395997273210900480.

Rancière, Jacques. 2010. *Dissensus: On Politics and Aesthetics*. Trans. Steven Corcoran. London: Continuum.

Siebers, Tobin. 2008. *Disability Theory*. Ann Arbor: University of Michigan Press.

Siebers, Tobin. 2010. *Disability Aesthetics*. Ann Arbor: University of Michigan Press.

Sins Invalid. 2021. La justiciar de lenguaje es justiciar para personas con discapacidades / Language Justice is Disability Justice, https://www.sinsinvalid.org/news-1/2021/6/8/la-justicia -de-lenguaje-es-justicia-para-personas-con-discapacidadeslanguage-justice-is-disability-justice.

Smilges, Logan. 2021. "Neuroqueer Literacies; or, Against Able-Reading." *College Composition and Communication* 73 (1): 103–125.

Sterne, Jonathan, and Mara Mills. 2017. "Dismediation." In *Disability Media Studies*, edited by Elizabeth Ellcessor and Bill Kirkpatrick, 365–378. New York: New York University Press.

Tuck, Eve. 2009. "Suspending Damage: A Letter to Communities." *Harvard Educational Review* 9 (3): 409–428.

US Copyright Office. n.d. "Definitions: Who Is an Author?" Accessed July 26, 2022. https://www .copyright.gov/help/faq/faq-definitions.html#:~:text=Who%20is%20an%20author%3F,entity %2C%20such%20as%20a%20publisher.

Waggoner, Jess, and Ashley Mog. 2020. "Visionary Politics and Methods in Feminist Disability Studies." In special issue, edited by Jess Waggoner and Ashley Mog. *Journal of Feminist Scholarship* 17:1–8.

Williams, Rua M. (@FractalEcho). 2021. "Open Letter for Citational Justice at ASSETS 21—on Behalf of Liz Jackson." Document attached to Twitter post, October 20, 2021. https://twitter .com/FractalEcho/status/1450860710293123082.

Wong, Alice. 2022. *Year of the Tiger: An Activist's Life*. New York: Vintage.

Yergeau, M. Remi. 2017. *Authoring Autism: On Rhetoric and Neurological Queerness*. Durham, NC: Duke University Press.

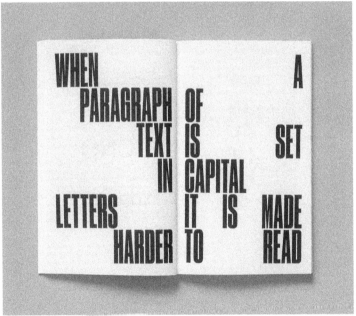

Sam Barclay, a designer based in London, published the first edition of *I Wonder What It's Like to Be Dyslexic?* in 2013. Some pages of the book model more or less accessible typography and the sociotechnical contours of reading. Other pages model dyslexic graphic design, evincing not only Barclay's experience of reading but also the disability aesthetics of unconventional print and even illegibility.

Image description: Sam Barclay, book cover and spread, "When a paragraph of text is set in capital letters it is made harder to read," in *I Wonder What It's Like to Be Dyslexic?*, 3rd ed. (self-published, 2019). Courtesy Sam Barclay, https://www.tobedyslexic.co.uk/.

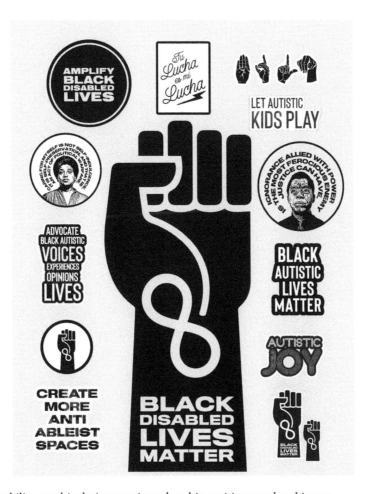

Black disability graphic design as crip authorship, uniting word and image.

The central symbol, created by disabled designer Jennifer White-Johnson in 2020, combines a black fist—representing protest and solidarity—with the infinity symbol, which Autistic communities use to depict the breadth of autistic experience as well as the larger neurodiversity movement. Arranged around the central image are a number of phrases: "Create More Anti Ableist Spaces," "Advocate Black Autistic Voices Experiences Opinions Lives," "Amplify Black Disabled Lives," "Tu Lucha es Mi Lucha," the letters "BDLM" represented by images of hands forming those letters in ASL, "Let Autistic Kids Play," Black Autistic Lives Matter," and "Autistic Joy." Small inset images of Audre Lorde and James Baldwin are haloed by quotes from those authors. Lorde: "Caring for myself is not self-indulgence. It is self-preservation, and that is an act of political warfare." Baldwin: "Ignorance allied with power is the most ferocious enemy justice can have."

White-Johnson writes, "In solidarity with my 7-year-old Black Autistic son and in virtual protest with my Black disabled community, I felt compelled to use my art to bring visibility to the facts. More than half of Black/Brown bodies in the US with disabilities will be arrested by the time they reach their late 20s. We don't see many positive stories or acts of #AutisticJoy among Black/Brown bodies because they don't make headlines. 'To Be Pro-Neurodiversity is to be Anti-Racist': this statement carries a lot of truth, which directly influenced the need to create the graphic."

Courtesy Jennifer White-Johnson, https://jenwhitejohnson.com/

SECTION I

Writing

1

Writing While Adjunct

A Contingent Pedagogy of Unwellness

MIMI KHÚC

I deserve to write.

This is a recent realization, after over a decade as a writer and scholar. Before, writing was something I had to do, something I wasn't doing enough of, something I wasn't good enough at, something other people seemed to do so much faster and better than me, something filled with dread and guilt and anxiety. Only recently has it become a thing of joy, a time that I carve out for myself, a space of creation that I have a right to access.

Life as an adjunct is not conducive to writing. Neither is being disabled. Contingency and disability: two forms of structural unwellness that intertwine with even more forms, such as racism, misogyny, and queerphobia, and leave us structurally abandoned, spoons most often dedicated to daily survival and trauma recovery. I am often too tired to write. I'm also often too poor to write. I'm not sure if able-bodied, tenured faculty understand this. Writing is a luxury many of us cannot afford, even as we are punished in the academy for not affording it. We adjuncts are failures from the outset and then are set up to continue failing. No one pays an adjunct to write, or to rest.

In a supposedly meritocratic system, I should be able to work my way out of precarity. Writing, or publishing, becomes the tool through which I prove myself and climb out of the academic underclass. *Academic hyperproductivity is not simply the means of belonging but its ideology as well.*

Unlike most folks in the contingent academic underclass, I decided to become an adjunct. I had no interest in the tenure track; I was already disillusioned by its treatment of women of color mentors who were doing everything "right" and still being denied tenure. I had no interest in doing everything "right" anyway. I wanted a relationship with academia on my own terms. It took several years, becoming deeply ill, being pushed out of a beloved contingent position, scrounging together multiple sources of income, and creating a wildly successful hybrid scholarly arts project to figure out what that would mean. I think

I'm still figuring it out.

How to write as a disabled adjunct queer woman of color and parent? Don't. No, really, don't. Prioritize your needs. Make sure your needs—physical, emotional, relational, spiritual, intellectual—are being met. Rest. Figure out what duties must absolutely be performed, especially if you have dependents, and what can wait or be off-loaded. Ask for help. Pay for help. Find joy. Invest in your own joy. And most importantly, do not feel shame—for needing help, for asking for help, for needing rest, for being "flaky" or "lazy," for prioritizing your own joy. Do not feel shame for not writing.

After all that, then maybe you can write.

In other words: come to know yourself as a human being with needs and limits, an interdependent being who inherently needs structures of support to survive. Come to know yourself as a being within systems that take your time and energy and spoons in varying ways and to varying degrees. Come to know yourself not as a perpetual failure within neoliberal capitalism but as something more than your productivity. Come to know yourself from what I have termed a "pedagogy of unwellness," an idea first drawn from my teaching (specifically teaching unwell Asian American students as an unwell Asian American adjunct), but eventually extending, epistemologically, to all of our structural encounters and dynamics. You are differentially unwell at all times, endlessly navigating your shifting needs, limits, and the demands placed on you. Come to know yourself as inherently worthy whether or not you write another goddamn word for the rest of your life.

The question to ask shouldn't be, "Why am I not writing?" or "How can I become more disciplined as a writer?" *The advice to "write every day" is ableist bullshit.* Stop trying to figure out how to write every day, or to force more hours into the day, and instead ask yourself: What enables me to write? What do I need in order to write? What would make writing feel joyful, full of possibility, full of wonder and creation?

In other words: What structures need to be in place to shift my relationship to work, to writing, to my needs, to my capacities?

The myth of independence extends to the myth of the independent writer, the scholar who produces simply by hard work and commitment and brains. But we do not write through sheer willpower in vacuums. Writing requires structures of support. It must be actively enabled. We write when we have structures of care supporting us. We write when a community builds these structures.

So I ask again: What are the structures you need?

And how might you build them or ask for them to be built? How might the institutions we work in be made responsible for building these structures?

Somewhere during this pandemic, I taught myself to be a baker. I baked every day in the first six months or so, teaching myself bread-making, cakes, pastry, and especially allergy baking to meet my kids' food restrictions. Somewhere along the way, baking became a huge part of my identity and the way I move through the world. It brings me joy. It feeds my creativity but also the technician in me. It literally feeds my loved ones and brings them joy. It even brings joy to my communities on social media.

Baking is something I make time for, and it is enabled by my not needing to do a bunch of other duties, like work for pay more, or provide childcare to my three kids, or perform various forms of domestic labor. In the summer of 2020, I stopped nearly all forms of work—teaching, writing, creating, public speaking—and just baked. I didn't just pick up baking as a "hobby," or even simply as a form of additive self-care. I baked instead of doing almost anything else. I baked because I needed to—and because I was able to *stop doing everything else.*

Like baking, "making time" for writing isn't simply willpower. And we don't do it just because we "love" it—*the romanticization of academic work invisibilizes the role of structure and the dynamics of enablement and disablement.* The dual narrative of will and love invisibilizes power, privileges, and differential obstacles, as sacred myths of meritocracy usually do.

Nowadays I mark days for baking and days for writing. And I build those times in by opting out of or deferring or off-loading other responsibilities. And I opt out, defer, and off-load by relying on other people, structures of support, and different structures of feeling.

In my work on mental health, I ask people to feel differently. It is a tall order, I know. But mental health doesn't make sense until we examine and disrupt our attachments to capitalist productivity, to "wellness" as moral, to work as proof of our value. It doesn't make sense until we recognize meritocracy as ableist. Until we allow ourselves to need. To break. To rest. And to never be whole, if wholeness means perfectly able and independent and self-reliant and the right kind of personhood

that systems of power demand us to be to keep those
systems going.

Rejecting meritocracy requires an intervention into
these ideas but also into these structures of feeling—the
ways we are told we are supposed to feel, about work,
about ourselves, about each other. I've asked people to
shift their ways of feeling, and being, to reunderstand
their mental health—but not specifically around writing
and scholarship and creative work! Perhaps I didn't
zero in on academic research and writing because
it may be one of the most difficult arenas to engage
disruptively. Academics love their hyperproductivity,
their achievements. Tenured faculty need to reassure
themselves they belong in their institutions, that they
deserve their positions (of power and privilege). Otherwise, they might be like me—

just an adjunct.

As an adjunct, I wrote because I wanted to. And I wrote
only when I could. This is not to romanticize writing
while adjunct—it's a pretty fucked-up deal. No incentives,
no support structures, too many demands on my time,
no access to institutional resources, no respect from
colleagues, no fucking sabbaticals.[1] I have been disabled
in more ways than one in my ability to write. And so I try
to no longer feel shame when I'm not writing. If I'm not
writing, that means the conditions are not present for it;
I am not enabled to write because life is too fucking hard
and has taken all my time and spoons.

But *I deserve to write.* I deserve the time, the energy, the
protection, the nurture, the care. I deserve to create and
to have my work out there. I have a right to access the joy
and meaningfulness of creation.

This is what opens up when we write from a pedagogy of
unwellness and the structures of feeling that space induces.
We shed the shame, the relentless hyperproductivity, the

ableism against ourselves and others. We build structures
to support our access to writing. And maybe we even
make projects like *Open in Emergency*.

From 2013 to 2016, I, with my partner
Lawrence-Minh Bùi Davis, developed *Open
in Emergency*, a hybrid scholarly arts project
decolonizing Asian American mental health,
a gigantic collaborative curation involving
over seventy-five contributors and a whole
lot of community crowdfunding.[2] *OiE* was
a box, a kit, a care package, intervening
in how we think and feel and do mental
health. Those same years, I taught as an
adjunct in an Asian American studies
Program That Must Not Be Named; I was
pushed out in 2017.
I made *OiE* not because it would get me
tenure
or promotion
(in fact, the opposite happened),
nor was I paid to make it. Which means
at least two things: one, I had very few
resources and very little enablement
to make it happen; and two, I had no
institutions or even field-wide structures
I was beholden to. And so I turned to
community, for both resources and that
accountability.

Writing while adjunct
reminds you who you are writing for, and why you're writing.

And it shapes the very questions you write about. Adjunct writing
is writing that happens because it needs to, because the questions
    matter, and the stakes are there
    right in front of you. It is writing
    that shapes itself around questions
    of need and joy, because
    why the fuck else would I be writing?

I find myself now writing a book. With a university press. This feels much closer to "real" academic writing than anything else I've done in the last few years. It has been with this book project that I've really had to reflect on the role of both unwellness and joy in writing, because I've been deeply unwell throughout its process—barely employed, managing depression and anxiety and PTSD, navigating wildly escalating family law litigation, surviving a global pandemic with a school-age kid at home—and because academic writing is something I've never found joyful. And so to continue working on this project, I've had to remember

that I deserve both care and joy in my work—and to reorient the *how* of my work toward both of those things. I remind myself that it's OK to be unwell, it's OK to need. That

writing comes second, third, fourth, to my being able to move in the world in safe and satisfying ways—or perhaps, better, that

writing should be part and parcel of my being able to move in the world in safe and satisfying ways.

I remind myself to not be seduced by academic systems of valuation, not to measure myself or others by those violent yardsticks. I reflect on how to remain unwell and

creative and

lazy and

joyful and

restful, all at once.

I remember to keep baking.

I remember to not write, too.

NOTES

1 Let's not forget that it's the adjuncts who cover the classes of those on sabbatical.

2 Mimi Khúc, ed. "Open in Emergency: A Special Issue on Asian American Mental Health." Special issue, *The Asian American Literary Review* 7, no. 2 (2016). From 2018 to 2020, I developed an expanded second edition, while adjuncting part-time across several institutions: "Open in Emergency: A Special Issue on Asian American Mental Health, Second Edition." Special issue, *The Asian American Literary Review* 10, no. 2 (2019/20).

2

Chronic Illness, Slowness, and the Time of Writing

MEL Y. CHEN

This chapter is about writing and forms of chronic illness, anchored in considerations of temporality, and thinking pragmatically about the time of publishing and the question of access. It ends with concerns about clarity and the possibility for poetics.

Chronic illness is a vagary. *Illness* itself is a descriptive catch-all in terms of experiences, sensations, challenges. Short of a diagnosis, of which allopathic medicine, for its sake, tends to have little to offer, chronic illness's only generic specification is a kind of adjectival patterning: the illness, whatever it is and whatever it entails, has a *chronic* shape. The temporal quality is, at the least, durative and lingering. And perhaps whatever "it" is, if it ever was perceived as an externality or an insult, has at some point become more known, more ordinary, more constitutional, perhaps even more customary. Let's remember, too, because it is all too often forgotten, that chronic illness is equally subject to the revisions disability studies offers for any disability: only in a certain fantasy can it exist as an individual property. That is, what emerges out of a state of chronic illness is not its "own" virtuosic or agentive production; illness itself works in situated conditions, and what it produces is of them as well.

To the extent a response is needed, to the extent one's body sends up signals for action or reception, something known emerges in response. That known/ knowing response is script, ritual. When I think of my own chronic illness—my repeated experiences (or my experiences of *near* repetition, of family resemblance) collected into a bounded time that I mark as the time of illness, first retrospectively, then in anticipation—the trial and error in the attempt at a goal while under its influence has yielded something of a method. It's a method for "management" or survival or sustaining or the prevention of an acceleration or an experiential spread or sensory overwhelm or all of the above.

For something so vague, then, it seems a curiosity to further bind its theorization to that of something "else": writing. But writing is a pragmatic reality for so many of us; there it is. It can be vocational or avocational. And in conditions of illness, it can further serve as a means of externalization, stabilization, registration, or sequencing, the way rock or wood records environment whatever the insult, whatever the extremeness. Though I suspect I wrote before I "was" ill, my attachment to writing has remained steady throughout. This is not to say, however, that writing comes easily or simply out of that attachment. Things are happening while you're writing, and many of them challenge the continuity of your experience as a thinking subject. Some require a distinct turn away from the activity or make it otherwise impossible—pain, sensory displacement, bodily or mental urgencies. Some constitute an accompanying hum, a buzz that comes in to set a novel pace. I've written elsewhere about brain fog, and one of its common characteristics is . . . difficulty with word recall. It takes substantial time to bring it forth. Consider that ellipsis: it marks a pause in the otherwise temporal fluidity of writing. It also expresses an intimate marker of chronic being. The ellipsis also marks a departure from the linearity of an argument, where my contiguity bends into someone else's jump.

Chronic illness writing is both writing and not writing. Thinking, and not thinking. Being active and inactive (consider the phrase "the inactivity of writing" and its spaciousness—there is a reason I no longer consider my first book a secular project). These can be experienced as disjointed ways of being, all the more when one feels they don't meet some fantasied bodyminded choreography—a definition of required fluency—that came with whatever habitus was trained into us (and each of us differently, very differently, the one that whatever schooling we had, or movement training, had a role in modulating). There may come a moment in the foregoing when a reader thinks, "Well, there's nothing remarkable about that. Writing is like that. Also, all writing is slow and all writing is uneven." I'm not claiming there's anything remarkable here, and we've all seen movies about tormented writers. Rather, my wish is to sit (not stand) with the activity of writing in chronic illness and see what it reveals, what else it leads to.

The first quandary concerns the question of writing crip (or being crip) in what amounts to a unilateral medium like writing, the kind of writing that is not occurring in live exchange (imagine a chalkboard, phone texts) but as the result of a drawn-out and often institutionalized process that is called "print": a dilatory, distributive, reached, functionally propositional kind. If my own cognitive disabilities translate into something that is possible for me—not in a selfish way but simply possible from whatever nexus my individual boundedness (which is always bound up with others) presents (deeply associative, nonlinear, but difficult for others)—then what kind of crip is it? Then it's paradoxically a question of crip elaboration with the goal of meeting convention. I recently found an assignment of singly authored writing unbearable, and in lieu of turning down the invitation, I turned to a friend; writing together broke the tyranny of the demand that pressed down not only on the sequencing of publication but on solo writing and the responsibilities I'd have to hold on my own. Instead, we wrote the project together, finding our mutually crip ways and reflecting on their integrality to the project.

A note on time: *Slowness* is what is imagined of crip writers who may well "write" quickly, writing for the sake of writing, but then, subject to the unforgiving needs of publication, must enter another painstaking elaborative process that is designed to de-crip many aspects of what has emerged. The "greater good" rendered under capitalist production standards forces a 1:*n* relationship between a text and an aspirationally large audience; convention becomes a mandate of sorts, and the written product must get closer and closer to communicative convention. That laborious process, which proves impossible for many would-be writers, is what makes it "slow." To be clear, I am not discussing the romanticized communicative ideal of extending the self in the ethical generosity of writing for the other; though that too is a goal worth considering, it is a separate matter.

Time also, tellingly, becomes more incalculable or illegible in scenes of entanglement, collaboration and other forms of togetherness. Slowness as a capitalist indictment fades and the shared project takes precedence. Writing for/with each other (these two paragraphs also appear in Kafer's text), Alison Kafer and I turn to Mia Mingus's (2010) call for "crip solidarity" (and these two paragraphs also appear in Alison's chapter):

> "I want to be with you. If you can't go, then I don't want to go. If we are traveling together, sharing political space together, building political family together, then I want to be with you. I want us to be together." Can we imagine this way of being as a mode of crip authorship? And how might such being make space for more expansive, capacious approaches to collaboration? We learned to wait on each other—for the migraine to lift, the fatigue to ease, the energy to return—as we wrote the introduction to *Crip Genealogies* together (with Eunjung Kim and Julie Avril Minich), in spite of our training to do otherwise.
>
> Inspired by those experiences, we invite an explicit turning toward collaboration and acknowledge the fundamentally collaborative nature of thinking in making that collaboration known. From this perspective, cripping authorship might mean cripping single authorship, even as we recognize that it must not be a cloak indictment: that in fact, single authoring may necessarily be someone else's best and only crip mode. But when single authorship is a proprietary accumulation of intellectual property that should have been shared (which, we note, goes hand in hand with intersectional theft), then it could be seen as "ripping off." Instead, we wonder what possibilities are made by messing with this formula, with unknown risks, erotics, and consequences: "cripping off." While the risks lean toward precarious positions vis-à-vis the academy, we commit to making more and more places where cripping off is imaginable and recognized.

My first book, *Animacies*, has been described as a theoretical text. It has also been described as a difficult text, perhaps for some impenetrable. But I think back to the sense, while writing it, that it was all I could do. In my blur, a blur that was cognitive but also disciplinary, a blur of being (wonderfully) departmentally reseated into gender studies from linguistics and finding new languages from that center, certain forms of sharing rose into awareness and demanded profiling. It was written in the brain fogginess of my most marked period of immersive illness, and came about in part by an act of desperation—not just to keep my academic job, where I nevertheless found some kind of fit (the equation wasn't publish or perish so much as publish while perishing, or perishing for publishing!)—but also to *let in* the sensemaking of the sensory, cognitive, and emotional elsewhere where I lived. There was something to trust in that sensemaking. It had become the only way I could possibly make sense of my living being at that time; it also became a technique, a technology, and maybe, if I dreamed well, a pedagogy. As the book's writer, then, I didn't experience it as theoretical. I perceived and willed it as a transdisciplinary bridging text, performing translational work by positioning commonly interested fields in explicit relationship to specific objects, because from the blur I knew there was more between them than they admitted, shared wishes, shared commitments. At a basic level, the phrases that came out were the only way for me to imagine. They came out as I did—evasive to the command, reluctant to the mastery of the word, always at a side reach, equivalent in some coarse way to my inability to experience a direct gaze without great risk. "It was all I could do." But I also knew the resultant text would be "difficult," and I felt shame. After all, I was committed to some form of disability studies and had the sense that "accessibility" was something to strive for.

Eventually, a member of the disability studies circles I was part of, and a friend connected to a publisher, approached me and quite generously welcomed me to pursue another publication, but this time rendering *Animacies* in the most accessible language possible. This was someone who, at least at that time, advocated for "plain language" scholarship, the idea being that there existed some form of common language that could be called plain, presumably also maximally shared by virtue of some lowest common denominator. It's not my place to scoff at this, perhaps, because I see where it comes from, and I write as someone who is highly trained, has credentials, is at ease in many academic languages, and, despite childhood troubles with reading, writing, and hearing, is given the "model minority" benefit of the doubt as an East Asian American person writing puzzlingly rather than being punished for it. But I do have some distress at "plain language" nevertheless, the first reason being that the plain language expected is a truly, honestly, still-colonizing language called English, with coercive grammaticalities that I wrote about in *Animacies*. I think of Michel Foucault's discourse, what he called a set of possible statements. Plain language, to me, with its commonest goal, is kin to clarity, which has been weaponized against so many even as it has assisted others; the two groups it divides fall neatly into neither "nondisabled" and "disabled" nor "dominant" and "subordinated." While many, including me at times, have felt great relief when clarity was needed at a given moment, others have been traumatized by its demand (and I use the word *traumatized* deliberately). Standardized language—too clearly the source of plain language, even if they are not the same—has killed living languages, small and large, in cities, suburbs, and plains, at borders, minoritized or assaulted by colonization and domination. Indeed, "accessibility," which disability studies scholars all too deeply understand to be a vexed wish, has too easily conspired with an unthought universal standard. Asserting the dominance of plain language (not what my colleague was doing at that moment, which was simply a sweet invitation) in access contexts, in the name of access, is a lot more racialized and nationalistic than the modest image of its presentation. As my dear and, for the purposes of this text, anonymous disability studies colleague wrote me the other night: To hell with accessible writing.

These exertions, wheelings, stoppages, and other tribulations of writing described earlier, only touched on here and otherwise still too rarely narrated, can be thrilling or, more often, they can be anxious and questioning, driven by real sensations of fragile security. In the end, writing with chronic illness, or "with disability," is not the same as writing crip; and writing crip isn't the same as writing accessibly. Writing crip isn't necessarily related at all to access, except perhaps to trace the figure of a departure from conventional choreographies that may happen to be shared with someone else or some others, and I'm not sure I would call that access so much as an occasion to live together profoundly. If crip obfuscates the problematic of scale, such that it seems to reject the hierarchical preferences by which "inclusion," "access," and "accommodation" are organized (or even more so, "inclusive," "accessible," and so on as properties of a thing), then I would hope for it to thrive all the more—to attain in the writing and not be scraped away by the requirements of publication. The troubled time of writing in conditions of chronic illness and under conditions of institutionalized publication intensifies the need for a poetics, a generative worlding that also makes its own way into that worlding, a poetics that can be lived as much as it can be written. I don't know the shape of that poetics, and it must not be prescriptive, but I feel that it is needed more than ever.

BIBLIOGRAPHY

Chen, M. Y. 2012. *Animacies: Biopolitics, Racial Mattering, and Queer Affect*. Duke University Press. https://www.dukeupress.edu/animacies.

Chen, M. Y., Alison Kafer, Eunjung Kim, and Julie Avril Minich, editors. 2023. *Crip Genealogies*. Duke University Press. https://www.dukeupress.edu/crip-genealogies.

Mingus, Mia. 2010. "Wherever You Are Is Where I Want to Be: Crip Solidarity." *Leaving Evidence* (blog). May 3, 2010. https://leavingevidence.wordpress.com/2010/05/03/where-ever-you-are -is-where-i-want-to-be-crip-solidarity/.

3

Composing Perseveration / Perseverative Composing

M. REMI YERGEAU

M&Ms on the table, organized by color. A line of toys, arranged according to size. A thought that needs to burst—that needs to expel, to wrench itself free, to crunch against your esophagus and career its way into the sonic world. An obsession with the Electric Light Orchestra, one that dominates all interpersonal contact and structures daily life. (Have you seen them on tour yet? They have a light show!) A deep-seated need to flap your fingers, an embodied priority that ranks higher in the body queue than sneezing and urination. A life-shattering fear that you improperly disposed of a battery in 2017, and perhaps the battery exploded and started a fire . . . or injured a jogger . . . or killed a sanitation worker . . . or irreparably poisoned an entire ecosystem.

Desire, distress, requirement, repetition, release, repetition.

In many ways, this chapter offers more of a provocation about neurodivergent composition than it does a tidy argument. For what these repeated acts tic us toward is perseveration, or what I might otherwise describe as a bodymind's compulsion to ruminate and rehearse. Perseveration is sticky. Its Latin origin, *perseverat*, translates as "strictly abided by" (Lexico, n.d.; *Oxford English Dictionary* 2022). Autistic author Judy Endow (2016) describes perseveration as "repeat[ing] things over and over." Perseveration is typified by capital-*R* Redundance, by excess, by insistence, by sameness, by stuckness. According to psychologist Timothy Pychyl (2009), perseveration is an action that persists "beyond a desired point."

Redundance, excess, insistence—beyond a desired point.

Arguably, being alive and disabled is already persistence beyond a desired point. Typically, perseveration is represented as a negative, as a symptom that many disabled people involuntarily experience. Even outside the domain of disability, perseveration harbors negativistic flair. Initially emerging in relation to the words *perseverance* and *persistence* (which arguably may hold more positive or value-neutral connotations), *perseveration*'s contemporary definitions rely on behaviorist strands of psychology (*Oxford English Dictionary* 2022). Indeed, its emergence as a psychiatric term in the early twentieth century is tightly interwoven with clinical work on sensoria, cognition, and bodily movements.

In the *Diagnostic and Statistical Manual of Mental Disorders*, perseveration is described in the language of "repetitive and ritualized behaviors and interests." In the parlance of mental disability more broadly, perseveration is also often bound up in descriptions of obsessions, compulsions, tics, self-stimulatory behaviors, and stereotypies. Stereotypy in particular has historically not only referenced the stereotyped movements of neurodivergent people (e.g., embodied motions such as body rocking, finger flicking, head banging, or verbal scripting) but also the stereotyped movements of gender-nonconforming people (e.g., the movement of hands on hips, flexed elbows, limp wrists). Where perseveration is concerned, the impulse to pathologize is strong, signifying embodied configurations that traverse disability, gender, and perception.

In this essay, I contend that perseveration is not (merely) the pathology that psychiatry suggests. In saying that perseveration is not merely pathology, I am not saying that it is never experienced as bad or terrible (because it often does feel just plain bad and terrible, especially when you can't stop mentally tallying how many times you've checked your stove and fear you might have burned down your entire neighborhood). Rather, I propose that perseveration may at times provide us a performative framework—an unruly, indecorous framework—for writing and multimodally composing, for creating scenes and disrupting, for cripping and defying and spiraling. Importantly, I approach this framework from a disability rhetoric perspective. In summoning rhetoric, I mean to suggest that relationships and power dynamics are central to thinking about how bodyminds write and express (Dolmage 2014). Disability rhetoric, as a field, pays particular attention to how any composition is embedded in normative, often violent understandings of how we communicate, interact, and dwell. So too does disability rhetoric provide us methods for rethinking pathologized forms (such as compulsions, tics, and obsessions) as means of communicating, expressing, or signifying. As Christina Cedillo (2018) notes, disability rhetoric's attention to power and communicative acts troubles binaristic notions of writer and reader, of designer and user, of doctor and doctored. Drawing on critical race studies and critical disability studies, Cedillo highlights the ways in which racialized and neurodivergent rhetors' "distinctive embodied identities . . . are rhetorical arrangements of and in the flesh, for they literally, corporeally, and spatially disrupt normative order." In other words, any socially just approach to communicating demands an understanding of writing that compasses us toward nonnormative embodiment. Cedillo further encourages readers to "make room for bodily diversity in composition by highlighting race and disability as critical means of embodied invention that gainfully unsettle habituated expectations." Building on Cedillo's work on race, disability, and writing, I am hoping we might think about perseveration as an awkward arrangement of the flesh—a compulsive mode of persisting within and against normative space.

I keep returning, then, to persistence "beyond a desired point." I am thinking about the ways in which the lives of neurodivergent people are bound up in endless acts of repetition, repetition that is stigmatized, denigrated, and sometimes born of trauma—and exponentially so for those whose perseverations are entwined in experiences of racism, classism, and antiqueer bias. *Persistence beyond a desired point.* Whose point is desired here? Far from viewing perseveration as an act of composing, clinical literature represents those who perseverate as trapped between thought and action, as dysphoric ticcers and the sadly obsessed (Grossi et al. 2013). (To be fair, many of us *are* sadly obsessed, but that doesn't mean our sad obsessions aren't modes of creation. Routinely checking behind one's car for dead bodies might be distressing, but it's also enaction, a series of motions that modulate spatial conditions.) In many ways, disability rhetoric is uniquely primed to unsettle how we think about perseverating, given what we know about nonlinearity, writing, processing, knowing, and repetition. If rhetoric isn't about repetition, then what the hell is it about?

My provocation, as it were, is to suggest that perseveration exceeds symptom- atology: What would it mean to consider perseveration as a way of writing oneself hypervigilantly, to think about perseveration as a mode of rhetorical invention or access creation? Indebted to Jay Dolmage's work on retrofitting, I suggest that perseveration might be more capaciously understood as actions disabled people engage in to maintain relations within, toward, around, or in defiance of a given space. These actions might be experienced as pleasurable, painful, embarrassing, entertaining, transgressive, involuntary, purposeful, or a number of any other affective modes—because persistence and space and relating are complicated things. In other words, I want to ask, absent broad systemic change, how do neurodivergent people, often of necessity, create access in inaccessible terrain? How do neurodivergent people body-as-verb? Where and when are we getting (un)stuck in communicative exchange?

For our purposes, I'm hoping we can think through—and trouble— perseveration in a couple of different ways. First, my hope is that it might show us where our own assumptions, as well as our methods and our institutions, tend to value the neurologically normative in their very design. Second, as we together perseverate on perseveration, my hope is that we might consider moments in which there might be value in reclaiming retrofitting as a practice. What would it mean to think about crip composing practices, such as trigger warnings, interaction badges, or collective hand-flapping, under the banner of the retrofit? Does perseveration lend *retrofit* more potential, more possibilities beyond afterthoughts, failtastic revision, and exclusion?

The work of Dolmage, as well as crip technoscience scholars such as Aimi Hamraie, has done a great deal to show us how retrofits are the result of inac- cessible design practices. Rather than think about neurodivergence from the inception of design, neurodivergence remains an afterthought. Retrofitting, per Dolmage (2017), is an additive rather than reimaginative ideology (78). Retrofits, per Hamraie (2017), are the postdesign deviations from otherwise "normate tem- plates," templates that are often based on the bodyminds of cis white nondisabled men (20). In other words, retrofits are about additive deviations. We typically think about retrofits in the context of a nondisabled entity (a business, a school, a community) begrudgingly adding a ramp for those poor disabled folks; it is less common for us to think about retrofitting as disabled folks crip-composing normative space, or as a "necessary strategy" in an inaccessible world (Hamraie, 150). *Additive deviations.* There is something compelling in thinking about obsessions and compulsions as wily deviants that latch onto normative space, cripqueer style.

I'm not sure that all perseveration at all times is always a neuroqueer retrofit. But I wonder what it might mean to sometimes think about perseveration in this way, in a broader morass of composing practices, as one means of perverting the retrofit (perhaps as a kind of neuroqueer misfitting, à la Hamraie). We might call to mind stimming, or self-stimulatory behavior, as one such perseverative example. Essentially, stimming is bodily movement that holds sensorial significance. We might think about stimming as a kind (or relative) of perseveration because stimming is often known for its bodily persistence, for its bursts of awkward repetition. Jason Nolan and Melanie McBride (2015, 1075) refer to stimming as "sensory utterances," highlighting how stimming can sometimes function as a mode of communicating or composing. Showcasing its environmental dimensions, Lydia X. Z. Brown (n.d.) notes that "stimming is a natural response to cope with overwhelming emotions. It is also a coping mechanism for sensory overload." All bodies stim—we fidget, twirl our hair, chew our pens, crack our knuckles, and so on. Stimming accrues its pathological power, and becomes marked as neurodivergent, when its repetition, disruption, or other nonnormative features reach a clinical threshold of excess. In other words, a neurotypical person's finger-tapping isn't generally categorized as pathological stimming, yet the finger-tapping of a person with ADHD generally *is*.

I'm calling attention to stimming as a perseveration, as a potential neuroqueer retrofit, because stimming is at times compensatory. That is, while stimming holds many sensory meanings, it is frequently a means of seeking sensory balance in an overwhelming, stressful, or painful situation. A neurodivergent person might rock their body hard against a wall in order to remain in a room; the rocking, in this instance, is a way to create access in an inaccessible situation, a way to relate within or around normative space. It is for these reasons that attempts to make people stop stimming are particularly violent in their attempts to norm. Trying to prevent a person from stimming too often assumes an errant body rather than an inaccessible environment.

As with any theory of disability and space, perseveration echoes elements of those theories that precede it, and at some junctures overlaps with more widely embraced ideas about environmental design. Like theories of participatory design, perseveration centers those most affected by a given environment as that very environment is being (re)composed or (re)constituted. But perseverative compositions, I suggest, begin to diverge from more well-known concepts that attend disability, such as universal design, in that its composers-who-are-also-composed bear direct lived experience in, with, and through disability. Importantly, perseveration remains attuned to one particular event. It is uniquely kairotic and often immediate. That is, perseveration's exigence derives from specific, often urgent, bodily need. It is a response toward that which has yet to receive adequate response. Disability justice scholars and activists such as Leah Lakshmi Piepzna-Samarasinha (2018), for example, have long drawn our attention to such needs under the frameworks of interdependence and self-care, in which disabled people work together to reinvent, retrofit, or hack a space or situation in order to make it more dwellable, more traversable, more breathable, less painful, and more attuned to the coalitional work of BIPOC (Black, Indigenous, and people of color) and queer disability design. Self-care and other access maneuvers could be understood as perseverative when they require redundancy, compulsion, and an urgent need for release. In this vein, Naomi Ortiz (2018) underscores the urgency and necessity of self-care in spaces designed by those in positions of power—whom Ortiz terms "Rule-bearers," or those for whom everyday situations are comfortable, welcoming, and hospitable (e.g., spaces designed for white nondisabled cis men) (19). In this, Ortiz reminds us that "safe spaces for non-Rule-bearers are a myth. We are constantly in negotiation to bring who we are into the world" (31). This negotiation is perhaps one such way of thinking about perseveration and/as retrofit. Following Ortiz, we might ask how, where, and when multiply marginalized neurodivergent people bring their very being into a world that is fundamentally unsafe.

In this way, perseverations are often, though not always, access maneuvers, incredibly *rhetorical* access maneuvers at that, and they complicate previously held ideas about retrofitting and environments that theories of universal design typically draw our attention toward. The 504 sit-ins in the mid-1970s, for example, show us perseveration at work. As Corbett O'Toole (2015, 56) reminds us, nearly 150 disabled people and allies took over the San Francisco Federal Building, occupying the space for twenty-six days. The occupation was compulsive interdependence at work, requiring a host of repetitive, embodied moves in the face of deeply hostile and inaccessible terrain: Deaf people signed to each other through the windows to get messages to outsiders and circumvent the FBI; bipedal disabled people attended to the care of wheelchair users; protesters pooled their medications and created access and care schedules; the Black Panthers delivered food (61). These were rhetorical strategies born out of bodily exigence and urgent need for redundancy (lest someone die or face dire injury).

Perseveration also departs from theories of universal design in other key ways. First, universal design deploys the social model of disability in ways that deny disability's value and insights. The social model dictates that disability is the product of an environment rather than an entity that can be localized within an errant bodymind. In other words, (bad) design creates disability. Stairs impede access; curbs impede access; fluorescent lights impede access. Disability comes into being via these designs because some bodyminds are given entry while others are denied. To locate disability as an individual pathology rather than as a political condition constituted by an inaccessible terrain is to adopt a medical model of disability. Here, universal design endeavors to imagine a universe of users whose needs and modes of entry require equitable prioritization—from the inception of design. In other words, universal design (in theory) *eradicates* disability by eradicating inaccess.

There have been notable critiques from disability studies scholars about how theories of universal design represent the social model, as well as its embrace of an unquestioned universality. Here I wish to echo Hamraie's argument that universal design is a shifting signifier. Universal design's very appeal to universality has the effect of decentering disability; if universal design is good for the entire universe, then what matter is disability? As Hamraie (2017, 11) points out, "Post-ADA narratives insist that Universal Design is disability-neutral: the focus is not on disability but rather on everyone. This claim is confusing, however, because it does not clarify what 'everyone' means in a world that devalues particular bodies." In other words, universal design de-emphasizes disability, whereas perseveration thrives on (and from) it.

As we meditate on how perseveration composes our bodyminds and the spaces we encounter, I'm going to suggest we shift directions slightly and think about perseveration in a more specific context: the workplace. While the COVID-19 pandemic initially brought with it a remote-work landscape that was new to many people, the fraught dynamics of workplace encounters—virtual and non—have long been experienced by disabled people. Whether we are on Zoom, in a cubicle, on a sidewalk, or on a retail floor, inaccessibility and sensorial hellscapes abound at work. Lealani Acosta, Ira Goodman, and Kenneth Heilman (2013, 181) describe perseveration as "failure to terminate an action." Were we to consider perseveration's failtastic possibilities in office settings more specifically, we might call to mind any number of unending mundane potentials. Offices are inhospitable spaces: thermostats run on normate (typically male) standards; inadequate ventilation, chemical contaminants, and interpersonal stressors can make employees physically ill; cubicles, windowless rooms, and sterile furniture arrangements contribute to the artificiality of office spaces. As with the embodied effects wrought by office spaces, the neoliberal demands of office work—efficiency, productivity, loyalty—bristle against disabled ways of moving in the world (and, arguably, run counter to conditions of life and living). In response to the somatic hostilities that offices rouse, designers typically appeal to universal design practices as a method for achieving twin goals: increasing workers' overall sense of well-being as a means of increasing workers' output. In this sense, failure to terminate an action—for example, laboring and producing and assembling until punch-out time—becomes reconfigured as a normative desire.

As Hamraie (2017, 41) reminds us, universal design's appeals to flexibility and inclusion are typically deployed as normalization in workplace contexts. This dynamic is particularly present in discourse on autism and employment. In the past decade, a number of employment firms and major corporations (such as Microsoft, Walgreens, and Freddie Mac) have spearheaded autism-at-work initiatives, actively seeking to recruit autistic employees. These programs, it should be noted, typically promulgate clichéd portraits of autistic people in their attempts to represent autistics as ideal employees; and, relatedly, these programs typically invoke the rhetoric of universal design to suggest that, with a few tweaks, any standard office can accommodate an autistic worker. The stereotype of autistic people (white cis men, it's almost always white autistic cis men) as technology- or mathematics-obsessed savants persists unabated in universal design discourse on autism employment, as does the notion that math and technology are the sole provinces of the future. Universities that partner with corporations on autistic job placement are overwhelmingly STEM oriented in nature, and autistic placement firms such as Aspiritech became well known by hiring autistic people as software testers. As Shannon Walters (2010) makes clear, the rhetoric of autism employment circulates well-worn figurations of autistic people as computeristic "conveyer[s] of information, with efficiency, accuracy, and clarity being [their] only attributes." Indeed, even a cursory glance at Aspiritech's website bears this out. At once appealing to autism stereotypes and the neoliberal valorization of productivity, Aspiritech's (n.d.) praise of autistic work habits sounds very much like praise of perseveration: "Lack of boredom with highly-repetitive tasks" and "High levels of intellect and an intense desire to do work that is commensurate with their skills" are among the items listed under the heading "unique talents."

Of course, the perseverative practices I wish to foreground aren't necessarily the savory ones. For what of Ortiz's non-Rule-bearers? While a love of boredom might indeed be the heartthrob of the workplace, I am more interested, following Ortiz, in how weirder perseverative potentials might transform normative space (rather than normative space transforming weird perseverative potentials). My weirdnesses, for instance, run plenty. Echolalia, the repetition of words and phrases, orders many of my conversations; the only way I can stop myself from verbally ticcing what others say is to mouth or mutter words, to mask the compulsion with silentish lip movements. But when I do echolalize, I weird up social spaces; interpersonal awkwardness inheres in my ticced rigidness; the contours of the space I'm in change; echolalia transforms how my conversation partner and I engage across, move within, and use a given space. To be clear, this weirding is not always (or often) experienced as a positive: rather, my weirdness is a condition by which I emerge and exist in dialogic space. In fact, through my verbal perseverations, I sometimes even predict the future: my body, in its urge to get the echoes out quickly, at times predicts and emits the echoes before the other person has even finished speaking. When spaces are not retrofitted for me, my body works (however [un]successfully) to retrofit space for itself. Rather than focus on perseveration's import to social conformity and the workplace, then, I want to draw our attention to perseveration's possible impacts on interpersonal exchanges and spatial configurations: its crip potentials, its repetitive retrofits.

To offer a more extended example of perseveration as neurodivergent retrofit, we might turn to autistic-led blogging and social media discourse. Bev Harp, an autistic author and curator of the blog *Square 8*, writes frequently about her own perseveration: Squawkers McCaw, an animatronic parrot. Describing Squawkers as an "ambassador of Autism Acceptance," Harp (2015) notes that Squawkers has accompanied her to work and community functions since 2007. *Square 8* boasts a dedicated tag for Squawkers, who appears in a variety of video posts, computer-generated images (memes, faux newsletters, and comics), and written reflections on autism and perseveration. In her 2007 introductory post about Squawkers, Harp highlights his programmability: he is capable of repeating words and phrases and doesn't require training to respond to questions. Squawkers's ability to perseverate and produce echolalic speech leads Harp to quip, "Scripts, anyone?"

Recall that perseveration is characterized by endurance and saturation: it is repetition that finds its expression across a multitude of embodied, obsessive, and relational means. Squawkers, in many respects, functions for Harp as a rhetorical commonplace: his very company is perseveration, but so too is his recurrence as a character in Harp's blog a perseverative act. Indeed, the very design of Harp's blog relies on Squawkers as a metonym (that is, a substitution or stand-in) for autism. For instance, in a mock holiday card that satirizes rhetorics of regressive autism, Harp (2009) represents Squawkers as a "Sibling of Neurotypicality," implicitly suggesting that Squawkers is, in toto, autism. In another post, Harp (2008) details a trip to Chicago in which fellow travelers react negatively to Squawkers's presence and echolalic scripts. Harp subtly juxtaposes the repeated refrain made by others—is the parrot real?—against similar claims about autism itself (are you really autistic?). So threatening was Squawkers's autistic presence that, at one juncture, a passerby "in front of the art gallery had jumped as if he might bite her."

What I find noteworthy in Harp's work is her openness about perseveration's embodied effects: social spaces are not designed for neurodivergent bodies, much less for the creatures, objects, and scripts that perseveratively accompany us. The crippily uncommon is perceived as deviant; museums, restaurants, grocery stores, and schools are not prepared for the parrotic awesomeness of a script-loving Squawkers McCaw. But Harp's work also gestures toward something more. Even though perseveration is socially beheld as intrusive, and even though it is not conceived as a condition of daily life (much less a condition of public space), it is nevertheless a form of access creation. In other words, perseveration can mean the difference between being in a space and being forcibly absented from a space. Perseveration is as much about coping as it is about distress.

What do we do when the tools we use to create accessible spaces are, in and of themselves, in some way inaccessible? What do we do when existing theories of design *still* foreground ability (minus the *dis*) in their appeals to universality—designs that force disabled people to perseverate in order to gain access, as opposed to designers perseverating on being and doing better in their jobs as designers? When are our bodyminds the safest (or even the most dangerous) vehicles for, of, or around access? Is there something more to be said about retrofits, or perseveration, or the Electric Light Orchestra? How are we persisting beyond a desired point?

BIBLIOGRAPHY

Acosta, Lealani Mae Y., Ira J. Goodman, and Kenneth M. Heilman. 2013. "Unilateral Perseveration." *Cognitive and Behavioral Neurology: Official Journal of the Society for Behavioral and Cognitive Neurology* 26, no. 4 (December): 181–188.

Aspiritech. n.d. "About." Accessed September 1, 2019. https://www.aspiritech.org/about.

Brown, Lydia X. Z. n.d. "Autism FAQ." *Autistic Hoya* (blog). Accessed September 1, 2016. https://www.autistichoya.com/p/introduction-to-autism-faqs-of-autism.html.

Cedillo, Christina. 2018. "What Does It Mean to Move? Race, Disability, and Critical Embodiment Pedagogy." *Composition Forum* 39. https://compositionforum.com/issue/39/to-move.php.

Dolmage, Jay Timothy. 2014. *Disability Rhetoric*. Syracuse, NY: Syracuse University Press.

Dolmage, Jay Timothy. 2017. *Academic Ableism: Disability and Higher Education*. Ann Arbor: University of Michigan Press.

Endow, Judy. 2016. "Autism, Perseveration and Holding onto Thoughts." *Ollibean* (blog), November 10, 2016. https://ollibean.com/autism-perseveration-and-holding-onto-thoughts/.

Grossi, D., R. Marcone, T. Cinquegrana, and M. Gallucci. 2013. "On the Differential Nature of Induced and Incidental Echolalia in Autism." *Journal of Intellectual Disability Research* 57 (10): 903–912.

Hamraie, Aimi. 2017. *Building Access: Universal Design and the Politics of Disability*. Minneapolis: University of Minnesota Press.

Harp, Bev. 2007. "Super-specialized Favorites List." *Square 8* (blog), December 13, 2007. http://www.8square8.com/2007/12/super-specialized-favorites-list.html.

Harp, Bev. 2008. "Autism. Really." *Square 8* (blog), July 26, 2008. http://www.8square8.com/2008/07/autism-really.html.

Harp, Bev. 2009. "Siblings of Neurotypicality Suffer the Most: A Holiday Letter from Squawkers McCaw." *Square 8* (blog), December 15, 2009. http://www.8square8.com/2009/12/siblings-of-neurotypicality-suffer-most.html.

Harp, Bev. 2015. "Celebrate Autism Acceptance Month and Win Your Own 'Squawkers McCaw.'" *Square 8* (blog), March 26, 2015. http://www.8square8.com/2015/03/celebrate-autism-acceptance-month-and.html.

Lexico. n.d. "Perseverate." Lexico (Powered by Oxford). Accessed June 1, 2022. https://www.lexico.com/en/definition/perseverate.

Nolan, Jason, and Melanie McBride. 2015. "Embodied Semiosis: Autistic 'Stimming' as Sensory Praxis." In *International Handbook of Semiotics*, edited by Peter P. Trifonas, 1069–1078. New York: Springer.

Ortiz, Naomi. 2018. *Sustaining Spirit: Self-Care for Social Justice*. Berkeley, CA: Reclamation Press.

O'Toole, Corbett. 2015. *Fading Scars: My Queer Disability History*. Fort Worth, TX: Autonomous Press.

Oxford English Dictionary. 2022. "Perseveration." March 2022. https://www-oed-com.proxy.lib.umich.edu/view/Entry/141447#eid30936913.

Piepzna-Samarasinha, Leah Lakshmi. 2018. *Care Work: Dreaming Disability Justice*. Vancouver, Canada: Arsenal Pulp.

Pychyl, Timothy. 2009. "Perseveration: The Deep Rut of Change Procrastination." *Psychology Today* (blog), March 5, 2009. https://www.psychologytoday.com/us/blog/dont-delay/200903/perseveration-the-deep-rut-change-procrastination.

Walters, Shannon. 2011. "Autistic Ethos at Work: Writing on the Spectrum in Contexts of Professional and Technical Communication." *Disability Studies Quarterly* 31 (3). http://dsq-sds.org/article/view/1680/1590.

4

Mad Black Rants

LA MARR JURELLE BRUCE

Part One: Confined

"He's balmy!" a white man said. "Make 'em take 'im outta your cell. He'll kill
you. He went off his nut from studying too much at the university. He was writing a book on how colored people live and he says somebody stole all the facts
he'd found. He says he's got to the bottom of why colored folks are treated bad
and he's going to tell the president and have things changed, see? He's *nuts!*"
—Wright [1940] 1993, 343

Confined to a cell in Cook County Jail, Bigger Thomas awaits his doom. The
beleagured black protagonist of Richard Wright's 1940 protest novel, *Native Son*,
Bigger is held behind iron bars.[1] Deeper still, he dwells behind an existential
wall he has erected around himself, "a barrier of protection between him and
the world he feared" (Wright [1940] 1993, 343), a petrified hardness to keep out
"racial hurt" (King 2008, 39).[2] Nineteen years into a life rife with that hurt, and
amid the bleak backdrop of Depression-era Chicago, Bigger accidentally kills a
wealthy white heiress named Mary Dalton. While on the run, in a fit of spite and
desperation, he rapes and intentionally kills Bessie Mears, a woe-weary black
woman who is sometimes his girlfriend. Bigger is soon exposed, declared public
enemy, deluged with public hatred, violently apprehended, convicted of Mary's
(not Bessie's) rape and murder, and quickly condemned to death.[3]

Bigger's jailhouse malaise is interrupted by the arrival of the "balmy" figure
described in the epigraph: a mad black scholar writing a book. Hurled into the
cell, the balmy man breaches Bigger's existential wall so that Bigger's "hate and
shame vanished in the face of his dread of this insane man turning suddenly
upon him" (Wright [1940] 1993, 343). Considering all the brutality Bigger has
endured, all the harm he has inflicted, all the peril he faces from guards and
inmates inside that jail, all the animus from mobs outside, it is remarkable that
he is so utterly unsettled by a solitary black man seeking social transformation.
Maybe Bigger agrees with that white inmate shouting warnings nearby. According to that white man, the urge to battle antiblackness and the will to seek racial
justice bespeak a nutty mind: "He says he's got to the bottom of why colored folks

are treated bad and he's going to tell the president and have things changed, see? He's *nuts*!"

Meanwhile, the balmy man screams truth to power and literally rattles the cage. Bigger beholds that "the man's eyes were blood-red; the corners of his lips were white with foam. Sweat glistened on his brown face. He clutched the bars with such frenzy that when he yelled his entire body vibrated. He seemed so agonized" (Wright [1940] 1993, 342). The balmy man's madness entails an unruliness of bodily surges and eruptions: blood rushing into his eyes, foam bubbling from his mouth, sweat seeping from his face, shouts flying out his throat, convulsions coursing through his body, agony emanating from his flesh. Remarkably, though, his madness is as thoughtful as it is visceral, as politicized as it is agonized. When the mad scholar finally speaks for himself, he claims he has uncovered a vast antiblack conspiracy:

> "You're afraid of me!" the man shouted. "That's why you put me in here! But I'll tell the President anyhow! I'll tell 'im you make us live in such crowded conditions on the South Side that one out of every ten of us is insane! I'll tell 'im that you dump all the stale foods into the Black Belt and sell them for more than you can get anywhere else! I'll tell 'im you tax us, but you won't build hospitals! I'll tell 'im the schools are so crowded that they breed perverts! I'll tell 'im you hire us last and fire us first! I'll tell the President and the League of Nations." (344)

While others may dismiss these words as rant and rave, I regard them as a condensed research report—orated in a brilliant flourish of rant and rave, just the same. The balmy man's findings are the fruit of interdisciplinary investigation into (infra)structural antiblackness in Chicago. He describes a collusion that spans housing, medicine, education, foodways, taxation, and employment, all systematically degrading black life. Based on his own declarations and the admonitions from that white inmate, it would seem that the balmy man's crimes are as follows: amassing damning evidence against city government, alerting others to his findings, expressing his fury aloud in public, planning to petition the president and League of Nations, and mobilizing to battle the evil he's exposed. These acts are treasonous transgressions against antiblackness and white supremacy.

If that white inmate knows so much about the balmy scholar, let's suppose he knows the allegations against Bigger—including the false charges that Bigger raped a white woman. Since fantasies of black rapists enthralled white supremacist imagination in early and mid-twentieth-century America, one might expect the white inmate to treat Bigger with special enmity. Yet in this scene the inmate shows no sign of malice toward Bigger. Instead, he regards Bigger as a sympathetic figure whose safety is in jeopardy, who ought to be warned. Why this sympathy for an alleged rapist and antipathy toward a scholar-activist?

I venture this answer: To the logics of white supremacy and antiblackness, Bigger's actual and alleged crimes are less menacing than the balmy man's revelations. White supremacists and antiblack racists may loathe Bigger, but their loathing is likely mixed with a smug sense of rectitude. After all, Bigger would seem to affirm their fantasies of black male brutality and thus justify their regimes of segregation, pathologization, criminalization, and annihilation. The mad black scholar-activist, on the other hand, belies their fantasies of black depravity and inferiority. He announces that black people are not constitutionally depraved or inferior but rather are subjected to depraved machinations and inferior conditions wrought by antiblackness.[4] Furthermore, as antilynching heroine Ida B. Wells had insisted decades earlier, there is no factual basis for white supremacist fear of black bogeymen ravishing white damsels in droves (Wells [1900] 2010). There is, however, ample cause for white supremacists to dread black radical planning and struggle. The balmy black man is so terrifying because he conducts such planning and struggle. Alas, he has no time to detail his findings or elaborate his agenda: "Soon a group of men dressed in white came running in with a stretcher. They unlocked the cell and grabbed the yelling man, laced him in a straitjacket, flung him into a stretcher and carted him away" (Wright [1940] 1993, 344).

During his brief appearance in *Native Son*, the balmy black scholar manifests four modes of madness: *phenomenal madness, furious madness, psychosocial madness*, and *medicalized madness*. I have theorized this four-part schema at great length elsewhere (Bruce 2021);[5] for now, I will sketch how each applies to the balmy man. His madness is phenomenal madness: an intense unruliness of mind experienced in the consciousness of a madperson (here accompanied by an unruliness of bodily surges and eruptions). It is furious madness: an acute and aggressive displeasure (here provoked by the systematic degradation of black people). It is psychosocial madness: a radical rupture from a given psychonormative status quo (here, in particular, it is a black insurrection against the pernicious logic of antiblackness). Furthermore, those white-clad orderlies will carry the balmy man into psychiatric confinement. There he will likely be branded with medicalized madness: severe mental illness, as codified and diagnosed by psychiatry.

In total, the madman's presence persists for about two pages. Nevermore does he appear in the book, nor is he ever mentioned again. And yet, for all his textual transience, he leaves a monumental impression in my imagination. Mad, black, reviled, exiled, deviant, defiant, critical, ethical, radical, writhing under the threat of annihilation, and quickly receding from view, he deserves all the care and rigor that *mad methodology* brings to bear.

Mad methodology, as I propose and practice it, is an ensemble of epistemologies, political praxes, interpretive techniques, existential orientations, affective dispositions, and life strategies that activate madness and center mad subjectivity.

In this paradigm, madness informs and infuses critical, ethical, radical ways of thinking, ways of telling, ways of protesting, ways of interpreting, ways of feeling, and ways of life. Mad methodology seeks, follows, and rides the unruly movements of madness. It reads and hears and amplifies *idioms of madness*: those purported rants, raves, rambles, outbursts, mumbles, stammers, slurs, gibberish sounds, nonsense noises, and unseemly silences that defy and deform the grammars of hegemonic Reason.[6] It historicizes and contextualizes madness as a social construction and social relation vis-à-vis Reason. It ponders the sporadic violence of madness in tandem and in tension with the structural violence of Reason. It cultivates critical ambivalence—a willingness to forgo affective resolution, cognitive closure, or ideological certitude and to harness the energetic tension and friction in ambivalent feeling—all the better to reckon with the simultaneous harm and benefit that may accompany madness (Bruce 2019).[7] It recognizes and sometimes harnesses "mad" feelings like obsession, rage, and paranoia as stimulus for radical thought and practice.

While normative Reason discredits madpersons, mad methodology affirms that they can be critical theorists and decisive protagonists in struggles for liberation. To be clear, I am not suggesting that madpersons are always already agents of liberation. I am simply and assuredly acknowledging that they can be, which is a heretical admission amid antimad worlds. I propose a mad methodology that neither vilifies the madperson as evil incarnate, nor romanticizes the madperson as resistance personified, nor patronizes the madperson as helpless ward awaiting aid. Rather, mad methodology respects the complexity and variability of mad subjects.

Most urgently, mad methodology extends *radical compassion* to the purported madpersons, queers, ghosts, freaks, weirdos, imaginary friends, disembodied voices, unvoiced bodies, and unReasonable others who trespass—like stowaways and fugitives and insurgents—in Reasonable modernity. Radical compassion is a will to care for, a commitment to feel with, a striving to learn from, a readiness to work alongside, and an openness to be vulnerable before a precarious other, though they may be drastically dissimilar to yourself. Radical compassion is not a naïve appeal to an idyllic oneness where difference is blithely effaced. Nor is it a smug projection of oneself into the position of another, consequently displacing that other.[8] Nor is it an invitation to walk a mile in someone else's shoes and amble, like a tourist, through their lifeworld, leaving them existentially barefoot all the while. Rather, radical compassion is an exhortation to ethically walk and sit and study and fight and build and suffer and celebrate with another whose condition may be utterly unlike your own. Radical compassion strives to impart care, exchange feeling, transmit awareness, embolden vulnerability, and fortify solidarity across circumstantial, sociocultural, phenomenological, and ontological chasms. It seeks to forge an existential entanglement not easily loosened. It persists even and especially toward beings who are the objects of contempt and condemnation from dominant value systems. For those who experience profound self-alienation—who are existentially estranged from their own selves, who endure internal rupture and fragmentation—it is vital to extend radical compassion to one's own self. I hasten to mention that radical compassion is no panacea: as intently as it strives, it sometimes falls short. After all, it is subject to the limits of human understanding, imagination, and will. Moreover, some chasms are too wide to cross. These limitations should not be cause for resignation or despair. We sometimes fail, but we keep trying.

A parapositivist approach, mad methodology does not attempt to wholly, transparently reveal madness. How could it? Madness, after all, tends to frustrate interpretation, elude understanding, refuse resolution. To study madness is to become accustomed to uncertainty and irresolution. To study madness is to discover that one can ethically encounter and engage a thing without purporting to know it. As mad methodologist, I relinquish the imperative to know, to take, to capture, to possess, to master—to lay bare all the world with its countless terrors and wonders—that drives much scholarly inquiry.

Now we return to that dreadful scene in Cook County Jail. As mad methodologist, I linger with Wright's black captive–cum–mad prisoner: his data stolen, his work dismissed, his arms strapped into a straitjacket, his body hurled onto a stretcher, then laid supine, then wheeled away into a paratextual elsewhere. I dream a subjunctive scenario where this mad black scholar regains his freedom. I imagine him finding his stolen data, then finishing his manuscript, then publishing it to great fanfare and controversy, then delivering it to the president and the League of Nations, then appealing to justice and liberation movements with greater moral authority, then organizing mad and black masses, and eventually achieving something like revolution or relief. I picture his book on a shelf of volumes about black Chicago in the mid-twentieth century, nestled between St. Clair Drake and Horace Cayton's 1945 ethnography, *Black Metropolis*, and Gwendolyn Brooks's 1945 poetry collection, *A Street in Bronzeville*. In this subjunctive world, the book is bound and the man is free.

I want freedom for him and for the mad and black prisoners held in real-life Cook County Jail today. In 2015, an estimated one-third of the jail's one hundred thousand inmates were living with some form of mental illness. This means that Cook County Jail was effectively the largest psychiatric "facility" in the United States. For a jail to lead the nation in housing mentally ill persons is a devastating testament to the failure of the US public health infrastructure to grapple with mental illness. Also in 2015, 67 percent of the jail's inmates were black, though only 25 percent of Cook County's residents were black, a devastating testament to the racialization of America's carceral state (Ford 2015).

As mad methodologist, it is my business to abide with the balmy man and his real-life counterparts; to discern the wisdom of his mad black rants; to highlight the insight in his "nutty" outburst; to amplify his rebuke of state-sanctioned antiblackness; and to extend radical compassion to him and to others who endure such struggle. Beneath and beyond my radical compassion, I also feel something like *ordinary affinity* for him. If radical compassion is driven by political imagination and resolve, ordinary affinity is far more rudimentary; it is solidarity born of likeness and shared experience. I feel this kinship because I am a mad black scholar, too.

In fact, I am a mad methodologist in at least two senses. First, I am a scholar who theorizes and mobilizes mad methodology. Second, I am a madman devising methods for critical, radical, ethical living. I know, firsthand, the ordeal of being a mad black scholar while writing a mad black book while braving an antimad-antiblack world.[9]

Incidentally, *balmy* means both "insane" and "soothing."

Part Two: Open

My own madness is a conspiracy of cruel ironies that won't let me rest: a need for cleanliness that erupts into mess; an urge for order that careens to disorder; a tendency toward doubt that will undoubtedly surface; a tyrannical self-rule that is utterly unruly; intrusive thoughts that are as much indigenous as they are invaders to my mind; ghastly obsessions that are as repulsive as they are transfixing; an ineffable feeling that demands constant explanation; a past-glutted regret that wants to devour my future; a drive toward perfection that fucks things up. And then there are the ritual practices: the rinses, revisions, rehearsals, recountings, countings, meditations, medications, inspections, prayers, atonements, and confessions militated against that anguish but only ever providing provisional relief. Eventually, the sheer dirtiness, the strangeness, the bloodiness, the meanness, the nastiness of this world comes rushing or creeping in.

If there is a spectrum of stigma about mental illness in US popular imagination, obsessive compulsive disorder (OCD) is typically treated as a lesser mental illness, a milder madness. It does not incite the terror that swarms around schizophrenia and dissociative identity disorder (often confused and conflated in popular representations). Nor does it inspire the pathos that seems to solemnly gather around major depressive disorder. Instead, OCD is cast as mere idiosyncrasy: an irksome tendency to nitpick and split hairs, or, more favorably, an admirable perfectionism. This spectrum of stigma is vividly displayed in popular cinema, where caricatures of mental illness abound. Schizophrenia and dissociative identity disorder are frequent fixations of horror films, where schizophrenic and dissociative "psychos" spawn mayhem and murder. Depression is depicted in melodramatic and sentimental movies, often the consequence of heterosexual heartbreak and healed by romantic redemption and cheerful friends. Meanwhile, OCD is frequent fodder for comedy, where symptoms become foibles and compulsive rituals resemble comic routines.[10] OCD incurs less social stigma than do schizophrenia and depression—but this knowledge yields little relief when I am scrubbing my skin down to the soul.

My first book, *How to Go Mad without Losing Your Mind: Madness and Black Radical Creativity* (Bruce 2021), ponders the role of madness in black radical art-making, self-making, and world-making. Not merely a study of madness, *How to Go Mad* is symptom and fruit of its author's madness. In other words, the book both suffers and benefits from my own balminess. The suffering comes from my dogged dread that the book will fail. When I read my prose in print, I see—with a marvelous singularity of vision that could be mistaken for divination or hallucination—errors and omissions that prod me toward unruliness of mind. I do not believe that I will ever finish that book, no matter that it is published. I will never feel that it has achieved closure or completion. It is endless. No copy-edit, no print run, no smell of fresh pages under elegant cover, no esteemed award, no slot on a bookshelf, no pages spread wide on an eager lap will ever convince me that the book is done. There's this aching feeling that some essential example or insight is missing; that a remark unwittingly degrades a community or misrepresents a lifeworld; that a misplaced quotation mark or lost footnote will unhinge the integrity of the work; that some flamboyant typo will show up, uninvited, to an utterly important sentence, enthralling your attention while the embarrassed sentence bows and disappears.

But what of the benefit? Madness suffuses the ethical, critical, and radical impetus for *How to Go Mad* and my broader practice of mad study. What I mean is that the work is devoutly ethical, trained by a superego that demands and relishes (before it questions and discounts) good deeds. The work is painstak-ingly critical, sharing my propensity to question everything, to take nothing for granted, to seek the secrets buried underneath every placid surface, to find fault everywhere, to try to make it better. The work is intensely radical, inheriting my inclination to think and dream at the limits, beyond the limits, and further still, but never *still*, because my mind keeps darting, keeps pacing. OCD might inten-sify another elemental force coursing through that book, its most vital feature of all, its care. At the palpitating heart of *How to Go Mad* is care: both careful and caring, both exacting and loving.

I considered composing a book manuscript in the format of my madness. Such a book would sometimes forgo grammar and sometimes adhere fanatically to it. It would veer between immaculate eloquence and impenetrable ramblings. It would occasionally dispense with the left-to-right, top-to-bottom, front-to-back trajectory typical among English-language books, moving in zigzags, spirals, and wormholes instead. It might include blank pages, murals' worth of marginalia, obsessive lists to rival telephone books, volumes of parenthetical digressions, miles of strikethroughs, drafts of paragraphs juxtaposed with their revisions, sprawling gaps and blackouts interrupting the narrative—all deteriori-tizing decipherability in order to achieve phenomenological fidelity. Or maybe my madness demands precisely what I poured into that mad black book: chaos condensed into one hundred thousand words of mostly coherent, sometimes resplendent sentences. Sentences born of profound violence and care. Sentences that want desperately to be held in your mouth and memory. Mad black rants rendered artfully.

I sometimes wonder whether I accidentally actualize Frantz Fanon's prayer at the end of *Black Skin, White Masks*: "Oh, my body! Make me always a man who questions" (1986, 206). If I am a man, I am a man who always questions, who is driven to ask with a visceral urgency as irresistible and insatiable as an itch in a fold of my brain. Every belief, every word, every phrase, every observation, every proposition, every citation, every punctuation mark is subjected to ruthless doubt and vicious interrogation. The conventions of grammar oblige me to end most of these sentences with periods, but there are ghostly invisible lines curling and hovering over most of these tiny dots. What I mean is that most of these periods are interrogation marks in disguise; most of these declarations are really restless questions underneath.

This restlessness thwarts tranquility—but thankfully, it also refuses complacency. This restlessness is an eternal doubting—and also, fortunately, a tireless probing. My refusal of respite resembles what dancer-choreographer and movement theorist Martha Graham describes as the artist's "queer divine dissatisfaction, a blessed unrest that keeps us marching" (de Mille 1991, 264). I sometimes slow my march, though I will not stop. This is a procession without end, without rest, without satisfaction, without closure. It is always underway, always awake, always longing, always open.

NOTES

This essay is adapted from the introduction and afterword *of How to Go Mad without Losing Your Mind: Madness and Black Radical Creativity* (Durham: Duke University Press, 2021).

1   In this essay, I do not capitalize "black" as a racial signifier. My intention is to center a "lowercase blackness" and "improper blackness" that resists reification as a proper noun. For further insight on my grammatical ethos, see *How to Go Mad without Losing Your Mind*, 6.

2   In *African Americans and the Culture of Pain*, Debra Walker King theorizes "racial hurt" as racialized violence that poses an existential threat to its victim. She writes, "Pain is a personal experience, a feeling that is uniquely our own. . . . Racial hurt, however, is not something we own. Racial hurt owns us. It, not pain, attacks the soul and renders its victims wounded or worse—soul murdered" (Charlottesville: University of Virginia Press, 2008) 39.

3   Bessie's remains are carted out as evidence in the trial for Mary's murder, but no trial is convened to pursue justice for Bessie's murder. Alas, Bessie is a poor black woman whose death and life are treated as inconsequential and contemptible—not meriting a trial or redress—by an antiblack legal system.

4   This "balmy" man would find powerful alibi in St. Clair Drake and Horace Cayton's monumental 1945 study, *Black Metropolis: A Study of Negro Life in a Northern City* (Chicago: University of Chicago Press, 1993). Based on research conducted in 1930s Chicago, *Black Metropolis* exposes a city structured by de facto segregation and infrastructural antiblackness.

For a study examining the racial inequity in contemporary Chicago, see Natalie Moore, *The South Side: A Portrait of Chicago and American Segregation* (New York: St. Martin's, 2017).

5 For a detailed account of these four modes of madness, see *How to Go Mad without Losing Your Mind*, 6–9.

6 I have defined "Reason" elsewhere as follows: "Reason is a proper noun denoting a positivist, secularist, Enlightenment-rooted episteme purported to uphold objective 'truth' while mapping and mastering the world. In normative Western philosophy since the Age of Enlightenment, Reason and rationality are believed essential for achieving modern personhood, joining civil society, and participating in liberal politics . . . However, Reason has been entangled, from those very Enlightenment roots, with misogynist, colonialist, ableist, antiblack, and other pernicious ideologies." (Bruce 2021, 4).

7 Regarding "critical ambivalence," I have written elsewhere that "Sometimes it is useful, even crucial, to tarry in the openness of ambiguity; in the strategic vantage point available in the interstice (the better to look both ways and beyond); in the capacious bothness of ambivalence; in the sheer potential in irresolution . . . Lingering in ambivalence, we can access multiple, even dissonant, vantages at once, before pivoting, if we finally choose to pivot, toward decisive motion. To be clear, I am not describing an impotent ambivalence that relinquishes or thwarts politics. Rather, I am proposing an instrumental ambivalence that harnesses the energetic motion and friction and tension of ambivalent feeling. Such energy might propel progressive and radical movement." La Marr Jurelle Bruce, "Shore, Unsure: Loitering as a Way of Life," *GLQ* 5, no. 2 (2019): 357.

8 In *Scenes of Subjection: Terror, Slavery, and Self-Making in Nineteenth-Century America*, Saidiya Hartman unpacks the epistemic violence wrought by hegemonic "empathy." She writes: "Properly speaking, empathy is a projection of oneself into another in order to better understand the other" or 'the projection of one's own personality into an object, with the attribution to the object of one's own emotions.'" Hartman further writes that "by exploiting the vulnerability of the captive body as a vessel for the uses, thoughts, and feelings of others, the humanity extended to the slave inadvertently confirms the expectations and desires definitive of the relations of chattel slavery . . . empathy is double-edged, for in making the other's suffering one's own, this suffering is occluded by the other's obliteration." Saidiya Hartman, *Scenes of Subjection: Terror, Slavery, and Self-Making in Nineteenth-Century America* (New York: Oxford University Press, 1997), 18–19.

9 That book is *How to Go Mad without Losing Your Mind*. In this disclosure of "madness," I am especially influenced by and indebted to disclosures of "madness" (whether medicalized or not) in Patricia J. Williams, *The Alchemy of Race and Rights: Diary of a Law Professor* (Cambridge, MA: Harvard University Press, 1991); Ann Cvetkovich, *Depression: A Public Feeling* (Durham, NC: Duke University Press, 2012); PhebeAnn Marjory Wolframe, "The Madwoman in the Academy, or, Revealing the Invisible Straightjacket: Theorizing and Teaching Saneism and Sane Privilege," *Disability Studies Quarterly* 33, no. 1 (2013), https://dsq-sds.org/article/view/3425/3200; and Keguro Macharia, "On Quitting," *The New Inquiry*, Sept. 19, 2018, https://thenewinquiry.com/on-quitting. I am also emboldened by Margaret Price's book-length study of "madness" in academic discourses and spaces, *Mad at School Rhetorics of Mental Disability and Academic Life* (Ann Arbor: University of Michigan Press, 2011).

10 Jack Nicholson won the 1998 Academy Award for Best Actor for playing a comically insufferable obsessive-compulsive author in the romantic comedy *As Good as It Gets*. Nicolas Cage earned great acclaim for playing an obsessive compulsive con man in the 2003 heist comedy, *Matchstick Men*. In television, Tony Shalhoub won three Primetime Emmys for Lead Actor in a Comedy Series for his portrayal of an obsessive-compulsive detective in the comedic crime procedural, *Monk*, which ran from 2002 to 2009.

BIBLIOGRAPHY

Brooks, Gwendolyn. 1945. *A Street in Bronzeville*. New York: Harper.

Bruce, La Marr Jurelle. 2019. "Shore, Unsure: Loitering as a Way of Life." *GLQ* 5 (2): 352–361.

———. 2021. *How to Go Mad without Losing Your Mind: Madness and Black Radical Creativity*. Durham, NC: Duke University Press.

de Mille, Agnes. 1991. *Martha: The Life and Work of Martha Graham*. New York: Random House.

Drake, St. Clair, and Horace Cayton. (1945) 1993. *Black Metropolis: A Study of Negro Life in a Northern City*. Chicago: University of Chicago Press.

Fanon, Frantz. (1964) 1988. *Toward the African Revolution: Political Essays*. Translated by Haakon Chevalier. New York: Grove.

———. 1986. *Black Skin, White Masks*. Translated by Charles Lam Markmann. London: Pluto.

Ford, Matt. 2015. "America's Largest Mental Hospital Is a Jail." *Atlantic*, June 8, 2015. https://www .theatlantic.com/politics/archive/2015/06/americas-largest-mental-hospital-is-a-jail/395012/.

King, Debra Walker. 2008. *African Americans and the Culture of Pain*. Charlottesville: University of Virginia Press.

Wells, Ida B. (1900) 2010. "Lynch Law in America." BlackPast.org, July 13, 2010. https://www .blackpast.org/african-american-history/1900-ida-b-wells-lynch-law-america/.

Wright, Richard. (1940) 1993. *Native Son*. New York: HarperCollins.

5

Plain Language for Disability Culture

KELSIE ACTON

Summary: Sometimes people in disability culture and activism use big words and complicated ideas. Big words and complicated ideas mean some people can't be part of disability culture and activism. Plain language is a way to include those people. Plain language is a way of writing or speaking so people understand you the first time they read or hear it. People have been using plain language for a long time in a lot of different places. This means that there are a lot of different ways of using plain language. These include using short sentences, common words, and headings. Critical disability researchers point out that some disabled people don't communicate in ways that are quick and easy to understand. Sometimes disabled people communicate in ways that have more than one meaning. Maybe plain language can exist with this. Maybe disabled people can make their own way of using plain language. This could make disability culture and activism accessible for more people.

Note on writing: This chapter is written in what I call a semi-plain language style. This means I do the following:

- Use an active voice
- Mostly use the 6000 most common words in the English language
- Use short sentences
- Use 14 point font
- Use "I" and "you"

There's some places in this chapter where I've used words that aren't among the 6000 most common English words. This is because some words mean very specific things and I want you to read that one meaning. For example, in this chapter

I use the words **disabled** and **impairment**. This is because I often find it helpful to think about disability using the social model. The social model of disability explains that everyone has differences in the ways their bodies and minds work. Some of these differences are considered unusual or not "normal." These differences are called impairments. Society creates barriers for people with impairments that prevent them from participating in the full range of human experiences. These barriers can be people's attitudes or inaccessible architecture, processes, and policies. So people are disabled by society (Shakespeare 2006). Often, making the world accessible means removing barriers. I don't think the social model is the only way to understand disability. But it often works well when I'm thinking about access. Any other uncommon words I've explained in the text.

I hope you find this chapter clear and easy to read.

WHY IS PLAIN LANGUAGE IMPORTANT?

"Disability advocacy spaces can be unfriendly to people who don't know all the right words" (Luterman 2020, 4). Sara Luterman wrote this at the start of the plain language translation of "Disability Visibility" by Alice Wong. When I read this, I thought about all my disabled friends who aren't interested in the ideas coming from disability culture and disability activism. These friends had told me that when they read these ideas or hear people talk about them, they feel like the ideas aren't for them. My friends can't hold complicated ideas in their minds long enough to understand them because of brain fog or pain or cognitive impairment. Big words reminded them of university. There were a lot of barriers to my friends' doing well at university. This made them feel bad about themselves. Now, when they read ideas that are new and complicated, sometimes they feel like they are back in university. They feel like they can't have conversations with people using long sentences and words they don't know. When Luterman wrote, "Disability advocacy spaces can be unfriendly to people who don't know all the right words," I felt the truth of that. I also knew I had made disability culture and activism spaces unfriendly because I love big, complicated ideas and I sometimes write in ways that aren't clear.

I care about accessibility. Accessibility is when someone can take part in an experience in a way that feels meaningful to them (Ellcessor 2017, 6). This means the way the content is shared and the content itself has to be accessible. Accessibility is one of the ways disabled people get to have the experiences they want to have. I want to make disability culture and activism spaces and ideas more accessible. Plain language is a tool that can make disability culture and activism more accessible to people who feel like complicated language and ideas aren't for them.

Plain language is a way of writing and designing text. Plainlanguage.gov says, "Plain language (also called plain writing or plain English) is communication your audience can understand the first time they read or hear it" (n.d., para. 1). This means that people reading plain language don't have to work to understand the text. Usually, people creating plain language documents want to make knowledge available to people who are not experts (Myers and Martin 2021, para. 7), often so they can make better decisions (Jones and Williams 2017, 415; Sims 2020, 14). Usually these decisions are about practical things like what to buy, whether someone should sign a contract, how to fill out a form for the government, what kind of medical treatment to try first, or who to vote for.

In this chapter I'm going to tell you some of the things I've learned about plain language. This includes some of the history of plain language. Plain language is used in a lot of different places. Because it is used in so many different places, there are a lot of different ways to write plain language. I talk about some of the ways critical disability researchers (McRuer 2006; Price 2011; St. Pierre 2015, 2017; Yergeau 2018) have thought about disability and communication. These researchers say that disability communication can have multiple messages and can take a lot of work to make and understand, and we don't always know what people are trying to say. Often, people think good communication is the opposite of this.

One of the reasons we think it is important for communication to be clear and easy to understand is that we live in a capitalist society. Capitalism is a system in which we give people money in order to get the things we need to live. It's useful for communication to be quick and easy in capitalism because then people can buy and sell things more quickly and people can make more money. Capitalism is not kind to disabled people. Disability communication doesn't work well with capitalism. But plain language is all about communicating clearly and easily. So does plain language support capitalism and reinforce "normal," nondisabled ways of doing things? At the end of the chapter I talk a bit about why we might still practice plain language and the future of plain language in the disability community.

HISTORIES OF PLAIN LANGUAGE

I found that plain language has complicated histories. For the most part those histories do not include disability. Researchers trace plain language back to many different starting points. Russell Wilterton (2015) says people in the fourteenth century cared about clear communication. In 1948, Rudolf Flesch developed the first version of his Reading Ease test. This test scores documents for how long the words and sentences in it are.

Eleanor Cornelius (2015) says that in the 1960s and 1970s people in Australia, Canada, Ireland, Sweden, Denmark, France, Germany, Italy, India, Singapore, South Africa, Hong Kong, Papua New Guinea, and New Zealand all started to ask for consumer information in plain language. This means information like whether a company will fix something you bought from them if it breaks, what companies will do with information you give them, and whether you can return something that doesn't work.

Today, plain language is used in a lot of different areas, including government documents, legal writing, technical writing, and medical information. The US government has passed several laws saying the government must communicate clearly. The most recent is the Plain Writing Act of 2020, which requires each federal agency to monitor documents released for plain language and give their employees training and resources in plain language (Sims 2020, 13). Plain language is also an important part of legal writing in Canada, the United States, and Australia (Balmford, n.d, para. 54; Wilterton 2015, 7). Plain language has been adopted as a tool in technical writing. This is because people doing technical writing are starting to think about how their work can help create a more just world (Jones and Williams 2017, 427; Sims 2020, 17). Finally, some medical researchers have started including plain language summaries in their articles (Myers and Martin 2021, para. 7). This means medical researchers write a few sentences at the start of the article so people who are not doctors can understand it. The idea that people should communicate clearly has been around for a long time. So there are many different places and fields where plain language is practiced. There are also a lot of different places and fields where people say plain language should be used.

Karen Shriver (2017) reviewed over a hundred documents related to the development of plain language in the United States. She found that over the past seventy years, there has been a shift from thinking about how easy the document is to read based on sentences and words, to thinking about the whole document (2017, 368). This includes thinking about how the text is laid out and designed—for example, how big the letters are and the font used. There is now a focus on whether people can use the information in the document and also whether people trust the information.

Researchers who want to know if people can trust and use the information in a document often call this a "human-centered design approach" (Jones and Williams 2017, 427).

This means that the people who will be using the document should be involved in creating the document. This is because confusing content is not the only way writing creates problems for people. For example, Natasha Jones and Miriam Williams (2017) looked at the documents people use to decide whether they should borrow money from a bank to buy a house. They found that one of the issues with these documents was that they left out important information. The information that was there was understandable, but people needed more information to actually decide whether they should borrow money. The people who will use the documents should be involved in the process of creating them, right from the start, so they can have a say in everything involved with the documents.

In the 1960s and 1970s people thought plain language was mostly for people making decisions about what to buy. Now people who write plain language think of their work as being for a lot of different people. Shriver (2017, 375) says people who write plain language started thinking about disabled people using plain language in the 2000s. It's difficult to trace the history of disabled people using plain language. Lots of disability groups, such as the Autistic Self Advocacy Network (n.d.) and the Green Mountain Self-Advocates (2020), provide plain language information to their members. Alice Wong asked Sara Luterman to make a plain language translation of "Disability Visibility" (Luterman 2020). Just because some people writing plain language didn't think about disabled people needing plain language until the 2000s doesn't mean that disabled people weren't using plain language before then.

People who write plain language want people to make good decisions for themselves (Maaß 2020, 41). This is a value shared by disability rights activists who demand independence and decision making for disabled people (Charlton 1998, 128). Disabled people need clear, easily available information in order to make decisions too.

HOW TO WRITE PLAIN LANGUAGE

Plain language is used in many different fields and places. So there are a lot of ways to write it. I read five pieces of writing that explain how to use plain language. I chose the "United States Federal Plain Language Guidelines" (plainlanguage .gov, 2011), the "Plain Language Commission Style Guide" from the United Kingdom (Carr, 2019), "Five Steps to Plain Language" from Center for Plain Language in the United States (n.d.), and the Australian government's "Style Manual" (2021) because people writing about plain language often talk about these pieces of writing. They also come from different places in the English-speaking world. I included Luterman's foreword to the plain language version of "Disability Visibility" as an example of using plain language to share disability culture. When I read through all of these guides, I found 72 ways to write plain language. Only 14 of these ways are in two or more guides. The following are the 14 ways to write plain language:

- Know who you are writing for.
- Put your information in an order that makes sense.
- Use headings.
- Write short sentences.
- Use the active voice.
- Use contractions like **don't** and **couldn't**.
- Use **you** for the reader and **we** for the organization preparing the document.
- Don't use unnecessary words.
- Try not to use abbreviations.
- Use words to mean what they usually mean.
- Write short sentences.
- Write short paragraphs.
- Use words or phrases that help the reader move between paragraphs.
- Ask the people you want to use your documents to test them.

All these suggestions are good suggestions. But generally, people don't agree on how to write plain language. Shriver (2017, 348) notes that there is a lot of research that could tell us how to write plain language. But this research is spread over many different areas of study like linguistics, education, and technical writing. People who write plain language need someone to bring together all this research and tell us how to write plain language based on research. Until then, most people won't entirely agree on how to write plain language.

CRITICAL DISABILITY STUDIES, PLAIN LANGUAGE, AND COMMUNICATION

No matter how we write plain language, we want clear writing that people understand quickly. This way of writing is very different from the way some critical disability studies researchers have thought about writing and communication. Critical disability studies researchers are often interested in how disability can change the way the world thinks we should speak or write. Critical disability studies researchers like Robert McRuer (2006), Joshua St. Pierre (2015, 2017), M. Remi Yergeau (2018), and Margaret Price (2011) often write about nondisabled people assuming that everyone should write or speak:

- clearly
- quickly
- in an order that makes sense to a lot of people
- so there is only one meaning, and
- efficiently, so that other people don't have to work to understand.

As I mentioned earlier, the world assumes people should write or speak in these ways because of capitalism. Capitalism teaches us to value speed and efficiency (Adam 2004, 64). For example, think of a factory. The factory owner wants to increase the speed of production and to eliminate any pauses in making the product. This is because if the factory can produce more of the product in a shorter time, then the factory can make more money. Capitalism also teaches us that time needs to be linear and there should be a direct movement from past to present to future. This way of thinking about time is everywhere in Western culture. We want to be as efficient and direct as possible. But often disabled people are not efficient or direct.

St. Pierre (2015), Yergeau (2018), and Price (2011) all explain how disabled people's communication can be different from the ways people are generally expected to communicate. These differences between how disabled people communicate and how they're supposed to communicate can help us imagine how the world could be different. In particular, they help us imagine a world that is not about efficiency and directness. A world without efficiency and directness could be a better world for disabled people.

St. Pierre (2015, 2017) is a researcher who writes about stuttering and fluency. For him, **fluency** is a word that is related to the world's ideas about what is normal. Fluency is about time. Fluency is the smooth movement from the past to the present to the future at a pace that most people feel OK with (St. Pierre 2015). People who are fluent don't look like they're working hard when they speak. Fluency creates a singular meaning. Disabled people may have a hard time creating fluency. Sometimes disabled people speak at a speed that is not expected by other people. For example, someone who stutters speaks at an uneven pace. Or someone who types to speak will create long pauses in the conversation. Sometimes disabled people have to work really hard to make other people understand them. For St. Pierre (2017), **disfluency** is a word for the way people who speak with a lot of effort, or who speak at an unexpected speed, or whose words can mean a lot of different things force us to consider different ways of speaking and communicating from our usual, fluent ways. It's important to note that St. Pierre (2015) is talking about speech, but I think what St. Pierre (2015, 2017) says is often true of writing as well.

Sometimes we value writing that takes time to read or has multiple meanings. But often we are taught to write in ways that will be quick to read and have one clear meaning. McRuer (2006) describes the university composition classroom as "intent on the production of order and efficiency" (151). Composition class is a class where students learn to write. McRuer means that university writing classes teach people to write in a very specific way that can be quickly and easily read. He also points out that:

> Composition theory has not yet recognized (or perhaps has censored the "imagined possibility") that the demand for certain kinds of finished projects in the writing classroom is congruent with the demand for certain kinds of bodies (2006, 158–159).

McRuer is saying that disabled people have a hard time producing the kind of writing that the people who write composition theory and teach composition class demand. This is similar to St. Pierre (2015, 2017) saying that disabled people have a hard time speaking in the ways the world expects them to. In both cases the world expects people to write and speak in ways that are easy and quick to understand.

Yergeau (2018) is a researcher who has written about autistic rhetoric. Autistic rhetoric includes the ways people write and talk about autistic people and how autistic people actually communicate. Yergeau writes about echolalia. Echolalia is the repetition of words and phrases. Yergeau says that the repetition of words and phrases is often not about the words and phrases themselves. The words and phrases are tools to communicate a wide range of feelings and meanings. Echolalia uses words or phrases to mean many different things. But the world doesn't value ways of speaking or writing that create multiple meanings.

If the way you communicate has multiple meanings or is confusing, then people will say you don't make sense. Price (2011, 26) also writes about teaching writing to university students. She points out that one of the ways the world recognizes people as people is to ask if they make sense. Making sense can mean communicating only one meaning. It can mean communicating with only the right amount of emotion. If a writing student doesn't make sense, then writing teachers might decide the student is disabled. But deciding a student is disabled doesn't mean that the teacher will make their classroom more accessible or try to help the student. Instead, the teacher might create more barriers. This is because if people don't make sense, the world is unkind to them.

St. Pierre (2015, 2017), McRuer (2006), Yergeau (2018), and Price (2011) all talk about how disabled people can't communicate the way the world expects them to. If people can't communicate the way the world expects them to, then they are discriminated against. This could mean that there might be more barriers to their finishing university, getting a job, and connecting with other people. So critical disability researchers want to make it OK for disabled people to communicate however they communicate. They want to make it more than OK. They want all the ways disabled people communicate to be respected.

In many ways plain language is the opposite of the kinds of communication St. Pierre (2015, 2017), McRuer (2006), Yergeau (2018), and Price (2011) are talking about. Using short sentences, lists, and the most common words possible are all ways of writing to make reading quick and easy. Using the most common words possible is also contrary to the ways disability communities have consistently reclaimed and reshaped language. In other chapters of this book, you might have read words like **crip** or **mad** or **neurodivergent**. The people who wrote those chapters used those words because they mean very specific things. But they also used them because they are unfamiliar, or they are used in unfamiliar ways. They are meant to stop the reader. These words slow the reader and make them consider ways of understanding disability and the world that the reader has not previously considered. These words change the pace you read at, the same way St. Pierre (2015) says stuttering changes the pace you listen at. Plain language is all about being quick and direct and asking the reader to do as little work as possible.

Disability could change the world because it forces us to question our focus on speed and efficiency. I also kept thinking about the ways I had seen disability culture and disability activism be unfriendly to many disabled people because of the ways we ask people to read. If there is one thing I have learned from disability culture, it is that there is never one right way of being, doing, or communicating. Usually the best way to make things accessible is to have lots of different ways of communicating.

I think plain language documents should exist alongside complex text, much the same way we might make sound recordings of writing, caption videos, or have important information translated into our local sign language. Critical disability scholars need to think about how we write and who we write for. Is complex language the only way we can imagine new ways of thinking and being? Who do we exclude from new thinking about disability when we use big words and complicated sentences? I can be excited about the ways disabled people communicate that make me work to understand. And I can understand that for other people that can be a barrier. I don't want disability culture and activism to only be for some people; I want everyone to be welcome.

DISABILITY CULTURE PLAIN LANGUAGE

Beyond this, I want disabled people to claim and imagine plain language for ourselves. Nondisabled people don't agree on how to write plain language. So maybe disabled people can develop a version of plain language that is for disability communities.

When I was describing the history of plain language, I mentioned that some researchers want plain language to take a human-centered design approach where the people who will use the documents are involved in the creation of documents. Involving disabled people who need plain language in making plain language documents could lead to new ways of writing plain language. Developing new access tools and better ways of creating access is one of the things disabled people do best.

I think Luterman (2020, 3) is right that everyone should have access to what disabled people think about disability. Plain language shouldn't just be for making decisions about what to buy, what medical treatment you should have, or who to vote for. Those are important. But so are the ideas coming from disability culture. Everyone should be able to read writing that is about how incredible disabled people are. Everyone should be able to see or listen to art about the ways disabled people care for each other. Writing that celebrates and loves disabled people can make people much happier. It can be life-saving.

Plain language can be an important tool in sharing disability culture with everyone who needs it. Involving people who need plain language to understand disability culture and new ways of thinking about disability could help me, and other people, find a version of plain language that is for disability culture.

BIBLIOGRAPHY

Adam, Barbara. 2004. **Time**. Hoboken, NJ: Wiley-Blackwell.
Australian Government. 2021. "Clear Language and Writing Style." *Style Manual*. Accessed May 28, 2021. https://www.stylemanual .gov.au/writing-and-designing-content/clear-language-and -writing-style.
Autistic Self Advocacy Network. n.d. "Accessibility Resources." Accessed September 28, 2021. https://autisticadvocacy.org /resources/accessibility/.

Balmford, Christopher. n.d. "Plain Language: Beyond a Movement." Plainlanguage.gov. Accessed July 27, 2021. https://www.plainlanguage.gov/resources/articles/beyond-a-movement/.

Carr, Sarah. 2019. **Plain Language Commission Style Guide**. Plain Language Commission. Accessed June 7, 2021. https://clearest.co.uk/wp-content/uploads/2021/09/PLCstyleguide7Oct2019_mf.pdf.

Center for Plain Language. n.d. "Five Steps to Plain Language." Centre for Plain Language. Accessed June 9, 2021. https://centerforplainlanguage.org/learning-training/five-steps-plain-language/.

Charlton, James I. 1998. **Nothing about Us without Us: Disability Oppression and Empowerment**. Berkeley: University of California Press.

Cornelius, Eleanor. 2015. "Defining 'Plain Language' in Contemporary South Africa." **Stellenbosch Papers in Linguistics** 44:1–18.

Ellcessor, Elizabeth. 2016. Restricted Access, Media, Disability and the Politics of Participation. NYU Press.

Green Mountain Self-Advocates. 2020. "COVID-19 Vaccine Information in Plain Language." December 15, 2020. https://gmsavt.org/resources/covid-19-vaccine-information-in-plain-language.

Jones, Natasha N., and Miriam F. Williams. 2017. "The Social Justice Impact of Plain Language: A Critical Approach to Plain Language Analysis." **IEEE Transactions on Professional Communication** 60 (4): 412–429.

Luterman, Sara. 2020. "Plain Language Translation of **Disability Visibility: First-Person Stories from the Twenty-First Century**." In "Disability Visibility Anthology," **Disability Visibility Project** (blog), June 30, 2020. https://disabilityvisibilityproject.com/book/dv/.

Maaß, Christiane. 2020. **Easy Language—Plain Language—Easy Language Plus: Balancing Comprehensibility and Acceptability**. Berlin: Frank & Timme.

McRuer, Robert. 2006. **Crip Theory: Cultural Signs of Queerness and Disability**. New York: New York University Press.

Myers, Beth, and Teukie Martin. 2021. "Why Plain Language? Linguistic Accessibility in Inclusive Higher Education." **Journal**

of Inclusive Postsecondary Education 3 (1). https://doi.org/10
.13021/jipe.2021.2953.

Plainlanguage.gov. n.d. "What Is Plain Language?" Accessed
August 15, 2021. https://www.plainlanguage.gov/about
/definitions/.

Plainlanguage.gov. 2011. Federal Plain Language Guidelines.
Accessed June 11, 2021. https://www.plainlanguage.gov/media
/FederalPLGuidelines.pdf

Price, Margaret. 2011. Mad at School: Rhetorics of Mental Disability and Academic Life. Ann Arbor: University of Michigan
Press.

Shakespeare, Tom. 2006. Disability Rights and Wrongs. London:
Routledge.

Shriver, Karen. 2017. "Plain Language in the US Gains Momentum
1940–2015." IEEE Transactions on Professional Communication 60 (4): 343–383.

Sims, Michaela. 2020. "Overcoming Tools of Oppression: Plain
Language and Human Centered Design for Social Justice." MA
thesis, University of Minnesota.

St. Pierre, Joshua. 2015. "Distending Straight-Masculine Time:
A Phenomenology of the Disabled Speaking Body." Hypatia 30 (1):
49–65.

———. 2017. "Becoming Dysfluent: Fluency as Biopolitics and
Hegemony." Journal of Literary and Cultural Disability Studies 11 (3): 339–356.

Wilterton, Russell. 2015. Plain Language and Ethical Action:
A Dialogic Approach to Technical Content in the Twenty-First
Century. New York: Routledge.

Yergeau, M. Remi. 2018. Authoring Autism: On Rhetoric and
Neurological Queerness. Durham, NC: Duke University Press.

6

Peter Pan World: In-System Authorship

Isolation Nation

JIM: Great! Maybe you can create a science article about that for me!
INGRID: Certainly! *I think the species can also create an article about itself!*
—Michael Gluzman[1]

Introducing

Isolation Nation was a six-week multimedia arts project undertaken "in-system" in fall 2020 by artists with a broad array of neurodivergent and developmentally disabled experiences. *In-system* refers to the fact that everyone involved receives significant support from a Medicaid-funded, not-for-profit organization. The twelve artists who took part all participated voluntarily and joined from several agencies across the northeastern United States. Isolation Nation includes people with a range of ages, races, religions, and genders. Throughout the project, group members refer to themselves using both identity-first and person-first language, and this is reflected in the writing. Most of the content comes directly from the disabled artists, and any external reflections or questions are indicated by the use of italics. Where people communicate an idea using poetry, art, or photographs, that is included.

Before starting the process, everybody was sent a description, release form, and agreement stating that whatever was discussed and created would not be censored or altered in any way by the participating agencies or involved guardians. Artists would retain all rights to their work. The goal of the project was to collectively fuse the accrued multimedia work into a short film, now publicly available (https://tinyurl.com/8uwsfwem). The final film is an amalgamation of the visual, sound, and written work submitted by the artists. The intention was for the completed project to be accessible in multiple ways: visually, aurally, or a mixture of both. It was edited and reviewed several times by all group members before being released publicly.

This chapter contains reflections that were collected through multiple written and verbal interviews, a transcribed reunion conversation about the experience of collective creation, and contemporaneous notes and the art itself. In the world around in-system disability authorship, the bubble of creativity is carved out of the system, against the odds, the permissions, the fatigue, the pandemic, the schedules, and the staffing.

Artists have given specific permission for their work to be reproduced for the purposes of this chapter. Every part of the original project and this chapter has been subject to multiple group revisions and edits, to ensure that the work reflects the intentions of those involved. The reflections have been broken down into the dominant themes that emerged. This is in order to highlight the non-verbal and fugitive conversations that occurred adjacent to the main discourse.

From the curator, Cathy James: I have worked for about twenty-five years as an arts facilitator alongside developmentally disabled adults. Because of the nature of the Medicaid system, I have had long relationships with many artists and over time we have developed both a mission and set of working practices that attempt to emphasize group-directed processes and minimize my footprint. However, it is impossible to remove myself from the power dynamic or deny that my role is rarely held to scrutiny. I have no vote in company matters, and creative projects are selected based on two group-identified goals: to make money and to have artists be recognized as capable, worthy, and fully human. This is the engagement sought by my colleagues, and thus these are the organizing principles of our work. In the introduction to her book *Geontologies*, Elizabeth Povinelli discusses how certain populations "only lightly scratch the retina of dominant ethical and political discourse" (21). So it continues to be with the more segregated existences of those people with an intellectual or developmental disability who live in-system.

Artists all selected how they wished to be credited—by full name, first name, or initials.

Venting

ALEX: *(From a poem)* We all make mistakes and none of us are perfect. So why do I need to be better than I am in order for people to accept me? We should not have to try to change just to be loved and accepted by others. Why does my behavior need to be perfect and wonderful so people will love me? Despite all my flaws, I have just as much right to be loved and accepted as any other person. So why doesn't everyone accept me? Is it because I'm too emotional? Is because I struggle to communicate with others? Because that's what people have often told me. And when they have told me these things, pointed out my flaws, this made me feel bad. It gives me a sense I'm just not good enough, that I need to change who I am as a person just for them to accept me.

MARIA: Slow down is safety. At work I was employee of the month. I miss work. I have to explain myself to them a lot. They need disability awareness. Sometimes I have to say leave me alone, let me have my bad days. Let me sometimes be upset. I have feelings too. I am not made of stone. I have a heart. I can only be angry in my room, alone. No *(I cannot be angry in front of other people)* I would even run to the bathroom and cry. But then they can go suck it. We don't want to feel like the outcasts. We are almost like the lost kids. Like Peter Pan. We're almost like Peter Pan and the lost boys. We feel as though we live within a Peter Pan world almost.

CATHY: *That's a really interesting thing to say. What makes you feel like the lost boys?*

MARIA: Well, the thing is, I feel as though people don't listen to us. We were never allowed to even grow up, we were always treated as though we were children. And that's gotta stop. That Peter Pan fantasy? Oh, that's gotta stop.

JORDAN: Oh, I was ready to go out again months ago. I am angry about how it was handled. That's putting it mildly, assuming Trump was handling it at all. Because I imagine they, the majority of disabled people, probably had some sort of spots they frequented, and that they would really rather be. That's their sense of normalcy. Maybe the closest thing to companionship I think. Even if it's with an inanimate object like a comic book or pen or some colored marker or something. That's my general interest is comic books, art supplies, movies.

CATHY: *Did making things help you to get through?*

JORDAN: Mostly, yes. I guess at this point costume making to pick up some fabric.

MIKE: There is a staff person that meant a lot to me. She is close like family. I miss that connection. It has been three months since I seen her. She touches my heart. I like cooking for her. She loves food.

MAX: There are so many places in the workplace, in art spaces whatever, where they are like "We don't talk about politics here, there are people who would freak out." That's another thing there are people who have outbursts but they're treating disabled people like "He can't know about bad things he'll freak out!" And the truth is, we should be angry, we should freak out. During Isolation Nation was one of the few spaces where I felt listened to and respected as a disabled person. There is a tendency when working with disabled folks to censor them or not to allow them to have their own thoughts and actions. This was a very free and open exchange.

Community Building

CATHY: *What does it mean to you to make art with other disabled people?*

MAX: The solidarity between all the artists who have different disabilities and all of us have different struggles, but we can find a commonality. Not all of us are going to be treated differently so we're building a space that is radically accepting and everyone tries to build that space. We're in this *(online)* space that we've created. And in here is built for people who are not neurotypical or have a disability or are different.

BRAD: (9,5) Makes you forget, makes you forget the pain, and how you feel. (9,1,1) You don't know. (1,1,6) You don't sit. (1,8,0) You don't sit at home.

(Brad communicates using a typing system, and the transcriptions of our inter-
views included the voice of his support worker Ayanna speaking numbers and
letters aloud. These have been included where recorded.)

CATHY: *So, art is an escape?*

BRAD: *(Nods)* Yes. Yeah.

ALEX: I feel that it is different with other disabled artists. I feel like, I feel like
they can kind of understand me better. 'Cause I'm one of them. I'm disabled
just like them. It just gives me a sense of community, a space where I belong.
I think the disabled art environments allow me to express myself differently.
They accept all my most important pieces. I am working and sharing feelings
without anybody judging me. I haven't always been, haven't always been able
to do that. Sometimes in life when I try to express myself, I feel like people
aren't really willing to listen clearly to what I have to say. I feel they don't
really understand me.

MAX: *(From a poem)*

> But within these hallowed halls of artists and folks with similar brain patterns
> who diverged.
> My experience has been radically free,
> not tokenized as most people with disabilities seem to be,
> but more so actually heard,
> listening to and valuing what I have to say
> interested in art and poetry.
> Like today.
> An actual interest.
> Fascination with anything, me or my comrades might have to talk about
> our own experiences even without relying on . . .
> "Oh, isn't that cute. Oh, you're an artist, or at least you're trying."
> Now, with you, it's different.
> Within these halls of Isolation Nation staring at this screen.
> We feel heard accepted and seen.
> Thank you.
> From the inside of my mind to the outside of my body or here hearing what
> I have to say,
> maybe let the light of creativity shine another day.

MIKE: It helped me create in that I want to create more art.

CATHY: *Tell me about the use of the chat function on Zoom. It was really a space*
without intervention. There were very few staff using it. What did it mean to
you? What happened in that space?

MARIA: OK on what I'm seeing, I'm seeing that, that we're all not the same.
We all have our own feelings and opinions about things and in the chat box

right, a lot of us we cannot say it verbally so this is why we have to have that chat box there. So we will be able to express how we feel by writing it down. That's like our voice.

EZ: We like to be funny and supportive.

PARIS: I use the chat to say hello. Give compliments.

MAX: I didn't actually use the chat box very much, but I like that it teaches people how to self-govern . . . I use voice-to-text, that's how I communicate so I don't really use the voice chat box as much . . . We are being told what to do a lot. We can have trouble doing things on our own. It's culturally a thing to have someone tell us what to do. And I love it when people have their own authority, their own rule.

CATHY: *Uriel used the chat function to make suggestions and to confront me in a way that seemed to feel safer than speaking his concerns directly. The chat function made it more comfortable for him to address the inescapable complexity of hierarchy.*

Persuading

CATHY: *When you make art, do you feel like you're trying to persuade other people, or do you create just for yourself? Do you work in the hopes that other people will understand you? Or both? Or neither?*

ALEX: Well, I do hope the other people will hear what I have to say . . . more like for community at large. I just want the world to be more accepting of me and other disabled people. I think it *(art)* allows me to share my message to the community at large. Hopefully it'll help. It'll help people understand. We need to be more understanding of disabled people like me.

MARIA: The reason I write for myself, it's because I want to feel comfortable in my skin for one, and then for two and I also want to educate those who are not like . . . what's the word I'm looking for? Education. I'm trying to educate the world. I'm saying look, I'm exactly like you. Don't look at me. I may need help in some things, in being myself, even though sometimes I need you. That's why I show them my poems. I don't feel good about myself sometimes right? Sometimes people don't see me as a person. I think that I don't want them just to see me with my challenges, right? I also want them to see me as a person.

CATHY: *Do you feel like you have to educate people, and does that ever get tiring?*

ALEX: I feel I have to educate people? Yes, I do. It's really about trying to have people accept you as you are.

MARIA: Yes. I feel as though they don't understand me. I feel as though they're trying to fix me.

They want me to be what they want me to be. And I'm like no, I'm not gonna be whatever you want me to be. Okay, let me just be myself. Let me have these feelings. I'm the teacher. I'm the teacher. And they're the students in a way. I do get angry. I think there isn't such a thing as normal.

MAX: I don't know, I feel like there's always going to be some sort of outsider looking in, when we're showing disabled folks and disabled artists to people who are not disabled. I don't know I always feel a little weird about it, but I'm glad we're able to do that. I think I would like to make art that's accessible for everyone.

BRAD: I feel bad for cerebral people. They want to, look to, (7 2 6 7 6) they look down (3 C 6) they look down on cerebral palsy. I see art as a way of showing people CP differently. Yes.

MIKE: Yes, it is important to relate to my work. But the art speaks for itself. I make art for the people.

JORDAN: I make art for myself. Anyone else who gets to see it is just lucky, I think. People don't have to understand what my work's about, but if they like it, good for them.

EZ: I want people to know more about me and stop judging me.

Imagining

CATHY: *What belongs in the future? What belongs in the future for disabled people?*

URIEL: *(Uriel made videos and took photographs of his ropes [figure 6.1] when imagining disabled futures. He described what they meant to him.)* It helps me yes. They help me concentrate on my art and they help me calm down. It helps me concentrate on my shredding business. *(Uriel and a friend have a business shredding documents.)* If somebody took them away that would make me freak out. Yes.

MIKE: *(This was from a song written shortly before the 2020 presidential election.)* Please vote for Joe Biden. For a loving heart. Love and guide you. Do it for me. Mom and dad always love you. Thank you so much. Let's stop the violence and stop the madness. Please God tell every one of the people that love you and care for you always. Please, please, vote Joe Biden. Thank you. God bless everyone else.

MAX: Radical freedom, radical accountability, egalitarianism. Prioritizing safety. Refuse corporatization. We are at a tipping point. Without rulers, exploitation, oligarchs, ableism. A place where we are not fetishized. No racism. Replace governments with you and me. Mutual aid. Zoom. Networks. Strength. Love. Kindness. Each according to ability and need. Choice. Community. Help each other. Capitalism doesn't care about you. Organization. Communities like this meeting. Radical love and acceptance. We're tired. We want change. We are planting seeds of a tree that we will never sit in the shade of. We need to build.

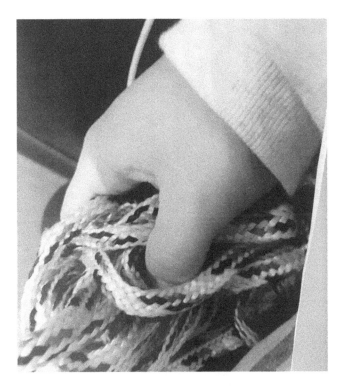

Figure 6.1. Uriel took a self-portrait of his hand holding a set of yellow ropes that have been looped together so they are held more easily.

PARIS: Smell the tree. Listen to the tree. The tree will save us. The tree will save us from warming in the world. We breathe because of the trees *(figure 6.2)*.

EZ: The future is about kindness and respect.

BRAD: I would open a new business. CP would be allowed in schools. I want to educate. Travel. Spread awareness of disability. Cerebral palsy. People think we are dumb. We are not dumb. I am lucky I have my wheelchair. And my apartment.

URIEL: I would camp with my best friend. Best buds. I have my ropes. Good friends. Families. My ropes help me concentrate. Ropes for all. I love ropes. I want to share my love of ropes.

MAX: I think community is going to be a big part of this. Just like the community we have now with these little Zoom meetings. The community that we're going to build is going to eventually become its own organism and we gotta make sure it's built in a way that is fair to all, equal to all and it doesn't stoop to the violence of what other systems stoop to. We have to organize ourselves and I realize I'm being recorded don't know what I'm saying. I mean I know what I'm saying but it's very hard 'cause this is a very emotional thing for me.

BRAD: We work too much.

Figure 6.2. Paris drew an image of a tree, a leaf, and a hand side by side. They are surrounded by floating leaves and words that read, "Feel the tree, touch the tree, kiss the tree, the tree is alive, hug the tree, listen to the tree, see the tree, taste the tree." The drawing is made with marker, and the main focus of color is the variety of shades of green used on the leaves and trees. The outline of the hand blends into a spiral in the center of the palm, where the words, "Have fun with the tree," can be seen.

CATHY: *What should we be doing instead of working, Brad?*
BRAD: (9 9) Having fun. (9 8) Go (1 9 7) on more vacations, travel everywhere. (2 3 0) I (2 3 W) I went traveling before the pandemic. (8 0) I (1 0) like (1 2 4) work. (1 2 4) Working (1 0 5) makes (1 2 1 3 5 E) makes me (9 3) feel (2 1) happy.
MAX: Profit over relationships, that needs to change.
BRAD: I want a girl to date. CP. Sexy hotness. *(There is much agreement that we want sexy hotness in our futures.)*
CATHY: *What kind of touch do you experience? What does it mean to you?*
MAX: I had a partner and sometimes it was shaming. I feel comfort and discomfort with my body, the fear that comes with being non-binary. Passion comes with hurt and manipulation. Then negotiation of touch is important when you're neurodivergent.

(The foregoing paragraph was a reflection from 2020, and Max wanted to update this during our editing session for this chapter. They wanted to add details of a more recent relationship that was newly fulfilling.)

Wild eyes and DIY patches all over her vest. Non-binary trans and ready to throw hands. My God she's beautiful. You should see the way she smiles when she talks about Anarchism, skirt swaying in the wind. I see the trauma in her eyes. It's the same trauma I carry in a town that says we don't exist or if we do exist it's as a fetish . . . as long as I'm with her I can finally feel safe. Frankly I don't care what labels we use so long as I get to spend time with her, whether it's taking down fascist stickers with our pocket knives, skateboarding through the neighborhood or just cuddling underneath the tree, I finally found someone I can trust.

PARIS: I speak for the tree, hug the tree, touch the tree, the tree is alive. Love the tree, kiss the tree.

JORDAN: I used to touch the subway pole, park benches, summer breezes, hot dog vendors, open hydrants, ice cream trucks.

URIEL: Ropes are touch. Lake. Touch of water. It feels good. It is warm. I swim like a fish. On the dock I sit and feel peaceful. Touch is comfort.

PARIS: I had manicures. She touched my hands, and I touched her hands.

MAX: I miss getting tattooed. Now I use henna. Tattoo is intimacy.

URIEL: Ropes for all.

MAX: I drop a curtsey with my friends. That's how we touch. Without touch.

MARIA: Sassy is the closest thing I have to an angel. Sassy is a stuffed cat. I want her in the book because she is my comfort. I hold her when I am upset.

JORDAN: I would create a virtual world. Everyone can interact with one another without the fear of contracting any physical viruses. I can't speak for virtual ones. This way everyone can be safe and indulge or get their wildest fantasies without little to no consequences. It's a basic win/win scenario this week. Plus, you have a way to settle online debates once and for all. My interest in science fiction, that was kind of the easiest thing that come up on. You think that, when you think about the virtual world. Then you figure out that the atmosphere will probably be too toxic to really go outside anyway. Which means we're going to have to pick up into virtual worlds anyway. All the clothes being made in factories, destroying the rain forests, then the parks, killing all the trees, destroying the atmosphere. Pollution.

MAX: We float, we swim, we crawl, we fly, we walk, we stagger, we wobble, we drive, we project.

MC: We need more naps, because it's good for your health when your body feels sleepy. It's good for your health especially on cloudy, rainy days when you feel so comfortable. My body feels so refreshed. I need rest and I don't worry so much about my health issues 'cause I need my rest. Otherwise, I get coughing gags or something.

CATHY: *So, this project has reminded you to kind of slow down and take care of yourself and remember that coziness is important?*

MC: Yes, I am super comfortable with naps, and you have all witnessed it! And I am not the only one. I said to my friend I said do you feel sleepy? Because she gets sleepy with the cloudy weather thing.

CATHY: *Do we need a new flag for the future? A new anthem?*

MIKE: I have written a new national anthem. *(Mike wrote a song that was a plea for tolerance, love, respect for your parents, and a stop to violence, as well as a request that everyone vote for Joe Biden.)*

JORDAN: The new flag is a peace sign. With a rainbow. The stripes are melting. There is a beaver escaping. *(This is Jordan's symbol for Donald Trump; a beaver represents his hair.)*

MARIA: This is a picture of a loom. All the pegs together. We need to be as one. We knit everyone together.

PARIS: I change the flag. It shows Black Lives Matter, equality, and the earth.

MIKE: This is an alien. It is friendly. This is a flag of all colors *(figure 6.3).*

Amplifying

"In system" habilitative spaces emphasize learning over teaching. To live on a kind of "competence probation" is an everyday reality for many; to be required to continually, repetitively demonstrate capacity. Education is clearly a space of agency and self-definition that can be elusive. To be an expert is to upend the hierarchical positioning of people with developmental disabilities and to carve out a valued role that speaks back to traditional abled values in subversive ways.

Community building is made complex by the bureaucratically required implementation of goals and plans that often prioritize living skills over relationships. Yet community grows both intentionally and through the cracks. Mutuality is often an act of fugitivity, a secondary and unexpressed intention inside disabled systems where gatekeeping remains entrenched.

The chat box function on Zoom has emerged as a place that exists without typical oversight or habilitation. It contains a second layer of communication that supports, encourages, and clarifies. Within it lies the potential for the assertion of a self-defined subjectivity that communicates its truth loudly in its own styling. Herein lies a space where venting and flirting occur alongside the more traditional expressions of peer support. It also became a space where the artists corrected, challenged, and guided me [Cathy] in ways that may have felt risky if done directly.

The artists of Isolation Nation expand and contribute to the ongoing dialogues around disability justice. However, contributions are often expressed in ways and spaces that remain underexposed and disregarded. Our understanding of what constitutes language has always been inadequate. In moving away from the complete sentence toward fragments, sound, art, outburst, image, and action, we are able to comprehend more fully the impressions, critiques, and desires of those who can barely "scratch the retina" of even mainstream disability culture.

Figure 6.3. Mike designed a new flag that incorporates more colors and a visiting alien. The flag is mixed media and shows two large black semicircles surrounded by a frilly, red border. The flag itself has blue, yellow, red, pink, and gray stripes. In the middle is a shape that resembles a flower, a planet, and a sun all at the same time. Underneath the flag are visiting aliens drawn in green.

MIKE: I am gonna eat my lunch now, I am gonna go. I love you all so much.

Artists: Alex Aerni, Arianna Priddle, Brad Goldman, Cathy James, EZ, JCW (Jordan), Johnny Mattei, MC, Maria Zulic, Max Maven, Michael Gluzman, Michael John Vecchio (Mike), Paris Victoria, Rayna, Uriel Levitt, and WS.

NOTE

1 Michael did not participate in Isolation Nation but is a neurodivergent poet, writer, and performer who participates weekly with Outside Voices Theater Company and Poets, of Course. Quote from his script is used with permission.

BIBLIOGRAPHY

Povinelli, Elizabeth A. 2016. *Geontologies a Requiem to Late Liberalism.* Duke University Press.

7

LatDisCrit and Counterstories

ALEXIS PADILLA

LatDisCrit is a mode of counterstorytelling about disability, race, and Latinx identities. It brings together the literatures of Latinx critical legal theory (Lat-Crit) and disability critical race theory (DisCrit), and its driving aims are emancipatory. LatDisCrit is a theory of pedagogy as well as writing. It emphasizes the significance of double consciousness in classroom ecologies (Annamma and Morrison 2018), especially as they foster spaces for decolonial solidarity (Annamma and Handy 2019; Padilla 2021a, 2021b, 2022). This chapter offers an illustrative example in which a special education teacher is, paradoxically, the dysfunctional antagonist with regard to inclusion and anti-ableist classroom dynamics for a five-year-old prekindergarten Latinx autistic student, Billy, in an urban district located in the midwestern United States (see Padilla et al. 2021 for further details and theoretical considerations regarding this example). An alliance between the student, his mother, and a Latinx psychologist yields a Lat-DisCrit counterstory about his education.

In formulating LatDisCrit, I also borrow two ideas from the critical hermeneutics of Paul Ricoeur: (1) the notion that authors are the first interpreters of their own work (1981), which has powerful implications for the analysis and facilitation of coauthorship and counterstorytelling as movement building; and (2) the concept of collective action as a social text (1971, 1974). The enactment of this latter idea entails that knowledge workers and activists in emancipatory movements read through specific identitarian lenses. In my case, blindness and Latinx identity are always at work in my authorial and interpretative endeavors. As an advocate, I had the privilege of both observing and helping enact a collective-action counterstory along with Billy's mother and his bilingual therapist.

LatDisCrit is a decolonial project concerned with intersectional disability agency and justice. As such, it deals with identity and alterity as manifestations of intersectional justice in action. It operates in practice as the enfleshment of resistance and emancipation against subaltern-marginalizing discourses and actions. LatDisCrit pursues (Padilla 2021a, 2021b, 2022) a critical integration of the literature strands associated with LatCrit theory[1] (Bernal 2002; E. Dávila and de Bradley 2010; Solórzano and Bernal 2001; Valdés 1999, 2000; Yosso 2000, 2006) and DisCrit[2] (Annamma, Connor, and Ferri 2013, 2016; Annamma, Ferri, and Connor 2019; B. Dávila 2015). The main contribution of LatCrit theory, which emerged as part of the critical legal studies movement (Unger 2015), was to emphasize the racialized nature of Latinx identities, even when white supremacist structural mechanisms tried to couch multiple forms of Latinidades as purely ethnic, often nationalist and nonracialized or politically neutral modes of being (Valdés and Bender 2022). DisCrit, on the other hand, has emerged primarily within schooling spheres. Still in the making, its original seven core tenets underscore the interlocking nature of race and disability as intersectional dimensions of oppression. DisCrit thinkers stress that these intersectional oppression spheres mustn't be couched merely in terms of interlocking modes of identity or representation, since that takes away their core social justice ethos (e.g., Connor Ferri, and Annamma 2021). Thus, both LatCrit and DisCrit stress the interplay of race/ethnicity, diasporic cultures, historical sociopolitics, and disability in conjunction with the multiple possibilities of Global South and Global North Latinx identities. Most of their explorations take place within Global North contexts, although Global South epistemologies (Santos and Meneses 2020) are an important part of the emerging political embodiments enacted through LatDisCrit, especially if one pays attention to decolonial Latinx and intersectionally grounded critical feminist political philosophers (Alcoff 2009; Calderón 2014; Castro-Gómez 2002, 2007; Mignolo 2000; Mignolo and Tlostanova 2006; Mignolo and Walsh 2018; Sandoval 2000; Wynter 2003; Yosso 2006).

Latinxness as authorship must therefore be seen as a possibilitarian justice-seeking thirdspace (Soja 1989; Waitoller and Annamma 2017). It's made up of waves and wakes of converging diasporas. These diasporic identities are constituted by what Robert Young (2001) calls tricontinentalism (alluding to Africa, Asia, and Latin America as neocolonial sociopolitical spaces). Often, these diasporic waves and wakes are filled with mixtures of extreme violence and pockets of hope; they embody alterity in the very making of continuous identitarian birth through border-crossing dynamicity. Blackness studies has been indispensable for understanding and explaining the interimperialist legacies of coloniality that make up LatDisCrit's contemporary manifestations of collective action as they enfold, for example, in Global North and Global South classrooms (Dei 2017; Dei and Hilowle 2018; Dei and McDermott 2014). Also shaping the process of decolonial emancipation is the cripping abjection associated with the embodiment of disability (Shildrick 2002), an often-neglected example of what Alejandro Vallega (2014) calls radical alterity or extreme otherness. Even in trans-Latinx embodiments of indigeneity and mestizaje, one needs to consider the vestiges of anti-Black and ableist sentiments. They proliferate through micropolitical, epistemological, and sociocultural oppression (Padilla 2021a, chap. 6).

In sum, in the tricontinental making of trans-Latinidades, there are pervasive macropolitical forces. Modes of interimperialism get enacted via what Nelson Maldonado-Torres (2007) calls the coloniality of power, knowledge, and being. This multifaceted configuration of coloniality translates at the micro level to internalized racism combined with deficit thinking and learned helplessness for most students of color with disabilities, their families or guardians, and even many of their advocates. Not surprisingly, it's common for anti-Black sentiment to drive intra-Latinx interactions among communities as well as white-dominated organizations for disabled people (Padilla 2021a, esp. chaps. 6, 8).

There are trans-Latinx students with ancestry from virtually all countries as well as racial and ethnic configurations in the Latin American tricontinental spectrum of sociopolitical diasporas. As such, they're endowed with what W. E. B. Du Bois (1924, 2007), alluding specifically to Black folks, called double consciousness (see also Rabaka 2010). Double consciousness is a paradoxical gift. Within dysfunctional classroom ecologies (Annamma and Morrison 2018), it "is most keen for those that exist at the intersections of multiple marginalized identities. . . . In a system of interlocking oppressions rooted in white supremacy, multiply-marginalized People of Color are most aware of how those oppressions function" (Annamma and Morrison 2018, 71–72). Hence, these multiply marginalized people of color, with or without disabilities, must be the center of analysis when one seeks to dismantle racially disparate outcomes and disabling modes of normalizing practices in and around classrooms (2018, 72). The focus on students of color without disabilities here is very significant. They are core allies for students of color with disabilities and their families to carry out their justice quests. They understand via double consciousness the racialized contours of oppression, and even when their understanding of disability dynamics may be partial or polluted with ableist or normalizing ideologies, their practical help is often paramount to concretize emancipatory victories.

As the example of Billy will show, to disrupt dysfunctional classroom ecologies, teachers aren't indispensable. Unfortunately, some of them are at the root of dysfunctional dynamics. But even when their role as emancipatory catalysts is preeminent, they shouldn't become messianic figures. They simply need to open doors to the collective gifts already present among their students and their families and advocates. Teachers and other students are invited to become coauthors and counterstorytellers. In Latinx and Chicanx circles, the concept of counterstories is interchangeable with that of *testimonios*, which, as defined by Cherríe Moraga (2011), are theories in the flesh. This means that counterstories are always embodied, and they're much more than mere narrative exercises. They theorize complex ways to disrupt and resist oppressive modes of domination through alternative knowledges and ways of undoing things that aren't right. In the emancipatory context of counterstorytelling, teachers are to roll up their sleeves and enact their power in the classroom as equals, as catalyzing forces in the process of creativity inherent to subaltern intersectionality. The rich legacy of witnessing (and experiencing) genocide and microaggressions among Indigenous, Black, pan-Asian, and trans-Latinx students with and without disabilities in the classroom will do the rest. In line with the theme of writing underscored in this section of the book, it's paramount to add here that teachers' writing is a tool of power. Even those notes that children bring home from their teachers are perceived by parents and guardians, especially among Latinx families, as statements of power. For children with disabilities, little ones like Billy, the diagnostic power of teachers' written and spoken words is immense. These words have the potential to either empower or leave terrible scars on a child's identity that lead to internalized deficit thinking, low self-esteem, and ableist self-perceptions.

In Billy's emancipatory counterstory, the initial source of ableist dysfunctionality came from his prospective special education teacher. Billy's counterstory illustrates the importance of thinking creatively about classrooms in terms of spatial justice, race (Bonilla-Silva 2006), and disability ecologies that transcend the physical classroom walls.

I met Billy's mother, Viviana, at Graciela's office. Like Viviana, Graciela was from Mexico. Graciela was a psychologist who provided bilingual therapy services for Latinx families in our community. Billy was five years old when I met him, and he was in the process of entering public school. During the latter part of prekindergarten, Billy's parents were convinced by Billy's prospective special education teacher (in a manner that wasn't so transparent) to have Billy psychologically evaluated. The results indicated that he exhibited an "extreme" mode of "nonverbal autism." Graciela strongly disagreed. Graciela felt that it was crucial to demonstrate the inaccuracy of the nonverbal proclamation via one-on-one therapy with Billy in order to prepare the family for a second evaluation. Indeed, in a matter of months Billy started speaking a number of words. Despite the exclusive use of Spanish at home, the bulk of Billy's emerging vocabulary was in English.

Based on recommendations from other Spanish-speaking neighbors, the family had chosen a Spanish-English dual-language school for Billy, and they did not want him to have to move to another school for kindergarten. When they shared this decision with the school, the special educator—a white individual embedded in a primarily nonwhite context—took on an antagonistic attitude aimed at dissuading Billy's parents, going as far as contacting Graciela to request her help in convincing the parents to take Billy elsewhere. Eventually, this educator was removed from the school, presumably for health reasons.

In terms of agency and awareness raising—that is, double consciousness in action—Viviana and Graciela's almost daily interactions generated a relational bond. The choreography of this bond acquired paramount significance since it allowed listening and even risk-taking strategies that were discussed at length within the safety of Graciela's therapeutic spaces. Moreover, Graciela's recent involvement with high-profile district administrators on account of another early childhood episode of overt ableist discrimination directed against Latinx families paved the way for the prompt removal of the special education teacher who attempted to block Billy from attending the school of his family's choice.

It was Billy's embodied intersectionality as a seemingly nonspeaking autistic and brown Latinx student that triggered the animosity from his prospective special education teacher. Regardless of the microdynamics at work, one must keep in mind that this classroom reflected broader macrosocietal issues. Thus, while removing the white supremacist and ableist instructor in this case was relatively easy, it's crucial for Latinx families with disabled children in this district to remain on guard. Perhaps harder to accomplish, it's also crucial for fellow teachers, emerging teachers, and teacher educators to contest similar racist and ableist episodes.

NOTES

1 LatCrit theory evolved as a Latinx version of the critical legal studies movement of the 1960s and 1970s, e.g., Unger (2015).
2 DisCrit centers its sphere of analysis on issues of disability studies in education at the intersection of race and disability. Overwhelmingly, DisCrit has been concerned with schooling matters in the U.S. and Canada. See, Migliarini et al. (2018) for an example of DisCrit works outside North American contexts.

BIBLIOGRAPHY

Alcoff, Linda M. 2009. "Comparative Race, Comparative Racisms." In *Race or Ethnicity? On Black and Latino Identity*, edited by Jorge J. E. Gracia. Ithaca, NY: Cornell University Press.

Annamma, Subini A., David J. Connor, and Beth A. Ferri. 2013. "Dis/ability Critical Race Studies (DisCrit): Theorizing at the Intersections of Race and Dis/ability." *Race Ethnicity and Education* 16 (1): 1–31.

Annamma, Subini A., David J. Connor, and Beth A. Ferri, editors. 2016. *DisCrit: Disability Studies and Critical Race Theory in Education*. New York: Teachers College Press.

Annamma, Subini A., Beth A. Ferri, and David J. Connor. 2019. "Cultivating and Expanding Disability Critical Race Theory (DisCrit)." In *Manifestos for the Future of Critical Disability Studies*. Vol. 1, edited by Kate Ellis, Rosmarie Garland-Thomson, Mike Kent, and Rachel Robertson. New York: Routledge.

Annamma, Subini A., and Tamara Handy. 2019. "DisCrit Solidarity as Curriculum Studies and Transformative Praxis." *Curriculum Inquiry* 49 (4): 442–463.

Annamma, Subini A., and Deb Morrison. 2018. "DisCrit Classroom Ecology: Using Praxis to Dismantle Dysfunctional Education Ecologies." *Teaching and Teacher Education* 73:70–80.

Bernal, Dolores D. 2002. "Critical Race Theory, LatCrit Theory, and Critical Race-Gendered Epistemologies: Recognizing Students of Color as Holders and Creators of Knowledge." *Qualitative Inquiry* 8 (1): 105–126.

Bonilla-Silva, Eduardo. 2006. *Racism without Racists: Color-Blind Racism and the Persistence of Racial Inequality in the United States*. Lanham, MD: Rowman and Littlefield.

Calderón, Dolores. 2014. "Anticolonial Methodologies in Education: Embodying Land and Indigeneity in Chicana Feminisms." *Journal of Latino/Latin American Studies* 6:81–96.

Castro-Gómez, Santiago. 2002. "The Social Sciences, Epistemic Violence and the Problem of the 'Invention of the Other.'" *Nepantla: Views from the South 3 (2)*: 269–85.

Castro-Gómez, Santiago. 2007. "The Missing Chapter of Empire: Postmodern Reorganization of Coloniality and Post-Fordist Capitalism." *Cultural Studies* 21 (2–3): 428–448.

Connor, David, Beth A. Ferri, and Subini A. Annamma. 2021. "From the Personal to the Global: Engaging with and Enacting DisCrit Theory across Multiple Spaces." *Race Ethnicity and Education* 24 (5): 597–606.

Dávila, Brianne. 2015. "Critical Race Theory, Disability Microaggressions and Latina/o Student Experiences in Special Education." *Race Ethnicity and Education* 18 (4): 443–468.

Dávila, E. R., and A. A. de Bradley. 2010. "Examining Education for Latinas/os in Chicago: A CRT/LatCrit Approach." *Educational Foundations* 24 (1): 39–58.

Dei, George J. 2017. *Reframing Blackness and Black Solidarities through Anti-colonial and Decolonial Prisms*. Cham, Switzerland: Springer.

Dei, George J., and Shukri Hilowle, editors. 2018. *Cartographies of Race and Social Difference*. Cham, Switzerland: Springer.

Dei, George J., and Mairi McDermott, editors. 2014. *Politics of Anti-racism Education: In Search of Strategies for Transformative Learning*. New York: Springer.

Du Bois, W. E. B. (1924) 2007. *The Gift of Black Folk: The Negroes in the Making of America*. Vol. 20 of *The Oxford W. E. B. Du Bois*. Oxford: Oxford University Press.

Du Bois, W. E. B. 1965. *The Souls of Black Folk*. New York: Avon Books.

Maldonado-Torres, Nelson. 2007. "On the Coloniality of Being: Contributions to the Development of a Concept." *Cultural Studies* 21 (2–3): 240–270.

Mignolo, Walter D. 2000. *Local Histories/Global Designs: Coloniality, Subaltern Knowledges and Border Thinking*. Princeton, NJ: Princeton University Press.

Mignolo, Walter D., and M. Tlostanova. 2006. "Theorizing from the Borders. Shifting to Geo- and Body-Politics of Knowledge." *European Journal of Social Theory* 9 (2): 205–221.

Mignolo, Walter D., and Catherine E. Walsh. 2018. *On Decoloniality: Concepts, Analytics, Praxis*. Durham, NC: Duke University Press.

Moraga, Cherrie L. 2011. *A Xicana Codex of Changing Consciousness: Writings, 2000–2010*. Durham, NC: Duke University Press.

Padilla, Alexis. 2021a. *Disability, Intersectional Agency and Latinx Identity: Theorizing LatDisCrit Counterstories*. Abingdon, UK: Routledge.

Padilla, Alexis. 2021b. "The Metanarrative of Blindness in the Global South: A LatDisCrit Counterstory on the Bittersweet Mythology of Blindness as Giftedness." In *The Metanarrative of Disability*, edited by David Bolt, 16–29. Abingdon, UK: Routledge.

Padilla, Alexis. 2022. "LatDisCrit: Exploring Latinx Global South DisCrit Reverberations as Spaces toward Emancipatory Learning and Radical Solidarity." In *DisCrit Expanded: Inquiries, Reverberations and Ruptures*, edited by Subini Ancy Annamma, Beth A. Ferri, and David J. Connor, 147–162. New York: Teachers College Press.

Padilla, Alexis, Paulo Tan, Renita Evans, and Pamela Vasile. 2021. "Exploring Listening Frequencies through Listening for, Listening with, and Consciousness Formation Archetypes: The Case of Relational Inclusive Education Situatedness." *Multiple Voices* 21 (2): 48–65.

Rabaka, Reiland. 2010. *Against Epistemic Apartheid: W. E. B Du Bois and the Disciplinary Decadence of Sociology*. Lanham, MD: Lexington Books.

Ricoeur, Paul. 1971. "The Model of the Text: Meaningful Action Considered as a Text." *Social Research* 38:529–562.

Ricoeur, Paul. 1974. *The Conflict of Interpretations: Essays in Hermeneutics*. Evanston, IL: Northwestern University Press.

Ricoeur, Paul. 1981. "What Is a Text? Explanation and Understanding." In *Hermeneutics and the Human Sciences: Essays on Language, Action, and Interpretation*, edited and translated by John B. Thompson, 107–128. Cambridge: Cambridge University Press.

Sandoval, Chela. 2000. *Methodology of the Oppressed*. Minneapolis: University of Minnesota Press.

Santos, Boaventura de Sousa, and Maria Paula Meneses. 2020. Preface to *Knowledges Born in the Struggle: Constructing the Epistemologies of the Global South*, edited by Boaventura de Sousa Santos and Maria Paula Meneses, xv–xvii. New York: Routledge.

Shildrick, Margrit. 2002. *Embodying the Monster: Encounters with the Vulnerable Self*. London: Sage.

Soja, Edward W. 1989. *Postmodern Geographies: The Reassertion of Space in Critical Social Theory*. Brooklyn: Verso.

Solórzano, Daniel G., and Dolores Delgado Bernal. 2001. "Examining Transformational Resistance through a Critical Race and Latcrit Theory Framework: Chicana and Chicano Students in an Urban Context." *Urban Education* 36 (3): 308–342.

Unger, Roberto M. 2015. *The Critical Legal Movement: Another Time, a Greater Task*. Brooklyn: Verso.

Valdés, Francisco. 1999. "Afterword: Theorizing 'OutCrit' Theories: Coalitional Method and Comparative Jurisprudential Experience—RaceCrits, QueerCrits and LatCrits." *University of Miami Law Review* 53:1265–1306.

Valdés, Francisco. 2000. "Race, Ethnicity, and Hispanismo in a Triangular Perspective: The 'Essential Latina/o' and LatCrit Theory." *UCLA Law Review* 48:1–41.

Valdés, Francisco, and Steven W. Bender. 2022. *LatCrit: From Critical Legal Theory to Academic Activism*. New York: New York University Press.

Vallega, Alejandro A. 2010. "Out of Latin American Thought from Radical Exteriority: Philosophy after the Age of Pernicious Knowledge." In *The Gift of Logos: Essays in Continental Philosophy*, edited by David Jones, Jason M. Wirth, and Michael Schwartz, 143–162. Newcastle upon Tyne, UK: Cambridge Scholars.

Vallega, Alejandro A. 2014. *Latin American Philosophy: From Identity to Radical Exteriority*. Bloomington: Indiana University Press.

Waitoller, Federico R., and Subini A. Annamma. 2017. "Taking a Spatial Turn in Inclusive Education." In *The Handbook of Research on Diversity in Special Education*, edited by Marie Tejero Hughes and Elizabeth Talbott, 23–44. Hoboken, NJ: John Wiley and Sons.

Wynter, Sylvia. 2003. "Unsettling the Coloniality of Being/Power/Truth/Freedom: Towards the Human, after Man, Its Overrepresentation: An Argument." *New Centennial Review* 3 (3): 257–337.

Yosso, Tara J. 2000. "A Critical Race and LatCrit Approach to Media Literacy: Chicana/o Resistance to Visual Microagressions." PhD diss., University of California, Los Angeles.

Yosso, Tara J. 2006. *Critical Race Counterstories along the Chicana/Chicano Educational Pipeline*. New York: Routledge.

Young, Robert J. C. 2001. "Preface: Sartre: The 'African Philosopher.'" In *Colonialism and Neocolonialism*, by Jean-Paul Sartre, 9–20. New York: Routledge.

Research

8

Virtual Ethnography

EMILY LIM ROGERS

Virtual worlds are of particular importance to disabled and chronically ill communities, for whom public, physical space is often inaccessible. As such, virtual ethnography has become a crucial method in disability studies. While conventional evidentiary hierarchies within the social sciences place virtual worlds as inferior proxies to embodied ones, there is no question that virtual methods allow access to groups that other methods cannot (Boellstorff 2012; Gold 2008). This raises the question of who has been left out of the knowledge production emerging from empirical research. Bedbound and homebound communities whose sociality takes place primarily online, for instance, constitute a group for whom traditional modes of ethnography are inadequate. These chronically ill and disabled communities have created "network[s] of like-minded people" from their homes (Ginsburg 2012, 110). To distinguish between online life and "real-life" interactions would be to relegate these communities outside the realm of study. Thus, without methodologies that can encapsulate these worlds, traditional ethnography's methodological apparatus is exclusionary by definition.

Virtual ethnography is not "virtually" ethnography: it is ethnography. In my work, I studied a community of largely bed- and homebound people over my six years of research with people with myalgic encephalomyelitis / chronic fatigue syndrome (ME/CFS). It drove home the fact that, in the case of ME/CFS and likely other disabilities and chronic illnesses, virtual ethnography did not "approximate" but was rather truly reflective of the worlds of my interlocutors. People with ME/CFS used video chat platforms like Zoom—made ubiquitous during COVID-19—long before the pandemic. Because around a quarter of people with ME/CFS are bedbound (Institute of Medicine 2015), remote technologies, digital or otherwise, have been a critical means of community-building for decades. The need to build community across physical space is compounded not only by the debilitation they endure from the disease itself but also by the stigma that comes along with a contested and frequently disbelieved illness. Even before widespread internet access, support groups used newsletters and informational mailings to access chronically ill people: facing an extreme deficit of specialists, with most doctors concentrated in a handful of major cities, people with ME/CFS accessed information on such topics as disability, diagnosis, and treatments despite the fact that their bodies were located across the country.

As early as 1996, before Web 2.0, people with ME/CFS had developed a robust listserv culture. Now, social media groups, patient-led wiki-style encyclopedias, and conference calls constitute much of the day-to-day lives of people with ME/CFS. Long before COVID-19, these remote means of socialization were a crucial link for disabled and chronically ill people.

In addition to providing access to disabled interlocutors, virtual ethnography can be an accessible methodology for disabled *researchers*. As the anthropologists Devva Kasnitz and Russell P. Shuttleworth point out, anthropologists who are themselves disabled are the ones most likely to study disability. Yet they must navigate the challenges of a profession with "a lightly veiled connection to images of adventure. Indiana Jones in a wheelchair?" (Kasnitz and Shuttleworth 2001). The stereotypical image of an anthropologist—able-bodied and typically white—roughing it out in a far-flung, in-person field site is frequently unfeasible for disabled ethnographers, leading some to argue "ableism is inherent" to anthropology's bread-and-butter method (Durban 2022, 8). Navigating inaccessible public spaces, flying on airlines that may destroy their wheelchairs, spending hours on the go, or severing themselves from necessary care networks or medical devices at home all contribute to the myriad ways traditional ethnography is inadequate not only to the task of accessing of disabled subjects but also for disabled ethnographers (Bradley 1997; Brown and Boardman 2010; Hartblay 2018). Virtual ethnography can thus eliminate some of these barriers to participation in research. In my own experiences as a chronically ill ethnographer, following my interlocutors and their mix of online and embodied interactions assisted me in pacing myself while conducting my research.

While virtual ethnography allowed me to capture the fabric of everyday life with ME/CFS, both my training in conventional ethnographic methods and my associated fantasies of what fieldwork should look like sat uneasily with my experience of doing the research. Some of this is ideological. Michelle Friedner, Devva Kasnitz, and Zoë Wool point out that disabled anthropologists feel that they are not doing "real" anthropology, no matter how rich the insights their fieldwork yields (Friedner, Kasnitz, and Wool 2018). But there are real practical challenges to designing a virtual ethnographic research strategy in the context of a field predicated on in-person interactions. My preconceived notions of gaining entrée and building rapport, in particular, were strained by the online platform on which my research took place. In conducting ethnography through a mix of online and offline interactions, too, fieldwork felt "patchy" (Günel, Varma, and Watanabe 2020). It took place in fits and starts, as I went months without seeing or talking to my interlocutors, who were frequently too crashed to come to events with consistency. Meetings would get canceled. Close interlocutors whom I had longed to meet in person would be too exhausted to make it out. Or I would meet people several times online in group settings yet be unable to reach them to have a smaller, more personal conversation. Obviously, ME/CFS presents unique challenges for fieldwork, but some of these insights are illuminative for virtual ethnography as a whole. Two main issues arose: building trust and maintaining contact. First, trust is difficult to build in online environments, especially when determining whether a space is public or private is not a clear proposition. Initial fieldwork consisted of "lurking" at technically public, yet often intimate, events. An ethnographer has to make a judgment about such spaces, and whether and when it is ethical to attend without announcing one's presence. Second, maintaining contact with someone can be difficult online. People may pop in and out of video calls. Casual day-to-day interactions are absent, as side conversations are near impossible. Hardly anyone lingers after virtual events, making it hard to decipher what people really take away from them. Someone could trust me enough to do an interview, yet we were not at the level of familiarity that regular texting or phone calls, for instance, felt appropriate for the dynamic. There was often a dizzying discrepancy between the intimacy of our conversations and the remoteness of our bodies.

I was once told that the distinction between sociology and anthropology is that in sociology, you get to go home at the end of the day, whereas in anthropology, you sleep in your field site. This observation reflects anthropology's colonial roots, but to stay with it for a moment reveals something about the trouble and richness of virtual ethnography. The idea that fieldwork can be "always on" comes from subject positions that are increasingly recognized as untenable: they presume a nondisabled researcher without care obligations, with unmitigated access to the field, and with the funding to perform the work. Fantasies of the field as a unified and discrete place—which I myself held—might provide comfort and legibility, but they are simply not suited to the study of chronically ill communities. Ultimately though, in a funny way, I both got to sleep in my own bed at night and felt as if I never left the field. My life indeed began to mirror the lives of my interlocutors. I logged hours of Zoom calls from a tiny bedroom in Brooklyn and grew socially isolated from my academic networks.

This situation changed during the COVID-19 pandemic. What was everyday life for people with ME/CFS became generalized, in many ways, to a nondisabled public with the advent of COVID-19. As disabled scholars and activists have pointed out, quarantine gave the nondisabled a taste of what it is like to be chronically ill, disabled, and homebound (Barbarin 2020; Schuller 2020): socializing only over FaceTime and Zoom, leaving the house only a couple of times a month to get groceries, and feeling disconnected from society. Within academia, agencies "pivoted" to funding at-home ethnography while universities switched to online learning. In both, these virtual worlds were heralded as opportunities for "innovation" rather than practices that disabled and chronically ill people had been doing for decades.

This forgetting has been duly corrected by disabled scholars and activists. The recent Remote Access Archive initiative, for example, aims to "gather stories, documents, and other information about how disabled people have used technology to interact remotely"—emphasizing that this socialization predates the pandemic (Critical Design Lab, n.d.). Disabled students have pointed out that they had asked for accommodations to take classes online, previously held to be "unreasonable," that now were part of a pivot so unremarkable that their professors needed little if any training in online pedagogy. There is hypocrisy to this, but also what some see as a silver lining: the pandemic has taught nondisabled people just how inaccessible physical spaces were. As of spring 2022, it seems that even as "in-person learning" begins to return, online or hybrid programming remains common, if not the norm, within academia and beyond it. In part because these events are typically recorded, services such as remote live-captioning are more common than they were before COVID-19. In this regard, COVID-19 has brought unexpected benefits, with some important accessibility features built into virtual spaces and a newfound attentiveness to the accessibility and importance of virtual spaces.

Are these developments cause for celebration? As virtual programming tends to reduce costs, for instance, it is prudent to ask whether austerity, rather than accessibility, is the driving factor at play. To take one example, it remains to be seen whether universities and other institutions will internalize these lessons and provide more resource-intensive access features for in-person events (for instance, setting up a separate projector for CART [Communication Access Realtime Translation] captioning or making sure to include accessible seating), or whether the (implicit or explicit) expectation is for disabled attendees to attend online. Moreover, digital settings do not a priori provide greater accessibility—for either interlocutors or ethnographers. Generational differences and access to a good computer and solid internet access play a role: most of my older interlocutors did not participate in video calls, and none of my housing-insecure interlocutors did. And as someone with brain fog, I often found online worlds difficult to research, without spatial and temporal markers that helped me keep things straight. Even before the pandemic, day after day blended together as virtual ethnography began to burn me out. Being relegated to my home and spending all day at a computer created a special kind of loneliness.

This raises an issue my interlocutors emphasized: though they did not currently have it, they *wanted* access to in-person, public space, especially during the pandemic. ("I see so few people already," my interlocutor Noor told me, "that it's been extra isolating.") A fortunate consequence of the pandemic has been that all sorts of institutions have reckoned with just how inaccessible their events were before the pandemic. An unfortunate potential effect of this realization is foreclosure of the imagination when it comes to making in-person events accessible, a model of access that would segregate rather than truly include. (The home as the new asylum?) Being homebound, for my interlocutors, is hard, and it is lonely. It is not the life that they wanted. The rich cultural worlds they create online—and the importance of virtual ethnography in capturing them—do not negate this fact. Just as Simi Linton (1998) pointed out disability studies' historical reluctance to acknowledge impairment, so too may a narrow focus on the accessibility of online spaces overshadow the very real things people with ME/CFS miss out on when they can only participate in life from their beds, the proverbial site of liberal privacy. Disability is not a tragedy, but inaccessibility is. While some have questioned whether pain and chronic fatigue, in particular, stretch the social model past its limits (Kafer 2013), societal changes in attitude and architectures may indeed improve the lives of people with ME/CFS and other chronic illnesses in ways that better allow them to inhabit public space. For instance, accessible architecture might look like "healthy buildings" (Allen and Macomber 2020) with increased ventilation and filtration that would help immunocompromised people beyond COVID, or it could include reclining chairs that allow people with ME/CFS to rest while making community in-person. Changing the dismissive attitude toward "contested" chronic illnesses may lead to better resources to manage symptoms—not toward a medical "cure" or elimination, but toward greater access to social worlds.

Another one of my interlocutors told me about something he called "healing touch." A keen observer with a bit of an ethnographic eye, Brad spoke at length about the variations in hugging cultures in his immediate versus extended family, and the significance of physical touch for someone with chronic illness. His wife and in-laws are not so "huggy," and Brad notices his health worsens when he hasn't been hugged for a while. As a nurse, he explains firmly his conviction that touch is necessary for care: "There is something where it has to be skin on skin, and you have to give that *moment* at least, where I recognize you as a human being. You know, my soul recognizes your soul, the *touch*. There's something very spiritual about that and people miss out on that." For Brad, hugs were constitutive of incorporation into humanness itself, and he even described "the dearth of touch" he experiences as someone with chronic illness as "horrific": "It's practically like not feeding someone."

Poignant in their own context, Brad's remarks also suggest what might be lost through virtual-only fieldwork. Bodies, in other words, make a difference. Bodies coexisting, conspiring (literally: breathing together) in public space makes a difference. Interacting in networked online spaces rather than engaging in organic contact in physical, public space (Delany 1999) affects the shape of social worlds and thus the findings that can be generated from virtual ethnography. Just the same, embodied ethnography is also marked by its own exclusions: it only examines the bodies that *can* show up, which, especially in the case of ME/CFS, should never be taken for granted. In this respect, virtual ethnography—in addition to its accessibility for both informants and researchers—may also have something to teach traditional ethnography about itself, just as the COVID-19 pandemic illuminated the inaccessibility of much of our world.

BIBLIOGRAPHY

Allen, Joseph G., and John D. Macomber. 2020. *Healthy Buildings: How Indoor Spaces Drive Performance and Productivity*. Cambridge, MA: Harvard University Press.

Barbarin, Imani (@Imani_Barbarin). 2020. "Me watching Ableds rebrand ableism as 'COVID Gaslighting' because it affects them now too." Twitter post, December 1, 2020. https://twitter.com/Imani_Barbarin/status/1333952237312290817?s=20.

Boellstorff, Tom, editor. 2012. *Ethnography and Virtual Worlds: A Handbook of Method*. Princeton, NJ: Princeton University Press.

Bradley, Candice. 1997. "Doing Fieldwork with Diabetes." *CAM Journal* 9 (2): 1–8.

Brown, Lindsey, and Felicity K. Boardman. 2010. "Accessing the Field: Disability and the Research Process." *Social Science and Medicine* 72 (1): 23–30.

Critical Design Lab. n.d. "The Remote Access Archive." Accessed October 3, 2022. https://www.mapping-access.com/the-remote-access-archive.

Delany, Samuel R. 1999. *Times Square Red, Times Square Blue*. New York: New York University Press.

Durban, Erin L. 2022. "Anthropology and Ableism." *American Anthropologist* 124 (1): 8–20.

Friedner, Michelle, Devva Kasnitz, and Zoë Wool. 2018. "What I Wish I Knew about Anthropology and Disability: Notes toward a More Enabling Anthropology." *Anthrodendum* (blog), January 10, 2018. https://anthrodendum.org/2018/01/10/what-i-wish-i-knew-about-anthropology-and-disability-notes-toward-a-more-enabling-anthropology/.

Ginsburg, Faye. 2012. "Disability in the Digital Age." In *Digital Anthropology*, edited by Heather A. Horst and Daniel Miller, 101–128. London: Berg.

Gold, Gerald. 2008. "Disability Culture and the Internet." *Anthropology News* 49 (4): 27–28.

Günel, Gökçe, Saiba Varma, and Chika Watanabe. "A Manifesto for Patchwork Ethnography." Society for Cultural Anthropology, June 9, 2020. https://culanth.org/fieldsights/a-manifesto-for-patchwork-ethnography.

Hartblay, Cassandra. 2018. "Cyborg." Society for Cultural Anthropology, March 29, 2018. https://culanth.org/fieldsights/cyborg.

Institute of Medicine. 2015. *Beyond Myalgic Encephalomyelitis/Chronic Fatigue Syndrome: Redefining an Illness*. Washington, DC: National Academies Press.

Kafer, Alison. 2013. *Feminist, Queer, Crip*. Bloomington: Indiana University Press.

Kasnitz, Devva, and Russell P. Shuttleworth. 2001. "Introduction: Anthropology in Disability Studies." *Disability Studies Quarterly* 21 (3): 2–17.

Linton, Simi. 1998. "Disability Studies/Not Disability Studies." *Disability and Society* 13 (4): 525–540.

Schuller, Kyla (@KikiSchoonz). 2020. "#COVID-19 is teaching the ableds what the disabled and chronically ill already know: your ability to leave the house is a privilege that can be lost at any time." Twitter post, March 13, 2020. https://twitter.com/KikiSchoonz/status/1238456960418275329?s=20.

9

Learning Disability Justice through
Critical Participatory Action Research

LAURA J. WERNICK

i.

I'm not formally a disability studies scholar, but I am a neurodivergent and learning-disabled social work scholar with chronic illnesses. I'm a white, queer, nonbinary, disabled, Ashkenazi Jew with class privilege, originally from unceded Dakota land (Minnesota) and currently living in the Lenape and Canarsie lands (Brooklyn). I have spent much of my adult life walking the line between my passion for justice and my love of researching, cocreating, and sharing knowledge. I have been a movement activist and organizer, mostly around issues of racial and economic justice, but also queer and disability justice. As an organizer, I was trained to support the leadership of those most affected, which was critical to developing an understanding of the intersection of the privileges and oppressions I hold. My background and political commitments led me to community-based critical participatory action research (CPAR)—"a framework for engaging research *with* [*or by*] communities interested in documenting, challenging, and transforming conditions of social injustice" (Fine and Torre 2021, 3. Emphasis and parenthetical comment are mine).

ii.

As a child, school was mostly a site of struggle and trauma. I was regularly harassed and bullied for my gender expression and Jewishness, and I also had reading and writing disabilities, attention deficit hyperactivity disorder (ADHD), and depression. Teachers considered me "bright" in class, but they also assumed I was lazy, not applying myself even though I worked many more hours than my peers, consistently struggling with my reading and writing. I wasn't officially diagnosed until college, when I was *accused* of having a learning disability "or something." Meanwhile, I had internalized my language-based struggles, considering myself to be stupid and feeling like an imposter. These combined traumas made me fearful that one day "they" would "figure me out." A professor was the last thing I thought I would become.

Despite the fact that reading and writing were painful, and that I feared being identified as a person with a learning disability, I was enthralled with all the knowledge that I found in books, at school, and in community. I was obsessed with analyzing intersectional systems of power, loved to talk about ideas, and had a passion for creating change. My trauma, depression, and ADHD gave me a keen ability to empathize with others, and coupled with my power and privilege, my ADHD gave me a passion to think about and consider multiple perspectives at the same time. I asked a lot of "why" questions—"Why was I seeing and experiencing all of these injustices? How can things change? What role can I play as a disabled person with class and white privilege?" I was also very strong at math and social sciences. As I got older, I gravitated toward opportunities to participate in analyzing and strategizing within movements. Because reading and writing continued to be difficult, I tended to be drawn to listening to other people's stories and found that I communicated best through storytelling. My combined disabilities made some fields intimidating and less accessible, while they also opened doors to unique combinations of skills and interests—analysis, storytelling, and critical inquiry.

iii.

Academia is not designed for people with learning disabilities or ADHD. There are not many academics with reading and writing disabilities on the tenure track in the social sciences—or at least ones who are open or visible. There are a lot of reasons for this. Primarily, it's a profession where one is expected to be well-read and well-spoken in jargon, to speak in soundbites, and where value is based on the number of articles and books written, especially as first author.

Who is usually first author? The one who does most of the writing, which is privileged over all the other elements of research, including building relationships, theorizing, analyzing data, outlining an argument, and developing a paper. There are also several stigmas around learning disabilities. People with learning disabilities are often called (or assumed to be) stupid and lazy, especially when we mix up our words, or our experience is minimized when others tell us they too "read slowly." Sometimes, it is hard for us to speak in short soundbites, so we struggle with not taking up too much space in meetings. People, including fellow professors, often assume that learning disabilities are a scam to get extra time on tests or other accommodations. The truth is that there are a few parents, mostly white and wealthy, who leverage their power and privilege to game the system. Doing so enables their kids to be diagnosed with learning disabilities and to get extra time and other accommodations that help them gain admission to higher-ranked colleges (Taylor, Smith, and Shallish 2020). This tactic is rooted in white supremacy culture and ableism, while at the same time it is ableist that we even have timed tests to begin with, because it implies that reading and comprehending faster is better. Additionally, white folks with disabilities are less likely to be labeled stupid or told they are lying than are students of color, and as a result, there are fewer disabled students of color who self-identify as such in college. These students often don't receive accommodations until it's too late (Banks 2014; Dolmage 2017; Lombardi, Murray, and Kowitt 2016).

Academia is an uphill battle for faculty with learning disabilities or ADHD. When speaking in academic meetings, we are told that we are not concise enough, that there is a correct, concise way of speaking. Even assuming we have received adequate accommodations through grade school and college (something that isn't as common as one would guess, given the many barriers for receiving diagnoses and accessing accommodations) and haven't internalized the stigmas of learning disabilities, academia is still not designed for us. There are not adequate accommodations for people who are neurodivergent and have learning disabilities in PhD programs. Most of us are not provided with dedicated offices that we can set up in a way that works for us, with the software we need, editors, large screens, and other tangible accommodations, not to mention extra time to graduation and additional funding to enable the potential extra time to graduation.

I have race and class privilege, and thus was able to get some additional support from family, friends, and colleagues to finish my PhD. It does take a community and a network of mutual aid to get through a PhD program, especially with a disability. The injustice lies in the reality that it is disproportionately disabled folks with race and class privilege who complete their PhDs and get tenure. This might be why faculty who have disabilities, who face chronic illnesses, or who are neurodivergent (and who have been open about it) are disproportionately white. Not all, but most. And once we get a tenure-track position, we don't get time and a half to tenure, nor a reduced course load per semester, as we might have received as students. Nor are we granted smaller classes with fewer students and papers to grade or, at the very least, a teaching assistant. In rhetoric, colleges and universities insist that people with disabilities are "encouraged to apply." They want to count our numbers in their ranks while not providing an accessible workplace that will allow us to thrive. Nondisabled and neurotypical scholars may engage in research about people with disabilities, but we are not invited into the room, and our knowledge and expertise are not valued.

*Inter*dependent collaborations with the community members most directly affected by disability research have neither been traditionally valued nor funded. Academics are expected to be *the* experts and hold the research money and the power. Collective writing is not as valued, and grants tend to have just one principal investigator. Within this hierarchy, power and individualism are embedded in both ableism and white supremacist culture, and this ignores the powerful and transformative impact that interdependent collaborations can have. It's been a struggle figuring out how to navigate academia in a way that aligns with my social justice values, my disabilities, and the often-inaccessible demands of academia.

Nevertheless, many faculty with disabilities have *cripped* the academic process—we work interdependently in collaborative partnerships, engage in mutual aid, and develop creative approaches to produce and disseminate innovative scholarship. Unlike other scholars in this volume who use or develop crip methods to study disability, I have found CPAR to be a research method that also accommodates disabled academic researchers and activists.

iv.

Interestingly, it was a combination of community collaborations and mutual aid that propelled me into academia and moved me through with integrity—in a way that was intentionally more democratic and participatory, and less hierarchical and individualistic. As a crip scholar deeply involved in movement work, I have engaged in CPAR in all my research (see Cahill 2007; Fine and Torre 2021; Hutchinson and Lovell 2013; Kemmis and Wilkinson 1998; Wernick, Woodford, and Siden 2010; Wernick, Kulick, and Woodford 2014; Wernick, Woodford, and Kulick 2014). I first learned community-based CPAR not in school but through my work as a community organizer. At its best, CPAR is research that is rooted in and led by those most affected by the issue being researched. It fundamentally shifts power from the outsider (e.g., an academic, government organization, or policy institute) to the insider—those who know and experience these systems. Collective action is embedded in all parts of the research: naming the problem or issue; developing the research questions and methods; using the data collection (qualitative, quantitative, autoethnography, photovoice, etc.) as a way to say we are here, this is our story, these are our lived experiences; and building power. The act of participating in the research can agitate and raise questions for the participant, and the data are used by those most affected to create change. Further, the act of engagement at each of these steps builds capacity to act and have a real impact. Those who are not as directly affected often still participate—these can be organizers, academics, organizational staff, and consultants—drawing on the combined knowledge and skills of all who participate, while intentionally centering those most affected as leaders.

My point of entry emerged when I was organizing with Community Voices Heard—a member-led organization made up of mostly poor and low-income women of color in Harlem and the South Bronx, building power to secure racial, social, and economic justice in New York State. My role was to support member leaders in their first CPAR: support them to collect and use research data for their campaign work against workfare and for real jobs, while using the process to increase membership and build leaders to fight for their demands. It was this work that propelled me to get my PhD. Community members were asking very sophisticated intersectional research questions, including questions about economics, poverty, labor, race, gender, and union worker displacement. I didn't have the research or statistical or analytical skills to answer the important questions they were asking. For this reason, I decided to go back to graduate school in social work and political science. I knew I had an enormous amount of privilege to take this route, and still do. I continue to stay committed to addressing intersecting issues and roles of power, privilege, and oppression throughout my career. Because of my disabilities, however, I did not think I would actually complete the program (especially writing a dissertation), let alone become an academic. I assumed I would learn what I needed and then go back to my work as a community organizer.

V.

It took eleven years to finish my PhD, and years later I now have tenure. It was only possible because I was engaged in community-based CPAR throughout my academic career, tied to ongoing and influential movement work, which allowed me to align my values with my career. I struggled with clearly communicating my ideas through words, particularly with writing, spelling, and grammar, and the writing process frequently brought up pain and trauma. Through this process, I developed an intertwining mutual aid network that included a team of editors, emotional support providers, and a handful of professors who (sometimes secretly) would give me a key to their office while on sabbatical, or sign forms allowing me to extend my time to tenure, and who finally got me adaptive software to help me read my own interview transcripts. I also stayed very active in movement work throughout. This kept me grounded in why I was doing academic work and the importance of bringing the research and academic tools together with movement work, all the while creating a space to build on and accommodate my disabilities.

One of the most exciting projects I worked on was with a group of LGBTQIA youths in Michigan beginning in the mid-2000s while I was in graduate school and later doing postdoctoral work. Because of my combined organizing and CPAR background, I was asked to consult with Riot Youth, a queer and trans youth program of the teen center Neutral Zone, on "a survey project," as they called it. Riot Youth drew queer, trans, and allied youths from all over southeastern Michigan, as there were still very few gay/queer–straight alliances in schools at that time. I ended up working with Riot Youth for five years, as their adult program adviser and organizer. They wanted to do a survey because their experiences of harassment and combined invisibility and visibility were not believed or taken seriously. They also felt that existing surveys did not capture their own experiences, including hetero- and cisnormativity, along with the intersection with racism and other systems of domination.

I was able to support them to use their own stories and knowledge to create a survey that both addressed their questions and developed processes that would get a more representative sample. Each step of the process of developing and implementing the survey was an action step. The process of developing the survey built their own critical consciousness about intersectionality and how power was operationalized within their own group and in their schools. We held meetings with administrators and school board members that intentionally centered youth voices; this literally meant that when administrators only talked with me, I would direct their eye contact to the youths as the experts in the conversations and negotiations to get the survey into the schools. Some of the most influential work included being transparent, at appropriate moments, about my own experiences being harassed in school, as well as my disabilities, and how they related to the work we were doing. We talked about how we all have important knowledge, experiences, and roles to bring to the process and acknowledged that this was a collective effort. Each role was important, including that of the young person whose primary duty was greeting new kids entering the drop-in space and making them feel welcome.

In the end, the survey was administered in either all English or homeroom classes across five schools. The act of taking the survey was also educational for students. The survey included definitions of different types of harassment and LGBTQIA-related terms (such as *cisgender*). The student activists and I analyzed the data together. They asked important questions about the differential impact of school climate for trans youths and LGBTQIA youths of color, as well as a number of other questions about the data that I would not have known to ask without this crucial partnership. During our meetings, I held tutorials about means and averages, medians, and statistical significance. By the end, many of these originally math- and school-averse kids knew how to use and interpret Stata, a sophisticated statistical program. While they did write and disseminate a report, the primary form of dissemination was through theater—which they called Gayrilla. They combined storytelling with numbers and concluded by role-playing how to create change. The youths had separate scripts for youth and adult audiences, and they performed for school boards, elected officials, teachers, social workers, and finally both high school and middle school students. They added small postperformance dialogue groups that they facilitated with no adults in the room. Gayrilla had between six and eight roles, and any young person could perform with script in hand. All they needed to do was attend one rehearsal to learn their blocking. When performing in schools, they would also share data and gather stories from the school at which they were performing, and incorporate it into the performance. It was a very effective and influential form of data dissemination. They wanted to know whether their work was having an impact, so they engaged in additional research using pre- and postperformance surveys. They used these data to get into additional schools whose administrators were originally apprehensive about allowing the performances. They also interviewed one another and held focus groups to assess the impact of engaging in CPAR and theater to create change that affected themselves. Many of these young people went from feeling isolated, depressed, and suicidal and skipping school to feeling more self-confident and happier and believing that they had the capacity to create change while reimagining their futures.

These youths changed policies on the state, city, and school levels; changed the curriculum content and practices by teachers; and affected the behavior of other youths in their communities. They wanted to affect schools of education and social work, so they could train future educators and social workers to be less hetero- and cisnormative and create safer spaces. This led to performing and speaking at local universities, and eventually some of the participants became interested in writing academic papers. In turn, this resulted in a long series of truly collaborative journal articles and book chapters. Many of these youth participants were much better writers than I, and our writing collaborations turned into comentoring and colearning spaces that pushed our collective scholarship to new levels and affected multiple academic disciplines, including social work, education, psychology, sociology, and queer and gender studies. This work has even been cited in multiple Supreme Court briefs on transgender bathroom usage rights.[1] These Riot Youth leaders have gone on to become amazing leaders in academia, law, public policy, social work, music, organizing, art, and theater, and one of the trans youths of color is now an actor on *The L-Word*.

As a crip scholar, I have continued to use CPAR throughout my career, including collaborating with disabled people and elders who employ domestic workers to fight for an interdependent feminist economy with both domestic worker justice and affordable care (Hand in Hand and the NY Caring Majority); wealthy young adults to redistribute wealth, land, and power (Resource Generation); mostly low-income youths of color organizing in Brooklyn (Girls for Gender Equity, Red Hook Initiative, and the Center for Anti-violence Education); and Jews for Racial and Economic Justice. In all these projects, I work interdependently and collaboratively with organizers.

vi.

The question I'm left with is, What does it mean to be a crip author and scholar? And what does it mean to be a crip author and scholar who engages in CPAR? What if one collaborates in all aspects of the research, including theorizing, researching, developing, and outlining an article, but someone else writes up the notes, bullets, fragments, and so on and turns them into paragraphs? What if someone or multiple people talk while someone else writes it down—who is considered the author? Who is considered the "expert"? Am I still an author? What happens when the line between community-based and academic knowledge creation is intentionally blurred?

Moreover, is knowledge dissemination considered crip authorship when we publish academic, peer-reviewed journal articles or academic books that very few people read? Who are considered our peers? What about press releases, testimony, theater performances, protests, reports, Supreme Court briefs? What actually has greater "impact," and who gets credit for each aspect of the collective building and dissemination of knowledge? What determines order of authorship when we are working as a collective to do truly influential interdependent work?[2] Does one need to be a primary author to be considered engaged in the act of knowledge development, analysis, and dissemination? Does one need to be the "spokesperson" to be the author, and does one need to be the author to be considered a leader or an expert in the field?

For years, I felt shame and embarrassment that I mostly engaged in scholarship and writing by doing collaborative work. I would hear, "You are a beautiful writer," and not know how to respond when actually my collaborator is the beautiful writer and I am "just" a collaborator who, along with everyone else, brings my own set of knowledge, skills, experiences, research, and analytic skills to the table to listen and cocreate with everyone else. While I have been involved with disability activism since the 1990s, it was only when I read about disability justice (Berne et al. 2018; Piepzna-Samarasinha 2018) a few years ago that I realized that as a movement activist and scholar with learning disabilities, I had been doing—or trying to do—disability justice my whole academic life. Disability justice is a framework based on ten principles: intersectionality, leadership of those most affected, anticapitalist politics, commitment to cross-movement organizing, recognition of wholeness, sustainability, commitment to cross-disability solidarity, interdependence, collective access, and collective liberation (Berne et al. 2018). It dovetails with CPAR, centering the leadership, knowledge, and experiences of those most affected in research and action within an intersectional and interdependent lens—which mirrors the well-known disability rights movement saying "Nothing about us without us." CPAR and learning disability justice have become elements of a writing strategy that allows me to align my social justice movement values and my crip scholarship. My hope is that this will not only help pave the way for future interdependence among crip scholars and their allied colleagues but also move us closer to cripping academia at large: centering knowledge and scholarship on those most affected, while valuing all the ways we collectively, and interdependently, build knowledge and have a meaningful impact.

NOTES

1   Research cited by: Brief for The National Education Association; American Federation of Teachers, AFL-CIO; National Association of Secondary School Principals; American

Federation of State, County, and Municipal Employees, AFL-CIO; Service Employees International Union; and School Social Work Association of America as Amici Curiae in Support of Respondent. The Supreme Court of the United States, Gloucester County School Board v. G.G (2017) (no. 16-273), and Brief for American Bar Association. Supreme Court of the United States (no. 16-273) in, Gloucester County School Board v. G.G (2017).

2 See Liboiron, M, et al. (2017). Equity in Author Order: A Feminist Laboratory's Approach. *Catalyst: Feminism, Theory, Technoscience*, 3(2), 1–17 for a feminist example of determining authorship order.

BIBLIOGRAPHY

Banks, J. 2014. "Barriers and Supports to Postsecondary Transition: Case Studies of African American Students with Disabilities." *Remedial and Special Education* 35:28–39.

Banks, J. 2019. "Are We Ready: Faculty Perceptions of Postsecondary Students with Learning Disabilities at a Historically Black University." *Journal of Diversity in Higher Education* 12 (4): 297–306.

Berne, P., A. L. Morales, D. Langstaff, and Sins Invalid. 2018. "Ten Principles of Disability Justice." *WSQ: Women's Studies Quarterly* 46 (1): 227–230.

Cahill, C. 2007. "Repositioning Ethical Commitments: Participatory Action Research as a Relational Praxis of Social Change." *ACME: An International E-Journal for Critical Geographies* 6:360–373.

Dolmage, J. T. 2017. *Academic Ableism: Disability and Higher Education.* Ann Arbor: University of Michigan Press.

Fine, M., and M. E. Torre. 2021. *Essentials of Critical Participatory Action Research.* Washington, DC: American Psychological Association.

Hutchinson, A., and A. Lovell. 2013. "Participatory Action Research: Moving beyond the Mental Health 'Service User' Identity." *Journal of Psychiatric and Mental Health Nursing* 20:641–649.

Kemmis, S., and M. Wilkinson. 1998. "Participatory Action Research and the Study of Practice." In *Action Research in Practice: Partnerships for Social Justice in Education*, edited by B. Atweh, S. Kemmis, and P. Weeks, 21–36. New York: Routledge.

Lombardi, A., C. Murray, and J. Kowitt. 2016. "Social Support and Academic Success for College Students with Disabilities: Do Relationship Types Matter?" *Journal of Vocational Rehabilitation* 44:1–13.

Piepzna-Samarasinha, L. L. 2018. *Care Work: Dreaming Disability Justice.* Vancouver, Canada: Arsenal Pulp.

Taylor, A., M. D. Smith, and L. Shallish. 2020. "(Re)producing White Privilege through Disability Accommodations." *Spark: Elevating Scholarship on Social Issues*, July 30, 2020. https://medium.com/national-center-for-institutional-diversity/re-producing-white-privilege-through-disability-accommodations-4c16a746c0dc.

Wernick, L. J., A. Kulick, and M. R. Woodford. 2014. "How Theater within a Transformative Organizing Framework Cultivates Individual and Collective Empowerment among LGBTQQ Youth." *Journal of Community Psychology* 42 (7): 838–853.

Wernick, L. J., M. R. Woodford, and A. Kulick. 2014. "LGBTQ Youth Using Participatory Action Research and Theater to Effect Change: Moving Adult Decision-Makers to Create Youth-Centered Change." *Journal of Community Practice* 22 (1–2): 47–66.

Wernick, L. J., M. R. Woodford, and J. Y. Siden. 2010. "Youth-Led Participatory Action Research: Fostering Effective Youth-Adult Partnerships—a case study." In *Participatory Partnerships for Social Action and Research*, edited by L. Harter, J. Hamel-Lambert, and J. Millesen, 165–186. Dubuque, IA: Kendall/Hunt.

10

Decolonial Disability Studies

It is important to ask, when considering a new community research project,
"What can research really do to improve this situation?" The answers might
reveal that . . . it is not the research that will make the difference but, rather,
who participates in the research, who poses the questions, how data are gathered, and who conducts the analysis.
—Tuck 2009, 423

Introduction

This chapter begins by critically revisiting what Indigenous scholar Eve Tuck calls
"damage-centered research"—a type of research focusing on exploring Indigenous communities' "damages" without necessarily empowering them. Tuck calls
for an epistemological shift from how research with Indigenous communities
has been historically conducted to a framework of desire that recognizes complex aspects of personhood and struggles in shaping the lived experiences of
Indigenous youths and communities.

Tuck's argument is useful for us to interrogate the ways damaged-centered
research has been widely applied in Western research that reinforces social
othering (see also Smith 1999). Social science research has utilized damaged-
centered research to evaluate the degree to which communities have been
affected by humanitarian crises. Consequently, disabled people in the South are
usually known to the West through numbers or statistics (which focus primarily
on their health condition, poverty, and impairments) and through representations of their victimhood (as illustrated in human and disability rights monitor-
ing reports). As Leslie Swartz (2018, 281) observes, "Most of academic writing
about disabled people in the global south is written by people from the global
north, some of them disabled and some not. Disabled people in the global south,
whether written about, or filmed or photographed, commonly enter the world
of the 'global' through the intervention of people in the north." And yet, why
research disability, what is researched and by whom, and who is excluded
from research are political questions. They remind us how research has material-
ized the "coloniality of power" (Quijano 2000) through the universalization of
Western theories and methodologies in the global context.

Questions regarding who "we" are, what epistemological framings we use, and where we stand in order to do research make the politics of disability theorizing challenging. As a discursive and material practice that produces social relations, disability studies has been dominantly conducted by researchers in the Global North. This question of authorship unveils epistemological challenges to research conducted in the Global South (Santos 2018). Disability studies, written by scholars situated in the Global North, has been powerful in disrupting the modernist thinking about disability as an individual problem, and it has created sociopolitical foundations for reframing disability and difference as historically produced by colonial, imperialist, and capitalist social forces (Erevelles 2011). Critical disability studies sees disability and ability as discursively coconstituted by the intersections of racism, colonialism, ableism, and other forms of oppression. Its struggles for disability justice have created more radical spaces for resisting these intersectional forms of oppressions and, in so doing, reframing the question of access for all bodies and minds (Sins Invalid, 2019). As Dan Goodley (2013) puts it, disability is *the* space from which we think about political, theoretical, and practical issues that are relevant to all of us.

At the same time, Western disability studies writings assume the spaces located in North American and Western European nation-states as universal; thus, disability discourse from the Global North tends to be universalized in disability studies writings. There is an implicit assumption that disabled people share similar experiences with oppression across nation-states and transnational spaces. At the same time, there is a hierarchy of knowledge that frames understandings of disability across these geopolitical spaces in that disability discourses in the Global North are centered on questions of access, representation, citizenship, and identity, and as such are perceived to be more valuable in the pursuit of disability justice. In contrast, the Global North's framing of disability discourses in the South is usually constructed through the discourses of poverty, development, and inclusive practices in ways that marginalize the geopolitical production of disablement in Southern spaces (see, for instance, Barnes and Sheldon 2010; Shakespeare 2012; Wissenbach 2014). Such discursive practices have reinforced unequal relations of power between disability scholars in the Global North and South. By applying the epistemic and political implications of Western disability studies to the Global South without considering the South's distinctive epistemological and social positions, Western disability studies has reproduced epistemic injustice.

Crip is a keyword that attends to the radical act of resistance and reimagination in ways that create spaces for radical love and transnational solidarity. At the heart of crip theorizing is the political question associated with unsettling the structures of power and oppressions produced within a global neoliberal capitalist order. *To crip*, like *to queer*, means to get into the process of unsettling, to make something twisted and strange (McRuer 2018). *Cripping* denaturalizes the normative culture of compulsory able-bodiedness and able-mindedness and invents new ways to counter intersecting forms of oppression. As such, crip theorizing could offer an alternative way of addressing marginalized spaces in Western disability studies by decolonizing Western structures of power/knowledge (Foucault 1980) and creating other spaces for resistance, radical love, and transnational solidarity.

And yet, how can crip theorizing engage with and unsettle transnational colonial and imperialist practices without reinforcing damaged-centered approaches in Southern contexts? How can research make visible the colonial, imperialist, and epistemic violence that underpins power dynamics without prioritizing damage? How can we create decolonial spaces for inventing new forms of existence for disabled and marginalized bodies? What impacts do we want our research to have for communities experiencing sustained consequences of colonialism, imperialism, and transnational capitalism? In other words, how can disability studies and crip theory be *decolonial*?

Drawing on the lived experiences of women and girls with disabilities from Vietnam as a part of the Transforming Disability Knowledge, Research, and Activism (TDKRA) project, I raise epistemological and political questions regarding the ways research can unsettle the hegemonic structures of knowledge embedded within Western disability studies. I refer to this work as decolonial disability studies—a collective body of theories, knowledges, and praxis that engages with the lived experiences and struggles of disabled communities in distinctive contexts in the Global South to resist the colonial imposition of Western disability studies and create alternative spaces for knowledge production *with*, *from*, and *across* Southern spaces (see the Decolonial Disability Studies Collective, n.d.). I argue that decolonial disability studies can tackle gaps of knowledge in disability studies in the Global South by creating more inclusive and accessible spaces for disabled, minority, queer and transgender, and young people who have been excluded from the Western framing of disability studies. This approach resists damage-centered research in ways that invent new possibilities for reexistence and resurgence.

Decolonial Disability Studies

The uncritical transfer of Western disability studies from the North to the South has been problematic because it privileges theories and discourses from the Global North (Meekosha 2011; Mehrotra 2020; Grech 2015; Swartz 2018). Referring to the unquestioning application of Western disability models to Indian contexts, Nilika Mehrotra (2020, 2) argues that "Global North theories appear largely incompatible with ground realities of people with disability living on this continent." According to her, disability is deeply bound by cultural, historical, religious, and sociopolitical conditions; how disability is understood in these contexts is historical, cultural, and political.

Decolonial disability studies could be seen as a collective body of knowledge that resists the tendency to universalize the hegemony of Western theories and epistemologies in disability studies. A decolonial approach to disability studies offers resources for understanding the ways Western regimes of knowledge exercise power relations through, for instance, the production of "normate standards" that constitute difference, and it illuminates how such normative standards exercise violence on the Other's bodies and minds (Dirth and Adams 2019; see also Meekosha 2011; Nguyen 2021). A decolonial disability studies approach recognizes the geopolitics of power that shapes specific lived experiences of disabled people in the South. Edelweiss Murillo Lafuente and Mark Sherry (2021, 136) define a decolonial approach as "one that recognizes and challenges the geopolitics of power, including the continuing effects of racism and colonialism on knowledge production, and is committed to challenge such power through a focus on the unique experiences, knowledges, identities, and wisdom of the Global South, particularly Indigenous people." Emerging in the Global South from centuries of Indigenous struggles, decoloniality is an epistemic and political struggle to create an alternative paradigm for knowledge creation in ways that connect theory and praxis. Decolonial thought arises from non-Western ways of knowing and being in relation to the struggles of communities in the South to formulate their own knowledge and counter colonial violence. However, one cannot decolonize knowledge without engaging and questioning the very foundations of Western epistemology (Mignolo 2018). In fact, a fundamental task of decolonial theory and concepts is to recognize the complex structures of colonial management and control, or "the colonial matrix of power" (Mignolo 2018, 142), in constituting the very epistemic assumptions and principles that regulate our discourses, narratives, and conversations. In so doing, it seeks to reclaim non-Western forms of existence and reexistence, recognize difference, and foster transformation. The goal of decolonial theory, then, is to restructure social relations as a result of epistemic and political struggles with the global project of Western modernity (Santos 2018).

Western approaches in disability studies reinforce the coloniality of power through their uncritical application of the same concepts and theories to historically colonized spaces. Much of what we know about disability in the Global South is through Global North representation. Voices from the Global South are most often silenced; their actions and agency are usually stripped away from research design and implementation. Their stories are only mentioned when they represent what Western intellectuals value, such as human rights and democracy. Furthermore, applying Western disability studies to the Global South is epistemologically and methodologically challenging. Shilpaa Anand (2010, 157) explains, "Western modes of theorizing force us to evaluate such an absence [of disability] as evidence of Asian antiquity not being sophisticated enough to have treated and cared for its disabled people."

The decolonial disability studies approach offers an alternative to the colonial structure of knowledge. First, it shifts the power dynamic between researchers and researched by making the knowledge, experiences, and perspectives of disabled people in Southern contexts central to research direction and development. Second, its methodology can offer a decolonial space for reclaiming and reimagining disability as a form of existence and coexistence (Nguyen et al., forthcoming). Grounded in the interconnection between theory and praxis, a decolonial approach to critical disability studies is vital for resisting the hegemonic structures of Western modernity by engaging with the everyday struggles of disabled people in the Global South. As illustrated in the case study that follows, the use of creative methods such as participatory visual research within decolonial disability studies offers an opportunity to imagine alternatives to what currently exists, and in so doing creates a decolonial space for shaping the content, form, and method of artworks produced in collective and imaginary ways (Nguyen et al., forthcoming).

In short, while Western disability studies has been slow in tackling epistemic injustice between itself and Southern epistemologies, a decolonial turn in disability studies can interrogate the coloniality of power that is embedded within the universalization of Western disability studies. This approach engages in decolonial praxis by illuminating more complex, nuanced, and sometimes difficult experiences of disabled people and their communities in the Global South. In so doing, decolonial disability studies puts disability theory and praxis from the Global South into conversations with the Global North while refusing to accept the master's narratives about disability from the perspectives of scholars and activists in the North.

Research as a Decolonial Praxis

The Transforming Disability Knowledge, Research, and Activism (TDKRA) project has emerged as a step toward "unsettling" the boundaries between research and activism to build a more transformative approach to inclusion and social justice in the Global South. The project's main objective is to tackle the gaps in knowledge in relation to girls with disabilities in the Global South. Throughout the research process, we engaged disabled girls and women in three disadvantaged communities in Vietnam in knowledge creation and mobilization as a form of activism for inclusion. The researchers, disabled people's organizations (DPOs) in different regions in Vietnam, and participants worked together over four years, from 2016 to 2020.

Central to TDKRA is the politics of engagement (Nguyen 2016; Stienstra and Nguyen 2020)—the ways in which girls and women with disabilities in the Global South engage in research as a way of claiming their existence, building their social relationships and networks, and developing the potential for

Figure 10.1. Art produced by Meo, A Luoi, 2017.

Image description: A woman standing by a house with two chickens. At the front of the picture, a man is harvesting what appears to be paddy rice in the field. There are banana plants, mountain ranges, and a glimpse of sunshine in the background.

activism. TDKRA materializes forms of decolonial struggle by centering the voices and perspectives of disabled girls and women within the research and activist process. For example, in our conversations, disabled women and girls shared their collective struggles for livelihoods and survival as their embodied experiences within the social dynamics of the Global South (Connell 2011). Their stories and participatory approaches created a basis for framing the research direction.

The participants' experiences with different forms of marginalization were unique and contextually based. Disabled girls and women who lived in more urban areas shared challenging experiences with job opportunities after having left school or an institution. In contrast, ethnic women with disabilities in the mountainous region experienced shortages of food and resources within their homes and communities. Some were able to borrow money from the government with low interest rates and repay their debts after harvesting. However, with unpredictable weather and the regular flux of natural disasters, many shared that they were not able to repay their debts.

In a drawing produced in a community workshop (figure 10.1), a fourteen-year-old girl whose nickname is Meo drew a rural space with a banana plant, mountain ranges, and a glimpse of sunshine in the background. At the center is a woman standing by a house with two chickens on her right. At the front of the picture, a man is harvesting what appears to be paddy rice in the field. In her story, Meo revealed the invisible side of disablement when she talked about the meaning of her drawing: "My drawing is about my parents. My father works, and my mother stays at home. My mother is not able to work because of the pain on her hand."

Meo's reflection on her visual production illuminates her experiences with oppressions in a specific space in the Global South. Located in one of the three "dioxin hotspots" heavily destroyed by the herbicide Agent Orange during the US-Vietnam War, A Luoi Valley is a geopolitical space with constant struggles among different social forces. Intensive sociopolitical conflicts during the war caused widespread destruction to the local communities. Between 1965 and 1970, more than four hundred thousand liters of Agent Orange were sprayed in A Luoi, causing massive forms of debilitation and disability in the region (Tran et al. 2021). The herbicide targeted cultivated land, destroyed crops, disrupted rice paddy production, and caused vast damages in the soil, lake, and river systems (Meding and Thai 2017). Local people who lived in this community saw the disabling impacts of Agent Orange on their lived experiences—the food they ate, the water they drank, or the field in which they played with their peers. Furthermore, ethnic tensions between the Kinh majority groups and ethnic minorities who are indigenous to this land intensified the latter's experiences of oppression (see McElwee 2008; see also Nguyen and Stienstra 2021). The majority of girls and women in A Luoi are Ta Oi, Pa Co, and Co Tu minorities, who are invisible in the state's discourse on disability. Despite the "inclusion" of ethnic minorities into the nation-state, ethnic minority women and girls with disabilities faced continuous struggles in terms of access to food, health care, and livelihoods, as reflected in Meo's story:

MEO: We often don't have money and borrow from them [family members]. We can borrow money from the grandparents, because they have monthly retirement pension.
FACILITATOR: What do you use the loan for?
MEO: To buy rice.
FACILITATOR: Do you often or sometimes ask for money?
MEO: We do that constantly.
FACILITATOR: Money from farming is not enough for your family life?
MEO: We cultivate a field but it takes some months until we can harvest crops.

In their conversations, participants shared that they were in dire need of access to health care but could not get the certificate to be qualified for social assistance (Nguyen and Stienstra 2021). They also felt that they were invisible in community activities such as festivals because their difference was not valued or welcome. Meo told the researchers that she could not participate in her community's social events because she was worried about being looked down on by others due to prejudice against her disability.

Another TDKRA participant is Thanh, an ethnic woman who had a brain tumor believed to be caused by her father's exposure to Agent Orange during the US-Vietnam War. Thanh was able to go to a neighborhood school; however, her sight weakened and her body was debilitated, requiring numerous hospitalizations. She remembered being called "crazy" and encountered violence in school due to her difference (see also Nguyen 2019). Her experiences with intersectional oppression as a young woman with disabilities and a poor ethnic minority member illuminate complex layers of oppression in her everyday struggles.

Interestingly, however, her drawing (figure 10.2) shows a vivid reflection of her community survival through her desire to go to school.

The drawing shows a one-story house with yellow walls and a red roof. In front of the house, three children appear to be going to school. Critically, Thanh illustrates disability in her picture through an image of a child holding a cane. There are trees on both sides of the drawing. Thanh described her drawing to her audience: "I would like to present my dream. The topic of my painting is 'Hope.' It has a dream house with green trees. Students with disabilities are going to school. Their dreams will be fulfilled some day in the future" (drawing workshop in A Luoi, 2017). Through her art, Thanh expressed her desire for schooling. She seemed more willing to talk about her future than to recount her pain and trauma in the past. This is an example in which decolonial framing enables researchers to eschew the damage-centered approach, with participants instead centering their own perspectives. This does not mean that she does not remember or no longer wants to recall historical memories that caused her entire family pain; however, it may mean that she wants to reimagine her story of disability in a way that marks disabled children's presence in schools and communities. Decolonial disability studies reconfigures the dynamic of research and centers the voices and perspectives of participants, illuminating the internal strengths these communities possess.

In their gatherings, participants expressed the willingness and commitment to engage with one another to share their stories as a starting point for building broader social movements. One such praxis was a movement-building activity named Five Fingers, organized by our local partner, the Bac Tu Liem Organization of People with Disabilities in Hanoi. The activity began with participants slapping their one fingers from each hand against each other to make a sound. They then slapped two, three, four, and five fingers against each other, collectively, making loud, crisp, and forceful sounds with their hands. Figure 10.3 provides a snapshot of our act of engagement. We came together, worked together, and built

Figure 10.2. Art produced by Thanh, A Luoi, 2017.

Image description: A one-story house with yellow walls and a red roof. In front of the house three children appear to be going to school. The child in the middle is holding a cane. There are trees on both sides of the drawing.

Figure 10.3. An image of the Five Fingers activity, Bac Tu Liem District, Hanoi, 2018.

Image description: A screenshot of a group of women and girls holding their hands upward. There is an ASL interpreter on the bottom left of the screen. The term on the upper left of the screen reads: "Activism."

collective struggles to amplify the voices and power of women and girls with disabilities in the Global South.

We must still ask who participates in this space, why, and who is missing from it. A decolonial disability studies approach requires us to make visible the forms of exclusion and marginalization that have been sustained within these communities. For example, not all girls with disabilities equally participated in our space due to experiences with ableism, racism, classism, and patriarchy that they had had in various social locations. Some participants only partially participated because they had to work to sustain their livelihoods. Furthermore, while the DPOs took the main responsibility for recruiting participants in their communities as part of a decolonial approach, access to research and activism continued to be the privilege of those located in less remote areas who could be reached by the DPO staff members. This challenges us to make decolonial spaces more accessible for those unable to engage in the project because of their class, gender, disability, or ethnicity.

Furthermore, power dynamics emerged through the movement building. At a national workshop co-organized by the TDKRA research team in collaboration with the Hanoi Organization of People with Disabilities, we saw tensions arising between nongovernmental organizations (NGOs) and the disability community. We brought together representatives of DPOs and disabled women and girls in three project sites to articulate and frame their perspectives on inclusion. In the midst of a discussion, an NGO representative took center stage and recommended that disability communities be more "open" to nondisabled people, like herself, as a path toward their "inclusion." In response, one DPO partner resisted, saying that her community does not function in a charitable manner and challenging the NGO to see the difference between charity and community struggles for rights.

This material practice illuminates the challenges of applying Western ways of knowing to the Global South. There is a deep-seated assumption that international NGOs can assume power to "include" disability communities in the Global South through colonial and ableist practices such as seek foreign funding and overcome obstacles themselves. Within the context of the United Nations Convention on the Rights of Persons with Disabilities, rights-based discourse is contentious, as it has transnationalized the Western regimes of governance onto the local communities. At the same time, DPOs have utilized this tool in order to negotiate power with the governments and international development agencies. This illustrates another aspect of decolonial struggles.

Conclusion: Decolonial Disability Studies as an Alternative Option

JosAnn Cutajar and Casimir Adjoe (2016, 507) interrogate the one-way transfer of knowledge from the North to South, arguing that "while our everyday experiences are situated in the local context, the landscape we read and learn is based somewhere else." In contrast, a decolonial turn in disability studies pushes us to revisit the conceptual limits of Western and Eurocentric frameworks in rendering certain bodies of knowledge from the South invisible (Reed-Sandoval and Sirvent 2019). In this chapter, I propose that a decolonial approach to disability studies is important because it creates alternative spaces for knowledge production in ways that negotiate power and challenge epistemic injustice in the South. The example of TDKRA sheds light on the possibilities and challenges of decolonial struggles through research praxis. We engaged with research as a way of resisting the hierarchy of Western disability studies and reclaiming our engagement with women and girls with disabilities in the Global South from their ways of seeing. This praxis resists "damage-centered research" (Tuck 2009, 422) by building decolonial spaces and methodologies for these women and girls to engage, to reimagine their difference, and to set a stage for connecting their knowledges and movements.

Decoloniality is an option among many systems of thought and is not intended to be universal (Mignolo 2018, 115). It offers a creative approach for reclaiming crip authorship by centering the stories of women and girls with disabilities in the Global South in ways that resist the Western hegemonic structures of knowledge, thus creating new grounds for decolonial struggles.

BIBLIOGRAPHY

Anand, Shilpaa. 2010. "Corporeality and Culture: Theorizing Difference in the South Asian Context." In *South Asia and Disability Studies: Redefining Boundaries and Extending Horizons*, edited by Shridevi Rao and Maya Kalyanpur, 154–170. New York: Peter Lang.

Barnes, Colin, and Alison Sheldon. 2010. "Disability, Politics and Poverty in a Majority World Context." *Disability and Society* 25 (7): 771–782.

Connell, Raewyn. 2011. "Southern Bodies and Disability: Re-thinking Concepts." *Third World Quarterly* 32 (8): 1369–1381.

Cutajar, JosAnn, and Casimir Adjoe. 2016. "Whose Knowledge, Whose Voice? Power, Agency and Resistance in Disability Studies for the Global South." In *Disability in the Global South: The Critical Handbook*, edited by Shaun Grech and Karen Soldatic, 503–516. Cham, Switzerland: Springer.

Decolonial Disability Studies Collective. n.d. Homepage. Accessed October 3, 2022. https://carleton.ca/ddsc/.

Dirth, Thomas P., and Glenn A. Adams. 2019. "Decolonial Theory and Disability Studies: On the Modernity/Coloniality of Ability." *Journal of Social and Political Psychology* 7 (1): 260–289.

Erevelles, Nirmala. 2011. *Disability and Difference in Global Contexts: Enabling a Transformative Body Politic*. New York: Palgrave Macmillan.

Goodley, Dan. "Dis/entangling critical disability studies." *Disability & Society* 28, no. 5 (2013): 631–644.

Grech, Shaun. "Decolonising Eurocentric disability studies: Why colonialism matters in the disability and global South debate." *Social Identities* 21, no. 1 (2015): 6–21.

Foucault, Michel. 1980. *Power/Knowledge: Selected Interviews and Other Writings, 1972–1977*. New York: Pantheon Books.

Lafuente, Edelweiss Murillo, and Mark Sherry. 2021. "Disability in Bolivia: A Feminist Global South Perspective." In *Dis/ability in the Americas: The Intersections of Education, Power, and Identity*, edited by Chantal Figueroa and David I. Hernández-Saca, 135–166. Cham, Switzerland: Palgrave Macmillan.

McElwee, Pamela. 2008. "'Blood Relatives' or Uneasy Neighbors? Kinh Migrant and Ethnic Minority Interactions in the Trường Sơn Mountains." *Journal of Vietnamese Studies* 3 (3): 81–116.

McRuer, Robert. 2018. *Crip Times: Disability, Globalization, and Resistance*. New York: New York University Press.

Meding, Jason D., and T. M. Hang Thai. 2017. "Agent Orange, Exposed: How U.S. Chemical Warfare in Vietnam Unleashed a Slow-Moving Disaster." *The Conversation*, October 3, 2017. https://theconversation.com/agent-orange-exposed-how-u-s-chemical-warfare-in-vietnam -unleashed-a-slow-moving-disaster-84572.

Meekosha, Helen. 2011. "Decolonising Disability: Thinking and Acting Globally." *Disability and Society* 26 (6): 667–682.

Mehrotra, Nilika, editor. *Disability Studies in India: Interdisciplinary Perspectives*. Singapore: Springer, 2020.

Mignolo, Walter D. 2018. "The Decolonial Option." In *On Decoloniality: Concepts, Analytics, Praxis*, edited by Walter D. Mignolo and Catherine E. Walsh, 105–244. Durham, NC: Duke University Press.

Nguyen, Xuan Thuy. 2016. "Girls with Disabilities in the Global South: Rethinking the Politics of Engagement." *Girlhood Studies: An Interdisciplinary Journal* 9 (2): 53–71.

Nguyen, Xuan Thuy. 2019. "Unsettling 'Inclusion' in the Global South: A Post-colonial and Intersectional Approach to Disability, Gender, and Education." In *The SAGE Handbook of Inclusion and Diversity in Education*, edited by Matthew J. Schuelk, Christopher J. Johnson, Gary Thomas, and Alfredo J. Artiles, 28–40. London: Sage.

Nguyen, X. T. 2021. "Critical Disability Studies at the Edge of Global Development: Why Do We Need to Engage with Southern Theory?" In *Still Living the Edges: A Disabled Women's Reader*, edited by Diane Driedger, 349–371. Toronto: Inanna.

Nguyen, Xuan Thuy, Tammy Bernasky, M. Gonick, and M. Mitchell. Forthcoming. "Critical Disability Studies as Methodologies for Social Change: The Use of Participatory Research Methodologies in Social Research with Women and Girls with Disabilities in the Global South." In *Culturally Relevant Storytelling in Qualitative Research: Diversity, Equity, and Inclusion Examined through a Research Lens*, edited by J. Salvo, and N. Denzin. Myers Education Press.

Nguyen, Xuan Thuy, and Deborah Stienstra. 2021. "Engaging Girls and Women with Disabilities in the Global South: Beyond Cultural and Geopolitical Generalizations." *Disability and the Global South* 8 (2): 2035–2052.

Quijano, Anibal. 2000. "The Coloniality of Power and Eurocentrism in Latin America." *International Sociology* 15 (2): 215–232.

Reed-Sandoval, Amy, and Roberto Sirvent. 2019. "Disability and the Decolonial Turn: Perspectives from the Americas." *Disability and the Global South* 6 (1): 1553–1561.

Santos, Boaventura de Sousa. 2018. *The End of the Cognitive Empire: The Coming of Age of Epistemologies of the South*. Durham, NC: Duke University Press.

Shakespeare, Tom. 2012. "Disability in Developing Countries." In *Routledge Handbook of Disability Studies*, edited by Nick Watson, 282–295. London: Routledge.

Sins Invalid. 2019. *Skin, Tooth, and Bone: The Basis of Movement Is Our People*. 2nd ed. Berkeley: Sins Invalid.

Smith, Linda Tuhiwai. 1999. *Decolonizing Methodologies: Research and Indigenous Peoples*. London: Zed Books.

Stienstra, D., and X. T. Nguyen. "Opening to the Possible: Girls and Women with Disabilities Engaging in Vietnam." In *Creating Spaces for Engagement*, edited by S. M. Wiebe and L. Levac, 139–60. Toronto: University of Toronto Press, 2020.

Swartz, Leslie. 2018. "Representing Disability and Development in the Global South." *Medical Humanities* 44 (4): 281–284.

Tran, Thi Ai My, Nguyen Duy Dat, Kersten Van Langenhove, Michael S. Denison, Hoang Thai Long, and Marc Elskens. 2021. "Evaluation of the Dioxin-Like Toxicity in Soil Samples from Thua Thien Hue Province Using the AhR-CALUX Bioassay—an Update of Agent Orange Contamination in Vietnam." *Ecotoxicology and Environmental Safety* 212:111971.

Tuck, Eve. 2009. "Suspending Damage: A Letter to Communities." *Harvard Educational Review* 9 (3): 409–428.

Wissenbach, Lars. 2014. "Pathways to Inclusive Development: How to Make Disability Inclusive Practice Measurable?" Discussion Papers on Social Protection 21, Deutsche Gesellschaft für Internationale Zusammenarbeit, Bonn, Germany. https://www.giz.de/en/downloads/08 _Discussions%20Paper%20on%20Social%20Protection.pdf.

11

On *Still* Reading Like a Depressed Transsexual

CAMERON AWKWARD-RICH

Other, additional forms of support, solidarity, and intimacy are needed to grapple with the all-too-common experience of lag—a form of being out of temporal sync, left behind—and the negative affects associated with it.
—Malatino 2019, 639

Frequently, depressed time . . . is characterized by feelings of slowness, delay or stillness arising from a lack of such future orientation.
—Cavaletti and Heimann 2020, 272

Ever since, I have found myself stuck in, around, 2014. To me (and, I think, to many of us who are, for whatever reason, attentive to the rhythms of trans cultures and their representation in the United States), 2014 registered as a transitional moment; one situation gave way to another. This giving way has been narrated in a variety of ways: as an "unprecedented" tip of *trans* into visibility via media and art (Koch-Reid, Haschemi Yekani, and Verlinden 2020, 3); the proclaimed "flourishing" of the academic, interdisciplinary space of transgender studies (Kunzel 2014); the relatively widespread emergence of an intelligible transnormative subject (Snorton and Haritaworn 2013); a welcome ascendency of informed-consent models in the previously (and in some places presently) heavily gatekept arena of trans health care and the "(incomplete) depathologization of trans identity" (Pyne 2021, 346); and the intensification (a slow drip and then a deluge) of state-level anti-trans legislation, forms of speculator and mundane violence, and the mainstreaming of tacitly white supremacist and explicitly anti-trans rhetorics. Trans scholars and other writers have offered innumerable diagnoses and historicizations of this post-2014 situation, to which I have diminishingly little to add. And yet, each time I sit down to write, I find myself beginning here, as if no time had passed, as if nothing had happened (though much has happened) to fundamentally change the situation or my relation to it. What I'm trying to describe is my (our?) attempt to write both in and about a Berlantian *impasse*, "a space of time lived" without a horizon of expectation, "without a narrative genre . . . a holding station that doesn't hold securely but opens out into anxiety, that dogpaddling around a space whose contours remain obscure" (Berlant 2011, 199).

And so. Way back in academic year 2014–2015, I wrote an essay that would become the central chapter of my dissertation and eventually my first academic book. But first, that chapter was published as the essay "Trans, Feminism: *Or, Reading Like a Depressed Transsexual*," already years later, in 2017. It was received well, I think, not because it said anything new but because it was received by many as *timely*. That essay was and is about many things, but it is throughout animated by a question about mental disability and (trans) epistemology: How might the cognitive or affective styles of depression allow me to know about the impasse of trans feminism? Or, more precisely, the gambit of that essay was that thinking with (rather than against) the habits of thought and feeling that inhere in depression might allow for the narration of a real and imagined trans feminist "us" that hangs together, without obscuring the painful, dangerous—and more widely shared than most of "us" would care to admit—trans antagonism and transmisogyny embedded in past and present liberal, radical, and other feminist projects. There, I was (and am) interested in the idea—first opened for me by Ann Cvetkovich's *Depression: A Public Feeling* (2012), Eve Sedgwick's (2003) and José Muñoz's (2006) queer/brown/depressed reworkings of Melanie Klein's *depressive position*, and Merri Lisa Johnson and Robert McRuer's compiled *crip-istemologies* (2014)—that thinking reflexively as an avowed depressive might enable ways of approaching histories and presents of conflict without moving immediately toward their resolution. And further, that doing so might allow for a more adequate description of what is going on.

Asked to return to this essay years later—first in the process of revising it for the book and then for this anthology—I can't help but be struck by the persistence of its timeliness in some respects. "Trans, Feminism" glimpsed in 2014/2015, that period of optimism about *trans*'s tip into legibility, the resurgent mainstreaming of trans exclusion under the guise of feminist concern. Now, after the advent of popular and university-authorized "gender-critical feminism," Abigail Shrier's trip to Washington to testify against the Equality Act, and so on, things I had to actively argue in that essay seem utterly obvious. As a consequence, I've come to think of that essay as having been written in depressive time, a retrospective understanding glossed only very briefly in the revised manuscript as a sense "that if the conflicted history of trans/feminism tells us anything, it is that times recur." In the present chapter, I attempt to unfold this retrospective insight with a bit more care by inching toward an account of "depressive time" as a particular kind of crip time, one that undergirds my reading like a depressed transsexual.

In doing so, I hope to sit in conversation with the vast and growing writing on various minoritized, and especially crip, temporalities, entangled literatures that I cannot do justice to in this short chapter. Still, I will say that crip time, first a disability culture commonplace, has been widely taken up by critical disability studies scholars as a means of describing the temporal dimensions of ableist oppression and the construction of disability under capitalism, as well as a set of potentially resistant, creative, nonnormative ways of inhabiting socially patterned time that are often necessitated by embodyminded disability and nurtured by crip community (Kafer 2013; Samuels and Freeman 2021). In these renderings, crip time throws into relief the ways that dominant orderings of time actively *produce* disability as the name for the forms of embodyminded-ness that cannot or will not "operate according to capitalist logic and labor time" and, potentially, offers and prefigures modes of living otherwise (Fink 2019, 9). Ellen Samuels (2017) has complicated this hopeful account of life in crip time, however, by offering a partial inventory of its "less appealing aspects . . . [ones] that are harder to see as liberatory, more challenging to find a way to celebrate," precisely because they are shot through with bad feelings, by which I mean feelings that are (1) phenomenologically painful, (2) not easily harnessed for collective politics and world-making, or (3) regarded as potentially pathological in a diagnostic setting. And yet the bad feelings she describes as crip time's "less appealing aspects" cannot only be understood as the *consequence* of inhabiting crip time, of falling out of "the sheltered space of normative time" (Samuels 2017). Rather, crip time might and has also been theorized as the forms of phenomenological or lived time that inhere in forms of bad feeling, mental disability, madness, or neurodivergence that are often composed of or manifested as nonnormative temporalities.[1]

Indeed, Alison Kafer's oft-cited account of crip time in *Feminist, Queer, Crip* raises questions about this second sense of crip time, even as its most circulated passages focus elsewhere: "What would constitute a temporality of mania, or depression, or anxiety? If we think of queer time as involving archives of rage and shame, then why not also panic attacks or fatigue? How does depression slow down time, making moments drag for days, or how do panic attacks cause linear time to unravel, making time seem simultaneously to speed up and slam shut, leaving one behind?" (Kafer 2013, 37). The remainder of this brief chapter thinks alongside one of Kafer's questions, "How does depression slow down time . . . ?" as well as meditates on what depressive time might lend to the doing of critical trans cultural studies. I do so by first accounting for the place of depression within contemporary trans discourse and then by elaborating on what I mean by depressive time as a particular (lack of) "future orientation" (Cavaletti and Heimann 2020, 272).

Depressed Transsexuals

Depression has long been endemic to the representation of trans life in US contexts, including persistent studies emerging from the psy disciplines that attempt to quantify the correlation between trans identity, depression, and other forms of mental disability. Whether explicitly or implicitly, these studies make claims about the larger projects of trans medicine and social support; rhetorically, the value of both has been attached to the question of transition's efficacy as an anti-depressant, whether or not it actually works to alleviate depression (and other bad feelings) among trans people.[2] This has meant that trans-antagonistic commentators have been inclined to latch onto singular studies that evidence enduring trans depression and suicidality as a way of attempting to undermine the consensus view that transition is "an effective treatment" (Dhejne et al. 2011; Williams 2015).

Likewise, *trans* has been linked to depressive forms of feeling and thought through the saturation of trans characters and storylines with bad feeling. "Transgender identity," as Cáel Keegan has argued, "has been sutured to specific forms of negative affect. . . . The fictional transgender figure has traditionally been marked as vulnerable to or productive of extreme emotional states, portrayed either as the emotive center of a narrative (The Crying Game), as disturbed, erratic, or unstable (Silence of the Lambs, Ticked-Off Trannies with Knives), or psychotically violent (Dressed to Kill, Sleepaway Camp)" (2013). While we have now available to us a set of tacitly trans-affirmative representations—ones that depict trans narratives as "journeys from negative to redemptive affect, from psychosis to mental health, from self-hatred to a celebration of liberal individuality" (Keegan 2013)—these are nonetheless powered by the enduring sense that trans people are a uniquely depressed and suicidal population who might be cured via recourse to the "universalized trajectory of coming out/transition, visibility, recognition, protection, and self-actualization" (Snorton and Haritaworn 2013, 67). While Keegan has described this narrative structure in the context of millennial cinema and television, one likewise encounters it in legal briefs, academic and journalistic articles, and celebrity profiles alike. These documents tend to rely on a familiar set of statistics—40 percent of trans adults have attempted suicide in our lifetime (James et al. 2016, 5), trans students are nearly twice as likely to be depressed and nearly three times as likely to self-harm compared with their cis peers (Bauer-Wolf 2019), and so on—statistics whose endless repetition renders trans depression and its cure common sense.

Against this use of the common sense of trans depression to construct the trans subject as in need of cure, there has lately been an interest in understanding depression as instead indexing the deleterious effects of trans antagonism. In these accounts, depression is not inherent to trans life, not a symptom of wrong embodiment that can only be cured via somatic intervention. Instead, depression is positioned as one outcome of life under trans antagonism—it is a social and political rather than individualizable problem. This political account of bad trans feeling has, of course, long been present in critical trans studies and politics. Back in 1994, for example, Susan Stryker offered a reading of the suicide of a young trans woman as being the outcome of trans misogyny within a queer community, not some inherent unbearable trans feeling. Recounting the "despair" engendered in the young woman as she entered the data collected from a community survey on whether the Lesbian Resource Center where she volunteered should stop offering services to trans women, Stryker concludes with the pointed rhetorical question, "Did [she] commit suicide, or did the queer community of Seattle kill her?" (1994, 239–240). However, while sociopolitical accounts of trans depression are certainly not new, they have only recently come to structure more official discourse. As a part of this shift, recent studies of small cohorts of usually well-off youths increasingly report that trans and other gender-nonconforming kids who are supported in living out their genders socially are at no higher risk of depression then their cisgender peers. One such report insists that "the current findings do not negate the experiences of the many transgender people who face high rates of mental health challenges, but do provide further evidence that being transgender is not synonymous with these challenges" (Gibson, Glazier, and Olson 2021).

In short, decoupling trans identity from depression is part of a larger, multi-sited, and sometimes contradictory attempt to produce the trans subject as able-minded. "Yet," as Jake Pyne reminds, "the fact that a trans person can now be considered able-minded must also be understood as a means of distancing ourselves from disabled and mentally suspect others" (2021, 346–347). Further, as I have argued elsewhere, the "methodological distancing" of transness from disability in general and mental disability in particular is long-standing and has its roots not in official "expert" discourse but rather in trans community, activist, and intellectual life (Mitchell and Snyder 2000, 2; Awkward-Rich 2020). And as I have also argued, disability studies teaches me that we should, at minimum, be suspicious of this move insofar as it ideologically reinforces (while appearing to contest) the very ableism and sanism that has long undergirded the withholding of care, first-person authority, and bodily autonomy from trans, disabled, racialized, and other minoritized people. While distancing *trans* from *mad* has certainly been important for the project of authorizing trans knowledge projects, this distancing too often proceeds not by contesting medicolegal regulation per se but rather by merely contesting that the trans subject is its proper object. Under these conditions, "trans and [other] psychiatrized people saying that they are not disabled because there is nothing wrong with them . . . work[s] to reinforce the idea that there is something wrong with those disabled people they are trying to distance themselves from" (Withers 2012, 112).

But, and perhaps more to the point, the project of loosening the association between *trans* and *mad* paints depression, madness, mental illness, and neurodivergence as somehow separable from trans knowledge and ways of knowing. More forcefully, the common sense of trans depression contains a particular assumption that undergirds all of its uses—antagonistic and affirmative alike—which is that *depression* can only be understood as counter to life and knowledge: it is what indexes a wrong body, a wrong society, or a wrong kind of interpretation. But reading like a depressed transsexual means instead taking an interest in how depression has and might shape trans ways of knowing. Indeed, given their persistently tight coupling, refusing to think of trans and depressed epistemologies as interrelated seems to me, frankly, an absurd proposition. And so, both because I am invested in a trans studies that is *not* invested in a future in which *trans* is understood as able-minded at the expense of trans-crip coalitions, and because it simply seems true to me that trans cultural and intellectual production has long been saturated by depressive forms of feeling and thought—whether this is a side effect of life under unjust conditions or not—it seems worth it to me to linger for a while in the impasse even though it does not feel good.

Depressive Time

As Ann Cvetkovich remarks, "With its spatial connotations of being at a 'dead end' or 'no exit,' impasse captures the notion of depression as a state of being 'stuck,' of not being able to figure out what to do or why to do it" (2012, 20). Further, as Berlant's elaborations of *impasse* remind, *being stuck* is not the same as *nothing is happening*. Indeed, stuckness might be characterized by a flurry of activity: "dogpaddling," turning things over, "flailing" around for a new genre that might (or might not) take hold (Berlant 2018, 157). Trans philosopher Hil Malatino has theorized such non-future-bound activity—in his formulation, the nonteleological activity of transition—as characterizing life "in interregnum, in the crucial and transformative moments between past and future, between the regime of what was and the promise of what might be" (Malatino 2019, 644), whereas in his 2021 novel *Future Feeling*, Joss Lake terms this psychic time/space the Shadowlands, a trip through which, he posits, is a necessary part of transition, of reorienting oneself in and vis-à-vis the past and future. For both Malatino and Lake, "whatever being trans is about, it's decidedly characterized by upheaval and emergence into a social world with shifting and shifted parameters" (Malatino 2020, 3), an emergence that requires withdrawing one's attachments to scripted, anticipated, and "promissory futures" (Malatino 2019, 644).

If it is not yet apparent, depressive time in my formulation has to do with the future. Specifically, it is a name for time lived in the absence of a socially patterned horizon of expectation, an absence that accounts for the commonplace understanding that time in depression is experienced as slowed down, "making moments drag for days" or, in the case of the moment of 2014, for years on end (Kafer 2013, 37). Although researchers in the psy disciplines seem to agree that people in the midst of depression reliably report experiencing time as slow or even stopped, why this might be, the mechanism that underlies the felt experience, is a relatively open question: "Despite the large number of studies," Daniel Oberfeld and colleagues report in their 2014 overview, "a firm conclusion to the effect that depression does indeed alter time perception cannot be drawn" (1). That is, studies that set out to measure depressed participants' ability to estimate or produce particular time intervals—by, for example, estimating the time that passes between two sounds or producing a one-minute interval by pressing a button on either end—do not reliably suggest that those in depressions are actually inclined to misperceive short, actively engaged durations. In contrast to these studies, Ann Marie Roepke and Martin E. P. Seligman offer a different language for what I am, through Berlant, trying to describe when they propose that depression involves a loss of (or reduction in) ability to relate to the future as an open horizon and to project oneself into it; for them, depression is "prospection go[ne] awry" (2016, 24). This hypothesis, in turn, resonates with decades of phenomenologically inflected work on depressive time (Wyllie 2005; Fuchs 2013; Minkowski 1970), which has understood time as "*lived*, i.e. arising from our precognitive orientation towards the future and existentially shaping our subjective experience" (Cavaletti and Heimann 2020, 272). Time slows in depression, then, not because of a misperception but because of a lack of future orientation, a lack that might cause the present-past to stretch out indefinitely even as things continue to happen, other people move on. Although they approach depression through the framework of pathology, I find these phenomenologies of depressive time useful as descriptions; this is my experience of depression anyway, that time moves along without me in it.

In some ways, depressive time stands in direct opposition to many dominant and academic constructions of trans time, in which transness has to do with movement into open futures through "unexpected becomings" (Stryker and Currah 2014, 9), with "how *what could happen* haunts the present" (Keegan 2018, 3), with "futurity itself" (Halberstam 2005, 18). Of course, however, the conflation of transness with futurity enables trans oppression, undergirding the structure of recurrent moral panics that must regard trans women and children as perpetually new (and trans men as perpetually nonexisting in the present) for their emotional force. Further, as has been repeatedly argued, not all forms of trans life (not even all forms within the narrow Euro-American parameters) are regarded as future-bound. Clinical investigations into autistic trans populations, for example, are presently structured by a "prying apart of autistic and trans life" in order to foster the "hope that the trans future might leave autism behind" (Pyne 2021, 351). Or, as the editors of the "Trans Temporalities" special issue of *Somatechnics* remind, the overdetermined link between *Black trans woman* and shortened life-span indicates that "only 'some versions of transness' are associated with futurity while for others, having a future at all is not a given" (Fisher, Phillips, and Katri 2017, 3–4). Or, as Jules Gill-Peterson demonstrates in *Histories of the Transgender Child*, the 1930s understanding of "black children's sexed plasticity" as "atavistic" eventually led to the "withholding of the narrow parameters of . . . transsexuality from black children" in the 1960s (2018, 80, 160). Something peculiar happens, then, at the intersection of *trans* and social categories constructed as having to do with slowness, delay, backwardness, atavism, and so on—namely, those who inhabit such crisscrossing temporalities are always at risk of being declared *not really trans*. So, as Pyne points out, "trans communities" are often primed, by the experience of delays in care and social or legal recognition, "to welcome affirmation in whatever suspect form it arrives and, further, to disavow our relation to those who are deemed 'slow' or 'delayed'" (2021, 347). But also, and perhaps more fundamentally, the commonplace understanding of *trans* as—for better and for worse—future-bound has worked to narrow who can appear as subjects of trans pasts, presents, and futures. The story about *trans* as futurity itself is a story with racial, disabling effects.

Here is what I have been trying to say: since 2014/2015 we have moved increasingly into a future in which *trans* can be registered as *able-minded* and reading like a depressed transsexual is my way of trying to not orient myself toward the lure of that future. But reading as an avowed depressive is not a new method, nor is it one that I recommend universalizing; depressive epistemologies know many things very poorly, perhaps especially how to do the urgent political work of imagining and enacting some kind of futures we might actually desire. To this end, Kafer's discussion of crip time is embedded within a larger concern and "desire for crip futurity" (2013, 27). Tarrying with the queer temporalities on offer in Lee Edelman's *No Future*, Kafer echoes and extends Muñoz, Heather Love, Jasbir Puar, and others by insisting that a fuck-the-future stance is "untenable" for disabled, racialized, trans, and otherwise minoritized people because of the way that the future is already constructed without and against us: "The task, then, is not so much to refuse the future as to imagine disability and disability futures otherwise, as part of other, alternate temporalities that do not cast disabled people out of time, as the sign of the future of no future" (34). By suggesting that no future might be a crip time after all, I mean simply that a crucial part of the work of imagining other futures, as Kafer implores us to do, is simultaneously learning not to want the ones that are ready-to-hand and promise feel-good endings. And indeed, one thing that depressives know very well, for better and for worse, is how to not want the future on offer. This produces and reinforces often painful desynchronization, but it also is one more way of refusing to (or being, frankly, unable to) understand the statistically white, nondisabled, neurotypical, well-supported trans child—the ones for whom it is possible in the first place to occupy "the sheltered space of normative time" (Samuels 2017)—as *the* subject of trans history and futurity.

NOTES

1 In an essay I do not engage here but am clearly thinking alongside, Clementine Morrigan (2017) theorizes "trauma time" as one such form of crip/mad time.

2 Although its rhetoric and venue drew ire from many corners of the trans internet, Andrea Long Chu is in my view correct to be suspicious of the way that trans healthcare is justified, in liberal discourse, not because bodily-autonomy is good in itself but, specifically, because transition might deliver on the promise of happiness (Chu 2018).

BIBLIOGRAPHY

Awkward-Rich, Cameron. 2020. "'She of the Pants and No Voice': Jack Bee Garland's Disability Drag." *TSQ: Transgender Studies Quarterly* 7 (1): 20–36.

Bauer-Wolf, Jeremy. 2019. "Trans Students Often Struggle with Mental Health." *Inside Higher Ed*, August 20, 2019. https://www.insidehighered.com/news/2019/08/20/survey-finds-mental -health-issues-are-common-among-trans-college-students.

Berlant, Lauren. 2011. *Cruel Optimism*. Durham, NC: Duke University Press.

———. 2018. "Genre Flailing." *Capacious: Journal for Emerging Affect Inquiry* 1 (2): 156–162.

Cavaletti, Federica, and Katrin Heimann. 2020. "Longing for Tomorrow: Phenomenology, Cognitive Psychology, and the Methodological Bases of Exploring Time Experience in Depression." *Phenomenology and the Cognitive Sciences* 19 (2): 271–289.

Chu, Andrea Long. 2018. "Opinion | My New Vagina Won't Make Me Happy." *New York Times*, November 24, 2018. https://www.nytimes.com/2018/11/24/opinion/sunday/vaginoplasty -transgender-medicine.html.

Cvetkovich, Ann. 2012. *Depression: A Public Feeling*. Durham, NC: Duke University Press.

Dhejne, Cecilia, Paul Lichtenstein, Marcus Boman, Anna L. V. Johansson, Niklas Långström, and Mikael Landén. 2011. "Long-Term Follow-Up of Transsexual Persons Undergoing Sex Reassignment Surgery: Cohort Study in Sweden." *PLoS ONE* 6 (2): e16885.

Fink, Marty. 2019. "It Will Feel Really Bad Unromantically Soon." *TSQ: Transgender Studies Quarterly* 6 (1): 4–19.

Fisher, Simon D. Elin, Rasheedah Phillips, and Ido H. Katri. 2017. "Introduction: Trans Temporalities." *Somatechnics* 7 (1): 1–15.

Fuchs, Thomas. 2013. "Temporality and Psychopathology." *Phenomenology and the Cognitive Sciences* 12 (1): 75–104.

Gibson, Dominic J., Jessica J. Glazier, and Kristina R. Olson. 2021. "Evaluation of Anxiety and Depression in a Community Sample of Transgender Youth." *JAMA Network Open* 4 (4): e214739.

Gill-Peterson, Jules. 2018. *Histories of the Transgender Child*. Minnesota: University of Minnesota Press.

Halberstam, Jack. 2005. *In a Queer Time and Place: Transgender Bodies, Subcultural Lives*. New York: New York University Press.

James, Sandy E., Jody L. Herman, Susan Rankin, Mara Keisling, Lisa Mottet, and Ma'ayan Anafi. 2016. *The Report of the 2015 U.S. Transgender Survey*. Washington, DC: National Center for Transgender Equality.

Johnson, Merri Lisa, and Robert McRuer, editors. 2014. "Cripistemologies: Part I." Special issue, *Journal of Literary and Cultural Disability Studies* 8 (2).

Kafer, Alison. 2013. *Feminist, Queer, Crip*. Bloomington: Indiana University Press.

Keegan, Cáel M. 2013. "Moving Bodies: Sympathetic Migrations in Transgender Narrativity." *Genders* 57 (Spring). http://www.colorado.edu/gendersarchive1998-2013/2013/06/01/moving -bodies-sympathetic-migrations-transgender-narrativity.

———. 2018. *Lana and Lilly Wachowski: Sensing Transgender*. Urbana: University of Illinois Press.

Koch-Rein, Anson, Elahe Haschemi Yekani, and Jasper J. Verlinden. 2020. "Representing Trans: Visibility and Its Discontents." *European Journal of English Studies* 24 (1): 1–12.

Kunzel, Regina. 2014. "The Flourishing of Transgender Studies." *TSQ: Transgender Studies Quarterly* 1 (1–2): 285–297.

Lake, Joss. 2021. *Future Feeling*. New York: Soft Skull.

Lewis, Abram J. 2014. "'I Am 64 and Paul McCartney Doesn't Care': The Haunting of the Transgender Archive and the Challenges of Queer History." *Radical History Review*, no. 120, 13–34.

Malatino, Hil. 2019. "Future Fatigue: Trans Intimacies and Trans Presents (or How to Survive the Interregnum)." *TSQ: Transgender Studies Quarterly* 6 (4): 635–658.

———. 2020. *Trans Care*. Minneapolis: University of Minnesota Press.

Minkowski, Eugène. 1970. *Lived Time: Phenomenological and Psychopathological Studies*. Translated by Nancy Metzel. Evanston: Northwestern University Press.

Mitchell, David T., and Sharon L. Snyder. 2000. *Narrative Prosthesis: Disability and the Dependencies of Discourse*. Ann Arbor: University of Michigan Press.

Morrigan, Clementine. 2017. "Trauma Time: The Queer Temporalities of the Traumatized Mind." *Somatechnics* 7 (1): 50–58.

Muñoz, José Esteban. 2006. "Feeling Brown, Feeling Down: Latina Affect, the Performativity of Race, and the Depressive Position." In "New Feminist Theories of Visual Culture," special issue. *Signs* 31 (3): 675–688.

Oberfeld, Daniel, Sven Thönes, Benyne J. Palayoor, and Heiko Hecht. 2014. "Depression Does Not Affect Time Perception and Time-to-Contact Estimation." *Frontiers in Psychology* 5 (July). https://doi.org/10.3389/fpsyg.2014.00810.

Pyne, Jake. 2021. "Autistic Disruptions, Trans Temporalities: A Narrative 'Trap Door' in Time." *South Atlantic Quarterly* 120 (2): 343–361.

Roepke, Ann Marie, and Martin E. P. Seligman. 2016. "Depression and Prospection." *British Journal of Clinical Psychology* 55 (1): 23–48.

Samuels, Ellen. 2017. "Six Ways of Looking at Crip Time." *Disability Studies Quarterly* 37 (3). https://doi.org/10.18061/dsq.v37i3.5824.

Samuels, Ellen, and Elizabeth Freeman, editors. 2021. "Crip Temporalities." Special issue, *South Atlantic Quarterly* 120 (2).

Sedgwick, Eve Kosofsky. 2003. *Touching Feeling: Affect, Pedagogy, Performativity*. Durham, NC: Duke University Press.

Snorton, C. Riley, and Jin Haritaworn. 2013. "Trans Necropolitics: A Transnational Reflection on Violence, Death, and the Trans of Color Afterlife." In *Transgender Studies Reader 2*, edited by Susan Stryker and Aren Z. Aizura, 66–76. New York: Routledge.

Stryker, Susan. 1994. "My Words to Victor Frankenstein above the Village of Chamounix: Performing Transgender Rage." *GLQ: A Journal of Lesbian and Gay Studies* 1 (3): 237–254.

Stryker, Susan, and Paisley Currah. 2014. "Introduction." *TSQ* 1 (1–2): 1–18.

Williams, Cristan. 2015. "Fact Check: Study Shows Transition Makes Trans People Suicidal." TransAdvocate, November 2, 2015. https://www.transadvocate.com/fact-check-study-shows -transition-makes-trans-people-suicidal_n_15483.htm.

Withers, A. J. 2012. *Disability Politics and Theory*. Nova Scotia: Fernwood. Kindle edition.

Wyllie, Martin. 2005. "Lived Time and Psychopathology." *Philosophy, Psychiatry, and Psychology* 12 (3): 173–185.

12

On Trauma in Research on Illness, Disability, and Care

LAURA MAULDIN

Containing

At this moment, I feel this work in my body. I am simultaneously amped up and shaky, and exhausted, like I could just fall into a deep sleep. My reaction to triggering situations has often been wanting to sleep immediately. But oddly, I am also electric right now. It's a strange feeling, like it's all just sitting under the surface. I carry with me the things that broke me, all that I could not tell people because no one could understand, what I felt, how I coped, the darkness in that coping. And now I am carrying the things that my participants also feel they cannot tell people . . . because they are actually telling me. And I'm containing them all.

In the summer of 2020, I began virtual interviews with forty-four spousal or partner caregivers across the country. Because my late partner died in 2010, I was about a decade out from my own experiences, far enough to feel safe to do the work. My aim was to get the stories of caregivers, and when possible, to get stories from their partners as well. During 2021, I was able to make visits to four different couples in four different states. This provided me with additional observations to go along with caregiver interviews, as well as opportunities to interview disabled partners. I asked my participants to tell me what their caregiving looked like, how it was accomplished using technologies at home, as well as what they thought about disability and illness, their own disabilities (many caregivers were also disabled themselves and having to forgo meeting their own needs), and how they navigated health care and home care in the United States, where disabled people are largely abandoned structurally. It was especially powerful to hear how some caregivers, with disabilities stemming from conditions like multiple sclerosis or heart failure, were providing care in the context of near-total structural abandonment. There was no help from publicly funded programs, and because of the pandemic, they couldn't rely on the unpaid help of others out of fear of exposure. In addition to this, most struggled with depression, anxiety, and even PTSD before the pandemic. Years of caregiving in a society that devalues it meant that they were taking medications for depression and anxiety, many exhibited a flat affect, and some were emotionally labile during interviews. I am still grappling with how to talk about their trauma as intentionally debilitating (Puar 2017) and how caregiving in a society hostile to it disables people. This was particularly true for the participants in my study who were caring in the context of terminal illness. Several of my participants' partners died during the course of our conversations.

Throughout the project, I grappled with how to contain my own trauma and grief. I had a vague idea that my closeness to all this would be an asset in the work, but my disciplinary training in sociology also told me to never let it seep in, to keep it contained and controlled so that I could stay "professional." This makes me think of Katherine McKittrick's brilliant book *Dear Science and Other Stories*, where she writes, "Discipline is empire" (2021, 36). There is such baggage in the discipline of sociology about being a "legitimate" social science. In the past, the discipline tried to achieve this through claims of neutrality (Emerson 2001), as though neutrality were the same thing as rigor. But it was largely feminists in the field who intervened to challenge this kind of thinking, and the discipline's qualitative research standards took a "reflexive turn" (Biber 2013; Craven and Davis 2013; Jaggar 2013). As an interdisciplinary scholar, trained in feminist scholarship and disability studies, I have more freedom to be honest in my writing and to develop new ways of instituting rigor. Rather than an obsession with neutrality or the establishment of rigor through distance, I instead dive into my closeness as a way to engage more authentically with the project. This reflects feminist sentiments from these interdisciplinary enterprises that hold that the self we bring to the work is integral to the research process and "closeness" to the topic is not an assumed liability but rather simply something that needs to be accounted for, or even an asset. Being more honest about my own experiences and what I bring to the project also reflects my commitment to using research to make people's lives better, to center care, connection, and justice. How can we care, connect, and seek justice without bringing our full selves? Thus, in addition to navigating trauma, I also juggled navigating the various (inter)disciplinary spaces I work in, from sociology to disability studies. As a result of my emotional ties to the topic, some of the questions that emerged in fieldwork related to affective relations, connection, and rapport and at times complicated the vague goal of "professionalism."

Because of my own experience caregiving, I explored literature on trauma-informed research methods and trauma stewardship to guide me in developing a way to center care in my methods with other caregivers. To start, it might be useful to define care. Nancy Folbre and Erik Olin Wright (2012) talk about care as having distinctive features, that it is interactive and supportive. That is, the work is infused with concern for the well-being of those involved, and specific practices are undertaken to actualize this. Joan Tronto talks about care as "a species activity that includes everything that we do to maintain, continue, and repair our 'world' so that we can live in it as well as possible. That world includes our bodies, our selves, and our environment, all of which we seek to interweave in a complex, life sustaining web" (1993, 103).

To enact such care, then, I thought carefully about both my orientation toward it and the practical ways to infuse it. I drew from trauma-informed interviewing, which takes into account that participants might be experiencing trauma. This literature is generally embedded in social work or detective work in policing when interviewing crime victims; some of the techniques have to do with allowing for silence during interviews, having resources ready, carefully planning the phrasing and flow of questions, and so on. There are a few examples of people thinking through the application of some of the principles to qualitative research, especially as it relates to reflexivity (e.g., Dempsey et al. 2016; Bosworth, Hoyle, and Dempsey 2011; Mitchell-Eaton 2019). That is, rather than just think about care as an affective state I bring to the interviews, I embedded specific techniques, as I detail later, into the work. I also made sure not to frame everything related to disability and care as negative. Being trauma informed doesn't mean just focusing on loss or grief; it also means celebrating and documenting survival, creativity, growth. Besides, the concept of trauma stewardship (Lipsky and Burk 2009) states that trauma has impacts that can be named and managed. While it's important to be present with others in their experiences, we must also acknowledge the effects of trauma on ourselves while we do the work and pay careful attention to it.

Seeping

July 2020
I held back in today's interview. The tears welled up and a few fell, but it was through sheer force of will that I did not collapse into guttural sobs. When we ended the call, I came out of the bedroom where I had been interviewing, found my partner in the other room, and said, "That was intense. I just cried a little during that interview, but I didn't want to be unprofessional." How is it that that was my first thought? The word *unprofessional* echoes out.

In interviews, my participants and I talked together. I told every single one of them that I was doing the work because I care about and want to investigate the structural issues shaping their experiences, but also that I was once a caregiver. This was information I gave them matter-of-factly because I felt they should know the personal and professional reasons why I wanted to do the project. It felt respectful. After all, I was asking them questions that were deeply personal, intimate, and could be upsetting. All of them said to me how much of a difference it made to know I had been through a similar experience, how they felt they could tell me things because of this disclosure. A few of my participants' partners died during fieldwork. Sometimes we were done with our interviews and they'd reach out to tell me. For others, it happened between our phone calls.

I would speak with someone one week and by the next their partner was dead, and they were grieving, deep in the beginning stages. This too was familiar territory for me; I did not feel awkward or unable to respond. My experiences meant I could be supportive of my participants in ways that other researchers likely could not have. As time wore on, I became more comfortable with crying in front of them, with them. And some of them told me things they did not tell anyone, and they would say, "I know you understand." So I began to ask myself, what if when we are interviewing those we may share a similar experience with, we see these seepages of relationality, of connection, not as "unprofessional" (what does that mean anyway?) but rather as connective, authentic? As investment in our participants, tying their lives to ours and pushing back on more standard or commonplace social science narratives that advocate the idea of separating "the researched" and "the researcher," the "objective" or "neutral" social scientist and the data? Regardless of the topic, are we not also our lives? Our feelings? And when relevant, our traumas and what we bring to our work?

November 2020

In today's interview, tears flowed from both of us. I have learned to grieve with my participants. She told me a story about falling asleep standing up in the elevator in the hospital after a long, frightening few days there where the situation was brutal. There were only six floors to her stop, but she somehow slept for just a minute, standing up, between floors 1 and 6. And this hit me in the gut. I am often aware of how sometimes I can only recall the shape of a memory, a haloed feeling, gauzy. I'm sometimes separate, walled off from all that happened. And the treatment I had for trauma, eye movement desensitization and reprocessing, can also cause you to stop being able to remember things as clearly. While it's all still deep within me, it is not quite on the surface. But it can be surfaced in very specific situations. This was one of them. I was suddenly bone-tired and on the floor of urgent care trying to get some sleep while my partner was waiting to be admitted to a floor. I could feel the warmth of one of the crisply woven white blankets from the blanket warmers that the nurses kept in the back of that unit. The tidbits from participants in the interviews would lead me back to my own memories. Sometimes I would have to catch my breath, as I felt a memory, just a sensation really, rising in my torso. When the interview ended, I would squint backward, to bring it up again and sob. Other times it felt like it had slipped away from me, but then it would still hit me later without warning, usually that night in a dream. My late partner, J, has appeared in my dreams more in the last few months than in the last few years. There's a closeness to her I feel again.

The early interviews in the project were the beginning of my containing everything. I didn't just contain that hour-long interview, I contained the decades. I learned about myself during these conversations with participants. I discovered memories I had long split off from, confirming how far into a dissociative state

I had been in during much of the caregiving. In this way, I learned about my own grief from my participants. The more people I interviewed, however, the less panicked or concerned I became about any tears that might come. Early on, I tried to keep myself really walled off, trying to be as contained as possible, but the more interviews I did, the easier it got for me to be more emotionally authentic. If I felt tears, I let them come quietly, in a way that did not take up space from my participants. It was a slow seep. I learned to be real but not overtake the interaction. I would subtly reach my arm out to the table next to me for a tissue, dab my cheek, and keep going, nodding at my participants over video, letting them know I am listening, I am feeling, to please go on.

Mitigation Techniques

What I want to do now is turn to the obligation of care we have for ourselves and each other when we are engaged in research. In undertaking qualitative research, we are not only tasked with accurately representing participants' lives, but we must also do so with care and empathy. How can we accurately represent people's lives if we do not care for them and sustain them during our interactions with them in fieldwork? And if we do not care for ourselves, we cannot come to the material safely. For me, in this particular project, care was both the topic of the research and the guiding ethos. Forefronting and confronting my own trauma and how it was brought alive in the process of interviewing participants was crucial for mapping myself in the work, but also in order to learn how to care for myself and them. It means taking enactments of care for myself and my participants seriously and enacting them in a systematic way.

Self-Care in Research

I quickly learned that I was stepping into complicated emotional terrain and I needed to be equipped to navigate it. The first thing I did was institute practices of self-care. This primarily took the form of boundaries around the timing and scheduling of fieldwork, as well as the development of rituals before and after interviews. For example, interviews were limited to one, sometimes two, a day because I found them emotionally exhausting. So I learned how to pace myself and protect my emotional health. Thus, I limited interviews to specific hours of specific days. This meant that I could know that every Tuesday and Thursday afternoon would look a certain way and I could rest in between. I rarely broke my scheduling rules unless a participant's schedule just could not accommodate these limits. It was comforting to know I had boundaries around my days and when things were scheduled. I also always left room for interviews to go very long. One of my first interviews was one of my longest, lasting over two and a half hours. I started blocking off two and a half hours for every interview. Most did not go that long, but it was a way to care for myself, to give myself room, to build slowness into my calendar. These things helped to significantly lower my anxiety.

Taking care of myself by developing rituals for before and after interviews during my fieldwork was also key. Many of the interviews were deeply affecting and retraumatizing for me on multiple levels. I needed to take care of myself so that I could enter the interview space in a way that was safe and healthy for everyone involved. This required being deliberate about self-care before and after. I would set up a comfortable interview space, make a cup of tea, and take some calming breaths. I would have all the things I needed ready—my computer, my notebook, tissues. This created a bit of a sanctuary for me to do some reflection and check in on how I was feeling, center my breath, and enter into the interview in a calm state. I also built in time after the interview to decompress and to memo immediately after. In many qualitative methods, memoing is a strategy for capturing your thoughts and feelings after an interview, observations of how it went, how you felt, and what you thought. Once I finished my memo, I would often close my laptop and cry. Then I would move into a debriefing stage. To do this, I would reach out to a friend, a colleague, or my partner and ask for care; space to just cry and vent, to say aloud what some of my responses were. I was always careful to do so without breaking confidentiality; it wasn't about the content of the interview per se, but my response to it. Building in these emotional buffers around the work meant I could keep showing up to hear stories in a way that was safe.

Care for Participants

We have a responsibility as researchers to enact care for our participants. This is not about paternalism, but rather about creating a two-way flow of care, taking care of ourselves so we can have good boundaries in the work and taking care of each other so that everyone can participate in interviews or fieldwork and feel cared for and sustained while doing so. During my fieldwork, I developed a set of systematic techniques for providing care. This was not just the affective work during the interview itself but specific operational strategies.

The first time I interacted with my participants was a recruitment phone call. For this call, I asked them to set aside about fifteen minutes to talk with me so I could go over the project, make sure they met the study criteria, and talk about the consent forms and other logistics. I went over what the study was about and revealed to my participants that I have some personal familiarity with what they've been through. Disclosing this positionality was part of keeping them safe. I was asking them questions about things that may potentially be very traumatic, or something they are actively grieving about. I wanted them to know that they would not need to do the additional work of managing my responses or worrying about being judged. This came from my own experience; when my partner was alive, I was hesitant to talk to people who "didn't get it." So I just generally explained to my participants that I had been a caregiver for five years before my partner died; I did not go into any detail. Participants all told me that it was a relief to talk with a researcher who might "get it."

Another part of keeping participants safe and caring for them was being clear on the details. Since many were in complex and traumatic situations, I would care for them by telling them that they would not have to remember any of the details from the consent form I was about to go over because they would have a copy of it. I assured them I would email them with clear instructions. I went over the information smoothly and conversationally, and when it came time to set up the appointment for an interview, I reminded them the day before by contacting them. I then followed up after the phone call with an email that summarized what we said and what was next in terms of the appointment date. I gave them my cell phone number and encouraged them to call or text with any questions.

When it came time to do the interviews, I worked hard to create a safe interview environment through specific techniques. Drawing on trauma-informed interviewing techniques, I told them up front that I might ask questions that were upsetting or the conversation could get into areas that were difficult. I told them that we could stop at any time and that it was OK if they didn't want to answer something. I found it useful to open with getting a picture of their lives, how and when they met their partner, how they cared for each other. This helped participants to remember who they were, who their partner was, and it also gave me information about their personality, their class or education background, and so on in the process. I also made sure to expect nonlinearity. Trauma refracts time through a prism in ways where events can be split off and their stories might jump around in time or be told in circuitous ways. I did not problematize this or try to shape it into something linear when they were in the middle of talking. Rather, I gently tried to piece together any timeline puzzles, sometimes going back at the end of an interview and saying I wanted to clarify something.

The affective labor in interviews was also strategic. I stayed open and soft; I would ask a question but let them talk about what they wanted. It was important to let things unfold and to be patient. Most of all, I created space. It was OK to be silent, to cry. I followed them where they went while balancing this with moving through interview questions. A lot of this affective work is simply staying gentle. I also ordered my questions in particular ways. I started with these broader openings to get to know them, then moved into the middle section, where the more traumatic aspects are likely to be discussed. I ended with demographics or other questions that were "easy," because everyone was tired by then. It was important to not ask participants to answer traumatic questions at the end when they were tired.

The Potential Damage Caused by Weaponizing Trauma

For many caregivers and disabled people, there is indeed loss and grief, and sometimes trauma comes along with it. But it is crucial that we hold these truths without devaluing and disrespecting the experience of disability. While attending to trauma and caring for participants and ourselves is important, it should not be done in a way that contributes to narratives of disability as tragic. Disability, illness, and caregiving are whole and human experiences; and part of their wholeness might include trauma. But in an ableist society that often *only* sees disability as tragic, we must tread carefully. How can we acknowledge trauma without slipping into what we might call "trauma porn," or "perverse fascination with other people's misfortune" (Meley 2019)? How can we acknowledge trauma without promoting the idea that disability is misfortune, rather than simply human experience? As Keah Brown (2021) put so well on Twitter, "Pity is so cheap. The true way we can move disability and illness involved narratives forward is to stop treating [disability and illness] like they're the worst possible things and more like the lived experience that inform the way fully realized humans navigate the world."

In academic work on care, and in caregiver advocacy circles, there is a tendency to center "caregiver burden," which has become a dominant concept for understanding the experiences of caregivers. Caregiver burden as a concept is a product of ableism. It strips disability and illness from its social context, positions it as *only* burdensome, and positions caregivers as nondisabled (when many are disabled themselves) and burdened *because of someone's disability* rather than because disabled people and their caregivers are both largely structurally abandoned. Care could be conceptualized as something so much more nuanced than "burden" if context were meaningfully included. For example, one might note that if home- and community-based services and long-term support services were adequately funded, income caps for disabled people raised, and so on, disability and care would be far less of a "burden." Yet if I run a search for "caregiver burden" in Google Scholar, there are more than four hundred thousand papers, primarily reviews of caregiver burden literature and caregiver burden scales and inventories to measure how burdened someone is, and so on. In addition, caregiver narratives or memoirs often exploit this burden frame. In writing about a *New York Times* story that celebrated a man murdering his wife and then killing himself when she had Alzheimer's, Alice Wong reminds us of how caregiver burden is used to excuse such horrors: "[In] cases like this, many people cite caregiver 'burden' as an explanation, [but that] assumes that [one] spouse is solely responsible for care and decision-making" (Wong, Brown, and Leebron 2020). Once again, the "burden" is equated with disability, and it is seen as so bad that disabled people should die rather than someone (in this case a spouse) being left alone to carry that burden. But this frame completely erases the structural conditions that devalue both disability and care and therefore create these circumstances. In caregiver memoirs, trauma is easily engaged with shallowly, forgoing critical engagement with disability policy or social context. In these cases, caregiver burden tropes slip into the realm of trauma porn, which highlights *only* the trauma and individualizes it, removing all social context.

So how can we both acknowledge trauma and infuse care into our work, but do so in a way that doesn't rely on and perpetuate flattened narratives of tragedy? What I would like to talk about in this last section are strategies to take trauma seriously but that don't fall into the trap of individualizing disability and reducing it to a tragic, pitiable phenomenon. For example, during interviews, I was careful to use affective techniques that normalized what people told me. I did not respond in horror. I nodded and validated, and created an environment where participants could talk about bodies and needs, but this was not upsetting or pitiable. Instead, I responded as though these were perfectly expected aspects of life (which they are). Second, I balanced our focus. I did this by asking participants to send me photos of their homes and the technologies and tools they use in care and in making homes accessible. Inevitably, caregivers had not thought about these as creative practices, as disability world-making (Hamraie and Fritsch 2019). When they did send me photos and we talked through the novel things they and their spouses were crafting together, how they mastered or adapted certain technologies, they were astounded (indeed, many were delighted!) at their own inventiveness, their partner's inventiveness, and how disability spurred these ideas. Thus, we balanced talking about the hard things with the generative.

I also asked questions about how they cared for each other, how they collaborated with their partners because they cared and contributed too. As a whole, trauma-informed methods do not need to be about focusing solely on loss or grief; they can also celebrate strength, creativity, and relationality. I asked questions related to collaboration and creativity as a way to move from a damage-based to a desire-based frame. This reflects Eve Tuck's work, where she writes that desire-based frameworks push against narratives of damage: "In damaged-centered research, one of the major activities is to document pain or loss in an individual, community, or tribe. . . . Common sense tells us this is a good thing, but the danger in damage-centered research is that it is a pathologizing approach in which the oppression singularly defines a community . . . research that operates, even benevolently, from a theory of change that establishes harm or injury in order to achieve reparation" (2009, 413). In contrast, Tuck argues, desire-based frameworks are interested in "understanding complexity, contradiction, and the self-determination of lived lives . . . by documenting not only the painful elements of social realities but also the wisdom and hope. Such an axiology is intent on depathologizing the experiences of dispossessed and disenfranchised communities so that people are seen as more than broken and conquered. This is to say that even when communities are broken and conquered, they are so much more than that—so much more that this incomplete story is an act of aggression" (416).

Finally, in analysis, contextualize, contextualize, contextualize. The goal is to tell our participants' stories, but not at the price of ignoring the politics of how we got here. Attending to trauma does not necessitate a freefall into a "tragedy" narrative of disability or illness. The stories of participants can be used to reveal how unjust and inadequate our systems are. Furthermore, conceiving of care as only an emotional or affective process (trauma, damage, burden) without attention to the structural apparatuses is destined to be exploitative. Instead, we have to attend to the conditions that dictate the circumstances of disabled people's lives and the contours of care. Doing these things pushes back on ableism and limits the potential for stories that involve trauma and disability or illness to be "saturated in the fantasies of outsiders" (Tuck 2009, 412).

BIBLIOGRAPHY

Biber, Sharlene Hesse, editor. 2013. *Feminist Research Practice: A Primer*. 2nd ed. Thousand Oaks, CA: SAGE.

Bosworth, Mary, Carolyn Hoyle, and Michelle Madden Dempsey. 2011. "Researching Trafficked Women: On Institutional Resistance and the Limits to Feminist Reflexivity." *Qualitative Inquiry* 17 (9): 769–779.

Brown, Keah. 2021. "Pity is so cheap. The true way we can move disability and illness involved narratives forward is to stop treating D&I like they're the worst possible things . . ." Twitter post, March 21, 2021. https://twitter.com/Keah_Maria/status/1373689994133565440.

Craven, Christa, and Dána-Ain Davis, editors. 2013. *Feminist Activist Ethnography: Counterpoints to Neoliberalism in North America*. New York: Lexington Books.

Dempsey, Laura, Maura Dowling, Philip Larkin, and Kathy Murphy. 2016. "Sensitive Interviewing in Qualitative Research." *Research in Nursing and Health* 39 (6): 480–490.

Emerson, Robert M. 2001. *Contemporary Field Research: Perspectives and Formulations*. 2nd ed. Prospect Heights, IL: Waveland.

Folbre, Nancy, and Erik Olin Wright. 2012. "Defining Care." In *For Love and Money: Care Provision in the United States*, edited by Nancy Folbre, 1–20. New York: Russell Sage Foundation.

Hamraie, Aimi, and Kelly Fritsch. 2019. "Crip Technoscience Manifesto." *Catalyst: Feminism, Theory, Technoscience* 5 (1). https://doi.org/10.28968/cftt.v5i1.29607.

Jaggar, Alison M. 2013. *Just Methods: An Interdisciplinary Feminist Reader*. 2nd ed. Boulder, CO: Paradigm.

Lipsky, Laura van Dernoot, and Connie Burk. 2009. *Trauma Stewardship: An Everyday Guide to Caring for Self While Caring for Others*. San Francisco: Berrett-Koehler.

McKittrick, Katherine. 2021. *Dear Science and Other Stories*. Durham, NC: Duke University Press.

Meley, Chloé. 2019. "The Pointless Consumption of Pain in the Era of Trauma Porn." *Incite Journal: The University of Surrey Politics Magazine*, July 3, 2019.

Mitchell-Eaton, Emily. 2019. "Grief as Method: Topographies of Grief, Care, and Fieldwork from Northwest Arkansas to New York and the Marshall Islands." *Gender, Place and Culture* 26 (10): 1438–1458.

Puar, Jasbir K. 2017. *The Right to Maim: Debility, Capacity, Disability*. Durham, NC: Duke University Press.

Tronto, Joan. 1993. *Moral Boundaries: A Political Argument for an Ethic of Care*. New York: Routledge.

Tuck, Eve. 2009. "Suspending Damage: A Letter to Communities." *Harvard Educational Review* 79 (3): 409–427.

Wong, Alice, Keah Brown, and Cade Leebron. 2020. "If That's Love, I Don't Want It: The Impact of the 'New York Times' Validating Ableism." *Bitch Media* (blog), January 14, 2020. https://www.bitchmedia.org/article/disabled-writers-respond-new-york-times-murder-suicide-ableism.

13

Injury, Recovery, and Representation in *Shikaakwa*

LAURENCE RALPH

There I sat—tapping my foot, refreshing the web browser every minute, on the minute. I glanced at the upper right corner of my computer screen, then at my watch, then at my computer screen again to confirm. Time was indeed . . . passing.

Finally, I got up, deciding that fresh air would be a welcome distraction—or at least a better use of my time than staring at my inbox. I had just grabbed my blazer from the back of my swivel chair and walked to the door when I heard a ding. I rushed back to my seat.

The email's subject line read, "Book Cover." My editor, David Brent, had finally sent me the image I had been waiting for—only eleven minutes later than promised. I downloaded the photo and clicked on the file.

This wasn't what I was expecting.

Well, I sat for a while, mouth agape, looking at the famed Chicago skyline and its celebrated Sears Tower juxtaposed against an aerial view of a darkened street corner. The name of my book, *Renegade Dreams*, was sprawled across the cover in bold red letters on a bright yellow graphic resembling caution tape.

I took a breath.

After digesting the image, I sent it to a few trusted colleagues for their opinion. *Was I overreacting?* For a moment I thought so. But when my colleagues were just as outraged as me, I found myself emboldened.

I typed a message to David. "While I appreciate the effort the press put into this design, I am not comfortable with it. . . . This picture contradicts the larger argument I am making in the book. It is essentially a shot of Black Chicagoans on a street corner—literally in the shadows of greater Chicago. The picture makes people anonymous and suggests that the corner is a space of injury and not much else. This image disturbs me because I go to great lengths to show that my interlocutors are more than people who hang out on a corner inciting violence."

I closed my email by providing links to Chicago artist Carlos Javier Ortiz's work. I admired his photographs and hoped the press might contact him for an alternate book cover. "Will you please consider his work in relation to the concerns that I have expressed here?" I asked.

Fortunately, my editor advocated on my behalf. Together we selected a photograph from Ortiz's *We All We Got* series.[1] It depicts young Black Chicagoans holding candles and gathering in front of a tree where one of their peers was shot

Figure 13.1. A group of Black urban youths holding candles at a vigil that honors the life of a slain teenager.

and killed (figure 13.1). The young people are trying to heal from the trauma of urban violence.

Even after David and I settled on the image that we would ask for permission to use, I found myself online at my desk on several different occasions, looking at Ortiz's photographs for hours on end. Instantly, the pictures transported me from Cambridge, Massachusetts, where I taught at the time as an assistant professor, to the West Side of Chicago, where I conducted the research for my book.

I could see Ortiz in my mind's eye trotting behind me with a camera swinging from his neck. It was as if he was there, chronicling my fieldwork experience with me. I had waited for the bus on Ogden Avenue, one of the streets that Ortiz photographed. I had been inside St. Sabina Parish—one of the churches that Ortiz immortalized—for baptisms and funerals. Some of the people he photographed were my friends. Others were strangers but lived parallel lives to the people I had interviewed.

In centering my book on disabled gang affiliates who use wheelchairs, I highlighted the overlooked fact that most victims of gun violence do not die. Chicago is a prime example of this trend. As I wrote, "Between 1999 and 2014 [when my book was published], more than 8,000 people had been killed, while an estimated 36,000 had been otherwise debilitated" (Ralph 2014, 4).

In a context where community residents anticipate gun violence, the disabled young Black men I came to know were deeply conflicted. Gang members who were killed became martyrs. But disabled gang members, unable to contribute

Figure 13.2. Ondelee Perteet, dressed in a white tuxedo, poses with his prom date. Friends and neighbors take pictures of the couple.

monetarily in the manner most valued (that is, as street-corner drug dealers), were often forgotten about, marginalized, and neglected. They sacrificed themselves for a gang that had, sadly, left them behind.

I do not mean to suggest that all young people who are disabled in Chicago due to gun violence are gang members—or even Black men. Still, this demographic anchored my study of injury. I explored how painful it felt for someone to feel abandoned by a gang after being maimed because of his allegiance to it. The young men in my study carried a particular kind of grief. Their mothers and fathers, the people who constantly warned them about their criminal activities, were now their caregivers.

Admittedly, my book did not chronicle the lives of Black teenagers who were actively trying to *avoid* the dangers of the street. Yet I knew that some of them were victims of gun violence too. In this way, I believe Ortiz's work complements my own, especially his photographs of Chicago native Ondelee Perteet.

One of Ortiz's photos captures Ondelee outside on the sidewalk in front of an apartment building just before his senior prom, seated in his wheelchair (figure 13.2). The teenager is wearing a white tux. His dreads are parted neatly and braided. Ondelee smiles. Ondelee's prom date drapes her arm around his shoulder and leans into him. Her wavy black hair grazes her shoulders as they pose. Little kids stand on the sidewalk behind the couple. Family, friends, and neighbors surround them, snapping pictures like paparazzi. I imagine that Ortiz,

Figure 13.3. Family picture of Laurence Ralph with his two brothers.

pointing his camera lens between the crowd of onlookers, is the only one on that sidewalk with a professional camera.

When I clicked on this photograph from Ortiz's digital archive, it instantly struck a chord. But this feeling of déjà vu wasn't merely because Ondelee reminded me of the young men I knew in wheelchairs on the West Side of Chicago. It was because Ondelee looked like I did when I was his age. And yet, back then, I didn't know anyone who had been shot. The possibility of being gunned down and paralyzed at the age of fourteen after someone opened fire at a party—like Ondelee was—wasn't something I would have anticipated.

But now, Ondelee's broad smile, as Ortiz captured it, made me think of myself. I thought about an old family portrait that hung above my mother's fireplace for years (figure 13.3). Posing with my two older brothers, I have the same hairstyle as Ondelee and a similar grin.

Fast-forward seven years, and Carlos Javier Ortiz has become just "Carlos" to me, which is to say, my friend. Our friendship began after our first conversation on the phone. "I'll send you a file of my pictures," Carlos told me, "and you can use them in your lectures if you want."

Over the years, Carlos and I have updated each other on the progress of our work. We have collaborated on projects. And we've sat together in front of large crowds discussing the intersection of my scholarship and his art.

The last event Carlos and I participated in was during the summer of 2021 for a digital exhibition at New York University on the relationship between protests and mourning. That's when I found out Carlos had just completed a short film, which was months away from being screened at the Tribeca Film Festival. After writing about gang affiliates who used wheelchairs, I immediately recognized the importance of thinking through the ways mobility and immobility shape people's understanding of what's possible for them to achieve.

In the film festival's online program, Ortiz describes his film, *Shikaakwa*, as "an elegy for the landscape and people who inhabit the land now referred to as Chicago."[2] By using its Indigenous name—the name given to it by Native Americans—Ortiz invites us to pay attention to the place we now call Chicago not only as it is, but how it once was. In his synopsis of the film, Ortiz tells us that "despair, movement, progress, and stillness" have remained staples in the landscape across centuries. What he doesn't explicitly say is that violence by way of the gun also had a lasting impact on its inhabitants. The technology colonists wielded to displace the Potawatomi, Odawa, Sauk, Ojibwe, Illinois, Kiikaapoi, Myaamia, Mascouten, Wea, Delaware, Winnebago, Menominee, and Mesquakie still haunts the terrain.

The COVID-19 pandemic prevented me from seeing *Shikaakwa* in person. Still, I bought tickets to the virtual festival, made a bowl of popcorn, and projected the film on the large screen in my living room. As the short film started, I found myself leaning forward on the edge of my couch. Ortiz's style of cinematography immediately struck me. In *Shikaakwa*, he uses a "two-channel projection" such that parallel images appear on-screen simultaneously. The effect of this cinematic technique is to produce a series of striking juxtapositions.

Ortiz recorded the images that appear on channel 1, while Ondelee's mother, Deetreena Perteet, recorded the video on channel 2. Deetreena's grainy home videos were originally intended to document her son's recovery. She never intended for that journey to be featured in festivals.

As the short film begins, a dance drill team comprising young Black men in white T-shirts perform a precisely choreographed routine while twirling wooden replica rifles in the air, on the left side of the screen. The second channel is black, steering my attention to the dancers.

Then I hear a familiar voice—Pastor Pfleger from St. Sabina Parish: "God, we remember the life lost here earlier this week, senseless violence. We wrap our arms around his family. We wrap our arms around all his relatives. We wrap our arms around our community. Because when a life is lost anywhere, we all suffer. We all lose."

The drill team continues to dance as channel 2 transitions to a group of Black men marching while carrying a makeshift cross (figure 13.4). On the horizontal axis of the cross, where Jesus's arms would typically be, the words "STOP SHOOTING" are painted in red.

Figure 13.4. Drill team (*left*); protesters carrying a cross (*right*).

I hear Ondelee's voice for the first time, rapping a song he wrote:

> Shot and paralyzed at the age of 14
> The Lord's by my side, when somebody tried to smoke me like a crack fiend
> But I got to thank the man that the kid still breathing
> So I said my prayers and knew that everything happened for a reason . . .
> It wasn't easy trying to survive a bullet through the chin . . .

Ondelee's voice fades away.

On channel 1, Black teenage boys ride their bikes on the sidewalk. On channel 2, older Black men sit in wheelchairs on a Chicago street corner (figure 13.5). Of course, one group—the older men—*must* use their wheelchairs to navigate the environment, whereas at any moment the teenagers can discard their bikes and run through the uncut grass into the forest behind them. Yet and still, the older, disabled men foreshadow the lives that the seemingly carefree teenage boys *could have* one day. Put differently: if we regard debilitating gun violence as a kind of destruction that impedes a person's natural life course, then the wheelchair becomes a symbol of premature debility for Black urban residents—doesn't it?

As I ponder the symbolic status of the wheelchair in urban Chicago, I realize that my formulation works in reverse in another of Ortiz's scenes. An older Black woman sits in her wheelchair at a vigil, holding a framed photograph of a young man, presumably her dead grandson (figure 13.6). Watching her strength amid the tragedy surrounding her, I assume that her disability results from a long life—a "natural" part of aging. In this light, her wheelchair looks more like a throne that signifies her privileged status as an elder—especially when juxtaposed against the photograph she holds. At least she has lived. There is an aliveness, particularly in the face of violence, that becomes synonymous with mobility in Ortiz's film.

Like the dancers with their wooden rifles, the film's subjects sometimes perform violence (like actors on stage) to showcase their humanity. This *performance of violence* speaks against Pierre Bourdieu's (1991) formulation of symbolic

Figure 13.5. Boys riding bikes (*left*); men in wheelchairs (*right*).

Figure 13.6. A group of Black women protesting gun violence while holding pictures of slain teenagers.

violence, which refers to the dominance that a government or a privileged social class has over another. No. This kind of dramaturgy is more akin to a "renegade dream": "an aspiration rooted in an experience of injury, which reimagines the possibilities within injury" (Ralph 2014, v).

Lest I be accused of unduly projecting agency onto desperate situations or suggesting too rosy a picture, I should say that these dreams were not grandiose. These were not the genre of dreams that have been Disneyfied and squashed into the storybook realm. In fact, when I first moved to Chicago, I did not recognize residents' struggles as dreams because they were often quite banal. Safe passage to school became something to dream for, as did a stable job and affordable and livable housing. These dreams, it is critical to note, didn't always come true: children were gunned down on the way to school; adults searched for work endlessly; the threat of displacement haunted residents daily. In the face of these

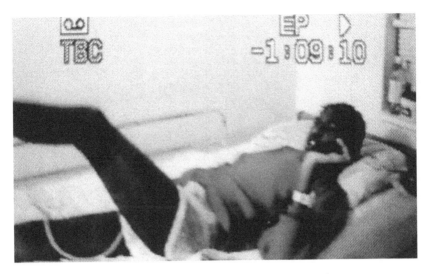

Figure 13.7. Ondelee kicks his leg on the hospital bed.

hardships, the most remarkable aspect of people's desires and the communal projects associated with them was the immense effort it took for Black Chicagoans to obtain resources that barely scratched the surface of actual need. The brutal honesty with which they acknowledged the difficulty of real change suggested that the power of such dreams is that working toward them, regardless of whether they come to fruition, have their own transformative capacities.[3]

After Ondelee was shot, a doctor told him that he had lost all sensation in his legs and would never walk again. And yet, in the film's climactic scene, Ondelee repeatedly kicks his leg in the air while lying on a hospital bed (figure 13.7), dramatizing violence and joy simultaneously.

"I will kick you in your face," Ondelee flails his left leg. Up and down, up and down, in defiance of his doctor's prognosis. "I will kick you in your face. Man, I swear . . . to . . . God. Look at that leg. Look at it. Man. . . . I will kick you in your *eye*." Ondelee continues to kick his leg on the hospital bed as his mother laughs at this miraculous play fight.

This scene allows the viewer to reimagine Chicago as a place where violence does not have to be routine or naturalized. Life could be different.

Cut to a dozen colorful balloons floating through an overcast sky. "Look there, that beautiful blue sky. God made it all, didn't he? He made all that sky," a disembodied voice says as the balloons float high above.

In Chicago, in a ceremony that has become commonplace, family members will gather to release balloons on the death anniversaries of loved ones. The balloons symbolize the act of their loved ones transcending the earth, ascending to a higher spiritual plateau. Only in this scene, Ortiz reverses the release of the balloons. They descend from the sky into the hands of the grieving family

Figure 13.8. Ondelee walks down sidewalk holding a friend's hand.

Figure 13.9. Ondelee's mother holding his baby as Ondelee watches.

members. What if God or fate granted their loved ones a second chance? What would that look like?

In another scene, Ondelee—the human embodiment of radical optimism—slowly and unsteadily walks while holding a friend's hand (figure 13.8). As he lumbers on, we hear his mother Deetreena's voice: "They say he'd never walked again. They said he'd never move his arms or legs again, but God said he will. I mean, we came to church today without the wheelchair. He decided to come on in. Cause God had a message for him today."

As the film comes to an end, the disparate channels give way to one full screen. Deetreena sits on her bed, holding her grandson—Ondelee's baby (figure 13.9).

Gazing at his mother and his newborn son, Ondelee looks ahead.

From the first moment I saw Ortiz's photography, I knew that it resonated with the theoretical concerns of my book, which has to do with the forms of violence and injury that open the way for political transformation and future-making. Ortiz's art also dovetails with how I engage with hypervisible social phenomena such as gangs and police through a grounded theory approach.

Traditional ethnographic methods reify the ideal of the "distanced" and "objective" ethnographer, often employing theories and concepts that "research subjects" are unfamiliar with or do not understand as a way to perform authority and expertise. By contrast, I employ theories and concepts that emerge from the fieldwork experience, deconstructing the self/other divide to which the traditional paradigm is indebted. My approach does not rest on a distinction between the ethnographic self and native other but instead draws its analytic leverage from an ethical commitment to "proximity" (Miller 2021).[4] In sum, my ethnographic aim is to break down the barrier between my interlocutors and myself by historicizing social problems *with* them. It is through this process that I build a subtle string of observations into powerful considerations of violence, debilitating injury, and death in the American inner city.

Watching Ondelee's family in that final scene, I better understood why the original cover of *Renegade Dreams* offended me so much. It was because my research interlocutors in Chicago cannot be adequately understood through familiar analytics such as "deviance" and "pathology." Such characterizations of urban life can become a reality of their own—a reality that too often forecloses the potential for injury to be a productive condition that sets new horizons in people's lives. An injury, after all, is not reducible to the violence that caused the pain and disappointment. Injury entails the possibility of recovery. That possibility, in Ortiz's work and my own, is coterminous with tenderness, hope, kinship, and love.[5]

NOTES

1 The photographs featured in this article are included with permission of the photographer, Carlos Javier Ortiz. They are published in Ortiz's 2014 book, *We All We Got.*

2 See https://tribecafilm.com/films/shikaakwa-2021, Last accessed on November 11, 2022 and also Bourdieu (1991), Miller (2021), Ortiz (2014), and Ralph (2014).

3 On the relationship between injury and disability, see: Livingston (2012), Kafer (2013), Crosby (2017), and Puar (2017).

4 On grounded theory and "proximity" see: Miller (2021).

5 See also: Rapp and Ginsburg (2001): 533–556.

BIBLIOGRAPHY

Bourdieu, Pierre. 1991. *Language and Symbolic Power.* Cambridge: Polity Press.

Crosby, Christina. 2017. *A Body, Undone: Living on After Great Pain.* Vol. 8. NYU Press.

Livingston, Julie. 2013. "Improvising Medicine." In *Improvising Medicine.* Duke University Press.

Kafer, Alison. *Feminist, Queer, Crip.* Indiana University Press, 2013.

Miller, Reuben Jonathan. 2021. *Halfway Home: Race, Punishment, and the Afterlife of Mass Incarceration*. Little, Brown.

Ortiz, Carlos Javier. 2014. *We All We Got*. New York: Red Hook Editions.

Puar, Jasbir. 2017. *The Right to Maim: Debility, Capacity, Disability*. Duke University Press.

Ralph, Laurence. 2014. *Renegade Dreams: Living Through Injury in Gangland Chicago*. Chicago: University of Chicago Press.

Rapp, Rayna, and Faye D. Ginsburg. 2001. "Enabling disability: Rewriting kinship, reimagining citizenship." *Public Culture* 13 (3).

14

Collaborative Research on the Möbius Strip

FAYE GINSBURG AND RAYNA RAPP

Introduction

Our collaborative writing is based on an enduring friendship and feminist academic partnership long preceding the diagnoses of each of our children (discussed later). Their new labels catapulted us into what we came to think of as disability worlds, a territory we encountered as parents that was previously unknown to us as "underimpaired" mothers and anthropologists (Davidson 2015). Our family lives took on new and unanticipated temporal trajectories with our children, including long stretches living in hospitals, endless searches for appropriate services and educational settings, and evenings and weekends devoted to supplemental tutoring and therapeutic regimens. In short, we were operating on what we later understood to be "crip time" (Kafer 2013). Additionally, we found ourselves reinventing family life with a difference, a process we recognized in other "disabled families." Eventually, after years of research described below, we came to understand that we and many others were forging "new kinship imaginaries," the creative transformations that families perform when disability catalyzes a departure from the typical normate life course. As for all mothers and others living in such disability worlds, an embrace of interdependence was crucial to our collective survival, an understanding prefigured in our feminist roots. These essential insights propelled our joint scholarship toward what we now think of as "cripping reproduction."

Our work started with our shared interests in the complexities of women's experiences of reproduction from the abortion controversy (Ginsburg 1998) to the rise of late twentieth-century reproductive technologies (Rapp 2011) as sites of constant contestation in American cultural life. In 1991 our first coauthored article on "the politics of reproduction" appeared in the *Annual Review of Anthropology* (Ginsburg and Rapp 1991), followed by a conference sponsored by the Wenner-Gren Foundation for Anthropological Research that we organized on that topic and a subsequent edited volume, *Conceiving the New World Order: The Global Politics of Reproduction* (Ginsburg and Rapp 1995).

The roots of our collaboration grew deeper and increasingly interdependent when a pregnant Faye served as a research subject for Rayna, who was then in the midst of her study of women's experiences and decision-making around amniocentesis genetic testing and the possibility of having an atypical fetus. It is an enduring irony of our long-standing research and writing partnership that when Rayna asked Faye back in 1988—when there were only a limited number of genetic tests available—how she felt about being the subject of such testing, she replied, "Well, now I know my fetus doesn't have three things wrong with it. And for the rest, we'll see." When her daughter Samantha was born a few months later, she had mysterious and life-threatening symptoms that landed Faye and Sam in the hospital for months on what medical anthropologists call "the diagnostic odyssey." At six months, Sam was diagnosed with a very rare autosomal recessive degenerative Ashkenazi Jewish genetic disorder, familial dysautonomia. From that point on, the two of us have been in a constant entangled conversation regarding the gaps between existential, cultural, religious, and biomedical understandings of what life with a difference—disability—is all about (Ginsburg and Rapp 2013).

Eight years later, Rayna's second child, Teo, was diagnosed with significant learning disabilities in his early school years. Our children went to the same "special ed" primary and middle schools, and we kept the conversation going about what it meant for them to live with disability as we navigated the labyrinth of bureaucracies necessary to procure the services to which they were entitled. Dealing with all the issues we faced, along with our kids—severe medical problems for Sam, and stigma faced by both—strengthened our teamwork: fierce advocates for our children, "accidental activists" (Panitch 2007) in our communities, engaged autoethnographers, disability studies scholar-advocates, and inseparable writing partners. Over the next decades, by necessity we followed the path of so many other parents of kids diagnosed with various chronic conditions—from learning disabilities to genetic disorders—as we sought support for our children and their alternative ways of learning about and engaging with the world. Rayna's son had a garden-variety diagnosis of dyslexia that nonetheless required hours of daily scaffolding to get him through schooling, not to mention lawsuits with the City of New York to secure funding for appropriate accommodations. Faye found that Samantha's familial dysautonomia affected her learning style, as well as causing a panoply of other, more severe complications that ranged from feeding tubes to the need for mobility support. Like most parents who discover that their kids need "special education" services, we were at first absorbed in a new reality for which we were utterly unprepared at both the pragmatic and existential levels. We dedicated ourselves to learning about our children's particular issues and locating educational settings and services that would meet their diverse needs. As close friends and longtime research partners, we were engrossed in constant discussion as we tried to make sense of our discoveries. The feminist motto "The personal is political" was our North Star.

In 1999, our essay entitled "Fetal Reflections: Confessions of Two Feminist Anthropologists as Mutual Informants" highlighted our growing concern that understanding the implications of a diagnosis of disability was thoroughly segregated from women's decision-making about prenatal testing (Ginsburg and Rapp 1999). How, we wondered, could potential parents possibly make an informed decision about whether to continue a pregnancy after receiving a "positive diagnosis" in the absence of any reality-based understanding of what it means to live with a family member with a bodymind impairment (Price 2015; Schalk 2018)? We began to write about these distinct discursive arenas as siloed "social funds of knowledge," segregating genetic diagnoses and "disability expertise" (Rapp and Ginsburg 2001; Hartblay 2020) that, we insisted, must be considered together. We began writing and teaching about the consequences of that segregation of knowledge, discovering that disability awareness and the practice of genetic testing—which both had escalated dramatically over the last few decades—were rarely brought into the same conversation. Ethical reflection in the realm of biomedicine, we found, is obscured in quotidian events such as the signing of routine consent forms where issues of the inclusion and exclusion of diverse bodyminds are too readily silenced.

We grew increasingly concerned with the tensions between these two powerful but contradictory aspects of contemporary life, what we have called the "doubled telos of modernity," a phrase we invented to describe this apparent contradiction (Rapp and Ginsburg 2001). On the one hand, biomedical progress, particularly around assistive reproductive technologies, continues to hold out the deeply American, neo-eugenic promise of perfectibility, given that fetuses found to have anomalies through prenatal testing are decreasingly brought to term. On the other hand, the rise of the disability rights and justice movement has created a robust ethical and political framework for democratic inclusion across the full range of human variability. Increasingly, we understood that these different and seemingly conflicting imperatives were reshaping life in the twenty-first century but their connections were rarely recognized. In response, we started "cripping reproduction" in our writing, calling for a more productive dialogue between aspirations for neo-eugenic exclusions in genetic testing and broader disability inclusion.

Birthing a Research Project

Out of necessity, our practical knowledge and capacity to provide what disability activist, writer, and educator Mia Mingus (2011) calls "access intimacy" for our children expanded. With that term, Mingus is indexing "that elusive, hard-to-describe feeling when someone else 'gets' your access needs." Along with other scholar-activists, we learned how different bodyminds are shaped by medicalized stigma, social policy, public neglect, and, increasingly, activism and lively cultural innovation built on many years of prior advocacy. Immersing ourselves in diverse domains of disability experience, our collaboration deepened as ethnographers of each other's journeys. In the process we became increasingly interdependent, finishing each other's sentences, no longer aware of where one of our ideas began and the other's ended. Further, our access intimacy extended to accommodating each other's experiences supporting our disabled kids. Many writing sessions were held in the family waiting room of the ICU, Samantha and Faye's second home for years. Sitting next to family members ordering Chinese takeout or receiving end-of-life counseling from a chaplain from their religious tradition, our conversations whiplashed between looking up alternative treatments and brainstorming our next article or presentation. Meanwhile, Rayna was sending communiqués from the front lines of what Teo called "The Board of Dread" as she took on her warrior-mom persona to get him learning support and respect. The concept of interdependence, foundational to feminism and disability studies, became our praxis. We came to understand and value that we were constantly operating on crip time, our pacing responding to the interruptions that interdependency demands. Our conversations—and minds—were melding, and we could no longer identify the source of our coproduced insights.

In 2006 we decided we were ready to go empirical. Although by then we had been writing together for over a decade, our first externally funded collaborative fieldwork project began the following year. We quickly discovered that research in New York City has locational advantages for ethnographers beyond our deep insider knowledge. The Big Apple is well known both for failed public support for disabled students in and out of school and for lively cultural innovation for people with disabilities in alternative education, the arts, and access to cultural venues. Further, the metropolitan area is famous for its broad spectrum of race, class, immigration, gender and sexuality, and religious diversity. In short, New York offers problems and possibilities that characterize the complexity of the experience of disability in the twenty-first century.

Our formal inquiry started with a foundational question that mirrored our own experiences: How do diverse families with a newly diagnosed child manage the logistics required to meet their youngster's school needs and social integration? Many informal encounters and conversations—in waiting rooms, on school playgrounds, and at community board meetings—enriched our structured interviews across New York's five boroughs with over fifty "disabled families" coming from diverse socioeconomic, cultural, ethno-racial, and religious backgrounds. All had children with learning differences requiring an individualized education plan, the federally mandated personalized roadmap outlining accommodations for each pupil diagnosed with a disability. We quickly learned that neither the children so labeled nor the label itself was easily domesticated or reified. "Learning disabilities," for example, was an often-fuzzy classification of disabling difference with its own genealogy, as it displaced profoundly stigmatizing terms such as "mild mental retardation," "minimum brain damage," and even "Mongolism" (Sleeter 1987). Indeed, the shifting, unstable nature of the category itself became part of our analysis and writing, as we came to understand our research in broader social and historical contexts (Ginsburg and Rapp 2010).

We have kept up with many families, reinterviewing over twenty-five of them as they passed through both the life course and the education system, balancing complex social situations—and sometimes medical diagnoses—and creating new understandings of family life. Their children, many of whom are now young adults and older, also increasingly became part of our conversations as they developed new understandings of what it means to live with disabilities and imagine "accessible futures" (Kafer 2013).

One of our earliest findings was that these families—and especially mothers—have been creating alternative kinship stories that reclaim their children from an exclusively medical diagnostic label as disability becomes a regular yet distinctive feature of kinship, domestic life, and public culture (see also Landsman 2009; Grinker 2021; Kittay 2019). With few available models for "life with a difference," they have produced story after story, what we think of as counternarratives. Often, these paralleled our own experiences cripping both reproduction and childrearing, imagined against the grain of conventional ideas of what constitutes appropriate parenting, a child's success and anticipated road forward, and expected cycles of family life. In other words, we began to recognize a particular sense of the present and future forged in dialogue with their children's differences as they drew their own roadmaps. We were not alone in tossing out typical child development books in favor of our hard-won knowledge of the roads less traveled. We have been writing about this shifting and more inclusive transformation as "new kinship imaginaries," reframing domestic lives lived with a difference (Rapp and Ginsburg 2001; Rapp and Ginsburg 2011). This paradigm shift—for ourselves and our interlocutors—often occurred as families realized their experiences didn't map easily onto preexisting models of American life. We were committed to writing about the radical potential of these stories to retrieve people with disabilities from the clinical framework of diagnosis and pathology. These collectively constitute an emergent terrain that encompasses the broad range of people whose narratives have been silenced until relatively recently. They also reframe the implicit norms and expectations of the life course as the experience of disability reverberates beyond the household, challenging taken-for-granted assumptions in unanticipated ways.

As our ethnographic research developed, we quickly realized that there is a yawning gap between the legislative promise of equity and inclusion for those with disabilities and the problematic realities most face: overwhelming bureaucracies, aging infrastructure, and ableist attitudes create enormous frustration, motivating parents like us to not only create new narratives but also, at times, undertake unanticipated action. We began writing about how this gulf between the legal mandate of inclusion and the reality of everyday discrimination was becoming the space of potential cultural transformation that interested us as both anthropologists and advocates. The activism on the part of many of our subjects across a broad range of backgrounds was particularly striking as they confronted the challenge of creating a more hospitable world for people with dis-abilities and their allies. Their experiences with disability turned many of them into accidental activists (Panitch 2007). As they learned about and demanded their rights, many developed new forms of courage and creativity, a process that we wrote about as "the social production of moxie" (Ginsburg and Rapp 2010). As one parent advocate put it, "The birth of our son with cerebral palsy brought the disability rights movement into our living room" (Habib 2008).

Lest this sound too celebratory, we also witnessed ongoing resistance, both passive and active, to this kind of change. Some negative encounters were infra-structural and part of daily life in the city: the all-too-frequent lack of compli-ance with curb cuts on New York City streets and chronically broken elevators in the subways. Others were bureaucratic and interpersonal, the kind of experi-ences we shared with our interlocutors. For example, families spoke indignantly of their run-ins with hostile educators who had mastered the fine art of counsel-ing children with learning disabilities out of their public, private, and religious schools without directly saying they were not welcome. Clearly, the passage of legislation such as the Individuals with Disabilities Education Act and Ameri-cans with Disabilities Act were necessary but not sufficient steps to creating a disability-friendly world.

Over time, our writing, initially focused on families, schools, and the world of special education, became more capacious. Beyond the accommodations required by law to integrate people with disabilities into public life, we encoun-tered remarkable creativity and diverse forms of cultural innovation. We plunged into the lively and unruly disability worlds inhabited by our interlocutors, explor-ing high school transition and alternative college programs, pediatric neuro-science and epigenetics labs, cultural activism in the arts, disability film festivals, and more. In short, our writing expanded to include the disability expertise of a wide range of respondents as we grappled with the complex questions raised by disability across the life course. The question of inclusion as well as social and infrastructural transformation hovered everywhere in our writing, as both utopian promises and a new normal. Over time we found again and again that the bureaucratic separation of disability categories—although a social fact—was contested in the emerging disability publics we encountered. What does it mean, we asked, to welcome all kinds of bodyminds, not only in schools but also in communities, places of worship, scientific and medical research, the arts and media, and ultimately American public life?

Adventures on the Möbius Strip

Our fields of disability and feminist studies, and our anchor in the discipline of anthropology, all share a long-standing embrace of reflexivity, encouraging us to theorize our own experiences as we navigated and wrote about the complex medical and educational bureaucracies as well as arts and politics that shaped our children's and family lives. We continue to find ourselves caught up reflexively in the projects we are studying, at times taking an active role in enabling the very activities we examine. This produces a sense of being simultaneously inside and outside the worlds we are exploring through interdependent ties of kinship and caregiving as well as our collaborative research, writing, teaching, mentoring, and advocacy. As a result, we have often experienced a vertiginous sense of our work as "adventures on the Möbius strip," in reference to the intriguing nineteenth-century mathematical figure that features a looped surface with a half twist in which the inside and outside are seamless and indistinguishable (Gunderman and Gunderman 2018).

As with many other disability and feminist scholars and anthropologists, our increasing involvement in this work has had a profound impact on us in several ways. The people with whom we work have often recognized us as allies because of our shared situation as parents of now-adult children with disabilities who are active in the broader disability world. Our students taught us to embrace another role as "accomplices" who can "enact social justice from positions of privilege" (Clemens 2017).

As members of a university community, we sometimes have institutional resources to offer in support of our mutual culture-changing work, providing campus meeting space for autistic activists, creating affiliations for disability artists, hosting a pilot transition program for students with learning disabilities finishing high school, organizing a steady stream of disability events from film screenings to book launches, and addressing the profound need for a more accessible campus. We have been deeply implicated from the outset in observing, participating in, and writing about such ventures. Our status as activist parents, researchers, teachers, organizers, and writing partners has been crucial to our commitments and credibility in a world justifiably suspicious of outside experts pronouncing on and too often pathologizing the circumstances of people with disabilities.

This chapter has offered us the opportunity to reflect on the significance of collaboration in our work together as feminist scholars and disability activists mutually engaged in research, teaching, writing, and world-building over three decades, what we have come to understand as our partnership in crip authorship. Following the shape of our central figure of the Möbius strip, each of our projects loops experientially into the next, propelling a dizzying sense of transformation, anchored in our ongoing conversations. The collaborative writing that results, we argue, serves as a microcosmic model of the feminist interdependency that not only is central to our own work and lives but also intersects with the broader pursuit of disability justice.

BIBLIOGRAPHY

Clemens, Colleen. 2017. "Ally or Accomplice? The Language of Activism." Learning for Justice, June 5, 2017. https://www.learningforjustice.org/magazine/ally-or-accomplice-the-language-of -activism.

Davidson, Cathy. 2015. "Handicapped by Being Underimpaired: Teaching with Equality at the Core." HASTAC, July 7, 2015. https://www.hastac.org/blogs/cathy-davidson/2015/07/07 /handicapped-being-underimpaired-teaching-equality-core.

Ginsburg, Faye D. 1998. Contested Lives: The Abortion Debate in an American Community. 2nd ed. Oakland: University of California Press.

Ginsburg, Faye, and Rayna Rapp, eds. 1995. Conceiving the New World Order: The Global Politics of Reproduction. Oakland: University of California Press.

Ginsburg, Faye, and Rayna Rapp. 1999. "Fetal Reflections: Confessions of Two Anthropologists as Mutual Informants." In Fetal Subjects, Feminist Positions, edited by Lynn M. Morgan and Meredith Wilson Michaels, 279–295. Philadelphia: University of Pennsylvania Press.

Ginsburg, Faye, and Rayna Rapp. 2010. "The Social Distribution of Moxie: The Legacy of Christine Sleeter." Disability Studies Quarterly 30 (2). https://dsq-sds.org/index.php/dsq/article /view/1239/1284.

Ginsburg, Faye, and Rayna Rapp. 1991. "The Politics of Reproduction." Annual Review of Anthropology 20 (1): 311–343.

Ginsburg, Faye, and Rayna Rapp. 2013. "Entangled Ethnography: Imagining a Future for Young Adults with Learning Disabilities." Social Science and Medicine 99 (December): 187–193.

Grinker, Roy Richard. 2021. Nobody's Normal: How Culture Created the Stigma of Mental Illness. New York: W. W. Norton.

Gunderman, David, and Richard Gunderman. 2018. "The Mathematical Madness of Möbius Strips and Other One-Sided Objects." Smithsonian Magazine, September 25, 2018. https:// www.smithsonianmag.com/science-nature/mathematical-madness-mobius-strips-and-other -one-sided-objects-180970394/.

Habib, Dan, dir. 2008. Including Samuel. Institute on Disability, University of New Hampshire. https://www.includingsamuel.com/.

Hartblay, Cassandra. 2020. "Disability Expertise: Claiming Disability Anthropology." Current Anthropology 61 (S21): S26–S36.

Kafer, Alison. 2013. Feminist, Queer, Crip. Bloomington: Indiana University Press.

Kittay, Eva Feder. 2019. Learning from My Daughter: The Value and Care of Disabled Minds. New York: Oxford University Press.

Landsman, Gail H. 2009. Reconstructing Motherhood and Disability in the Age of "Perfect" Babies. New York: Routledge.

Mingus, Mia. 2011. "Access Intimacy: The Missing Link." Leaving Evidence (blog), May 5, 2011. https://leavingevidence.wordpress.com/2011/05/05/access-intimacy-the-missing-link/.

Panitch, Melanie. 2007. Disability, Mothers, and Organization: Accidental Activists. New York: Routledge.

Price, Margaret. 2015. "The Bodymind Problem and the Possibilities of Pain." Hypatia 30 (1): 268–284.

Rapp, Rayna. 2011. "Reproductive Entanglements: Body, State and Culture in the Dys/regulation of Child-Bearing." Social Research 78:693–718.

Rapp, Rayna, and Faye Ginsburg. 2001. "Enabling Disability: Rewriting Kinship, Reimagining Citizenship." Public Culture 13 (3): 533–556.

———. 2011. "Reverberations: Disability and the New Kinship Imaginary." Anthropological Quarterly 84 (2): 379–410.

Schalk, Sami. 2018. *Bodyminds Reimagined: (Dis)ability, Race, and Gender in Black Women's Speculative Fiction.* Durham, NC: Duke University Press Books.

Sleeter, Christine. 1987. "Why Is There Learning Disabilities? A Critical Analysis of the Birth of a Field in Its Social Context." In *The Formation of School Subjects: The Struggle for Creating an American Institution*, edited by Thomas S. Popkewitz, 210–237. London: Falmer.

15

Lessons in Yielding: Crip Refusal and Ethical Research Praxis

ZOË H. WOOL

I wanted this bit of autoethnography to give you something, to be of use to you, to be user friendly, not knowing who the users might be. So I said in the abstract I initially wrote for this chapter that I would end with a set of lessons for yielding.

But who am I to give you lessons? Especially when writing a piece about my own failures. Of course, that right there is the problem, isn't it? The idea that mastery is a precondition for giving lessons. The idea of mastery itself (see Singh 2018).

The Skinny

I have been called many things in my life. I made a list of them once. I was cofacilitating a course called Disability Inside Out. The course was a series of modules led by disabled scholars, writers, and activists, some of whom I was also in community with. In a module led by one of the field's key figures, we were asked to write a long list of all the words we use to name ourselves. Then we were asked to write another long list of all the words others have used to name us. Finally, we were asked to write a paragraph or two about a word on one of these lists. I assumed I would write about a word related to gender or queerness. But the prompt was more specific than that. We were asked to choose a word that "has burrowed into your body."

I looked at my two lists. I noticed the words that appeared on both. I noticed the words that I called myself but others didn't. I noticed the words others called me that I didn't claim. I thought about what word had burrowed into my body. I was surprised by the word that presented itself—a word used by others and not by me: *skinny*.

Skinny is, of course (though not only), a gendered word. It describes the ideal embodied state for normative white femininity. This was always a problem for me as a white queer who cherished her female masculinity back when she was just a wee tomboy inseparable from her blue Benetton sweat suit and pirate sword. But *skinny* comes with other baggage too—the ideal embodiment of white femininity always also carrying the suggestion of weakness, which is in turn always also freighted with an aura of incapacity (Garland-Thompson 1997, 19–29). *Skinny* sits squarely at the intersection of hetero-femininity, whiteness, and disability. *Skinny* does a lot of heavy lifting.

I realized as I reflected on the word as it had named me, but not been claimed by me, that in my small-bodied queerness, I had always turned to feats of strength to manifest my queerness, because of the queerness of feats of strength performed by a small-bodied white girl. As a little kid, I would rearrange furniture, hauling my bed from one wall to another. As a bigger kid, I would armwrestle and ask young adults if I could try to pick them up, relishing their sudden change in expression as their toes left the ground with my small arms wrapped around their upper legs. As an adult, I always offered to do the heavy lifting, to move the couch up the stairs, to carry the groceries. I never asked others for extra muscle. I was reluctant to accept it when offered (which is how I once managed to drop a futon frame on my neck). In short, I rebelled against the imputed white hetero-femininity of *skinny* by doubling down on a form of boyish butchness underwritten by ableism. A version of what queercrip scholar Jess Waggoner calls "gaybleism" (Waggoner 2020).

This proclivity for queer feats of strength became central to my practices of worldmaking, caring for relations, and manifesting myself. It joined up with the modes of hospitality—particularly the hosting and feeding of beloved others—that are so important to me, and that also sometimes require heroic labor. It was braided together with my capacity to weather the punishing expectations of success in the academy (see Nishida 2016). It was a part of what allowed me to spread myself very, very thin while caring and laboring for the many projects and people to whom I understood myself to be obligated.

I have found all of these things nourishing, as well as exhausting. They are the things I understand myself to be made of. They are the substance of most of my relations.

I have also been rewarded for these things. Rewarded for my skinniness by a white world that equates it with health, by a white straight world that equates it with feminine desirability, by a queer world that ratifies my small-bodied performance of strength as a desirable form of queerness. Professionally, my exhausting, overextended academic labors have been rewarded with prestige and remuneration and almost unfathomably stable employment. My internalized ableism, born of a queer reaction formation, had set me up for success.

Crip Refusal

For about twenty years, I have been in relation to disability community. By which I mean it was then that I began to count disabled writers and scholars and activists and worldmakers among the web of relations within which I made myself. Introduced to these worlds by my partner, who lived in them, I cultivated friends and relations within them through forms of hospitality and care.

While my understanding of disability as an axis of embodied social difference became radicalized by these relations, and by the poetry and scholarship and activism that they introduced me to, disability didn't become part of my research until a few years later. I didn't start graduate school with research interests in disability or embodiment. I didn't plan to do dissertation fieldwork anchored in those topics either. Yet some months into my fieldwork, I found myself buying copies of the canonical book *The Ultimate Guide to Sex and Disability* for injured soldiers I was working with. I ended up writing a dissertation and then a book that dealt centrally with disability, masculinity, and heteronormativity in the contemporary United States.

This convergence of my world and my work brought a divergence into stark relief: the divergence between the generative and complex ways disability, gender, sexuality, and care were intertwined in queer crip projects I knew (those of Eli Clare and Sins Invalid in particular) and the paucity of disability imaginaries in the exemplarily heteronormative space of military and postmilitary life in the United States. Exploring this divergence, and creating traffic across it, became the crux of my next (and still ongoing) book project, tentatively titled *The Significance of Others*.

I began designing the project around the loose assemblages of mutual support known as care collectives (McArthur 2014) or care webs (Piepzna-Samarasinha 2018), one in New York City that I participated in and others in the Bay Area that I was connected to. I started talking to disabled friends about the project, asking if they might be interested in participating, if they had any feedback about the framing, if there were other people they thought I should talk to. My friends were excited about the project and echoed my own sense of the problematically deep divide between injured veterans and regular old disabled folks, a distinction between the worthy and unworthy disabled not unlike the distinction between the worthy and unworthy poor.

The friend whose care collective I was part of in New York City said he'd be happy to participate in the research. Incentivized by my new institution to apply for outside funding in my first two years as a faculty member, I began working on a big grant proposal for the project. I described doing participant observation in care collectives, as well as fieldwork with injured US veterans. I wrote about how my own involvement with or connection to these collectives would facilitate my research access.

And then I got a lesson in yielding.

I was talking on the phone to an acquaintance, A., an artist whom I knew through mutual disability networks and whose work had been formative for my thinking about disability and care. I expected A. to be on board with the project in the helpful and frictionless ways others had been. I hoped that she'd be willing to let me do participant observation as part of her care collective, and that I'd be able to say so in my grant proposal. I don't remember her exact words, but I do remember the mild sense of panic tinged with shame that I felt when she pointed out that it would hardly be worth the labor of training someone to do support work and integrating them into a care schedule if they'd only be there for a month or two each year—the standard summer research schedule I planned for the five-year project. I wanted to object that I was actually a quick study and very good support worker. But I was being insecure and defensive. Of course, she was right, expert as she was in coordinating her own care and participating in the care of others. It was a moment that reminded me that humility is an ethical and political research imperative (see Liboiron 2021).

I kept talking. I explained that I would compensate interview participants by barter, offering them two hours of my time for every hour they offered me. I had arrived at the idea of barter in conversation with disabled friends who helped me think through how to balance a spirit of reciprocity with the utility and value of transactional forms of compensation, even for exchanges situated within longer-term and more robust relations. I was pleased with this barter idea. A. was not impressed, but only because she took such a practice of reciprocity for granted. I realized that perhaps I had been so pleased with this barter idea because I measured it by the yardstick of prestigious grants, where such practices were valued, but not de rigueur, and therefore all the more special.

A. asked me why I chose to offer two hours of my time for every hour someone gave me. Again, mild panic. I explained that it seemed only fair, a matter of equity: I likely had a greater margin of energy, time, and money to spare than those I'd be interviewing. And their contributions would generate value for me in a sphere of (academic) capital to which they had no access, so I owed them some kind of surplus. It was a small way of addressing the irreducibly extractive nature of ethnographic research. But, she said, you have your own limits. Calling me in with real generosity, she pointed out that by offering double what I was being given, I was instantiating myself as doubly capacitated, as inexhaustible. That I was not allowing my own limits, my own vulnerabilities, into the transaction, into the intersubjective relation. That I wasn't attending to the possibility that I might become overwhelmed or burned out. That I was excluding myself as a subject of my own practices of care. This was an invitation to yield.

This was an invitation born of A.'s ethical refusal (see Simpson 2014).[1] A refusal to participate in a research project that wouldn't be worth the labor, despite the involvement of beloved others within her world, and despite being carried out by someone who was already positioned within it. A refusal to allow a certain logic of equity to pass untroubled when that logic relied on the myth of the invulnerable researcher. A refusal to allow my heroic forms of care to escape accountability for their ableism. This was a refusal anchored in crip ways of being and caring. A crip refusal (see also Lee 2021).

A few years after this conversation, when I was invited to contribute to this book, I asked A. if she'd like to cowrite this piece with me. She said she wasn't taking on any new writing projects and welcomed me to take ownership of the way that our conversation had felt like an invitation and made meaning for me. Another generous and generative crip refusal. A refusal I hope finds itself well met here.

Queer Failure

In his book *The Queer Art of Failure*, Jack Halberstam (2011) offers a scrappy and celebratory orientation to the ways queerness is coded as straight failure. Halberstam has been something of a posterchild for the unrequited relationship between queer and crip theory (Kafer 2013; McRuer and Mollow 2012), a "bad romance" (Johnson 2015) in which queer theory stakes its claim to differences of illness (HIV and AIDS) and madness and itinerant life course trajectories, ground already well tended and cared for by crip theory, without acknowledging that work or joining in that care. The relationship between crip and queer theory has changed dramatically in recent years, grown closer with the ascendency (some would say appropriation) of crip theory into the sharpest edges and coolest corners of critical theory, and the inclusion of disability as one of the canonical forms of embodied social difference, alongside race and gender.

But the embrace of failure as a queer art is still an embrace that simultaneously erases the "'feels like shit' dimension of failure" (Johnson 2015, 225) which remains a painful part of disabled life for those who can't or don't or won't measure up to standards of success or worthiness or desirability in heteronormative *or* queer worlds. The queer art of failure is a partial embrace of failure that doesn't recognize its partiality. In that, it risks undermining projects of disabled worldmaking, epistemology, and justice by making the "feels like shit" dimension of failure the "part that has no part" (Povinelli 2011, 47) in the inverted and reclaimed space of queer possibility that Halberstam's failure as art names. In this, queer failure manifests the friction between *queer* and *crip*, a queer reluctance to embrace the cripness with which it is intertwined.

The queer failure I want to name is my own. The failure of my own queerness to yield to the crip worlds I was part of. A failure to yield to the limits of my own capacities, despite my commitments to radical disability worlds, and despite the ways that my own capacities fall within most definitions of disability. My failure to see the way that my queer skinny ass had thrown the crip value of mutual vulnerability under the bus and called it reciprocity.

Ethical Research Praxis

I ended up offering an hour-for-hour barter in my research protocols. Only three participants took me up on it. One gave my hours to a friend who needed help running errands after a big move. I helped another edit some professional documents, but those hours blurred into the tasks of an ongoing professional mentorship. The third said it seemed silly since I already contributed to their life and work, but the promised labor eased the way for me to fill in when they were between care workers and needed support making dinner for friends.

I didn't end up doing participant observation in care collectives. The friend whose collective I was part of in New York City passed away the winter before we would have started. Learning from A.'s crip refusal, I decided to at least begin the project with interviews, which seemed less fraught, and perhaps less costly for others.

Throughout the fifteen years since my first fieldwork experiences gave me a sense of the particular mix of intimacy and extractivism that characterized the kind of ethnographic research I learned to do, I had been willing to "stay with the trouble" (Haraway 2016). I named ethnography as irreducibly extractive for my undergraduate and graduate students and tried to help them reckon with it in their own ways. But as my relations in and to the field became ever more "patchy" (Günel, Varma, and Watanabe 2020)—amid the exigencies of teaching schedules, the white antiracist commitments to institutional rabblerousing that came with joining the professoriate, my own small projects of worldmaking, and the urgencies of "sandwich generation" life—I found it harder and harder to build relations in the field thick enough to bear this ethnographic extraction in a way that felt justifiable.

These, of course, are not new troubles. We are lucky to have generations of insight and wisdom to help us grapple with the extractive nature of ethnographic research, from Zora Neale Hurston (1950), to Vine Deloria Jr. (1988), to Faye Harrison (1997), to Audra Simpson (2014), to Ryan Jobson (2020). Alongside this shining genealogy, and recent offerings within the emerging field of disability anthropology (Block et al. 2015; Block 2020; Hartblay 2020; Rogers 2020), when I grapple with the question of what ethical research praxis might be, I return to my conversation with A.

I consider the way crip life and crip time and crip politics infused her responses to my research protocols. The way crip accountability became a new measure, questioning a model of reciprocity valued because it was scarce within a domain of academic prestige anchored in mastery—a project whose racism, colonialism, and patriarchy have been generatively indicted (Singh 2018), but whose ableism still remains largely unnamed beyond explicitly crip critique.

When I think, as a feminist scholar, of what ethical research praxis might look like, I think of A.'s invitation, her lesson in yielding, that was also a reminder of standpoint theory's crucial linking of positionality and epistemology—the insight that we always know *from* somewhere (Harding 1986)—as her invitation surfaced the internalized ableism rooted in the reaction formation of my queerness that shaped my heroic gesture toward what I hoped was equity in a mode of research I knew to be irreducibly extractive.

The lessons here are not mine to give, they are mine to learn.

NOTE

1 In her ethnography of the political life of the Kahnawà:ke Mohawk polity, Audra Simpson elaborates the Kahanawà:ke refusal to take what supposedly good things are offered by the state (such as U.S. or Canadian passports) and allied forms of authoritative knowledge, such as anthropological categories of cultural difference and forms of multicultural "recognition," which ultimately discipline difference and undermine the political and epistemological sovereignty of those who are being made subjects (but not authors) of knowledge or "recognition." In her account, refusal, particularly the refusal of things that seem good from the perspective of the liberalism of settler states, becomes an ethical and political act. Her thinking about refusal from her particular location within Kahnawà:ke enactments of sovereignty has informed a broader way of thinking about the politics and ethics of refusal in other sites (See McGranahan 2016).

BIBLIOGRAPHY

Block, Pamela. 2020. "Activism, Anthropology, and Disability Studies in Times of Austerity: In Collaboration with Sini Diallo." *Current Anthropology* 61 (S21): S68–S75.

Block, Pamela, Devva Kasnitz, Akemi Nishida, and Nick Pollard. 2015. *Occupying Disability: Critical Approaches to Community, Justice, and Decolonizing Disability*. Dordrecht: Springer.

Deloria, Vine, Jr. 1988. *Custer Died for Your Sins: An Indian Manifesto*. Norman: University of Oklahoma Press.

Garland-Thompson, Rosmarie. 1997. *Extraordinary Bodies: Figuring Physical Disability in American Culture and Literature*. New York, NY: Columbia University Press.

Günel, Gökçe, Saiba Varma, and Chika Watanabe. 2020. "A Manifesto for Patchwork Ethnography." Society for Cultural Anthropology, June 9, 2020. https://culanth.org/fieldsights/a-manifesto-for-patchwork-ethnography.

Halberstam, Jack. 2011. *The Queer Art of Failure*. Durham, NC: Duke University Press.

Haraway, Donna J. 2016. *Staying with the Trouble: Making Kin in the Chthulucene*. Durham, NC: Duke University Press.

Harding, Sandra. 1986. *The Science Question in Feminism*. Ithaca, NY: Cornell University Press.

Harrison, Faye V., ed. 1997. *Decolonizing Anthropology: Moving Further toward an Anthropology for Liberation*. 2nd ed. Arlington, VA: American Anthropological Association.

Hartblay, Cassandra. 2020. "Disability Expertise: Claiming Disability Anthropology." *Current Anthropology* 61 (S21): S26–S36.

Hurston, Zora Neale. 1950. "What White Publishers Won't Print." *Negro Digest* 8 (April).

Jobson, Ryan Cecil. 2020. "The Case for Letting Anthropology Burn: Sociocultural Anthropology in 2019." *American Anthropologist* 122 (2): 259–271.

Johnson, Merri Lisa. 2015. "Bad Romance: A Crip Feminist Critique of Queer Failure." *Hypatia* 30 (1): 251–267.

Kafer, Alison. 2013. *Feminist, Queer, Crip*. Bloomington: Indiana University Press.

Lee, Crystal. 2021. "Who Gets to Refuse Technology (and How)?" Presented at the Prototyping AI Ethics Futures: Rights, Access and Refusal, Ada Lovelace Institute, June 22, 2021. YouTube video, 1:28:09. https://youtu.be/kwq4YaLCubk.

Liboiron, Max. 2021. *Pollution Is Colonialism*. Durham, NC: Duke University Press.

McArthur, Park. 2014. "Sort of Like a Hug: Notes on Collectivity, Conviviality, and Care." *Happy Hypocrite*, no. 7, 48–60.

McRuer, Robert, and Anna Mollow, eds. 2012. *Sex and Disability*. Durham, NC: Duke University Press.

Nishida, A. (2016). Neoliberal Academia and a Critique from Disability Studies. In: Block, P., Kasnitz, D., Nishida, A., Pollard, N. editors. *Occupying Disability: Critical Approaches to Community, Justice, and Decolonizing Disability*. Springer, Dordrecht.

Piepzna-Samarasinha, Leah Lakshmi. 2018. *Care Work: Dreaming Disability Justice*. Vancouver, Canada: Arsenal Pulp.

Povinelli, Elizabeth. 2011. *Economies of Abandonment: Social Belonging and Endurance in Late Liberalism*. Durham, NC: Duke University Press.

Rogers, Emily Lim. 2020. "Staying (at Home) with Brain Fog: 'Un-witting' Patient Activism." *Somatosphere* (blog), October 5, 2020. http://somatosphere.net/2020/staying-home-brain-fog-patient-activism.html/.

Simpson, Audra. 2014. *Mohawk Interruptus: Political Life across the Borders of Settler States*. Durham, NC: Duke University Press.

Singh, Julietta. 2018. *Unthinking Mastery: Dehumanism and Decolonial Entanglements*. Durham, NC: Duke University Press.

Waggoner, Jess. 2020. "'Dykes, Disability n' Stuff': Queer Ableisms and the Work of Disabled Lesbian and Cripqueer Print Cultures." Presented at the Disability Studies @ Rice Lecture Series, Rice University, Houston, TX, February 5, 2020.

16

Creating a Fully Accessible Digital Helen Keller Archive

HELEN SELSDON

The Helen Keller Archive at the American Foundation for the Blind (AFB, n.d.-a) is the largest extant collection of materials by and about Helen Keller (1880–1968). Currently on loan to the American Printing House for the Blind in Louisville, Kentucky, over eighty thousand items chronicle her life and the world she lived in, from the late nineteenth century to the middle of the twentieth. This chapter traces the journey that was taken to bring this physical collection to a global audience via digital technology and, most importantly, how over 186,000 digital images and thousands of pieces of metadata spanning Keller's life and beyond were made accessible to the blind, deaf, deafblind, and hard of hearing communities whose history they relate.[1]

As the archivist at AFB, I took care of the archival collections from 2002 until 2021. During that time, I witnessed growing attention to disability history and a recognition that people with disabilities must be able to access their own stories and shape and narrate their own past. What better place to start than by creating a fully accessible digital Helen Keller Archive?

Keller was among the most recognizable people with disabilities in the twentieth century. She not only used her extraordinary popularity as an advocate for disabled people but was also a feminist, social activist, and public intellectual. Keller's involvement in key cultural, social, and political events of the nineteenth and twentieth centuries was unparalleled. She was both a product of her environment and a driving force upon it, paving the way for a more inclusive society. Her advocacy resulted in legislation that benefited blind students and veterans and had profound ramifications for society as a whole.

Before Accessible Archives

Before the creation of an accessible digital archive, research at AFB necessarily took place in person. Visitors who could afford to do so traveled to New York City. Most of these visitors were sighted. For those with low vision, the AFB provided access to a closed-circuit television that can zoom in on text, and blind researchers were often accompanied by an assistant who read text aloud. Similarly, deafblind researchers had assistants who were familiar with tactile sign language.

The lack of accessible digital collections was discussed in Sara White's November/December 2013 *SAA Archival Outlook* article, "Disability: Uncovering Our Hidden History." This included a survey response from an individual with a disability. When asked if archives take disabled people into consideration when designing their websites, the individual noted that "digital collections are merely scanned images of archival collections without accessible mediums" (28). This is a problem.

Every time you create a digital record, or share an item online, you are either including or excluding users with disabilities, based on your approach. Web designers often inadvertently create barriers to assistive technology users, as well as users with low vision who aren't using assistive technology. These barriers include using color to indicate the sections of a page, labeling forms incorrectly, or not including captions, transcriptions, or descriptions for images (alt tags). For some individuals with low vision, it can be challenging to read web materials that are composed in unusual typefaces. Software that allows users to zoom in and out of an image may be useful to some users with low vision; however, these will be inaccessible to a user who is blind.

Accessible Websites

Accessible websites allow users to select text and transform it into a font of their choosing, and provide descriptions and text equivalents for images, video, and audio. These sites follow the web content accessibility guidelines of the Web Accessibility Initiative. The best mode for ensuring that digitized documents are accessible is to include a text version of the contents; this allows readers with vision loss to use assistive technology to access online materials. Screen-reader software programs, such as JAWS, VoiceOver, or NVDA, provide sophisticated speech or Braille output and a somewhat modified interface for both software and webpages. People with low vision may use screen magnification tools—like ZoomText or MAGic software—which enlarge text and images on the screen and often provide speech output.

A New Tool

AFB has long committed to making its website (www.afb.org) fully accessible to those who are blind or low vision. Because AFB did not find an adequate archival tool, it set out to design its own. Our web team—which was led by Cristal Earl, who is legally blind—made sure that the site can be smoothly navigated by those who can't see, as well as by those who can. In 2007, AFB designed and implemented an Encoded Archival Description web application software for its Talking Book Archive, which was fully accessible to both the software's administrators and its end users who were blind or visually impaired. Six years later, this Encoded Archival Description software was used in a pilot project as proof of concept to digitize and disseminate the Helen Keller collection at the item level. This initiative was key to securing funding in 2015 from the National Endowment for the Humanities (NEH) for a large-scale digitization project and to develop a robust archival tool that was fully accessible to people with disabilities.

In collaboration with digitization vendor Hudson Archival in upstate New York and New Zealand software designer Veridian/DL Consulting, tens of thousands of images and their metadata were digitized in multiple file formats. All images are posted as JPEG2000 (JP2) files, and the archive administrators have access to downloadable TIFF, JPEG, PDF, and JP2 image files. But this was just the beginning. Under the watchful eye of Hudson Archival's president, Toya Dubin, an army of metadata assistants viewed each digital item (often consisting of multiple digital images), wrote a brief description of it, and selected subject terms from drop-down lists (taxonomies) that best described the item. Countless spreadsheets were generated and their information exported and transformed into a searchable database.

All this work would have been of little use to people who are blind or low vision if the interface itself were not accessible. AFB staff, in conjunction with Veridian, made sure that the website was coded using valid and properly labeled HTML on every page and that all the multimedia controls, such as any buttons that you could click on with a mouse, had an easily discoverable keyboard equivalent. We believe that through careful use of transcriptions, image descriptions, captions, and audio description as well as fully compliant code, AFB has pioneered the most accessible online archive currently available.

June 2018 saw the public launch of the digital archive and a celebration of the successful completion of the first phase of the project. Our main event was a pizza party at the New York Institute for Special Education in the Bronx. Not only was this a celebration, the event was also intended to showcase the value of the digital archive as an educational tool for children with visual impairments. We even had a cake celebrating Keller's birthday (June 27) and invited broadcast media to attend, resulting in wonderful press coverage.[2]

It Takes a Village

The complicated process of developing an accessible digital archive was a highly collaborative one. A myriad of individuals and organizations were involved, including staff at AFB, digitization vendor Hudson Archival, software designer Veridian/DL Consulting (led by Stefan Boddie), the Helen Keller Digitization Project Advisory Board (volunteers), and dozens of professionals and volunteers around the nation and the disability community.

The "It takes a village" mentality was never more clearly shown than when we tested the site for usability and transcribed documents for accessibility. From December 2016 through February 2017, Elizabeth Neal, Associate Director, Web Content Strategy at AFB, conducted usability tests of the customized website. Nineteen volunteers were recruited to test the site, roughly double the average size of a usability participant group. A broad cross section of testers was involved and included historians; technology experts; blindness professionals; student; older adults who are blind, deaf, or deafblind; and hearing and sighted users. The feedback was invaluable in understanding how to deliver a site that works for seasoned archivists, historians, and the general public alike. As a result of the feedback from the accessibility testing, we identified significant changes to the site's nomenclature, organization, and layout, and the site was greatly improved.

The Helen Keller Archive is a treasure trove. Materials include correspondence from nine US presidents and leading figures such as Mark Twain, Pearl S. Buck, and Albert Einstein. Correspondence also includes letters to Keller from ordinary men, women, and children around the world whose stories have never been told. Beyond written materials, there are hundreds of gifts that Keller received during her lifetime, many from her trips around the globe. These, as well as press clippings, speeches, photographs, and film, form a massive archive with a wide range of formats. How do you make them all fully accessible?

The first important step in this process was the creation of text transcriptions of all typewritten pages using optical character recognition (OCR). OCR is a software program that enables computers to read scanned text and spits out accessible transcriptions. However, most handwriting cannot be deciphered by OCR, and typewritten text that is faded or uses unusual fonts can produce inaccurate transcriptions. In March 2018 we posted a request on Idealist.org for volunteers to transcribe handwritten documents (as well as poor-quality type-written documents). Over forty volunteers around the nation came forward, and each of them was individually trained by Hudson Archival's president to make corrections (including in French and German). As we became more proficient, we developed standards for transcription, ensuring uniformity and reducing inconsistencies. The only item each volunteer needed for the task was access to a computer with an internet connection.

Photographs and audio-visual materials required different treatment to be accessible. Over 1,500 images were studied and described for a visually impaired audience. Similarly, excerpts from the 1954 documentary *Helen Keller in Her Story* were captioned and audio-described, and full descriptive transcripts were provided to make the video content both more searchable and more accessible to blind and deafblind users. In addition, the video player controls themselves were high contrast and keyboard accessible, thanks to the open-source tool AFB developed in 2015, one of the first free, fully accessible, embedded video players with HTML5 controls.

Helen Keller Archive Curricula

Following on the heels of the success of the first NEH-funded project, in 2018 we received our second major grant from the NEH. This funding enabled us to complete the digitization process, further improve the customized site, and create accessible curricula for middle school students surrounding Keller's life and legacy. For too long, disability history has been overlooked and has remained inaccessible to our own communities. The digital Helen Keller Archive enables disabled students and scholars to see themselves in history and to shape that history through unmediated, independent research. Equally, it is important for sighted and hearing children, and indeed anyone in the public with access to a computer, to learn about the lives and achievements of disabled people.

Few collections can deliver such a wealth of primary and secondary source materials chronicling twentieth-century history. Our challenge was figuring out how to maximize the educational potential of the collection. In 2019, AFB began developing free lesson plans to teach middle and high school students about Keller's life, disability history, and the use, function, and value of digital archival collections. In January, we asked AFB's Helen Keller Advisory Board Committee, "What educational features should we develop for the Helen Keller Archive?" They responded, quite wisely, "Ask the teachers." That led us to create a focus group with educators at the Math and Science Exploratory School, MS 447, in Brooklyn to find out what tools they needed to bring the Helen Keller collection into their classrooms. Key themes for the lesson plans emerged, in support of specific Common Core curriculum standards. Recommended topics included the following:

- learning about digital and physical archives
- developing internet research skills, including how to use primary and secondary sources
- exploring disability rights and civil rights in Keller's lifetime

We created a team that included a project manager with experience creating curricula for museums, a curricula writer, a historian and college professor, our digitization vendor, AFB staff with accessibility expertise, and myself, the archivist. Over six months we hashed out our draft lesson plans, and in December 2019, sixty eighth-grade sighted and hearing students at Brooklyn's MS 447 helped AFB beta test the first lesson.

The curricula team observed how an experienced teacher adapted the lesson to fit available class time. It was fascinating to listen to students discuss the importance of preserving information, and the pros and cons of physical and digital archival collections. Some students had never heard of Keller, while others had in-depth knowledge of her as a political advocate.

Difficulties with the Search and Browse features revealed the need for usability improvements, as well as greater emphasis on teaching digital research skills. The students were fascinated by accessibility and wanted to learn more about how people who are blind, deaf, and deafblind access multimedia content.

Accessibility for All

In June 2020 we launched our first two lessons: Introduction to Digital and Physical Archives, and Primary and Secondary Sources. Little did we expect that a global pandemic would underscore the importance of accessible online lesson plans for distance learning. During the summer of 2020 we decided to record the first lesson so that students could follow along, guided by a "virtual" teacher (AFB 2020). The lesson is accompanied by captions and a complete transcript for students who are deaf or hard of hearing.

With 2020 marking the centennial of the Nineteenth Amendment in the United States, we were thrilled to receive a grant from Humanities New York to create a lesson devoted to Keller and women's suffrage using the digital archive. "Votes for Women, a Voice for All: Helen Keller, Suffragist" (AFB, n.d.-b) provided a golden opportunity to use the archive's documents to teach students how to contextualize historical events. For instance, Keller gave a speech at a 1916 women's conference in Chicago in support of women's suffrage. This speech provides contemporaneous reporting on the fight for equal representation. Students can discuss historical events concerning the creation of a more equitable society and relate them to today's actions to do the same.

As we developed this third lesson, we realized that we needed to address issues of race, class, and gender to provide broader context for Keller's role in the suffrage movement. It became clear that the lesson would benefit greatly from the expertise of educators skilled in teaching the complex issues surrounding race in the United States, and in this instance, the historical inequity between Black and white suffragists. As a result, AFB reached out to college and middle school teachers as well as academics at Learning for Justice (formerly Teaching Tolerance). The feedback helped determine the contents and shape of all three lesson plans.

All three lessons are available on the Helen Keller Archive website and are included on the EDSITEment.neh.gov website (a partnership between the NEH and the National Trust for the Humanities). Coinciding with Women's History Month in March 2021, the lesson plans and digital archive were included as a resource in the *Building a More Perfect Union* lesson plan book and are located in the subsection "The ADA & Taking Action for Access."

Make Your Collections Accessible!

The digital Helen Keller Archive is an award-winning website used by historians, writers, and researchers worldwide. It represents a powerful vehicle for continuing Keller's work to build a more inclusive society. Creating a fully accessible digital archive for materials in multiple formats was a herculean task involving numerous organizations, professionals, and volunteers, and very importantly, it required the vision and extraordinary generosity of the NEH as well as other forward-thinking donors—and the ongoing commitment of AFB.

The challenges of creating a fully accessible digital archive have resulted in innovative tools that can benefit all archival collections, including the following:

- a tool that enables volunteers to transcribe documents remotely
- digital tools to improve the security of digital information and facilitate the dissemination of online archival collections worldwide
- a digital preservation tool that checks and allows administrators to repair and replace corrupted digital files
- template updates that enable software designer Veridian to improve the accessibility for every collection it hosts

The digitization of Helen Keller's archival collection—as with that of many other collections—greatly assists with the long-term preservation of information and its dissemination. But many online collections are useless to those with vision loss. Just as the Talking Book pioneered by AFB in the 1930s brought information and literature to thousands of people with vision loss around the world, today historical collections must be available to both nonsighted and sighted audiences if we are to create equal access to the vast amount of learning, culture, and education that is increasingly available on the web.[3]

Within the disability community, Keller continues to arouse debate resulting from her iconic status and her "elevation" as a disabled person. Modern scholars such as Georgina Kleege (2006) have reflected on problematic aspects of her legacy. The importance of the digital archive in grounding the debate in facts and primary sources cannot be overstated. In early January 2021, a bizarre idea circulated on the internet—that it was impossible for Keller, a deafblind woman, to have achieved all that she did. AFB responded with posts on its blog and on Facebook. The posts reflected on the importance of education and knowledge—as embodied by the digital Helen Keller Archive—in the face of prejudice and ignorance, and the importance of access to verifiable knowledge and information in a time when historical facts are questioned on social media. Negative attitudes toward people with disabilities remain embedded in modern society—even toward a figure whose standing we thought unassailable. This powerfully underscores the value of creating fully digital archival collections that provide evidence of the role people with disabilities have played in shaping public policy and can teach schoolchildren as well as the general public about the past and, in our case, the abilities and extraordinary life of Helen Keller.

NOTES

1 This article originated with a short blog post for the Disability History Association (Selsdon, 2020).
2 Spectrum News, NY1. 2018. "Bronx students among first to access Helen Keller Archive." June 7. https://www.ny1.com/nyc/bronx/news/2018/06/07/bronx-students-among-first-to -access-helen-keller-archive.
3 For more information about the Talking Book historical collection, including digitized and transcribed audio examples, see Mara Mills, "A Listening Tour of the AFB Talking Book Archives," *AFB Blog*, May 28, 2021.

BIBLIOGRAPHY

AFB (American Foundation for the Blind). 2020. "Helen Keller Lesson Plan One: Introduction to Digital and Physical Archives." YouTube video, 15:15. Posted September 8, 2020. https://www .youtube.com/watch?v=T-NFaykMnkA.

AFB (American Foundation for the Blind). n.d.-a. Helen Keller Archive. Accessed October 5, 2022. https://afb.org/HelenKellerArchive.

AFB (American Foundation for the Blind). n.d.-b. "Lesson Three: Votes for Women, a Voice for All: Helen Keller, Suffragist." Helen Keller Archive. Accessed October 5, 2022. https://afb.org /HK-Lesson-3.

Kleege, Georgina. 2006. *Blind Rage: Letters to Helen Keller*. Washington, DC: Gallaudet University Press.

Mills, Mara. 2021. "A Listening Tour of the AFB Talking Book Archives." *AFB Blog*, May 28, 2021. https://www.afb.org/blog/entry/listening-tour-talking-books.

EDSITEment! 2021. "Building a More Perfect Union." National Endowment for the Humanities. https://www.nhd.org/sites/default/files/NHD_AMorePerfectUnion_LessonBook_FINAL.pdf.

Selsdon, Helen. 2020. "The Digital Helen Keller Archive: A Powerful Educational Tool." *All of Us* (blog), August 12, 2020. http://allofusdha.org/ada-turns-30/the-digital-helen-keller-archive-a -powerful-educational-tool/.

White, Sara. 2013. "Disability: Uncovering Our Hidden History." *SAA Archival Outlook*, November/ December 2013, 12, 28.

SECTION III

Genre/Form

17

Manifesting Manifestos

ALISON KAFER

I have written extensively about Donna Haraway's "Cyborg Manifesto" (1991). I have read countless articles, chapters, books, and interviews about it. I even participated in a symposium devoted to it. But before writing this chapter, I never once thought about it *as* a manifesto. Nor did it ever occur to me to position "A Cyborg Manifesto" within a larger history of manifestos, or to approach the piece as part of a literary or cultural genre, *the manifesto*. To the extent that I recognized it as part of any genre, I simply saw it as an example of feminist theory and criticism. What most interested me about the "Manifesto" was the cyborg figure and, especially, the feminist, queer, and trans of color critiques that had collected around it. I was drawn to the work the "Manifesto" was doing in the world, and how this work could inform disability theorists, artists, and activists as we grappled with cyborg technologies.

Perhaps this failure to register as a manifesto (despite its title), and to read instead as *feminist theory*, was by design. Haraway explicitly and repeatedly depicted the "Cyborg Manifesto" as an intervention in feminist thought, drawing heavily on women of color feminisms. The echoes I felt with other feminist theory and criticism were not mere coincidence. But Janet Lyon also locates a profound "wariness about manifestic discourse" (1999, 195) in Haraway's "Manifesto," highlighting her challenges to teleological narratives, her refusal to assert a unified feminist *we* or *us*, and her desire "for a complicated ironic myth" rather than a "specific agenda" (195, 196). "By calling her essay a manifesto," Lyon argues, "Haraway both invokes and plays ironically with the form's status as a foundational text," in part by subverting the conventions of manifestic writing (195). As a result, Lyon argues, Haraway's "Manifesto" is "a manifesto scorched almost beyond recognition" (195).

But another way of explaining my inattention is that I was too intently focused on tracing the histories, uses, and possibilities of "Cyborg" to make it to "Manifesto." In retrospect, I can see that in querying what work disability was doing for the cyborg, I neglected to ask the same questions of the manifesto: As a genre, rhetorical form, and cultural practice, what use does the manifesto make of disability, or disabled figures? To what extent does the manifesto form—and cultural or critical understandings of the form—draw on conceptualizations of disability?

Quite a bit, as it turns out. In critical and popular discourse, both the manifesto and the manifesto writer are understood to be *mad*, and mad in both senses of the word. As a form, the manifesto is described as "infectious, contagious," and uninterested in "rational back-and-forth discourse"; it "invites disorientation and distorts time" and is "not designed for remembering" (Fahs 2020, 5, 6). It "has a madness about it. It is peculiar and angry, quirky," even "downright crazed" (Caws 2001, xix). "Univocal, unilateral, [and] single-minded" (Lyon 1999, 9), as a genre it "radiates certainty well beyond the point of good judgment into the blind obsession of the *idée fixe*" (Alvarez and Stephenson 2012, 7). The manifesto borders on "lunacy" and harbors an "ardent disregard for good manners and reasoned civility" (Lyon 1999, 200, 12). It is "immodest and forceful, exuberant and vivid, attention grabbing," and "always in overdose and overdrive" (Caws 2001, xxi). "Lacking scholarly pedigree . . . bad tempered . . . [and] wonderfully cranky," manifestos "require mania and are intentionally and consistently extreme" (Fahs 2020, 5–6, 9). Full of "fervid, even violent, rage" (Lyon 1999, 14), they are "rude and forceful" (Alvarez and Stephenson 2012, 4) and "*loud*" (Caws 2001, xx). "Not an attractive piece of writing by existing norms or standards" (Ahmed 2017, 252), the manifesto can be understood as the "discursive model of the lunatic" (Lyon 1999, 198) or as a "schizophrenic scream" (Atkinson quoted in Fahs 2020, 10).

According to many writers, it is precisely the angry screams of the manifesto that make it such an appealing and necessary form, or what Sara Ahmed identifies as "a survival strategy" (2017, 249). Annie Hill describes her collection, "State Killing: Queer and Women of Color Manifestas against U.S. Violence and Oppression," as "releas[ing] an orchestra of furies that go by the name of *manifesta*" (2019, 5). Lamiyah Bahrainwala notes that she wrote her contribution to the collection both as and about a survival tactic: "Screaming is a vital response to white fragility, as I refuse to respond to this violence with rationality or silence" (2019, 21). For many feminist critics, the madness heralded in the manifesto is no mere metaphor. "Within the manifesto genre," asserts Breanne Fahs, feminists "*could be mad* (both emotionally and psychologically)" (2020, 9; emphasis in the original). Presumably this attention to those who are mad *and* mad is what led Fahs to include Claude Steiner's 1969 "Radical Psychiatry Manifesto" in her 2020 collection of feminist manifestos.[1]

But as much as feminist critics love the manifesto, compiling collections of them and generating their own, there are hints of discomfort with how the "crazed" dimension of the manifesto attaches to manifesto writers and readers, marking feminists themselves as "crazy," a marking that must be refuted or disavowed. Felicity Colman, for example, laments that "authors of manifestos are frequently dismissed . . . as nutters—demented or socially unstable people" (2010, 375–376), and although she acknowledges the societal stereotypes that undergird such characterizations, she also is quick to reassure readers that "the manifesto form offers more than just an insight into insane or schizo processual thinking" (376). If Fahs casts the manifesto as a place where a feminist can "*be mad*," Colman suggests that the *real* work of the manifesto is to be found else-where, far away from disability and madness.

One tack I could take here would be to interrogate this very dynamic, questioning the use of madness as a way of signaling passion, urgency, and power while simultaneously isolating feminist political work from (the experiences of) people who identify as mad or who are perceived as mad. The mad passion celebrated in many of these descriptions is not directed against the surveillance, institutionalization, containment, and removal done to mad and neuroqueer people, nor is it aimed against the use of psych labels to support such violence. Moreover, as scholars such as Moya Bailey and Izetta Autumn Mobley (2019), La Marr Jurelle Bruce (2021), Bettina Judd (2019), and Therí Pickens (2016) have noted, the slippage between *mad* and *mad* is often used to shore up anti-Blackness, positioning Black women in particular as "unhealthy or unproductive" (Pickens 2016, 16).[2]

Another potential project would be to highlight the continued reliance on *coherence*, *meaningfulness*, and *usefulness* in feminist manifestos and feminist manifesto criticism, even as those same writers and critics describe *incoherence*, *irrationality*, and *waste* in exuberant terms. Or perhaps I could contrast the frequency with which manifesto critics draw on disability metaphors with the relative absence of disability manifestos in their collections.

As necessary as all of that work is, I want to turn instead to manifestos written *by* sick, mad, autistic, Deaf, and disabled people *to* sick, mad, autistic, Deaf, and disabled people as well as those centering anti-ableist practices, politics, and imaginaries. For the remainder of this chapter, I take feminist manifesto scholars at their word: If the manifesto is indeed *mad*, an ideal site for expressing irrationality, refusing productivity, playing with language, naming oppression, and imagining otherwise, then what work have disability studies scholars, disability justice activists, and disability artists and cultural workers made of, from, and in relation to it?

For me, this work includes a suspicion about the use of the manifesto label as a way "to identify a text's foundational status" (Lyon 1999, 12). I am wary of any such moves for or in disability studies because of the way they obscure ongoing histories of unequal access, rely on and perpetuate a narrow view of the field's scope, and marginalize alternate histories and legacies of struggle. In naming the following texts manifestos, especially the ones that don't name themselves as such, I am not marking them as canonical or foundational but rather highlighting their disruption and refusal of such terms.

Crip Manifestos: Manifesting Sick, Mad, Autistic, Deaf, Disabled Futures Now

Critical access studies and movements for radical accessibility have been key sites of crip manifesting, in part because the manifesto form offers such a sharp formal and tonal departure from the institutional "access checklist." Aimi Hamraie suggests that the "first clue" to realizing disabled architect Ronald Mace had written "a covert manifesto for Universal Design" was that "not a single checklist was to be found" (2017, 203). Hamraie presents the access checklist, with its expectations of predictability, stability, and legibility (Price 2021), as diametrically opposed to the more radical manifesto, which "keep[s] misfits in mind" (Hamraie 2017, 203) rather than retroactively accommodating them after the fact. Carmen Papalia's (2018) "Accessibility Manifesto for the Arts" argues for "an anti-policy approach to accessibility" that "instead confronts ideas of agency and power"; Papalia's "Open Access" approach presents access as "a creative, long-term process," one that is "a perpetual negotiation of trust between those who practice support as a mutual exchange." Jos Boys (2020) argues for a similarly collaborative and iterative approach to design, using their "(Little) Manifesto" to articulate guiding principles for "doing dis/ability differently in architecture." And in her "Intersectional Disability Arts Manifesto," Alice Sheppard suggests that such work requires attending to "the beautiful complicated histories and cultures of disability, race, gender, and sexuality." Design by misfits, for misfits; access as an ongoing collective process; attending to intersectional relations of power: these are the very moves that have long circulated in disability justice manifestos, statements, gatherings, practices, and dreams (e.g., Sins Invalid 2015; Piepzna-Samarasinha 2018; Lazard 2019).

Manifesto writers committed to this kind of crip design have found Haraway's "Cyborg Manifesto" especially generative. Hamraie and Kelly Fritsch make brilliant use of Haraway in their 2019 "Crip Technoscience Manifesto." They strategically lay claim to her title and language, noting that their "manifesto calls attention to the powerful, messy, non-innocent, contradictory, and nevertheless crucial work of crip technoscience" (2). In so doing, they assert the crip potential of technoscience as "a transformative tool for disability justice" (3) and the centrality of disabled designers and makers to practices of "world-building and -dismantling" (2).

For these theorists and artists, the label *manifesto* serves to signal the radical dimension of the work under discussion or to position their own work within a larger intellectual tradition. But as a quick look at the table of contents of various manifesto collections will confirm, many texts widely regarded as manifestos do not declare themselves as such in their titles. As with Hamraie's interpretation of Mace, what makes a manifesto a manifesto is not (only) its title, but what it does, how it reads, and what it asks of readers. Fahs suggests, for example, that manifestos pose "a different set of questions," including a critical interrogation and active refusal of "the very painful ways in which feminist writing and thinking is often dismissed as trivial, overly emotional, and unsophisticated" (2020, 13). Colman shares Fahs's sense that a wide range of texts register as feminist manifestos based on their "critical appraisal of language" (Colman 2010, 382) and their ability to "provide a new syntax for thinking" (380).

Artists, activists, and students of disability offer a rich archive of such language work, highlighting exclusions and offering examples of how to approach communication otherwise. The new syntax of the "maddened" (Riley 2022), cripped manifesto makes explicit the ableist entanglements of language and power. Consider Lydia X. Z. Brown, E. Ashkenazy, and Morénike Giwa Onaiwu's editorial decisions in compiling *All the Weight of Our Dreams: On Living Racialized Autism*. Brown explains that the editors decided not to "focus on grammar, style, voice, punctuation, capitalization, or spelling, because we want to encourage and highlight all forms of communication, speech, and writing. We are aware that forced conformity to arbitrary standards of 'better' language usage has a violent and oppressive history, especially targeting poor people, those for whom English is not a first language, cognitively disabled people, and uneducated people (which is often related to class, race, and disability)" (Brown 2017, viii–ix). Brown, Ashkenazy, and Onaiwu demonstrate a keen awareness of the myriad ways linguistic norms determine whose experiences are deemed worthy, putting this awareness into practice in the very formation of their text (and their relations to authors). Sins Invalid's 2021 statement on language justice similarly intervenes in these modes of exclusion, radically expanding conceptions of language, communication, and presence:

> There are languages created and used specifically by disabled and Deaf people, as our bodyminds inform our means of expression. We use Augmentative and Alternative Communication (AAC), American Sign Language (ASL), Lengua de Señas Mexicana (LSM), Black American Sign Language (BASL), ProTactile Communication, with and through our trachs and our staccato breathing, through our brain fog and aphasia, through pain and pain meds, through masks and voice amplifiers, through text and videos, through our grunts and moans and sounding our worlds, through blinks and blowing through straws and more ways than we can outline.

In their "Manifesto," the Canaries, a collective of artists with chronic illnesses, note that language is a key site for the denial of their experiences with pain, illness, and disability: "OUR MALFUNCTIONING PARTS ARE SILENCED OR REPLACED WITH APPROXIMATIONS . . . WE SHRINK IN A DISCOURSE THAT DENIES OUR EXPERIENCE AND ITS CAUSES. . . . HOW CAN WE BE LEGIBLE WHEN DOMINANT LANGUAGE EXCLUDES US?" (Canaries 2016, 22; all caps in original).

Given the focus on manifestos as a particularly "crazed" form, I also want to highlight the work of those naming the possibilities of mad methodologies of reading, writing, and thinking that are committed to mad lives (Bruce 2021; Minich 2023). Take, for example, Lindsay Eales's "Loose Leaf" essay, in which she invites readers to "print these pages. Shuffle them. Read" (2016, 59). She describes her essay with the same words critics use to describe manifestos:

"Excess. . . . Non-linear. . . . Disjointed, unformed, messy, hurting, mad" (58), and the essay shifts widely, wildly, across different tonal registers and textual forms. Eales makes apparent how one can issue manifestic invocations while refusing definitive lists of guiding principles or coherent demands. Indeed, the thrust of Eales's essay is a refusal of coherence altogether.

In their 2019 "Queer Crip Mad Manifesta against the Medical Industrial Complex," Lzz Johnk and Sasha A. Khan deploy Leah Lakshmi Piepzna-Samarasinha's formulation of "echotextia, an autistic poetic form where others' words echo in our own and are in conversation" (Piepzna-Samarasinha 2018, 11). Johnk and Khan "disrupt and talk back to psychiatric and medical systems" (2019, 34) by taking in pathologizing language and spitting it back out, differently. They splice together "quotations, paraphrases, and subtext from and of conversations we and loved ones have had with doctors and with each other" in order to "craft coalitional resistance" (29).

If manifestos are intended to refuse capitalist logics of property and propriety, and to exhibit mad, incoherent multiplicities of voice and meaning, then collaborative writing is an essential mode of the crip manifesto; "singular, individual modes of cognition are not enough" (Young 2023, 37) for manifestic work. Writing for/with each other, Mel Y. Chen and I turn to Mia Mingus's (2010) call for "crip solidarity" (and these two paragraphs also appear in Chen's chapter):

> "I want to be with you. If you can't go, then I don't want to go. If we are traveling together, sharing political space together, building political family together, then I want to be with you. I want us to be together." Can we imagine this way of being as a mode of crip authorship? And how might such being make space for more expansive, capacious approaches to collaboration? We learned to wait on each other—for the migraine to lift, the fatigue to ease, the energy to return—as we wrote the introduction to *Crip Genealogies* together (with Eunjung Kim and Julie Avril Minich), in spite of our training to do otherwise.
>
> Inspired by those experiences, we invite an explicit turning toward collaboration and acknowledge the fundamentally collaborative nature of thinking in making that collaboration known. From this perspective, cripping authorship might mean cripping single authorship, even as we recognize that it must not be a cloak indictment: that in fact, single authoring may necessarily be someone else's best and only crip mode. But when single authorship is a proprietary accumulation of intellectual property that should have been shared (which, we note, goes hand in hand with intersectional theft), then it could be seen as "ripping off." Instead, we wonder what possibilities are made by messing with this formula, with unknown risks, erotics, and consequences: "cripping off." While the risks lean toward precarious positions vis-à-vis the academy, we commit to making more and more places where cripping off is imaginable and recognized.

To return to where I started, consider a text that offers wordplay akin to "A Cyborg Manifesto," Pickens's kaleidoscopic, textured, echolalic works of and on Black madness. Unafraid of committing "literary theorist blasphemy," Pickens knows that "get[ting] us to think about how we think when we think about Blackness and madness" requires a profound "distrust of linearity" (2019, 21, xi). She refuses a conclusion, approaches her arguments sideways, embraces messy contradiction, and frequently interrupts herself and her reader. The range of affect the text embraces and fosters is part of Pickens's method. Her footnotes, for example, "are not solely explanations of sources and methodologies, but they also signify, joke, pun, turn a phrase, explore. Both the footnotes and epigraphs are asides, witticisms, and musings," allowing us "to theorize from above and below" (Pickens 2019, xi). If "manifestoes disrupt the assumption of linear progress" (Czerwiec et al. 2015, 3), then the refusal of linearity found in *Black Madness :: Mad Blackness* might mark it as a contribution to the genre.

Given the generative theorizations happening under the name of crip time and disability futurities, the manifesto might be particularly enticing for the possibilities it offers in demanding more just, accountable, and accessible futures. Not only might manifestos offer a kind of crip time in their disruption of linear time, but they also are a site for speculating on what a crip future might be, or do, or allow. As Hill explains, manifestos "can move us toward the futures we desire" by fostering radical "consciousness and collectivity with the express purpose of changing lived conditions" (2019, 7). Other feminist theorists share Hill's position that the manifesto is concerned with naming ongoing oppressions, demanding change in the present, and expanding current conceptualizations of what is possible, thereby naming more just futurities into being (e.g., Ahmed 2017; Fahs 2020; Weiss 2018). As Karma Chávez explains, the imagined futures of the manifesto have effects *now*: "Their very existence is a present political action, a performative gesture that engages and alters the conditions of the public sphere" (2013, 26).

In "Femme Shark Manifesto!," Piepzna-Samarasinha names into existence a radical crip love: "FEMME SHARKS RECOGNIZE THAT FEMMES COME IN ALL KINDS OF SIZES AND EACH KIND IS LUSCIOUS. WE WORK TOWARDS LOVING OUR CURVY, FAT, SKINNY, SUPERSIZE, THICK, DISABLED, BLACK AND BROWN FINE-ASS BODIES EVERY DAY. WE REALIZE THAT LOVING OURSELVES IN A RACIST/SEXIST/HOMO/TRANSPHOBIC/ ABLEIST/ CLASSIST SYSTEM IS AN EVERY DAY ACT OF WAR AGAINST THAT SYSTEM" (2008; all caps in original). Jina B. Kim and Sami Schalk similarly understand crip self-care as "inextricably tied to the lived experiences and temporalities of multiply marginalized people, especially disabled queer people, disabled people of color, and disabled queer people of color," arguing that it points to the possibilities for "self-care outside capitalist imperatives" (2021, 327).

Crip artists Sky Cubacub (2020) and Sandie Yi (2020) have both turned to body adornment as a way to bring this kind of radical crip love into practice; they both center crip fashion as a site of care work. In Yi's framing, "makers follow Crip time: the design ideas do not arrive based on the production speed required by capitalism" but allow for continuous negotiation between maker and wearer; "the production process therefore is a form of providing care." While Yi and Cubacub have each published manifestos about their process, their manifesting exceeds the written word. Their adornments—built for the contours and needs of crip, trans, sick, fat bodies—carry out the mad, crip work of the manifesto, both in the sense of imagining disability otherwise and, perhaps especially, in highlighting the possibilities of nonverbal modes of relation.

Yi (2020) firmly places Crip Couture within disability culture, but she also calls into being a diverse, inclusive crip community: "Crip Couture's creations are based on the agenda and issues identified by people who are Sick (chronically ill), Mad, Autistic, Disabled and Deaf people (S.M.A.D.D.) who are from a diverse range of race, class, and gender identity expressions. Crip Couture also creates room for people who may not have had the opportunity to claim a disability identity or connect to a disability activist community. Crip Couture aims to hold a space for . . . those who are still questioning their disability identity." Sophia Maier, V. Jo Hsu, Christina V. Cedillo, and M. Remi Yergeau issue an even more expansive invitation in their trans, crip "Fractal Many-Festo" (2020), calling in those who are committed to trans disability justice, regardless of identity: "In writing this manifesto, we ask whether you would collaborate with us, whether you would tic with us, whether you would help us to invent and sustain and share trans, crip space. . . . Not because you're trans. Not because you're disabled. But because you share with trans disabled communities a project of world-building. Because you take pleasure in your tics, in your (gender)queerness, in your desire."

Maier, Hsu, Cedillo, and Yergeau's call for solidarity is, in part, a response to transphobic comments made by the editor of *Disability and Society*, Michele Moore, and the essay links to a petition demanding the journal's editorial board take action to affirm trans lives.[3] Their manifesto is one of many crip manifestos directed as much to those *within* disability studies and activism as those outside it; even as they invoke a collective "we," they insistently interrogate the exclusions such unifying language makes possible. Perhaps the most well-known internal critique of disability studies comes from Chris Bell, whose "Introducing White Disability Studies: A Modest Proposal" (2006) offered a searing indictment of the whiteness of the field's founding frameworks; as he noted in the essay—a manifesto in everything but name—his critique built on the earlier manifesto statements of the International and People of Color Caucuses of the Society for Disability Studies, statements that were themselves repeatedly revised and reissued in response to ongoing exclusions, erasures, and marginalization. Ahmed

(2017) suggests that this kind of iterative, recursive process is a necessary part of the feminist manifesto, particularly those manifestos speaking back to racism, imperialism, and white supremacy; she uses her looping wordplay to reveal how we keep coming against the same things, over and over and over again. The work remains undone.

Manifest Failures, Affective Shifts, and Necessary Imaginings

While it is true that I failed to register Haraway's text as a manifesto, manifestos have played a significant role in my scholarly life. For well over a decade I organized part of my Introduction to Feminist Studies course around them. In addition to reading a wide range of manifestos, I asked my students to spend several class periods writing their own feminist manifesto in small groups. The only requirements were that they create something they could share with the class (e.g., a poem, a list of demands, a map, a process) and that each group come to consensus on its own manifesto. The assignment was, in many ways, designed to fail. Despite their best intentions, with every articulation of what they wanted to create or become, they found gaps, unspoken assumptions, a narrowing of perspectives, erasures, and exclusions. Sometimes they recognized these failures in the moment; other students would return to their articulations later in the semester, or later in their studies, and exclaim that they would write a very different manifesto now. Fahs describes such realizations as part of the process: "Good manifestos . . . do not claim to know things *for all time*; they only claim to know things *for this moment*" (2020, 4).

As I tell my students, these very gaps and erasures are exactly what keep me coming back to the manifesto-as-feminist-theory / feminist-theory-as-manifesto, or what continues to fascinate and intrigue me about these forms. The erasures in any given manifesto remind me that I have my own exclusions and, more broadly, they remind me that no single manifesto (or theory, or practice, or formation) can get everything right. Moreover, as queer theory cautions, any naming of what we want always, inevitably, forecloses other articulations or namings. But rather than cast those concerns as condemning the manifesto from the start, might they instead be reasons to keep writing, and rewriting, and rewriting? As José Esteban Muñoz (2009) puts it, we are not yet queer, but there is great possibility in the aspirations of that "yet," and the "we" conjured in such documents is the "we" still to be imagined. The manifesto, he reminds us, is "a call to a doing in and for the future" (26), a place where we can imagine radical crip politics and radiating crip futures. Manifestos, in this queer framing, are relational—formed in relation to this moment—rather than prescriptive; they are about process rather than outcome. Audre Lorde describes this process as "*believing, working for what has not yet been while living fully in the present now*" (2009, 148). In other words, the manifesto—because of its incompleteness and its related promise of more manifestos to come—provides a place to counter the erasure of some bodies from our collective futures, an erasure that makes possible the ongoing evisceration of bodies in the present. As Joshua Chambers-Letson, Tavia Nyong'o, and Ann Pellegrini put it in their gloss of Muñoz, "That hope will be disappointed, and fail us, is not its negation but its condition of possibility" (2019, xiv).

When the editors of the present volume first invited me to reflect on the role of manifestos in my work, I thought that I would use this opportunity to create my own manifesto, to imagine the textures of a more just, accessible, and accountable present, a present and presence that fostered feminist, queer, antiracist, and anti-imperialist practices, one that recognized the importance of crip lives and crip deaths. Or perhaps a manifesto specific to life in Texas in 2021, a manifesto refusing the violence of manufactured power failures, rampant reproductive and trans injustices, voter suppression, anti-immigrant and anti-Black vitriol, and the ableism tangled within each. But I could never get myself to write those pieces, as necessary as I think they are. Instead, I wanted to revel in the crip imaginaries and futurities I've mentioned here, and many, many more. From Akemi Nishida's bed activism to Sunaura Taylor's speculative aquifers to Leroy Moore's Krip-Hop to HEARD's cross-disability abolitionist organizing to whatever it is you are doing right now: all of your everythings continue to carry me through much more than whatever I could create.

But if I'm honest, it's also that the more I read about manifestos as a genre, the less able I felt to write one. Everything I read about manifestos kept telling me that they are to be written quickly, fiercely, with passion and in rage; they are to be written with specific targets and clear agendas and razor-sharp precision. And the more I read these affect imperatives, the more tired, the more slow, the more stuck I felt.

I want to close, then, by returning to this question of what it might mean to take seriously the notion of the manifesto as a mad, crip form. What—and whom—do we exclude when we insist on particular affective modes and responses, especially if under the rubric of crip authorship? Sarah Orem (2021) encourages disability studies scholars to look carefully at the places where the field has failed to feel anger, recognizing that such moments often signal a failure to register the workings of whiteness, and that is certainly part of what I'm wanting here.

I'm also wanting to register the potential for more muted presences (E. Kim 2012) and affects (Chen 2014) to become sites of crip manifesting. I'm drawn to the possibilities of the nonverbal and the nontextual; I want both the excess of language and its absence. Quiet, inward, solo; anxious, worried, depressed; reluctant, uncertain, ambivalent; slow, hesitant, halting: don't the textures of crip lives, disability futurities, and disability justice require a recognition that protest can take many forms (e.g., Burch 2021; Hedva 2016; Nishida 2022)? As Bruce (2021, 236, 11) reminds us, mad methodologies include not only digressions, ramblings, and strikethroughs but also quiet "painstaking study" and "obsessive care," "a deft dance between release and hold, hold and release."

In imagining what this kind of careful interplay can mean, I am reminded of Ellen Samuels quietly writing haikus "in [her] head" while "laying stiffly in the rigid embrace of an MRI machine," "thinking, *how do I get through the next minute, the next hour, week, day, year of this?*" (2021, 69). Samuels's poems do the manifesto work of invocation, reaching out explicitly to "other sick and disabled people, to say: you are not alone. And neither am I" (76). With each silent haiku, Samuels imagines herself in relation, an imagining that not only gets her through the realities of the medical-industrial complex but also carves a crip space of community that exceeds it. Such quiet calling reminds me of the care scores by Park McArthur and Constantina Zavitsanos (2013) and Carolyn Lazard (2015) that guide readers through acts of care and touch between people and texts; *here*, they explain, are ways of being together: follow along, use these steps. Or, in the neuroqueer imaginings of Maier, Hsu, Cedillo, and Yergeau, "obsess with us. Echo with us. Perseverate with us. . . . Manifest with us" (2020).

Those involved in abolition movements have long insisted on the need for radical imaginations, for imagining futures without prisons, without racial capitalism, without carceral logics and practices; abolition requires thinking and acting as if it were possible (e.g., Ben-Moshe 2020; Davis 2003; Kaba 2021). In her "manifesta against U.S. violence and oppression," Caitlin Gunn explains that "a framework of radical speculation enables us to bypass mental hurdles of feasibility, freeing us to accept the challenge of imagining and building the futures we desire" (2019, 16). We cannot stop dreaming simply because we do not yet know how to bring those dreams to fruition.

Eli Clare provides exactly this kind of reminder in his poem "May Day, 2020":

It is time. It is time. It is time

to listen to our grief and soothe our jangled nerves—
we cannot afford to forfeit imagination. (2021, 256)

We cannot afford to forfeit imagination. The poem offers, all at once, a manifesto, an argument for the necessity of manifestos, and an exhortation to create our own. Join me; join us; begin. Manifest again and again and again.

Thanks to all those who have supported this writing, especially Lamiyah Bahrainwala, Susan Burch, Mel Y. Chen, Eunjung Kim, Julie Avril Minich, Dana Newlove, Lisa Olstein, Alexis Riley, Ellen Samuels, and Hershini Young; the editors of this collection, Mara Mills and Rebecca Sanchez; and my Introduction to Feminist Studies students.

NOTES

1 Hill makes a similar move with her inclusion of Lzz Johnk and Sasha Khan's "'Cripping the Fuck Out:' A Queer Crip Mad Manifesta against the Medical Industrial Complex" (2019) in her special issue. Both Fahs and Hill are unusual here, in that many manifesto collections draw on the language of madness without any attention to health care inequities, the role of psychiatry in carceral logics, or the experiences of people with mental illnesses, disabilities, and/or diagnoses.

2 As Bettina Judd wryly, furiously notes, "I have to make this point perfectly clear: Black women are no angrier than any other group of people. I'm pissed that I even have to tell you this" (180).

3 As of this writing, the petition is still accepting signatures: https://www.ipetitions.com/petition/ds.

BIBLIOGRAPHY

Ahmed, Sara. 2017. *Living a Feminist Life*. Durham, NC: Duke University Press.

Alvarez, Natalie, and Jenn Stephenson. 2012. "A Manifesto for Manifestos." *Canadian Theatre Review* 150 (Spring): 3–7.

Bahrainwala, Lamiyah. 2019. "Responding to 'White Fragility': A Manifesta of Screams." *Feral Feminisms*, no. 9 (Fall): 21–25.

Bailey, Moya, and Izetta Autumn Mobley. 2019. "Work in the Intersections: A Black Feminist Disability Framework." *Gender and Society* 33 (1): 19–40.

Bell, Chris. 2006. "Introducing White Disability Studies: A Modest Proposal." In *The Disability Studies Reader*, 2nd ed., edited by Lennard Davis, 275–282. New York: Routledge.

Ben-Moshe, Liat. 2020. *Decarcerating Disability: Deinstitutionalization and Prison Abolition*. Minneapolis: University of Minnesota Press.

Boys, Jos. 2020. "A (Little) Manifesto for Doing Dis/ability Differently in Architecture." *Journal of Architectural Education* 74 (2): 170–172.

Brown, Lydia X. Z. 2017. "A Note on Process." In *All the Weight of Our Dreams: On Living Racialized Autism*, edited by Lydia X. Z. Brown, E. Ashkenazy, and Morénike Giwa Onaiwu, viii–ix. Lincoln, NE: DragonBee.

Bruce, La Marr Jurelle. 2021. *How to Go Mad without Losing Your Mind: Madness and Black Radical Creativity*. Durham, NC: Duke University Press.

Burch, Susan. 2021. *Committed: Remembering Native Kinship in and beyond Institutions*. Chapel Hill: University of North Carolina Press, 2021.

Canaries. 2016. "Canaries Manifesto." In *Notes for the Waiting Room*, edited by Taraneh Fazeli, 22: n.p.

Caws, Mary Ann. 2001. "The Poetics of the Manifesto: Nowness and Newness." In *Manifesto: A Century of Isms*, xix–xxxi. Lincoln: University of Nebraska Press.

Chambers-Letson, Joshua, Tavia Nyong'o, and Ann Pellegrini. 2019. "Foreword: Before and After." In *Cruising Utopia: The Then and There of Queer Futurity*, by José Esteban Muñoz, ix–xvi. 10th anniversary ed. New York: New York University Press.

Chávez, Karma R. 2013. "Differential Visions of Queer Migration Manifestos." In *Queer Migration Politics: Activist Rhetoric and Coalitional Possibilities*, 21–48. Urbana: University of Illinois Press.

Chen, Mel Y. 2014. "Brain Fog: The Race for Cripistemology." *Journal of Literary and Cultural Disability Studies* 8 (2): 171–184.

Clare, Eli. 2021. "May Day, 2020." *South Atlantic Quarterly* 120 (2): 255–256.

Colman, Felicity. 2010. "Notes on the Feminist Manifesto: The Strategic Use of Hope." *Journal for Cultural Research* 14 (4): 375–392.

Cubacub, Sky. 2020. "Radical Visibility: A Disabled Queer Clothing Reform Movement Manifesto." In *Disability Visibility: First-Person Stories from the Twenty-First Century*, edited by Alice Wong, 90–100. New York: Vintage.

Czerwiec, M. K., Ian Williams, Susan Merrill Squier, Michael J. Green, Kimberly R. Myers, and Scott T. Smith. 2015. Introduction to *Graphic Medicine Manifesto*, 1–20. University Park: Pennsylvania State University Press.

Davis, Angela. 2003. *Are Prisons Obsolete?* New York: Seven Stories Press.

Eales, Lindsay. 2016. "Loose Leaf." *Canadian Journal of Disability Studies* 5 (3): 58–76.

Fahs, Breanne. 2020. "Introduction: The Bleeding Edge: On the Necessity of Feminist Manifestos." In *Burn It Down! Feminist Manifestos for the Revolution*, edited by Breanne Fahs, 1–21. New York: Verso.

Gunn, Caitlin. 2019. "Black Feminist Futurity: From Survival Rhetoric to Radical Speculation." *Feral Feminisms*, no. 9 (Fall): 15–20.

Hamraie, Aimi. 2017. *Building Access: Universal Design and the Politics of Disability*. Minneapolis: University of Minnesota Press.

Hamraie, Aimi, and Kelly Fritsch. 2019. "Crip Technoscience Manifesto." *Catalyst: Feminism, Theory, Technoscience* 5 (1). https://catalystjournal.org/index.php/catalyst/article/view/29607/.

Haraway, Donna J. 1991. "A Cyborg Manifesto: Science, Technology, and Socialist-Feminism in the Late Twentieth Century." In *Simians, Cyborgs, and Women: The Reinvention of Nature*, 149–182. New York: Routledge.

Hedva, Johanna. 2016. "Sick Woman Theory." *Mask Magazine*. http://www.maskmagazine.com/not-again/struggle/sick-woman-theory.

Hill, Annie. 2019. "Introduction: State Killing: Queer and Women of Color Manifestas against U.S. Violence and Oppression." *Feral Feminisms*, no. 9 (Fall): 5–11.

Johnk, Lzz, and Sasha A. Khan. 2019. "'Cripping the Fuck Out': A Queer Crip Mad Manifesta against the Medical Industrial Complex." *Feral Feminisms*, no. 9 (Fall): 26–38.

Judd, Bettina. 2019. "Sapphire as Praxis: Toward a Methodology of Anger." *Feminist Studies* 45 (1): 178–208.

Kaba, Mariame. 2021. *We Do This 'Til We Free Us: Abolitionist Organizing and Transforming Justice*. Edited by Tamara K. Nopper. Chicago: Haymarket.

Kim, Eunjung. 2012. "Why Do Dolls Die? The Power of Passivity and the Embodied Interplay between Disability and Sex Dolls." *Review of Education, Pedagogy, and Cultural Studies* 34 (3–4): 94–106.

Kim, Jina B., and Sami Schalk. 2021. "Reclaiming the Radical Politics of Self-Care: A Crip-of-Color Critique." *South Atlantic Quarterly* 120 (2): 325–342.

Lazard, Carolyn. 2016. "Score for Patient Interaction." In *Notes for the Waiting Room*, edited by Taraneh Fazeli. digigiid.ee/en/exhibitions-archive/disarming-language/canaries-2.

Lazard, Carolyn. 2019. "Accessibility in the Arts: A Promise and a Practice." Philadelphia: Recess Art / Common Field.

Lorde, Audre. 2009. "A Burst of Light: Living with Cancer." In *I Am Your Sister: Collected and Unpublished Writings of Audre Lorde*, edited by Rudolph P. Byrd, Johnnetta B. Cole, and Beverly Guy-Sheftall, 81–149. New York: Oxford University Press.

Lyon, Janet. 1999. *Manifestoes: Provocations of the Modern*. Ithaca, NY: Cornell University Press.

McArthur, Park, and Constantina Zavitsanos. 2013. "Other Forms of Conviviality." *Women and Performance* 23 (1): 126–32.

Maier, Sophia, V. Jo Hsu, Christina V. Cedillo, and M. Remi Yergeau. 2020. "GET THE FRAC IN! Or, The Fractal Many-Festo: A (Trans)(crip)t." *Peitho* 22 (4). https://cfshrc.org/article/get-the-frac-in-or-the-fractal-many-festo-a-transcript/.

Mingus, Mia. 2010. "Wherever You Are Is Where I Want to Be: Crip Solidarity." *Leaving Evidence* (blog), May 3, 2010. https://leavingevidence.wordpress.com/2010/05/03/where-ever-you-are -is-where-i-want-to-be-crip-solidarity/.

Minich, Julie Avril. 2023. *Radical Health: Justice, Care, and Latinx Expressive Culture*. Durham: Duke University Press.

Muñoz, José Esteban. 2009. *Cruising Utopia: The Then and There of Queer Futurity*. New York: New York University Press.

Nishida, Akemi. 2022. *Just Care: Messy Entanglements of Disability, Dependency, and Desire*. Philadelphia: Temple University Press.

Orem, Sarah. 2021. "Tangles of Resentment." *Signs: Journal of Women in Culture and Society* 46 (4): 963–985.

Papalia, Carmen. 2018. "An Accessibility Manifesto for the Arts." As told to Caoimhe Morgan-Feir. *Canadianart* (blog), January 2, 2018. https://canadianart.ca/essays/access-revived/.

Pickens, Therí Alyce. 2016. "The Verb Is No: Towards a Grammar of Black Women's Anger." *CLA Journal* 60 (1): 15–31.

Pickens, Therí Alyce. 2019. *Black Madness :: Mad Blackness*. Durham, NC: Duke University Press.

Piepzna-Samarasinha, Leah Lakshmi. 2008. "Femme Shark Manifesto!" Leah Lakshmi Piepzna-Samarasinha's website. https://brownstargirl.org/femme-shark-manifesto/.

Piepzna-Samarasinha, Leah Lakshmi. 2018. *Care Work: Dreaming Disability Justice*. Vancouver, Canada: Arsenal Pulp.

Price, Margaret. 2021. "Time Harms: Disabled Faculty Navigating the Accommodations Loop." *South Atlantic Quarterly* 120 (2): 257–277.

Riley, Alexis. 2022. *Patient Acts: Performance, Disability, and the Making of Mad Memory*. [Unpublished doctoral dissertation] University of Texas.

Samuels, Ellen. 2021. *Hypermobilities: Poems*. Brooklyn, NY: Operating System.

Sheppard, Alice. n.d. "Intersectional Disability Arts Manifesto." https://alicesheppard.com /intersectional-disability-arts-manifesto/.

Sins Invalid. 2015. "10 Principles of Disability Justice." *Sins Invalid: An Unshamed Claim to Beauty in the Face of Invisibility* (blog), September 17, 2015. https://www.sinsinvalid.org/blog/10 -principles-of-disability-justice.

Sins Invalid. 2021. "La justicia de lenguaje es justicia para personas con discapacidades / Language Justice Is Disability Justice." *Sins Invalid: An Unshamed Claim to Beauty in the Face of Invisibility* (blog), June 8, 2021. https://www.sinsinvalid.org/news-1/2021/6/8/la-justicia-de-lenguaje -es-justicia-para-personas-con-discapacidadeslanguage-justice-is-disability-justice.

Weiss, Penny A. 2018. *Feminist Manifestos: A Global Documentary Reader*. New York: New York University Press.

Yi, Chun-shan (Sandie). 2020. "The Crip Couture Manifesto." *Wordgathering* 14 (4). https:// wordgathering.com/vol14/issue4/disability-futures/yi/.

Young, Hershini Bhana. 2023. *Falling, Floating, Flickering: Disability and Differential Movement in African Diasporic Performance*. New York: New York University Press.

18

Public Scholarship as Disability Justice

JAIPREET VIRDI

We each become the protagonists of our stories of change and transformation.
—Judithe Registre (2018)

Public scholarship is, quite simply, scholarship for the public. It appears as different forms of engagement—blogs, social media posts, vlogs, websites, podcasts, museums, documentaries, op-eds, lectures, essays, activism, exhibits, television, and so on—and is predicated on making knowledge accessible to the public. It bridges academic expertise with public consciousness, circulating in spaces that are easily understood and available to address publicly identified needs. Public scholarship has always existed, but it has become an integral aspect of academic discourse over the past twenty-five years as researchers build relationships with their communities through social justice (Leavy 2019; Badgett 2015; Dodd and Garland-Thomson, 2013; Nightingale 2013; Gonzales 2019; Cann and DeMeulenaere 2020). As Adrianna Kezar, Yianna Drivalas, and Joseph Kitchen emphasize, "Public scholarship is connected and closely related to the words *diverse democracy, equity,* and *social justice*" (2018, 4).

If public scholarship is centrally about making knowledge accessible, then what does it mean for it to act as disability justice? That is, if justice is the "first virtue of social institutions," as philosopher John Rawls (1999 [1971], 3) declared, then how do we continuously ensure that disabled people, their lives, and their histories are represented in spaces that are made accessible to them? How can academics researching and writing about disability history democratically engage with disabled communities? Public history, a subset of public scholarship, affords such an opportunity: as citizens and scholars, historians possess responsibility for disseminating knowledge, clarifying past narratives and concepts, and preserving primary sources and factual analysis (Cauvin 2016). Digital spaces have especially provided tools for reaching a wider range of audiences, including those—such as disabled people—who tend to be excluded from academic institutions or restricted from obtaining historical resources on account of inaccessibility.[1] Moreover, the historical marginalization and silence, if not absence, of disabled people in the archive has prompted scholars to rethink "the archive" itself and how historical materials are collected and categorized. "Cripping the archive" not only prompts a critical reexamination of how ableness informs the politics of archives, it also presents multiple perspectives for evaluating the temporal, spatial, and material constructions of disability.[2]

Public scholarship, then, allows us to reimagine our audience and assumptions about what counts as "academic" scholarship. When I was a graduate student, I launched a blog to share aspects of my research on nineteenth-century cultural histories of deafness and medicine. Promoting the blog required crossposting on social media, not just the posts but also interesting tidbits I learned while browsing digitized collections for materials or searching for related historical images. As I tracked the engagements and blog statistics, I learned that most followers of my content were not academics—as I believed—but curious general readers, some of whom were deaf and eager to learn about their shared medical past. This forced me to confront my own assumptions about how academic scholarship can exclude the very people whose histories are being examined and exposed.

Sharing images with brief context soon became a form of engagement, a way to educate the public on historical aspects of diseases, vaccination, medical advancements, and cultural frameworks of health and healing. As with all forms of curation, this also became an ethical process. While some historical images can be fun and quirky, or informative, others require more nuanced and sensitive oversight to avoid being sensationalized or decontextualized. This becomes more crucial when we address the implications of *looking* at pictures of people's suffering and diseased bodies: Do we learn anything more? Is it appropriate? Is it meant to shock or discomfort the viewer?

Suzannah Biernoff (2017) has addressed the troubling liaison between medicine and art, focusing on photographs of plastic surgeon Harold Gillies's World War I patients with severe facial injuries. With the images in the public domain, Biernoff questions what the new frontiers of visuality will be when they are appropriated for public consumption without historical context. Medical images especially tend to become "an ethical borderland in which legal definitions of privacy, personhood, and human rights compete with the contemporary politics of witnessing, memory, and memorialization; a space of fantasy where fascination and aversion are found in equal measure" (Biernoff 2017, 169).

"What do we gain for seeing images like these?" Biernoff (2012, 187) asks. What do we gain by viewing suffering, especially when perceived through a medicalized gaze? And how do we, as historians, connect objectivity and historical value with the tendency for sentimentality and spectacle, which can become problematic? I confess that I, too, have made errors in judgment when sharing shocking images of medical injuries or disfigured bodies, unaware of how they could be read differently. These are images that can be fascinating and appealing to the medically curious, but they also continue to propagate freakery, a concept that has long served to diminish the value of disabled people.

We nevertheless still stare in astonishment, sustaining our gaze—sometimes in wonderment, other times in befuddlement. Staring, as Rosemarie Garland Thomson explains, is a "vivid form of human communication," one that is "an embodied and relational visual exchange that carries complex cultural and historical meanings" (2005, n.p). Nowhere is this embodiment so vivid as in discussions of disabled, disfigured, or deformed bodies, the histories of people whose perceived abnormality invited the medical gaze. But in the process of creating, viewing, categorizing, and exhibiting a "freak"—even if it offers academics avenues for theorizing how disability fits within medical history—we strip disabled people of control over their own narratives. We remove their agency, reduce their personhood to mere object of curiosity, and erase their lived experiences.

What happens, then, when we return autonomy to disabled people and center their stories? That is what disabled activist Alice Wong set out to do with the Disability Visibility Project (DVP), which launched in 2014 in partnership with StoryCorps. An online community dedicated to creating, sharing, and amplifying disability media and culture, DVP is written by disabled people, based on the notion that "disabled narratives matter and that they belong to us" (Disability Visibility Project, 2021).[3] Championing disability culture, history, art, media, and politics, DVP organizes and facilitates events and work by disabled people through blog posts by guest writers, oral history interviews, and social media promotion and hashtags. In 2017 DVP expanded to include a podcast, and an anthology, *Disability Visibility: First-Person Stories from the Twenty-First Century*, was published in 2020 (Wong 2020). The podcast was archived following its 100th episode in April 2021.

Wong's achievements in publicizing DVP demonstrate how narratives are crucial in the formation of identity creation and transformation, particularly for justice-based activism and politics. As David Engel and Frank Munger argue, "Perceptions of who one is and where one belongs in relation to others play a critical role in determining whether rights are understood as relevant" (2007, 86). Using life-story narratives becomes a powerful approach for conveying how individual experiences of disability can construct meaningful understandings for policy, such as how American disabled activists used their narratives—and especially bodies—to show the public how social and environmental barriers prevented their full inclusion into society and eventually led to the passage of the Americans with Disabilities Act (ADA) in 1990 (Pelka, 2012). These narratives add to the richness of our collective cultural heritage, but the struggles were not erased the moment that the ADA was signed into law. The "ADA Generation," a term coined by disability activist Rebecca Cokley, defines the first generation of disabled advocates who grew up at the intersections of disability rights legislation, "expecting its rights but also [finding] resentment instead—propelling a need to keep pushing back" (Shaprio, 2020). They are the people who work to "bend the arc of justice into a ramp" (Cokley, 2018). For them, disability is identity and pride. For disabled people of color like Wong, moreover, narratives position them in cultural discourses in which they have long been left on the sidelines (Wong, 2015).

Judithe Registre (2018) proclaims that narrative justice is a new era of advocacy, one that forms "the creation of a cultural awakening that seeks to shift representation, voice, and agency." Redefining the gatekeepers of scholarly knowledge and making space for the marginalized who have long been shunned from avenues of power enables us to dismantle existing power structures and social inequities. This includes citational justice, which acknowledges the inequities and power imbalances in the way work is credited and appropriated as a resistance to unethical hierarchies of knowledge production (#CiteBlack-Women is an example).[4] For we cannot achieve social justice when people are silenced: "Their own experiences and stories are never allowed to speak, never fully understood to self and others, and never connected with others to form allies and solidarity for social justice" (Lee and Johnstone 2021, 725). Narratives, then, lay the groundwork for justice. They use the power of the word enriched with emotion—written, spoken, articulated—to shape the necessary change for justice by cultivating resistance to oppression.[5]

For disability advocacy more specifically, narrative justice can serve as a form of affirmation: it ensures that disability narratives and disabled people are not erased in stories about them, and it presents their lived experiences as celebratory joy and individual experience, rather than the usual tale of trauma and overcoming. Moreover, it is imperative that these stories are made accessible to disabled people as well—these are *their* as well as *our* histories and experiences, after all, and providing access serves to both inform and confirm these narratives. Anthology collections like *Disability Visibility*, *About Us* (Catapano and Garland-Thomson, 2019), and *Resistance and Hope* (Wong, 2018) further outline the variability of human experience and the value of learning from disabled people themselves—echoing the community's long-standing slogan, "Nothing about us without us." And I believe narrative justice through essay writing becomes all the more crucial for addressing misinformation or for contextualizing social issues that could benefit from a disability perspective.

It is at this juncture that a bridge is needed between academic scholarship and public history: by making theoretical and historical writing accessible for general readers, we can dismantle barriers that prevent disabled people from accessing knowledge about their social, cultural, and political histories. Several institutional initiatives have achieved this with exhibitions on disability histories: Ryerson University's traveling exhibit *Out from Under: Disability, History, and Things to Remember*; Nineteenth-Century Disability: Cultures & Contexts, an online primary source repository; and the Disability History Museum, a virtual project with over three thousand primary sources, as well as exhibits in traditional brick-and-mortar museums such as the Smithsonian National Museum of

American History's *EveryBody: An Artefact History of Disability* (Virdi, 2020).[6] Yet as evident with DVP and the growth of public scholarship, public history has outgrown its traditional associations with museums and journalism, especially given issues of inaccessibility arising from physical and institutional barriers.[7]

That is, public history goes beyond simply writing or creating exhibits for a public audience. It demonstrates the past matters as more than historical memory—it is a tool for explaining how and why our societies are the way they are, and for better understanding the structural inequities that commemorate the "victors" and distort the experiences of the colonized and oppressed. Or, as Robert Kelly explains in his classic essay, the historian's perceptive is crucial, for "the historian has a special way of looking at human affairs, and a special way of explaining them" (1978, 16). As a historian of medicine and disability with a prominent social media platform, I especially feel the burden to address issues of public health, vaccination, ableism, and medical racism, issues that are structurally imbedded in our society and regularly used to convey misinformation. Yet I believe that historians—all specialists, but especially those studying disability history—have a responsibility to ensure their work is accessible outside the academy.

Public scholarship, then, can act as a form of activism for disability justice. Through Wong, I learned of Tressie McMillan Cottom's assertion that "the best essays build a public thought process and form," by which essay writing becomes an activist tool (Wong, 2022, xv).[8] For example, in February 2021, Nike announced its "hands-free" Go FlyEase sneaker, which was quickly praised for its accessibility features. Observing that the initial announcement failed to acknowledge the history of the FlyEase's collaboration with disabled people, I posted a tweet identifying the need to acknowledge and celebrate disability design, a point that I regularly incorporate in my own scholarship and teaching.[9] The tweet went viral, with 18.5 million impressions, but the responses nevertheless still failed to address that a shoe that was clearly designed for disabled people ended up erasing their participation. In partnership with disabled advocate and designer Liz Jackson, I wrote an essay for *Future+Tense* (a subsidiary of *Slate*) emphasizing the importance of marketing products to disabled people beyond tokenistic representation or inspiration. "And if we've learned one thing as disabled design critics," we emphasized, "it is that stories inform the way we design" (Virdi and Jackson, 2021).[10]

Jackson and I created an important discourse with our essay: marketing products to disabled consumers while erasing them is not a new phenomenon or entirely Nike's fault but rather part of a legacy of capitalism that tends to undervalue disabled people's full participation and inclusion in society. Positioning disabled people at the center of their own narratives—or better, making space for them to tell their own stories—affords us perspectives for better understanding the spectrum of human experience, especially that of disabled people of color and colonized people whose places in history have been written over, if not completely ignored.

Public scholarship, and public history, provides us with powerful tools to demonstrate the ways disability history matters. It reaches beyond the academy to the public directly, informs equitable museum and archive practices, intervenes into design process, and above all demonstrates the importance of representation. It is important for academic writing to be accessible to the people who are being written about, and moreover, as historians, we have a responsibility—perhaps now more than ever—to explain our collective past and clarify concepts. With public history, we can better understand the world we live in and incorporate a diversity of perspectives in order to create a more just and inclusive vision for ourselves, what Alison Kafer (2013, 24) terms "crip futurity": a longing for a future in which the collective knowledge and practices of disabled people shape all aspects of society.

NOTES

1 Angela Gallagher, "Archives and the Road to Accessibility," *Perspectives on History* (15 July 2019).
2 The concept of "Cripping the Archive" is the subject of Jenifer Barclay and Stefanie Hunt-Kennedy's forthcoming edited collection, *Cripping the Archive: Disability, Power, and History*.
3 Disability Visibility Project, "About." accessed August 30, 2021. https://disabilityvisibilityproject.com/about/ .
4 Diana Kwon, "The Rise of Citational Justice: How Scholars are Making References Fairer," *Nature* (22 March 2022).
5 Geeta Tewari, "Regarding Narrative Justice, Womxn," *Michigan Journal of Race and Law* 25 (2019): 61–75; Rafe McGregor, *Narrative Justice* (London: Rowman and Littlefield International, 2018).
6 *Out From Under* (www.ryerson.ca/ofu); *Nineteenth-Century Disability* (www.nineteenthcenturydisability.org); *Disability History Museum* (www.disabilitymuseum.org); *EveryBody* (www.everybody.si.edu). For more on digital exhibits and disability history, see: Jaipreet Virdi, "Materializing User Identities & Digital Humanities," in *Making Disability Modern: Design Histories*, Bess Williamson and Elizabeth Guffey editors (New York, NY: Bloomsbury, 2020), 225–241.
7 Alex Marshall, "Is this the World's Most Accessible Museum?" *New York Times*. September 11, 2019.
8 Tressie McMillian Cottom, "Why I am Building This Community," essaying (24 February 2021).
9 Jaipreet Virdi, "Disability Design for the Win!" Twitter Post, 1 February 2021, 3:02 pm. https://twitter.com/jaivirdi/status/1356332028212477952?s=20.
10 Jaipreet Virdi and Liz Jackson, "Why Won't Nike Use the Word Disabled to Promote Its New Go FlyEase Shoe?" Slate/Future Tense, 5February 5, 2021. The essay received over 115,000 page views. Our warning that the sneaker would be financially inaccessible for the consumers that need them the most realized a few months later as the initial limited release sold out and the once-priced at $120 sneakers were being listed online for upwards of $2,000. Despite criticism, as of October 2021, Nike has still not listed the new Go FlyEase on its website.

BIBLIOGRAPHY

Badgett, M.V. Lee. 2015. *The Public Professor: How to Use Your Research to Change the World.* New York: New York University Press.

Biernoff, Suzannah. 2012. "Medical Archives and Digital Culture." *Photographies,* 5 (2): 179–202.

Biernoff, Suzannah. 2017. *Portraits of Violence: War and the Aesthetics of Disfigurement.* Ann Arbor: University of Michigan Press.

Cann, Colette, and Eric DeMeulenaere. 2020. *The Activist Academic: Engaged Scholarship for Resistance, Hope, and Social Change.* Gorham: Myers Education Press.

Catapano, Peter, and Rosemarie Garland-Thomson, editors. 2019. *About Us: Essays from the Disability Series of the New York Times.* New York: Liveright Publishing.

Cauvin, Thomas. 2016. *Public History: A Textbook of Practice.* New York: Routledge.

Cokley, Rebecca. 2018. "Reflections from an ADA Generation." TEDx, University of Rochester, July 25, 2018.

Disability Visibility Project. 2021. "About," accessed 30 August 2021. https://disabilityvisibility project.com/about/.

Dodd, Jocelyn and Rosemarie Garland-Thomson. 2013. *Re-Presenting Disability: Activism and Agency in the Museum.* New York: Taylor & Francis.

Engel, David M., and Frank W. Munger. 2007. "Narrative, Disability, and Identity." *Narrative,* 15 (1): 85–94.

Garland-Thomson, Rosemarie. 2005. "Staring at the Other." *Disability Studies Quarterly,* 25 (4).

Gonzales, Elena. 2019. *Exhibitions for Social Justice.* New York: Taylor & Francis.

Kafer, Alison. 2013. *Feminist, Queer, Crip.* Bloomington: Indiana University Press.

Kelly, Robert. 1978. "Public History: Its Origins, Nature, and Prospects." *The Public Historian* 1 (1): 16–28.

Kezar, Adrianna, Yianna Drivalas, and Joseph S. Kitchen, editors. 2018. *Envisioning Public Scholarship for our Time: Models for Higher Education.* Sterling: Stylus Publishing.

Leavy, Patricia, editor. 2019. *The Oxford Handbook for Methods of Public Scholarship.* New York: Oxford University Press.

Lee, Eunjung and Marjorie Johnstone. 2021. "Resisting Politics of Authoritarian Populism during COVID-19, Reclaiming Democracy and Narrative Justice: Centering Critical Thinking in Social Work." *International Social Work,* 64 (5): 716–730.

Nightingale, Eithne. 2013. *Museums, Equality and Social Justice.* New York: Taylor & Francis.

Pelka, Fred. 2012. *What We Have Done: An Oral History of the Disability Rights Movement.* Amherst: University of Massachusetts Press.

Rawls, John. 1999 [1971]. *A Theory of Justice.* Cambridge: Belknap Press.

Registre, Judithe. 2018. "Why Narrative Justice is the Next Frontier for Social Change." *Inclusivus.* February 27, 2018. https://inclusivus.org/inpowered-perspectives/2018/2/27/why-narrative -justice-is-the-next-frontier-for-social-change.

Shapiro, Joseph. 2020. "Disability Pride: The High Expectations of a New Generation." *New York Times,* July 17, 2020.

Virdi, Jaipreet. 2020. "Materializing User Identities & Digital Humanities." *Making Disability Modern: Design Histories.* Bess Williamson and Elizabeth Guffey, editors. New York: Bloomsbury, 225–241.

Virdi, Jaipreet and Jackson, Liz. 2021. "Why Won't Nike Use the Word *Disabled* to Promote its New Go FlyEase Shoe?" *Slate/Future Tense,* February 5, 2021. https://slate.com/technology /2021/02/nike-go-flyease-shoe-disabled-design.html.

Wong, Alice. 2022. *Year of the Tiger: An Activist's Life.* New York: Vintage.

Wong, Alice, editor. 2020. *Disability Visibility: First-Person Stories from the Twenty-First Century.* New York: Vintage.

Wong, Alice, ed. 2018. *Resistance & Hope: Essays by Disabled People.* Disability Visibility Project.

Wong, Alice. 2015. "Telling Our Stories: Why I Launched the Disability Visibility Project." *Talk Poverty.* July 30, 2015. https://talkpoverty.org/2015/07/30/telling-stories-people-with -disabilities/.

19

Twenty-Seven Ways of Looking at Crip Autotheory

ELLEN SAMUELS

1. Autotheory is "work that engages in thinking about the self, the body, and the particularities and peculiarities of one's lived experiences, as processed through or juxtaposed against theory—or as the basis for theoretical thinking."[1] This emerging genre "takes one's embodied experiences as a primary text or raw material through which to theorize, process, and reiterate theory to feminist effects."[2] Autotheoretical writing presents "the lives [it] chronicle[s] as deeply enmeshed in other lives and in history, in power relations that operate on multiple levels simultaneously."[3]

2. There is no theory of autotheory that does not start with the ill and disabled bodymind. There is no theory of autotheory that is not already crip.

3. Is the opposite of life writing death writing? The theoretical term *necropolitics* crashed into the mainstream in the past two years, spreading its wide wings across a sky streaked with the colors of white-walled, overflowing ICUs and the deep crimson of Black blood staining the streets.[4]

Like many, I struggled with how to write during this time, how to make any sense of the world collapsing around us, what use my words could be to anyone, even myself.

4. I asked myself, is this autotheory? Is the real meaning of autotheory the attempt of the self to find meaning? And if I who am writing it is sick, disabled, crip, does that make this crip autotheory?

5. Like my invalid forbear Florence Nightingale, I took up my lamp and went in search of critical or craft writing about disability autotheory. To my great surprise, I found none.

6. I stopped to rest and strap on my wrist brace. Then I set off again, lamp held high, in search of the meaning of autotheory. I needed, I still need, to know if what I am doing is what this is.

Or do I?

7. My autonomic nervous system is slowly failing, my body forgetting the unconscious essential work of heartbeat and blood flow, digestion and sweat. I could write a hundred, a thousand metaphors out of this ragged collapse. None will help me as much as two liters of normal saline run intravenously over an hour. Theory has its limits. Words fail me.

8. *Autoimmune:* Allergic to self, the immune system attacks the body, mistaking it for an enemy.

Autonomic: Involuntary or unconscious, what the body does without us telling it to.

Autotheory: There is no body without mind or mind without body.[5]

Crip autotheory: Bodymind, mindbody, when have we ever drawn those lines?

9. It's disappointing, in 2022, to read thoughtful, informed, deep dives into autotheory that cannot conceive of, that do not bother to include, disability as a relevant category of analysis, one that must be theorized, one with its own bodies of knowledge, its communities, its politics, its *theories.*[6]

10. It's exhausting, in 2022, to read published, influential deep dives into autotheory that use disabled people's narratives and lives as their starting point, their raison d'être, their prime examples—Johanna Hedva's "Sick Woman Theory" (2020), for example—and still cannot seem to conceive of disability as a category of analysis in its own right.[7]

11. I think I have a name for this type of feminist theorizing, that which proceeds as if there had not been a quarter century of bold and brilliant crip interventions into feminist intellectual and political work.[8] I think we should call it Well Woman Theory.

12. I could not find a single published article on the topic of disability and autotheory, not one, only the unpublished but brilliant work of Iseult Gillespie (2022), a graduate student in my own department.[9]

13. It's not as simple as saying we are left out. We are not even marginalized. We are there at the very center, the heart of this work, but only as objects, never as subjects with the right to theorize our own experience, to be the authors of our own autotheory.

I think that is rather ironic.

14. But enough of these cantankerous musings. As I said, they're exhausting and I'm always already exhausted.

Maybe that's why autotheory appeals. Many days I can't even get out of bed. I have no tales to tell of where I go, what I do. The story of my life is the story of my thoughts.

15. Wait, stop, that's not what autotheory is. Autotheory is "a practice of the self that works to undo it: to write an ethics of self-unsaying in the end times generated by the Anthropocene."[10] Autotheory "offers a mode of resituating the subject within and against legitimated modes of knowledge production in solidarity with coalitional politics."[11]

16. Q: When is an autobiography not a theory?

A: When it is of no use.

17. Q: When is a theory not an autobiography?

A: When it has no heart.

18. Autotheory sometimes contains or intersects with, yet is also more than, autobiography, memoir, *testimonio*, diary, confessional, blog—all the forms we sometimes gather together under the genre of "life writing."[12] But how is it different or distinct from those broad and long-storied categories?

19. Many would cite two foundational recent texts, Maggie Nelson's 2015 *Argonauts* and Paul Preciado's 2013 *Testo Junkie*, as the ur-moments of contemporary autotheory. Nelson popularized the term, reflecting that she was "always looking for terms that are not 'memoir' to describe autobiographical writing that exceeds the bounds of the 'personal.'"[13]

But does autotheory weave together theory and personal experience, or does it make theory out of personal experience, thus redefining what we mean by theory . . . or experience . . . or person?

20. The importance of this question, I think, is not merely of genre or form, or even the effects of genre and form. It is about purpose and history. It is common in the (mostly white) writing about (mostly white) autotheory to at least acknowledge its deep roots in the writings of feminists of color, such as Audre Lorde, Gloria Anzaldúa, and Cherríe Moraga. But such mentions are usually brief, almost perfunctory, before the analytical and appreciative eye turns back to Nelson, Preciado, and other white authors.[14]

21. Exceptions occur, of course, and are important: Lauren Fournier's discussion of a number of Black and Indigenous artists in her 2021 book *Autotheory as Feminist Practice*, Kyle Frisina's 2020 analysis of Claudia Rankine's *Citizen*, So Mayer's brilliant 2018 exploration of racialized gaps and co-optations in Nelson's *Argonauts*. The special issue of *ASAP/Journal* on autotheory that appeared just as I was finishing this chapter notably centers "historically marginalized perspectives on autotheory, dialoguing across Black, Indigenous (Plains Cree, Métis), Asian American, Chicanx, and Mestizx epistemologies."[15]

But in many ways, how autotheory has been theorized as a form or genre continues to center whiteness and a particularly white genealogy and definition of what theory is and does.

A different genealogy for autotheory, especially crip autotheory, needs to do some of the similar excavation and braiding work that Michael Hames-García (2011) does in his crucial revisionary history of queer theory, creating a timeline that integrates the crucial work of queer women of color like Lorde, Anzaldúa, and the members of the Combahee River Collective with that of queer theory's canonized white scholars like Judith Butler and Michel Foucault.[16]

22. This work is not only genealogical but also crucially requires a reconceptualization of the auto/theory relationship: when we look at the feminist- and queer-of-color roots of autotheory, we see that those authors are not intertwining theory with experience so much as alchemizing experience into new theories, those necessary to understand and represent their own experiences.

"That self-connection shared," wrote Lorde in 1978, "is a measure of the joy which I know myself to be capable of feeling, a reminder of my capacity for feeling. And that deep and irreplaceable knowledge of my capacity for joy comes to demand from all of my life that it be lived within the knowledge that such satisfaction is possible, and does not have be called *marriage*, nor *god*, nor *an afterlife*."[17]

What is needed is not merely more sustained citation of and critical attention to works such as Lorde's, but an integration and transformation of how the genre and form of autotheory are defined, deployed, and potentiated in service of multiple liberations.

23. The recent *ASAP/Journal* special issue laudably sets out to do such crucial work with regard to race and indigeneity. Of course, this makes it even more frustrating to note how the issue continues autotheory scholarship's jarring, willed ignoring of disability as a category of analysis—even when the majority of authors and artists under discussion explicitly identify as mad or ill or crip or have been powerfully claimed as crip ancestors.[18] Indeed, autotheory's "politics of citation unveil its relations."[19]

24. Lazard's "In Sickness and Study," Hedva's "Sick Woman Theory," Lo Bil's presentation "Sick Theories," Gloria Anzaldúa's unpublished writings on health, Ann Cvetkovich's *Depression: A Public Feeling* . . . [20]

There is no theory of autotheory that is not already crip.

25. Who is creating crip autotheory today? Surely too many to name. Some, like Lazard and Hedva, have already been addressed in the field but without real recognition or engagement of their crip politics and contexts.

Others I could name include mixed-genre writers Eli Clare, Leah Lakshmi Piepzna-Samarasinha, Petra Kuppers, Molly McCully Brown, and Aurora Levins Morales; poets like Travis Chi Wing Lau, Jim Ferris, Kenny Fries, Cyrée Jarelle Johnson, and Kay Ulanday Barrett; essayists and memoirists including Esmé Weijun Wang, Keah Brown, Simi Linton, Corbett O'Toole, Anne Finger, Sonya Huber, and Sejal Shah; graphic novelists like Cece Bell, Ellen Forney, and Coyote Shook; performers like the Sins Invalid Collective, Terry Galloway, Lynn Manning, and Carrie Sandahl; visual artists including Riva Lehrer, Katherine Sherwood, and Sunaura Taylor; and films such as *When Billy Broke His Head*, *Crip Camp*, and *Invitation to Dance*.[21]

Alice Wong's 2020 edited collection *Disability Visibility* offers a marvelous sampling of many of these authors' works. Indeed, I suggest that the entire collection functions autotheoretically.

26. Back to oversharing: three years ago, I began receiving IV infusions to calm my nervous system when it goes especially awry.

I hate it: the dizzying car ride, the hospital's revolving door, the garish colors of the gift shop, the struggle to find a vein that will accept the needle. As medical experiences go, the infusion center is actually not bad. It's accessible, comfortable, covered by my insurance, and respectful of my body. What I hate is not so much the infusions themselves but the fact that I have to get them, that this has become the routine of my days.

So I started to take selfies in the infusion chair, selfies I cropped and filtered and posted on social media, annotated with mild puns: Infusion Noir. Chanuk-kahfusion. Diana Princefusion of Themiscyra. I needed to have something, anything, to take from the experience that was not purely biological, not purely about me being broken and needing to be fixed. I am still doing it. I just posted an infusion selfie last week.

Is this autotheory? Or simply "selfie theory"?[22] Or something else entirely?

27. Can a survival practice also be a theory? Can a theory ever be a survival practice? Is it ever anything else?

NOTES

1　Arianne Zwartjes. "Under the Skin: An Exploration of Autotheory," *Assay: A Journal of Nonfiction Studies* 6, no. 1 (2019). https://www.assayjournal.com/arianne-zwartjes8203 -under-the-skin-an-exploration-of-autotheory-61.html.

2　Lauren Fournier. 2018., "Sick Women, Sad Girls, and Selfie Theory: Autotheory as Contemporary Feminist Practice," *a/b: Auto/Biography Studies* 33, no. 3: 646, https://doi.org /10.1080/08989575.2018.1499495.

3　Stacey Young. *Changing the Wor(l)d: Discourse, Politics, and the Feminist Movement.* (New York: Routledge, 1997): 69.

4　Necropolitics, a term mostly deployed in academic realms, was coined by social theorist Achille Mbembe to describe how social power in modernity operates through the power of devalued life. Necropolitics describes "the capacity to define who matters and who does not, who is disposable and who is not" (Mbembe, 11). Both the COVID-19 pandemic and the Movement for Black Lives prompted discussion of necropolitics in the wider cultural realm, as in for example Namrata Verghese's article "What is Necropolitics" published in *Teen Vogue* magazine on March 10, 2021. https://www.teenvogue.com/story/what-is-necropolitics.

5　"There is an important emphasis on body in autotheory, on bringing physicality and embodied experience into the writing, in dialogue with the theoretical or other academic material . . . And there is a certain rebelliousness to working in the realm of autotheory: an assertive disregard of genre, category, boundary; a willingness to take on established fields of theoretical work and to say, we are body as much as we are brain" (Zwartjes, "Under The Skin: An Exploration of Autotheory").

6　See for example the 2020 special issue of *Arizona Quarterly* on "Autotheory Theory," including the introduction by Robyn Wiegman ("Introduction: Autotheory Theory"); the 2021 special issue of *ASAP/Journal on Autotheory* including the introduction by Alex Brostoff and Lauren Fournier, ("Introduction: Autotheory ASAP! Academia, Decoloniality, and 'I'"); Zwartjes, "Under the Skin: An Exploration of Autotheory."

7　Fournier. "Sick Women, Sad Girls, and Selfie Theory." In Fournier, *Autotheory as Feminist Practice in Art, Writing, and Criticism.* Cambridge, MA: MIT Press, 2021.

8　For example, Rosemarie Garland-Thomson, "Integrating Disability, Transforming Feminist Theory," *NWSA Journal* 14, no. 3 (2002); Alison Kafer, *Feminist, Queer, Crip* (Bloomington, IN: Indiana University Press, 2013); Schalk, Sami and Jina B. Kim, "Integrating Race, Transforming Feminist Disability Studies" *Signs: Journal of Women in Culture and Society* 46, no. 1 (2020): 31–55.

9 Iseult Gillespie, "A Dialogue in Pain: Autotheoretical Affinity and Disabled Coalition in *Bluets* and *A Body Undone*." Unpublished article, 2022.

10 Robyn Wiegman, "Introduction: Autotheory Theory," *Arizona Quarterly: A Journal of American Literature, Culture, and Theory* 76, no. 1 (2020): 10, https://doi.org/10.1353/arq .2020.0009.

11 Brostoff and Fournier, 493.

12 See G. Thomas Couser, *Signifying Bodies: Disability in Contemporary Life Writing* (Ann Arbor, MI: Univeresity of Michigan Press, 2009); Lauren Fournier, *Autotheory as Feminist Practice in Art, Writing, and Criticism* (Cambridge, MA: MIT Press, 2021); Susannah B. Mintz, *Unruly Bodies: Life Writing by Women with Disabilities* (Chapel Hill, NC: University of North Carolina Press, 2007).

13 Nelson quoted in Wiegman, "Introduction: Autotheory Theory," 2.

14 See for example the 2020 special issue of *Arizona Quarterly* on "Autotheory Theory." See also Shannon Brennan's critique of the white autotheory archive in her "Troublesome Knowledge: Autotheory in the Queer Classroom" (*ASAP/Journal* 6, no. 3 (2021): 727 n.8) and Daniel Peña's 2016 *Ploughshares* blog post, "The Argonauts Is A Direct Descendant Of Anzaldua's Borderlands/La Frontera And No One Is Talking About It," https://blog.pshares .org/the-argonauts-is-a-direct-descendant-of-anzalduas-borderlandsla-frontera-and-no -one-is-talking-about-it/.

15 Brostoff and Fournier, 492.

16 Michael Hames-García, "Queer Theory Revisited." In *Gay Latino Studies*, ed. Michael Hames-García and Ernesto Javier Martinez (Durham: Duke University Press, 2011): 19–45. Brennan also references Hames-García's genealogical work (728 n.9).

17 Audre Lorde, "Uses of the Erotic," *Sister Outsider: Essays and Speeches* (Freedom, CA: Crossing Press, 1984): 57.

18 For example, the reclaiming of Gloria Anzaldúa as crip ancestor, most notably by Aurora Levins Morales (who is herself often referenced in autotheory studies without mention of her disability identity and politics). Reflecting on the unavailability of disability community to Anzaldúa in her lifetime, Levins Morales writes: "Gloria, if you were here now, among us, with your endlessly bleeding womb and glucose making tidal waves in your blood, you would not be silent about this, because you would not be alone. I think if we called on you to bring the story of your body into this circle, you would come" (*Kindling: Writings on the Body*, 9).

19 Brostoff and Fournier, 490.

20 All works are referenced in the September 2021 special issue of *ASAP/Journal on "Autotheory"* and/or in Fournier, *Autotheory as Feminist Practice.*

21 Of course this is not an exhaustive list; there are dozens more authors and works that could be cited here. Indeed, the field of crip autotheory is deep and wide enough to support book-length exploration, which makes it all the more striking that I could not find a single published article on the topic. Also many of the authors/artists mentioned here work in more than one genre—Riva Lehrer recently published an acclaimed memoir, for example— but in order to provide some contextual groupings for readers new to the area, I placed each name here in proximity to the genre for which they are best known.

22 See Fournier, "Sick Women, Sad Girls, and Selfie Theory," 651–658.

BIBLIOGRAPHY

Brennan, Shannon. 2021. "Troublesome Knowledge: Autotheory in the Queer Classroom." *ASAP/ Journal* 6 (3): 707–730.

Brostoff, Alex, and Lauren Fournier. 2021. "Introduction: Autotheory ASAP! Academia, Decolo- niality, and 'I.'" *ASAP/Journal* 6 (3): 489–502.

Couser, G. Thomas. 2009. *Signifying Bodies: Disability in Contemporary Life Writing*. Ann Arbor: University of Michigan Press.

Fournier, Lauren. 2018. "Sick Women, Sad Girls, and Selfie Theory: Autotheory as Contemporary Feminist Practice." *a/b: Auto/Biography Studies* 33 (3): 643–662.

Fournier, Lauren. 2021. *Autotheory as Feminist Practice in Art, Writing, and Criticism*. Cambridge, MA: MIT Press.

Frisina, Kyle C. 2020. "From Performativity to Performance: Claudia Rankine's *Citizen* and Autotheory." *Arizona Quarterly: A Journal of American Literature, Culture, and Theory* 76 (1): 141–166.

Garland-Thomson, Rosemarie. 2002. "Integrating Disability, Transforming Feminist Theory." *NWSA Journal* 14 (3): 1–32.

Gillespie, Iseult. 2022. "A Dialogue in Pain: Autotheoretical Affinity and Disabled Coalition in *Bluets* and *A Body Undone*." Unpublished manuscript.

Goh, Irving. 2020. "Auto-thanato-theory: Dark Narcissistic Care for the Self in Sedgwick and Zambreno." *Arizona Quarterly: A Journal of American Literature, Culture, and Theory* 76 (1): 197–213.

Hames-García, Michael. 2011. "Queer Theory Revisited." In *Gay Latino Studies*, edited by Michael Hames-García and Ernesto Javier Martinez, 19–45. Durham, NC: Duke University Press.

Hedva, Johanna. 2020. "Sick Woman Theory." Originally published in *Mask* magazine. https://johannahedva.com/SickWomanTheory_Hedva_2020.pdf.

Kafer, Alison. 2013. *Feminist, Queer, Crip*. Bloomington: Indiana University Press.

Lorde, Audre. 1984. *Sister Outsider: Essays and Speeches*. Freedom, CA: Crossing.

Mayer, So. 2018. "Medea's Perineum." *Angelaki* 23 (1): 188–193.

Mbembé, J.-A., and Libby Meintjes. 2003. "Necropolitics." *Public Culture* 15 (1): 11–40.

Mintz, Susannah B. 2007. *Unruly Bodies: Life Writing by Women with Disabilities*. Chapel Hill: University of North Carolina Press.

Morales, Aurora Levins. 2013. *Kindling: Writings on the Body*. Cambridge, MA: Palabrera.

Nelson, Maggie. 2015. *The Argonauts*. Minneapolis: Graywolf.

Preciado, Paul B. 2013. *Testo Junkie: Sex, Drugs, and Biopolitics in the Pharmacopornographic Era*. New York: Feminist Press.

Schalk, Sami, and Jina B. Kim. 2020. "Integrating Race, Transforming Feminist Disability Studies." *Signs: Journal of Women in Culture and Society* 46 (1): 31–55.

Wiegman, Robyn. 2020. "Introduction: Autotheory Theory." *Arizona Quarterly: A Journal of American Literature, Culture, and Theory* 76 (1): 1–14.

Wong, Alice, ed. 2020. *Disability Visibility: First-Person Stories from the Twenty-First Century*. New York: Vintage.

Young, Stacey. 1997. *Changing the Wor(l)d: Discourse, Politics, and the Feminist Movement*. New York: Routledge.

Zwartjes, Arianne. 2019. "Under the Skin: An Exploration of Autotheory." *Assay: A Journal of Nonfiction Studies* 6 (1). https://www.assayjournal.com/arianne-zwartjes8203-under-the-skin-an-exploration-of-autotheory-61.html.

20

Disability Life Writing in India

MOHAIMINUL ISLAM AND UJJWAL JANA

Researchers in the social sciences have assembled a growing body of work on the sociology and politics of disability in India, but the academic investigation of disability in the fields of literary and cultural studies has mostly remained unexplored. There is evidence that the cultural representation of disability has historically occurred at the expense of disabled individuals because they have not been attributed any agency or subjectivity (Couser 2005, 603). In a previous article, we connect the problem of representation to a historical lack of authorship by disabled people themselves: "In the Indian context, the tradition of self-writing or life writing by people with disabilities has been a very recent and contemporary phenomenon. This has been a trend since 1990 when self-writing became a powerful mode of representation for individuals with disabilities to articulate their centuries-old silence and social, cultural, and economic oppression within a caste-ridden social structure" (Islam and Jana 2021, 204). Following the development of the life narrative genre in India over the last three decades, the concurrent emergence of the disability rights movement, a tremendously enlarged reading populace, and more numerous methods of publication than ever before, there is now no dearth of writings related to disability and disability studies. This corpus of writing consists of more than ten literary memoirs, in addition to innumerable smaller essays, oral traditions, web writings, and older theatrical performances such as Dharamvir Bharati's *Andha Yug / The Blind Age*, performed in 1962; *Togalu Gombeyaata*, created by Kathatha Puppet Theatre; *Bhagavad Gita on Wheels*, created by Syed Sallauddin Pasha; and Nondi Natakam, performed in Murugan Temple since the seventeenth century.

Barring some exceptions, disability life writing in India has exposed the link between disability and socioeconomic inequality and questioned the individualist ethos of public discourse regarding disability and the tendency to suppress rather than articulate diversity. In doing so, these writings engage in the cultural and educational polemics of various genres, spanning the fiction of social realism, bildungsroman, and oral traditions; celebrity autobiographies; survivor testimony; and documentary forms of social media and blogging. The narratives in disability life writing shape their authors' ideas of who they are, individually and collectively, and how their texts serve as a cultural repository with a major focus on the constitution of disability memories.

Surveying US and European literature, G. Thomas Couser argues, "A comprehensive history of disability life writing has yet to be produced, but it is safe to say that not much of such literature was published before World War II" (2005, 604). In India, Subodh Chandra Roy's *The Blind in India and Abroad* (1944) and Ved Mehta's *Face to Face* (1957) are the earliest attempts at Indian life writing in English on blindness. These life narratives played a crucial role in the emergence of a cultural history of Indian disability. In other words, Indian disability life narratives help to form our understanding of broader social and cultural issues in Indian disability history, of which the hierarchical and discriminatory caste system is an integral part.

However, there is a paucity of engagement in contemporary theoretical discussions regarding the convergences between disability and the broader sociopolitical context as represented in Indian disability life writings. Some writers (such as Anita Desai in *Clear Light of Day* [1980]) have examined Indian literary representations of disability as indictments of the nation's false promises and have pointed out the disabling metaphors used by British colonizers to justify their arguments against Indian self-rule. Unlike fictional texts that use disability as metaphor, Indian disability life narratives consider and represent a postcolonial, even anticolonial kind of "autoethnography or autoethnographic expression" as an instance "in which colonized subjects undertake to represent themselves in ways that engage with the colonizer's own terms" (Pratt 1992, 7).

Indian disability life writings, particularly in the postindependence period, have the potential to uncover the relationship between disability and social stratification, reshape the tropes of physical and social isolation, and question the institutional hegemony dominating private lives. Jane Buckingham rightly comments, "Written memoirs and academic writing on disability experience are an important element in the emerging historiography of disability in India. However, many people with disabilities are not able to read or write or access resources to support their academic and personal development. These memories and testimonials are as important as the written record in contributing to an historiography which speaks to the needs and hopes of those marginalised not only by disability but by poverty and low caste status" (2011, 425). These self-narratives, oral and written, represent the ways a society envisions and constrains embodied selfhood and disability community. Indian disability autobiographers interpret their individual experiences within colonial and postcolonial contexts thereby contributing to the emerging domain of intersectional and global disability studies. The genre challenges disability studies to go beyond a middle-class and primarily Anglo-Indian world view that is hindered by "a singular lack of specificity as to . . . the nature of cultures shaped by colonization and its consequences" (Barker and Murray 2010, 223).

Within this context, Mehta's *Face to Face* (1957) and Preeti Monga's *The Other Senses* (2012) are remarkable Indian life narratives on blindness. Both memoirs depict the struggles of visually impaired people who faced adversity from many facets of society. Mehta narrates diverse personal experiences of an intelligent and visually impaired man in a society separated by caste, gender, and economic status. Monga documents her difficult path as a woman in India who chooses to live life her own way, despite her disability and frightening societal and cultural restraints. *Face to Face* and *The Other Senses* offer frames for examining disability from a different sociocultural vantage in India, subverting the conventionally accepted notion of disability as an aberration from normalcy. These life narratives provide witness to the social and cultural marginalization of people who are blind or visually impaired and hence serve as a form of resistance.

The objective of this chapter is to show the contours of history, culture, and memory in Indian disability life writings. These writings challenge and deconstruct historical and cultural understandings in India of disability as "deceit" or "mischief," as well as mainstream Indian society's ableist binary framework of disability and ability, in a culture shaped by colonization and its consequences. By using memory as a tool, these writings provide alternative emancipatory spaces for preserving or recovering disabled perspectives and communities.

Mehta was born in 1934 into a Hindu family in Gujrat, in the province of Punjab in northern India. He lost his sight when he was three and a half years old due to cerebrospinal meningitis. This unanticipated incident looms large in his life, leaving him in a condition of uncertainty and mental instability. Nobody in his family imagined their three-and-a-half-year-old son would become blind because of his prolonged sickness. It was a shocking experience for him, as he could not cope with the idea of being blind. As he affirms, his blindness deprives him of certain experiences valued by the sighted world:

> I started living in a world of four senses—that is, a world in which colors and faces and light and darkness are unknown. . . . I started living in a universe where it was not the flood of sunshine streaming through the nursery window or the colors of the rainbow, a sunset or a full moon that mattered, but the feel of the sun against skin, the air just before the coming of the quiet night, the smell of the stubble grass on a warm morning. It was a universe where at first—but only at first—I made my way fumbling and faltering. (Mehta 1957, 3)

His blindness ultimately becomes a family tragedy, not just an individual problem. He encounters many unanswered questions in the everyday life of a blind person in a culture where the distinction between "normal" and "abnormal" is the norm. His narrative becomes "a saga of a man who is pushed down due to an existential crisis and stands defiant to fight all the trials and tribulations of life with calm" (Islam and Jana 2021, 205). His blindness was a social taboo, and people close to him ridiculed and discriminated against him for something that was no fault of his own. He recollects, "A state of complete inaction therefore followed my blindness. In part this was due to the immediate shock of the illness, but more important still, the impasse was caused by ignorance of the potentialities of a blind child, since the only blind persons my parents saw were beggars" (Mehta 1957, 4).

At that historical point in time in India, the universe of disabled people was very bleak, with blind people moving from one corner to another corner with begging bowl in hand. Hindus believe blindness is a punishment for misdeeds committed in a previous birth. The religious model interprets disability as a divine act, usually as vengeance for a transgression committed by the crippled person or his or her family (Mahanta 2017, 19). Mehta's mother did not have medical expertise like his father, so she always blamed her past life for his blindness. As a result, Mehta's mother consulted a pandit (priest) and decided to do penance for her previous misdeeds. The pandit took Mehta's hand in his and examined the lines meticulously. Then he stared at Mehta's mother's face and mumbled slowly as he scrutinized her forehead. Mehta writes, "He [the pandit] found himself inadequate, and more pandits would have to be consulted. At his request, they were called and questioned exhaustively as to what atonement could be made. Although their analyses and remedies differed considerably, they all agreed that by doing penance for her sins, my mother could improve my chance of regaining sight" (1957, 5).

Pandits recommended various means of cure ranging from intense prayers to arduous physical exertion, and for a fee, they consented to undertake a segment of the required ritual. Conversely, his father, a doctor, sought to combat superstition by providing him with an education, just like his other children, so that Mehta might become a self-supporting citizen of the world, as he used to say it. To quote Mehta, "Although in my case there was an obstacle which seemed insurmountable, he was determined to leave no avenue unexplored. He read all available literature on blindness. He learned that almost all India's blind people had turned to begging for their livelihood, or had become owners of *pan* and *biri* shops and spent their days rolling nuts and condiments in a betel leaf or tobacco in a cigarette paper" (1957, 10–11).

His father was determined that this would not be his son's fate, and he began to seek the assistance of numerous famous educational authorities. Nevertheless, before Mehta turned five, his father sent him to the Dadar School in Bombay, the country's premier school for the blind, which was nine hundred miles away from their home in Punjab. It turned out to be an orphanage, like the scores of other such schools around the country. In this school, he earned respect and learned the discipline of living life independently. As he recollects, "I preferred the new taste of independence in school, and even the taunts of [classmate] Abdul seemed more bearable than my sheltered, uneventful life at home" (Mehta 1957, 16). Mehta spent three years there, bedridden for most of the time, and then returned home because the school had nothing more to teach him. For years, he was unable to attend further schooling. All along, his father had been attempting to get him to the West, where blind people could get a good education, but no school there would take him because he was too young.

When Mehta was thirteen years old, India achieved independence, but at the cost of partition that killed a million people and displaced eleven million more, with no fewer than four million people evacuated. Mehta's family was among the refugees who fled from the newly formed Pakistan with only the clothing on their backs. Mehta was concerned that he would be stuck in India for the rest of his life, with little chance of receiving a proper education. Then he had the opportunity to study for a few months at a newly founded Institute in Dehra Dun, India, for World War II troops who had become blind (Mehta 1957, 150). He learned touch-typing there, among other things, and later he wrote a series of letters to blind institutions in England and the United States, informing them of his hardships. No school wanted to admit him, with the administrators now claiming that his training was inadequate and that, in any event, his moving overseas at such a young age would result in social maladjustment. The Arkansas School for the Blind, however, eventually accepted his application. When he arrived in New York, he had very little knowledge of the new world. He felt strange and bizarre in the new environment. But he was greatly astonished that his peers did not ridicule him for his blunders, unlike in India, where he would have been scorned or ignored for weakness or imperfection. So he experienced pleasures and warm friendship in the West, and his sense of sound, smell, and touch came alive. It occurred to him, "Living in America is an alluring prospect for me in so many practical ways: the freedom of movement" and "having enjoyed a more understanding, less superstitious, and certainly more educated attitude" (Mehta 1957, 305, 308). Mehta's *Face to Face* documents the intersection of class, caste, and disability in India, ultimately arguing against the religious model. As discussed in our previous article, "The idea of disability as a social stigma or as punishment for an individual's misdeeds in a past life or the consequence of disregarding gods were perpetuated in a caste-ridden dogmatic, and superstition-shaken society in India" (Islam and Jana 2021, 210). In this case, the narrator and his father unequivocally articulate their revolt against these societal norms.

The Other Senses, by Preeti Monga, offers a different trajectory of disability experience in India. Monga was born in 1959 in the holy city of Amritsar in India. She belonged to a touch-typing Sikh family. She was barely six years old when doctors eventually diagnosed her deteriorating vision as a result of optic atrophy. Her family sadly accepted the verdict that there was no treatment available for her condition anywhere in the world.

In her memoir, Monga chronicles numerous instances where she was considered naturally inferior due to her visual impairment. She draws attention to the gruesome realities of disabled women in India: her friends, teachers, and neighbors looked at her with pity. It seemed as if she had been "transformed into a strange pitiful object to be handled with extra consideration or simply left alone" (Monga 2012, 26).

Monga's initial reactions to her own blindness were a kind of remorse and subdued silence rather than the resistance or protest of her later years. She reminisces about difficulties with transportation and accessibility she experienced while attending primary school:

> I silently endured this horror, terrified at every step I took treading into the unseen, my tiny heart constantly thumping against my ribs. Even so, the thought of sharing my fears or staying away from school never occurred to me, probably because I saw no other child around me create a fuss about getting off the bus and walking to class. Instead, I endured this daily ordeal, thinking about the secrets that would unfold from between my books, the fascinating stories the lessons would reveal, the ramblings around the compound, the fun that I would have chattering and playing once I was through with this treacherous journey! (2012, 19)

Her narrative chronicles the intricacy of social responses to physical distinctions. As Shilpaa Anand has argued, "These responses cannot be precisely fixed as medical model, moral model or social model but suggest that a serious study of literary narratives of the Indian context may uncover conceptualisations of corporeal difference that are yet to be theorised" (2020, 241). Monga's story does not seem to reveal the details of her objectification, but it draws attention to the conflicting responses to the intersections of disability, gender, and education that frame everyday experiences of disablement.

When Monga was expelled from school at the end of eighth grade because of her blindness, she was forced to stay at home and learn music. Disability historian Aparna Nair explains, "As scholars have noted for other spaces, the Blind were popularly believed to have a peculiar affinity for music" (2017, 191). Many stories exist in India of blind musicians who gained expertise with certain instruments, such as the *dilruba*, sitar, *sarangi*, harmonium, tabla, and flute. But Monga did not move on to a musical career.

When she dreamed of marrying a trustworthy and compassionate man, she experienced social rejection and embarrassment for venturing into such a fantasy. Nevertheless, she got married in 1982, believing her dream of a "perfect match" had become a reality. But she soon found herself in an abusive relationship. Her memoir delves into the thoughts of a guilt-ridden husband to try to understand what makes him torture her. The answer is fear. In 1986, she took action to rescue herself and her kids from their domestic turmoil. Monga recollects, "Though I had decided to better my situation and had turned into a fight, life would sometimes seem so unbearable that I would catch myself contemplating poisoning the children and myself. . . . 14 September 1993 thus witnessed me weeping through the night with Keith relentlessly hurling all manners of vile abuse" (2012, 148).

At the same time, peers and family members made her life even more challenging. They questioned why a blind woman should walk alongside "competent," "non-defective" humans. According to mainstream Indian society, Monga may be offered sympathy and charity, but how can she be empowered to live on equal footing with sighted people?

The pain of being doubly ostracized—first as a woman and then as blind—and the painful abuse she experienced haunted her ceaselessly. But she managed to manifest many of her dreams as reality. She firmly believes, "When life gets cloudy, the trick is to look at the silver lining" (Monga 2012, n.p.). Monga was appointed as the India coordinator, and then nominated as a board member, for the Combat Blindness Foundation India, a US-based organization, working in the area of avoidable blindness in the developing world (2012, 176). She is currently an award-winning trauma counselor, writer, and aerobics trainer, having been the first Indian blind person to successfully clear the aerobic instructor training. Monga describes succeeding in her dreams "in the absence of the sense of sight, clutching on to the rope of faith, depending upon the wings of the other senses" (2012, 177). In 2006, she established a nonprofit organization, Silver Linings, to provide opportunities for blind women to complete their higher education and become equipped with necessary skills and flourish in society.

Mehta's *Face to Face* and Monga's *The Other Senses* have made a significant intervention into the literary-historical documentation of disabled people's experiences in India by challenging the stereotypical religious representations of disability and providing a corrective measure in the form of life narratives of schooling and employment. Furthermore, Monga has provided an ecosystem of new social opportunities for other blind people.

A close reading of these two life writings reveals the entwinement of disability with discriminatory practices of caste, religion, and economic factors. These two life writings open up new spaces of engagement with disability in India, far different from the traditional representations. The texts expose the lack of educational and other support systems for disabled people in India as a result of deep-rooted bias. While the government has provided little to no assistance to disabled people, some individuals have developed affordable creative devices, while others—like Mehta and Monga—combat social and cultural stigmas by publishing their own testimonies.

B. Mangalam rightly states that "narratives of self articulation by the disabled are marked by interrogation of social attitudes towards the disabled and documenting quotidian challenges and struggles of the disabled community" (2020, 149). The quotidian issues surrounding Indian disability have been obscured for so long that much more research is required to uncover the history, culture, and memory of disabled people. Present-day Indian disability life narratives serve as a significant factor in changing attitudes toward disability, and in shaping socio-cultural history and memory to come.

BIBLIOGRAPHY

Anand, Shilpaa. 2020. "Translating Rhetoricity and Everyday Experiences of Disablement: The Case of Rashid Jahan's 'Woh.'" In *Disability in Translation: The Indian Experience*, edited by Someshwar Sati and G. J. V. Prasad, 231–242. New York: Routledge.

Barker, Clare, and Stuart Murray. 2010. "Disabling Postcolonialism: Global Disability Cultures and Democratic Criticism." *Journal of Literary and Cultural Disability Studies* 4 (3): 219–236.

Buckingham, Jane. 2011. "Writing Histories of Disability in India: Strategies of Inclusion." *Disability and Society* 26 (4): 419–431.

Couser, G. Thomas. 2005. "Disability, Life Narrative, and Representation." *PMLA* 120 (2): 602–606.

Desai, Anita. 1980. *Clear Light of Day*. New York: Harper & Row.

Islam, Mohaiminul, and Ujjwal Jana. 2021. "Text as a Cultural Archive: A Close Reading of Madan Vasishta's Deaf in Delhi: A Memoir." *Journal of Literary and Cultural Disability Studies* 15 (2): 203–218.

Mahanta, Banibrata. 2017. *Disability Studies: An Introduction*. New Delhi: Yking Books.

Mangalam, B. 2020. "Negotiating Disability in/and Translation: A Reading of Two Tamil Short Stories." In *Disability in Translation: The Indian Experience*, edited by Someshwar Sati and G. J. V. Prasad, 146–158. New York: Routledge.

Mehta, Ved. 1957. *Face to Face*. New Delhi: Penguin Books.

Monga, Preeti. 2012. *The Other Senses*. New Delhi: Roli Books.

Nair, Aparna. 2017. "'They Shall See His Face': Blindness in British India, 1850–1950." *Medical History* 61 (2): 181–199.

Pratt, Mary Louise. 1992. "Introduction: Criticism in the Contact Zone." In *Imperial Eyes: Travel Writing and Transculturation*, 1–11. London: Routledge.

Roy, Subodh Chandra. 1944. *The Blind in India and Abroad*. Calcutta: University of Calcutta.

21

The History and Politics of Krip-Hop

LEROY F. MOORE JR. AND KEITH JONES

In this chapter the founders of Krip-Hop Nation discuss how and why they use music, history, politics, new language, and theory to uplift their Black disabled community and to educate Hip-Hop scholars, media creators, and the whole industry and culture about the absence of a disability framework.[1] Krip-Hop Nation's tagline is "*Krip-Hop is more than just music.*" Leroy F. Moore Jr. and Keith Jones are Black disabled activists, artists, and Hip-Hop and music lovers. Even their first face-to-face meeting was political—it was at the 2004 Democratic National Convention in Boston, where they got kicked out because of all the questions they were asking. Later, in a music studio recording Keith's latest CD, between songs Leroy asked Keith if he ever saw another physically disabled artist in Hip-Hop. They both laughed, then wrote out the framework of Krip-Hop Nation. "Krip-Hop" is a play on *Hip-Hop*. Although the "Krip" part of the name refers to "crippled," it is spelled with a *k* to avoid association with the Crips.

Since 2004 Krip-Hop Nation has become an international collective of Hip-Hop and other disabled musicians with a few chapters around the world as well as what we call Mcees With Disabilities (MWD) in Germany, the UK, Africa & more. Krip-Hop Nation has over 300 members worldwide. They have put out many music projects, performed internationally at festivals like DADAFest in Liverpool, UK, and created new terminology, theory, books, films and college lectures—so much that Krip-Hop today is a subculture of Hip-Hop. Krip-Hop is a community as well as style of music, an artistic space where people with disabilities can speak out and speak back to the social structures that exclude people based on disability, race, sexuality, and a host of other marginalized identities. Krip-Hop Nation has its own politics, lingo, culture, history, and of course music.

EXCERPT FROM "MESSAGE TO GANGSTER RAPPERS"
 (JONES AND MOORE 2021B)
You can't survive what I've been through
Got the strength of my Black disabled ancestors who created the Blues
Already tasted death so I've nothing to lose
Was that little kid on that short yellow bus with my cripple crew
We grew up and made Krip-Hop
To put Hip-Hop on the spot

But you don't like to be in the spotlight
Like Teddy Pendergrass it's a TKO referee called the fight

I was born D.O.A.
Get out of my way
Hard life from the start
Can't stand up against me you got no heart

The primary goal of Krip-Hop Nation is to increase awareness in music and media outlets of the talents, history, and rights of people with disabilities in the Hip-Hop industry. Moore hopes that by listening to his music the audience will understand the need to question authority and the information provided to them. He wants his listeners to learn about their community and become open to all people. Issues such as racism and sexism are commonly discussed in his music, and Moore hopes that people will examine possible ableism in their attitudes too. Krip-Hop Nation goes beyond producing music and the bling-bling associated with Hip-Hop; the movement is about advocacy, education, and overcoming oppression. The movement has sought to reclaim negative terms associated with the disabled (such as *crazy*, *lame*, *retarded*, and *cripple*), using them to shock people into understanding and respecting the disabled African American community. Krip-Hop Nation addresses discrimination against disabled artists in Hip-Hop by publishing articles and hosting events, lectures, and workshops.

There is a process to get to Krip-Hop politics: empowerment and deep education that is desperately needed in the Hip-Hop arena and in the Black community. What can Krip-Hop Nation offer to students and community members for a more inclusive Hip-Hop culture, Hip-Hop studies, and industry? Most important, an open and welcoming community locally, nationally, and on an international level.

Leroy F. Moore Jr. and the Roots of Krip-Hop

Krip-Hop founder Moore is an African American writer, poet, and community activist who was diagnosed with cerebral palsy. Moore was born in New York in 1967 to an activist father loosely connected to the Black Panthers. Moore's upbringing sensitized him to the challenges faced by African Americans and the disabled. As a youth, he discovered that most people had little knowledge of the historical impact of disabled African Americans. This led him to begin research, initially in the music industry.

Moore first spotlighted disabled Hip-Hop artists in the early 2000s. He coproduced and cohosted a three-part series on what he called "Krip-Hop" for a Berkeley, California, radio station. The Krip-Hop series appeared on KPFA's *Pushing Limits*, which focuses on news, arts, and culture for the disabled community.

The series' popularity inspired Moore to create Krip-Hop Nation for disabled musicians, since little cultural work or music by people with disabilities had been recognized. "The Krip-Hop movement really makes the pain of the people visible," Moore said. "It goes a lot deeper than what people can see."[2]

With two Black disabled friends back in 1980, Moore started a letter campaign to Black leaders about the lack of Black disability anything back then. That and many experiences as a Black disabled youth have led him to his work today. His father's record collection back in the late 1970s was his early education about being Black and disabled because he saw Black disabled male Blues, Jazz, and Soul singers, from blind Willie Johnson to Walter Jackson with his crutches, on their album covers. He saw the Black opera *Porgy and Bess*, which has a character who is a Black physically disabled man; that changed his life. Unfortunately he wasn't empowered until he brought what he saw at home into school—his father's records, *Porgy and Bess*, and the story of how Harriet Tubman became disabled and how she used it to guide other Black people to freedom—and felt oppression for the first time in an education institution, which attempted to hush-hush that history; that is, his full identity.

Black Ableism

Although the term *ableism* has been defined by disability advocates from the dominant culture, if you put *Black* in front of anything coming out of disability, it must first be stripped down, then reshaped in the experiences, histories, and words of the Black disabled experience. By now, we know that the Black disabled experience in America has different roots from our white disabled counterparts'. Because of the need of Black disabled people to heal the wounds inflicted by our Black community, it is imperative that—one by one or collectively—we tell our stories and define new terminology, definitions, art, music, and political views and provide education and resources for our Black community. That is why Moore has coined the term *Black ableism*, knowing that there are many Black disabled people who have asked, "What is ableism in the Black community?"

Ableism is defined as bias and discrimination against disabled people. As Talila A. Lewis (2022) explains, it is "a system of assigning value to people's bodies and minds based on societally constructed ideas of normalcy, productivity, desirability, intelligence, excellence, and fitness. These constructed ideas are deeply rooted in eugenics, anti-Blackness, misogyny, colonialism, imperialism, and capitalism."

If we take this definition and apply it to the Black experience in the United States, the long history of slavery and anti-Blackness helped shaped Black ableism toward Black disabled people. Due to the lack of awareness of race and the racism that continues to exist in the disability rights movement, it is not surprising that the Black community has not taken steps to recognize their own ableism.

Moore has defined Black ableism as discrimination and social prejudice against Black people with disabilities or who are perceived to have disabilities from Black nondisabled people as far back as slavery. For example, slave owners used disability as a reason to devalue a slave because of what he or she could contribute to the plantation. And we, a new people, emerged out of slavery and saw by the slave master's example that disability meant devalued.

Unchallenged Black ableism not only holds back the Black community from advancing, it also makes the Black community hurtful toward Black disabled people and their families. Yes, it is surprising that an oppressed group can oppress others in their own group. Black ableism can cause many deep-rooted problems in a Black disabled person. The problems range from having low self-esteem, to trying to reach the unreachable—also known as overcoming or hiding one's disability—to, most importantly, not having a community.

Ableism, like racism, manifests from the individual to the institutional level when it corrupts Black institutions. Black ableism can only be eradicated by stripping what the Black community has been taught about disability through the lens of oppression and then rebuilding. This rebuilding process must be conducted by coordinated teams of Black disabled people and family members who have had a presence in both the disability and Black communities.

Krip-Hop Nation's Politics

Krip-Hop Nation unlearns what has been forced on us about disability. We reject the erasure, exploitation, pity, and overcoming approaches to disability. We understand ourselves politically and culturally through speaking, singing or rapping, writing, and most importantly living with an activist lens on what affects us in our community, in institutions, and as allies. Through song, poetry, visual arts, and writing, we realize that we are stepping up and helping to correct how society views us as people with disabilities or artists with disabilities, and at the same time we know we wear many hats when we want to advocate and when we just want to party.

We learn from disability justice and its principles (see Sins Invalid 2015). The disability justice movement was begun by Black and Brown artists and activists with disabilities like the members of Sins Invalid, the National Black Disability Coalition, and the Harriet Tubman Collective. We also recognize our disabled ancestors from the Blues to minstrel shows to freak shows to the circus to Jazz all the way up to Hip-Hop.

As an international network, we realize that many times we will not agree and there will be conflicting politics, views, and goals; however, we try to stay open for the growth of our communities. Although we believe and uphold disability justice and our mission, we also are aware that we live under capitalism and we all need to eat and survive, so we also see Krip-Hop Nation as a venue where artists can display their art and receive some monetary value or investment and travel opportunities in their careers as musicians, activists, journalists, authors, and organizers.

Krip-Hop Nation tries to live up to our own standards:

1) Use politically correct lyrics.
2) Do not put down other minorities.
3) Use our talents to advocate and teach not only about ourselves but about the system we live under as it pertains to being a person of color in conjunction with having a disability.
4) Challenge mainstream and other media about the ableist ways they frame disability.
5) Increase the presence of voices that are missing in popular culture.
6) Recognize our disabled ancestors, knowing that we are building on what they left us.
7) Increase disability solidarity and collaboration around the world.
8) Help to increase the visibility in Black museums and cultural centers of Black disability art, music, and historical involvement in art and activism of the times.
9) Promote the disability justice movement's Ten Principles.
10) Be a space for the Black community to gain disability and Krip-Hop political education, cultural expression, and activism while understanding the importance of Black disabled individuals at various times in history.
11) Know that sometimes we fail to meet the preceding standards but continue trying.

Just as Hip-Hop can and is being used to educate and inspire people, especially Black and Brown youths and adults, Krip-Hop has been doing the same with our own terminology like *Krip-Hop*, *Black ableism*, *Afro-Krip*, and more, as well as our politics, journalism, and activism.

The Krip-Hop Institute

We close with a letter to Hip-Hop about our planned Krip-Hop Institute.[3]

MISSION

Krip-Hop Institute will be a cultural, activist, and inclusive platform meeting space for the community. KHI will specialize in the accurate representation of those who are marginalized, especially those who are disabled, Black, and at the intersection of the Black disabled community. This will be achieved both locally and internationally by having a music studio, visual art gallery, and archival historical material, as well as a Krip-Hop virtual reality and screening floor where Krip-Hop chapters all over the world can talk to each other. Ultimately, the goal of KHI will be to create an international hub for disabled and nondisabled activists, artists, and researchers around the world. It is essential that KHI be based in the Black and disabled community in order to truly represent it. Through adequate collaboration within the community, KHI will conduct outreach to educational institutions in the hope of gaining more allies and acquiring the institute's much-needed materials. Examples include but are not limited to hard-to-find books, scholarly articles, and specific types of art.

Dear Hip-Hop,

We, Krip-Hop Nation, an international collective of Hip-Hop artists and other musicians with disabilities, are writing this letter to you to not only give thanks for a platform but also to push this artistic international movement to become more politically aware and play an active role with us to reeducate the Hip-Hop and music industry and our communities about not only the ableism in Hip-Hop. We must go past the charity model of disability to step up and acknowledge what Krip-Hop Nation calls the politically and culturally disabled with disability justice and Krip-Hop politics, language, and international solidarity.

This process of unlearning ableism and the charity model of disability will take rebuilding relationships within the disability community. Although Hip-Hop from the beginning gave us a platform to see and express ourselves, it has become an ableist and harmful environment for not only disabled, especially physically disabled, artists but also people with disabilities who want to work in Hip-Hop, such as journalists, scholars, TV show hosts, and more.

Musicians with disabilities have always been here, but there has been a lack of cultural activism, especially in Hip-Hop, with a disability justice approach to continue to display the talents of musicians with disabilities and at the same time advocate and celebrate our history and intersectional cultures and politically educate ourselves and our communities locally, nationally, and internationally.

For almost thirteen years Krip-Hop Nation has provided public education through our music CDs, lectures, workshops, YouTube conversations, short video clips, activism, visual arts, articles, and political education locally and internationally. We have made strides, but it has been outside the mainstream Hip-Hop arena, so we are pushing ourselves in 2021 and beyond to collaborate in the Hip-Hop popular arena to help make Hip-Hop a more open political and cultural environment where disabled Hip-Hop artists and activists, journalists, and scholars can not only work but be proud to share and welcome others like them.

You ask how? Krip-Hop Nation knows that this process has to be bigger than a one-time event. It must be an ongoing process with local, national, and international Hip-Hop, organizations, partners like the United Nations, and others. It can start off as a conference that will spell out the goals of this ongoing reeducation with materials like books, films, curricula, and media campaigns. Considering that people with disabilities around the world are the poorest of the poor, Krip-Hop Nation knows if we want to make an impact that will change attitudes, institutional beliefs, and actions, the movement must be well funded and uplifted by local to international organizations and spokespeople.

Are you committed to partner with Krip-Hop Nation and pull in resources and institutional backing to spread Krip-Hop Nation's mission and work, not only to organize and hold this conference but most importantly to accomplish what comes out of this conference with Krip-Hop Nation's leadership? One of our big goals is to open what we call the Krip-Hop Institute and get into the upcoming Hip-Hop Museum in New York. We have work to do, and this letter is the beginning. We hope you will learn from our letter and our work and then join us in doing the work!

Leroy F. Moore Jr. and Keith Jones
August 9, 2021

NOTES

1 Some material in this chapter previously appeared on the Krip-Hop Nation website, kriphopnation.com

2 KQED. Interview with Leroy Moore, Founder of Krip Hop Nation. https://www.kqed.org /arts/43903/interview_with_leroy_moore_founder_of_krip_hop_nation.

3 This letter was previously published as an audio file on SoundCloud and can be accessed here: https://soundcloud.com/blackkrip/dear-hip-hop-audio-letter.

BIBLIOGRAPHY

Jones, Keith, and Leroy F. Moore Jr. 2021a. "Dear Krip Hop." *SoundCloud*, July 1, 2021. https://soundcloud.com/blackkrip/dear-hip-hop-audio-letter.

Jones, Keith, and Leroy F. Moore Jr. 2021b. "Message to Gangster Rappers." *SoundCloud*, May 19, 2021. https://soundcloud.com/blackkrip/message-to-gangster-rappers.

Hix, Lisa. 2011. Interview with Leroy Moore, Founder of Krip Hop Nation. KQED. February 14, 2011. https://www.kqed.org/arts/43903/interview_with_leroy_moore_founder_of_krip_hop _nation.

Lewis, Talila A. 2022. "Working Definition of Ableism—January 2022 Update." Talila A. Lewis's website, January 1, 2022. https://www.talilalewis.com/blog/working-definition-of-ableism -january-2022-update.

Moore, Leroy. n.d. *Krip Hop Nation*. Accessed October 6, 2022. https://kriphopnation.com.

Sins Invalid. 2015. "10 Principles of Disability Justice." September 17, 2015. https://www.sinsinvalid .org/blog/10-principles-of-disability-justice.

22

Verbal and Nonverbal Metaphor

ASA ITO

It is impossible for other people to experience your disability, but metaphors can help us to convey our feelings in verbal or nonverbal forms. Metaphors are devices to connect and merge different bodies that cannot be combined in essence. The purpose of this chapter is to describe a variety of examples of metaphor that allow people to meet their own body as well as others', and to clarify the practical meaning of metaphor as a technique for bodily communication.

The first section is about metaphors to understand one's own body and to illuminate differences in the subjective experiences of people who stutter. The second section discusses metaphors to meet other's bodies, using the example of the "cultural ears" of those born deaf and the coappreciation of artworks by sighted and visually impaired people. The last section deals with nonverbal metaphor through the example of the Sports Guide without Sight project.

1. Metaphor to Understand One's Own Body

There are many natural metaphors in crip communities. The following three metaphors are used by those who stutter. Stuttering is a reality we all experience, but each expression has a different emphasis.

The first example comes from a woman who speaks repetitively. She compares her body to a trembling fruit jelly: "When I repeat words, time seems to move slowly. I feel myself opening the container of trembling fruit jelly with great care and attention, which enables me to avoid stuttering blocks" (Aya Watanabe).

Her attentiveness to pronouncing a word is compared to the care needed to open the container of trembling fruity jelly without spilling it out. Her body easily gets out of control because of how unstable it is. For her, stuttering blocks are the worst, so she tries to avoid them by releasing her jiggly body. Meanwhile, her body seems to be dancing and trying to escape.

Another woman says her body is much stiffer: "When I speak in public, I get rigid and stop breathing, which seems to destroy the vital activity of my cells. My body feels like stone or ice. . . . I am horrified like I am at the end of the earth alone" (Naomi Takayama).

She describes how she feels when she cannot make her words come out of her mouth in front of other people. While Watanabe's main symptom is a repetition of parts of words, Takayama's body becomes dry, hard, and cold. Similar feelings of being apart from the world are prevalent in *The Temple of the Golden Pavilion*, a famous piece of Japanese literature by Yukio Mishima.

As a final example of metaphor, a man who uses the technique of switching words often to avoid stuttering blocks offers a metaphor regarding stuttering. For instance, if he wanted to say "water," he used a word with a similar meaning—say, "bottle." He explains, "Whenever I speak, I notice 'that guy' is approaching me like 'here, here, here comes the block!' As a child, I could not help but bump into it. Now I can avoid it from any side, which allows me to have room in my mind" (Chen Dominique).

He uses playful language to describe his technique to cope with stuttering. To avoid a threat that may put his life in danger, he jumps off the road and alters his course as if he were playing a video game. Because he has seen blocks knock him down over and over again, he is skilled at playing the game of stuttering.

A beautiful metaphor can help to illuminate people's subjective experiences with disabilities. In these examples, stuttering demonstrates that even those who are supposed to belong to the same disability community can have different experiences of disability. These subjective sensations are shaped by metaphors based on their recognition of or attitude toward the disability. According to George Lakoff and Mark Johnson, it is our physical experiences that generate metaphorical expressions, and a metaphor can only have meaning when it is related to physical reality: "In actuality, we feel that no metaphor can ever be comprehended or even adequately represented independently of its experiential basis" (1980, 23). Though these authors are strongly ableist in the sense that they assume our physical experiences are universal, their approach to metaphors from a cognitive perspective is still significant. By utilizing metaphors, we can express how we perceive things differently depending on how we feel.

Metaphors that fit crip experiences are important for two reasons. The first is that they allow us to compete with the dominant ableist language. Disability studies has criticized the use of several metaphors that contain disability expressions fostering a pejorative view of people with disabilities. As an example, people often convey the belief that visually impaired people are incapable of understanding beauty or truth when they say things like "She's blind to nature's beauty." If we have an inspiring metaphor to express the richness of the world without sight, it will help us refrain from presupposing ability based on a common cliché.

Another reason such metaphors are important is that they allow us to cultivate more precise language about crip experiences. Liz Crow highlights that in the social model of disability, we tend to avoid focusing on the diverse experiences of our bodies: "External disabling barriers may create social and economic disadvantage but our subjective experience of our bodies is also an integral part of our everyday reality. What we need is to find a way to integrate impairment into our whole experience and sense of ourselves for the sake of our own physical and emotional well-being, and, subsequently, for our individual and collective capacity to work against disability" (2014, 359–361).

In 1976 Gen-yu-kai, a Japanese stuttering association, published the *Declaration for People Who Stutter*. In it, people who stutter are encouraged to live with stuttering as a social normality. People who stutter, however, are not homogeneous, and they have a delicate nuance about them. As the declaration notes, some people choose to stutter in public, but others hide their impairment by using techniques like switching words so people will not recognize them as someone who stutters. The social model is indispensable, but we must compensate for it with nuanced language to take account of the diversity of subjective experiences and needs.

2. Metaphor to Understand Another's Body

Crip metaphor is a fundamental tool to describe our personal bodily experiences. This does not mean that certain metaphors must only be used by those whose bodies are qualified to use them. The general public should be able to access crip metaphors, regardless of their lack of experience with the reality on which they are based. In the same way, people with disabilities should be able to use expressions whose physical basis is unfamiliar to them.

Occasionally, people with disabilities are irritated by the issue of the "right to use certain expressions." Georgina Kleege, who is legally blind, describes the reaction her friend had when she used visual expressions:

> I was talking about a book I was reading and a friend said, "Don't you mean listening to? Don't you mean you were listening to the book on tape?"
>
> Of course, this was literally true; generally speaking, I do most of my reading aurally. But I'm not going to say, "I'm listening to such-and-such a book on tape," or "I scanned such-and-such a book into my computer so I could use its synthesized voice" when all I mean is that I am reading it. To specify the mode of access I happen to be employing implies that I have something to say about the particular mode, that the fact that I was listening to it (or touching it in Braille for that matter) significantly alters my understanding of it. Occasionally this could be true, I suppose. Mostly it's not.
>
> It's like I'm not going to say, "Later I will be in close proximity to you" instead of "See you later." How literal-minded can people be? (2006, 103)

As this example reminds us, sticking to precise expressions that exactly match the features of a speaker's body can cause a practical and ethical problem. If a visually impaired person said, "I will be in close proximity to you," we would be confused. Moreover, if they are forced to say such things, this means they are being excluded from mainstream culture. A language is a form of media. We chose certain expressions not only because they are fitting to our bodies and allowed but also because they are understandable in a particular situation.

Language is ambiguous. A word can be used literally or metaphorically depending on who uses the word. This ambiguity can indeed mask the differences in our bodies if we ignore the gap those who use that word metaphorically may feel. However, if we are conscious and creative in our use of language, this bilateral nature of words can be a way to meet each other's bodies. When hearing a speaker in this common space that includes many bodies, a mutual penetration may occur when the listener tries to understand the reality of the speaker that his or her body cannot experience directly.

Penetration can be found in a wide range of communication fields. This first example is from Tomotake Kinoshita, a researcher who was born deaf. His essay "Survival by Myself" describes the layered experience of walking through beautiful woods. He felt as if he was borrowing others' bodies while under the trees:

> While walking through the mixed forest of the park and arriving among the woods, a phrase of Musashino [a famous essay on nature in Musashino, a suburb of Tokyo, written by Doppo Kunikida in 1898] happens to occur to me. . . . Beyond the distance of 120 years, I heard the sound written in Musashino. Doppo's apprehension of Musashino as a sum of sensations that came from his various senses such as sight, hearing, and touching, which he had when he was walking there, was built inside me. Then I realized that I was accompanied by someone though I was standing alone in the grove. . . .
>
> By borrowing Doppo's apprehension, I listen to the sound, which fills the mixed forest. This ability to borrow others' apprehension has something to do with the fact that I am deaf. People with physical impairments have the hidden ability to borrow others' bodies with ease because they are lacking in certain functions. (2019, 208–226)

In contrast to physiological ears, we might call Kinoshita's borrowed sense of hearing "cultural ears" or "acquired ears." Because he cannot hear any sounds physiologically, he has learned how it feels to hear sounds in certain situations through the description of sounds in literature. He can imagine the sounds of woods as vividly as if he actually hears them. It might help him "feel" it since sound is a kind of vibration that is familiar to deaf people. In addition to being symbols, words are also media that connect different bodies beyond time and space. Through reading or listening, one can penetrate the body of another. The boundaries between bodies are blurred.

Another example of borrowing another's body can be found in a museum. With a special program held in various museums in Japan called Verbal Imaging Museum Tour with Visually Impaired People, the sighted and the visually impaired can enjoy exploring artworks together. Attendees are divided into groups of about six people, including those who are visually impaired and those who are sighted. They discuss the assigned work with their team members. In this program, a visually impaired staff member facilitates the discussion. Each work is admired for about twenty minutes and then you hop on to the next. People never touch a work during the program, but they exchange words.

Traditionally, visually impaired people enjoy art by touching it. The museum offers a variety of programs specifically designed for those with visual impairments, including an opportunity to touch a three-dimensional model of a work of art or the work itself. This type of program may have the benefit of helping visually impaired individuals correctly perceive the physical features of the work. However, it is important to distinguish perception from appreciation. To perceive a work of art is to understand a physical aspect of it. On the other hand, to appreciate is to enjoy the aesthetic value of it and to develop your subjective impression. Touching objects and concentrating only on their physical aspects tends to prevent people from having such an aesthetic attitude.

This kind of tour is designed so that sighted people do not have to explain the work to blind people. Hayashi was the designer of the program and held it in many museums around Japan. "I always encourage the sighted participants to discuss two things," he said to me in an interview. The first thing you notice is the size of the painting, its color, its motif, and so on. It is all objective information. Then there are the invisible things: your thoughts, your memories, and your impressions. It is all subjective meaning. Whenever someone tells you to describe the subjective meaning, the conversation becomes filled with metaphors. It is possible for visually impaired people to hear contradictory metaphors as the discussion proceeds. The color of an abstract painting can be green like cedar leaves, sliced pickles in sandwiches, weird witch soup, and horrible zombies. Each participant's cultural and personal background is crucial to understanding these metaphors. The Verbal Imaging Museum Tour can be described as appreciation through others.

The visually impaired staff and participants are not passive listeners. As a result of hearing various impressions of the sighted, they may ask why they are reminded of witch soup or they may express their own interpretation. The nonphysical aspect of the work is important, so they are welcome to engage in the discussion. They can also deepen discussions because their point of view is sometimes unexpected to the sighted. This collaborative process of appreciation benefits from the gap of information and perspectives among participants. A blind man put it to me in an interview, "[The] Verbal Imaging Tour taught me that having sight does not always mean to be superior. Sight does not assure them of the correct answer. The sighted can be blind" (Kenji Shiratori).

Here, the words and the practice of seeing seem to lose their literal meaning. This concept should not be limited to its physiological and literal meanings but should be extended to its cultural and metaphorical meanings. As metaphorically understood, seeing can be performed by people who cannot see physiologically. A disability can make us question the literal meaning of a word and make us redefine it.

3. Nonverbal Metaphor

The foregoing examples are evidence that beautiful metaphors can open common space for differently abled bodies where mutual penetration occurs due to its bilateral (literal and metaphorical) nature. Metaphors are more than just verbal, but we tend to use verbal ones. This section will shed light on nonverbal metaphors and see how the encounter and the mutual penetration of different bodies happen without using words.

Sports Guide without Sight is a collaboration between Junji Watanabe (Nippon Telegraph and Telephone Corporation's Communication Science Laboratories), Akiko Hayashi (Nippon Telegraph and Telephone Corporation's Service Evolution Laboratories), and me (Tokyo Institute of Technology) since 2018. This project began with the aim of developing a new approach for visually impaired people to enjoy sports games more vividly. However, our goal became the reproduction of the subjective experience of players using everyday tools such as towels that would be accessible to those with and without visual disabilities.

For visually impaired people, verbal live coverage of sports games has traditionally been an orthodox method of watching sporting events. As a flying ball travels through the sky, the commentator in a baseball stadium may describe the sharp line it draws against a blue sky with captivating narration. This type of verbal explanation is indeed popular and useful among visually impaired people, but some have complained that it is insufficient. There are primarily two problems.

One problem is that the verbal live coverage tends to be an explanation ex post facto of what is happening in the game. What excites spectators of soccer games is not the fact of scoring a goal but the process and the expectation leading up to it. However, verbal explanation takes too much time to catch up with the event. Some visually impaired people say they feel left behind amid the crowd in stadiums or sports bars because they cannot follow the course of events in detail.

The second problem relates to the quality of the information that words convey. It must be difficult to imagine what the athlete's jump was like when you hear "the athlete jumped." Did he jump like a cat without any preparation? Did he squat down and then jump high like a spring? This movement has infinite nuance but words cannot describe it all. People with visual impairments may be frustrated by the poor quality of the information.

Our first attempt to counter this weak verbal explanation was to translate judo into towel language using touch and vibrations (figure 22.1). It is a fairly

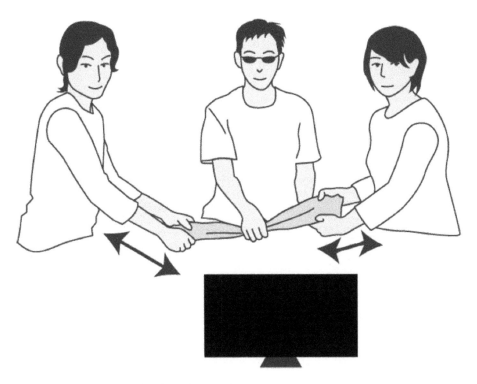

Figure 22.1. Translation of judo with a towel.

straightforward process. The blind spectator holds the center of a towel, which is held on each side by a sighted translator of each judo athlete. As the athletes move, the towel conveys the struggle and tactics of their movements to the spectators. A blind man claimed that he felt the thrill of live events as if he were part of the action. Although details of the sporting technique tend to be omitted, this method of translation is good for enjoying the excitement of the game.

Our experience reminded us of the importance of nonvisual aspects of sports games. We usually think of sports as something that can be seen, as evidenced by common phrases like "watching sports games." However, when athletes play, they also use their auditory and haptic senses. We might be better able to enjoy sports games in a more empathetic way if we borrow the perspective of visually impaired people and take nonvisual aspects into account. That insight led us to develop the Sports Guide without Sight project.

To create a "sports guide without sight," we interviewed athletes of twelve sports about the sensations they have during their games and tried to translate those using ordinary objects. Fencing players hold a foil lightly between their index finger and thumb. Wrist movements are crucial, as foils are very flexible. With trial and error, we found that entangled wooden blocks shaped like *C* and *H* were a suitable way to convey the sensation of engaging blades and

Figure 22.2. Translation of fencing with wooden blocks shaped like *C* and *H*.

Figure 22.3. Translation of baseball with a cord.

releasing to strike. Both players close their eyes as one attempts to wrest their block from the other (figure 22.2).

Additionally, such translated activities can convey a psychological aspect of the game. We tried to translate how a batter reads a pitcher's movements in baseball (figure 22.3). In the activity, both the pitcher and the batter close their eyes, and the pitcher pulls a cord. To read the pitcher's movements, the batter touches the pitcher's shoulder, and then grabs the cord. It is a home run if the batter grabs the red portion, it is a swing and miss if it is the black part, and it is a hit if it is the surrounding area.

The metaphor of touch takes us into the subjective experience of others that cannot be experienced literally. Despite not being trained as fencing players, we can experience the essence of what it is like to handle a foil. Although we have not mastered the skill of hitting, we can sense a pitcher's psychological tactics. Using nonverbal metaphors helps us see sports from the perspective of players and enables us to redefine what it means to watch sports.

BIBLIOGRAPHY

Crow, Liz. 2014. "Lying Down Anyhow: An Auto-ethnography." *Qualitative Inquiry* 20 (3): 359–361.

Dominique, Chen. 6/26/2027. Interview with the author.

Kinoshita, Tomotake. 2019. *"Survival by Myself," Switch of Wisdom*. (In Japanese). Tokyo: Iwanami-shoten.

Kleege, Georgina. 2006. *Blind Rage: Letters to Helen Keller*. Washington, DC: Gallaudet University Press.

Lakoff, George, and Mark Johnson. 1980. *Metaphors We Live By*. Chicago: University of Chicago Press.

Hayashi. 4/7/2017. Interview with the author.

Ito, Shinji. 1976. *Declaration for People Who Stutter*. Tokyo: Taimatsu-sha.

Shiratori, Kenji. 3/12/2014. Interview with the author.

Takayama, Naomi. 4/26/2017. Interview with the author.

Vidali, Amy. 2010. "Seeing What We Know: Disability and Theories of Metaphor." *Journal of Literary and Cultural Disability Studies* 4 (1): 33–54.

Watanabe, Aya. 3/12/2014. Interview with the author.

SECTION IV

Publishing

23

Accessible Academic Publishing

CYNTHIA WU

A few years ago, a friend completing her first book called me in a panic. She asked if her editor would cancel her contract if she missed her deadline for the revised manuscript. "No," I responded. "Just ask for an extension." A few weeks later, I received another call. Would her contract be withdrawn if one of the chapters turned out differently from how the proposal described it? At this point, I sat her down. "You're misunderstanding the relationship between you and your editor," I said. "He isn't your probation officer. He's your colleague." I explained that her editor had invested significant time and resources into getting her manuscript to this stage. He wanted to see it in print as much as she did. Moreover, she would continue to have a relationship with him long after her book came out. Even if she didn't work with him for her next book, he would ask her to review manuscripts and recommend up-and-coming authors he should be soliciting. "He needs you as much as you need him."

Authors and editors work symbiotically in shaping a field. They play different roles, but they each perform tasks needed by any academic discipline. Although many pretenure faculty imagine editors as mythical gatekeepers who make or break careers, our relationships with them are much more collaborative than we initially think. Getting the attention of an editor, developing an "elevator pitch," submitting a prospectus, responding to reader reports, signing a contract, attending to revisions, and managing every other step of publishing a book can be mystifying to early-career scholars. This is made more daunting by how high the stakes are when a book plays a significant part in one's job security. On the other side, though, editors invest equally in cultivating relationships with us. They want to acquire manuscripts that will become worthy books. These books will wind up in college and university libraries and in the personal collections of faculty and students. They might win awards or garner other recognition for the press. The professional advancement of editors is as tied to their track record with books as ours is. Authors provide crucial labor to editors once we have cut our teeth writing our own book. As peer reviewers, we give specialist feedback on manuscripts and guide revisions for authors. After a book is published, we might assign it in our classes. If we serve as a series editor at a press, we take a more active role in bringing authors and manuscripts to editors' attention. If we do a stint on our university's press board, we provide the final stamp of approval on book projects. Faculty and press editors work together.

The publishing process at university presses isn't perfect. The elevation of the book as the gold standard for presenting long-form work in most humanities fields contributes to an inequitable situation caused by uneven levels of resourcing. Research budgets, teaching loads, and opportunities for sabbatical leave, which vary widely from one institution to the next, affect the ability of individual faculty to write books. However, in the midst of these conditions, some of us in the field of disability studies would like to make publishing a book more accessible, and we interpret the word *accessible* in ways that are broad ranging. This chapter describes the birth of the book series Dis/Color at Temple University Press, which showcases titles that bridge the fields of critical ethnic studies and disability studies. Its founding in 2019 was a joint effort among three disability studies scholars who serve as the series editors and four acquisitions editors who, at various points in its development, handled the project from inception to proposal to actualization. This chapter also locates our process in a larger set of institutional concerns regarding the status of the book. Our attempts to make publishing more accessible are not a panacea for challenges such as the decline of tenure-track jobs, the increase of publishing expectations, and the casualization of labor in academia. Nevertheless, I imagine that modest changes, when made in a variety of places, might provide some respite and joy in a profession that could always use more of those things.

In September 2012, a senior scholar in a field adjacent to mine reached out. I had met her several years before when I was a finalist for a position at her institution, which I didn't wind up getting. She was the chair of that search committee, and she and I have kept in touch ever since. I consider her an informal mentor. She expressed her concern that, lately, I seemed frustrated and unenthused about my career path, which didn't seem to square with the excitement I should be feeling about the publication of my first book. She asked for details. I explained the situation. She expressed empathy, shared her own stories, and affirmed that institutional cultures can be very demoralizing. Then she presented a solution. "Build something that reminds you of why you got into this profession." Among the suggestions she presented was starting a book series at a press.

At the time, there were only two book series devoted solely to disability studies, Corporealities at the University of Michigan Press and The History of Disability at New York University Press. The former was founded by David Mitchell and Sharon Snyder, and it was influential in providing early visibility for books in the field, such as the series editors' own *Narrative Prosthesis: Disability and the Dependencies of Discourse*. The latter was founded by the late Paul Longmore and Lauri Umansky, and it published seven books from 2001 to 2014 (it stopped acquiring new projects after Longmore died in 2010). Cultural Front at New York University Press was another key player in the field. As disability studies expanded, four more series would emerge: Literary Disability Studies at Palgrave Macmillan, founded by David Bolt, Elizabeth Donaldson, and Julia Miele Rodas; Disability Histories at the University of Illinois Press, founded by Kim Nielsen and Michael Rembis; Crip at New York University Press, founded by Michael Bérubé, Robert McRuer, and Ellen Samuels; and Anima at Duke University Press, founded by Mel Chen and Jasbir Puar. At Temple University Press, I consulted with Janet Francendese, the editor with whom I worked on my first book, about her interest in a series that would bridge the fields of critical ethnic studies and disability studies. She voiced enthusiasm. On the cusp of retirement, Janet urged her successor to follow up with me. In the meantime, I asked Julie Minich if she would like to partner with me. Janet's replacement, Sara Jo Cohen, suggested that, given the interdisciplinarity of the field, we might find a social scientist to balance out Julie's and my training in literary studies. Nirmala Erevelles joined us in this capacity.

Getting a book series off the ground can be a long process. Both Julie and I were untenured when Dis/Color existed only as an idea. We waited until the time-consuming process of filing for promotion at our respective institutions was over. We had several conversations with, at any given time, the acquisitions editor whose portfolio in which Dis/Color would be housed. These interactions sometimes took place at conferences and sometimes happened over a phone call. After Sara Jo Cohen's departure from Temple, Sarah Munroe took over. Sarah worked closely with us in making a case to the press board for Dis/Color's relevance at a time when work in disability studies that engaged race was increasing in popularity. The late Chris Bell may have observed in his essay "Introducing White Disability Studies: A Modest Proposal" (2006) that the foundational scholarship had left the field's whiteness uninterrogated, thus presuming its universality. A decade later, however, much had changed. We saw Dis/Color as an opportunity to create an institutional platform for this burgeoning area of research.

The process of writing a proposal for a new book series is similar to that of writing a proposal for a book. We summarized its scope, located it in prevailing trends, and made an argument for how it would move the field forward. As with proposals for books, the series proposal also contained a section where we described existing series that might overlap and explained how we would avoid duplication. Another section noted book manuscripts in progress as potential titles we could solicit. We compiled this list by attending conferences to learn about new work and asking our disability studies colleagues about recent graduate students they had advised. Finally, we included an overview of the audience and market we envisioned. Once submitted, it was distributed to several external reviewers in much the same way a book manuscript would be read by external specialists. We used the feedback from these reader reports to hone the proposal further before it went before the press board for final approval.

From the beginning, the series editors believed very strongly that the concept of "access" should be interpreted expansively. In this day and age of the ebook, where software can transform written material into audio, access for people with low vision and blind people is fairly easy. Because of advances in technology, any press can make books accessible in this way. However, we also wanted to expand the reach of disability studies scholarship to readers who might not ordinarily read books from a university press. To be sure, not every book will have a trade audience, and not all research needs to court one in order to legitimize itself. But given that the fields in which Dis/Color is located have their origins in community-based movements, we wanted at least some of the books in the series to appeal to readers outside the academy. In general, all scholars might try writing for an audience like this occasionally, even if this writing doesn't take the form of a book.

Our commitment to access extends to authors as well. We have agreed to prioritize work by first-time authors who are junior faculty, non-tenure-track faculty, faculty at institutions that downplay the monograph in their tenure and promotion structure, and independent scholars. There is a lot of valuable research being done outside the usual contexts, and we wanted to give it a platform. This doesn't mean we discourage proposals from authors who fall outside these categories. For instance, the second book published in Dis/Color is by a senior scholar at a research university. What matters most to us is the quality and fit of the work. If it comes from an author whose position in the academy is not secure or an author whose voice is not usually amplified, we take special interest in reading the manuscript and marshaling it through the rigorous peer-review process for which Temple University Press is known.

Also, we must remember that publishing has presented barriers for many disabled people. First, people with physical, sensory, intellectual, or psychosocial impairments have historically been limited in their access to formal education. Second, biases—conscious or not—on the part of gatekeepers associated with publishing may cause book projects authored by disabled people to be overlooked. Third, authors who might need to work at a different pace may find themselves shut out because of the untenability of expectations about productivity. These absences in the publishing record are a multigenerational gap that will take many years to correct. The solutions need to be holistic, with many different players addressing the issue at different levels. The series editors and Shaun Vigil, the acquisitions editor who currently oversees Dis/Color, have agreed to abide by what Ellen Samuels calls "crip time" when communicating with authors about deadlines. The nonnormative temporality many disabled people inhabit "forces us to take breaks, even when we don't want to, even when we want to keep going, to move ahead" (Samuels 2017). Authors with unpredictable bodies and minds or those who are caregivers for people with unpredictable bodies and minds often can't anticipate the timing of a project's completion. We understand that deadlines may be missed, extensions should be granted, and flexibility needs to be built into any process of accessible publishing.

As of this writing in November 2022, Dis/Color has published three books, pushed two more into production, and signed advance contracts for two more projects. Several more proposals and manuscripts are in various stages of review. I love the genre of the monograph. It is schematic, but the form illuminates more than it constricts. The joy lies in seeing what authors do with it: how they seduce me, surprise me, frustrate me, unsettle me, make me hungry, make me think, make me laugh, and leave me spent. The experience of writing a book resembles reading one, except multiplied by several hundred times. However, my love is troubled by an undercurrent of guilt because of the unsustainability of academic publishing. It feels like loving a gas-guzzling SUV.

In 2002, Stephen Greenblatt alerted the humanities to this crisis. The requirement to publish a monograph for tenure, Greenblatt observed, had surged in recent years. Meanwhile, university library budgets nationwide have diminished. These opposing trajectories have placed the humanities on a path to disaster as presses scale back acquisitions in response to decreasing book sales. Junior faculty left scrambling for a publisher, Greenblatt warned, would suffer the direst consequences. His open letter to the Modern Language Association resonated with many people. From the vantage point of authors, the institutional elevation of the monograph actually contributes to its distortion as a generic form. As David Perry argues, when we turn books into mandatory professional benchmarks, we warp their purpose as sustained, long-form contributions to a field (Perry 2015). Taking my earlier metaphor further, I say that when we buy SUVs for cruising on highways, we forget they were meant for slow approaches over rough terrain. The truth is, research in the humanities can take many shapes. The form of the book suits some types, but others may be better served otherwise. These means may include a cluster of related articles, art shows and exhibition catalogs, consultations for museums or interpretive centers, webpages and other digital projects, performances, podcasts, documentaries, smartphone apps, or many other possibilities.

What has happened in the two decades since Greenblatt issued his open letter? For a while, there was no movement to solve the humanities publishing crisis even as some ways of alleviating the pinch emerged, such as the American Literatures Initiative, a Mellon-funded project that provides subventions to several university presses to offset the cost of books by first-time authors. The problem Greenblatt observed actually became worse for a while. Some research universities began demanding two books for tenure as they jockeyed for position in the rankings game, and some teaching colleges that did not previously require one had yielded to mission creep. This was not surprising. After all, academia is risk averse. Most faculty and administrators succeeded in this profession by following the well-trodden path instead of venturing into the unknown. However, this is all changing. A recent article in *Inside Higher Ed* by Charles Watkinson, director of the University of Michigan Press, and Melissa Pitts, director of the University of British Columbia Press, provides an overview of what presses are now doing to support research that takes nonmonograph forms. This includes launching peer-reviewed podcasts and other audio texts, designing platforms for collaboration with community partners, and providing infrastructure for open-source publications (Watkinson and Pitts 2021). Because presses are taking the lead in creating alternate ways to package knowledge, the hope is that department chairs and deans, who might need the legitimizing factor of a university press, would be more willing to regard these options as on a par with books.

This brings us to our role as faculty in these transformations given that, as I mentioned at the beginning, we work collaboratively with press editors. We need to think and act broad-mindedly when reading the work of our colleagues if prevailing attitudes about the monograph are expected to change. If you serve on the committee that keeps your department's guidelines for tenure and promotion up to date, consider adding language that recognizes research contributions across a wide range of formats. This may be easier in an interdisciplinary department, but even the most staunchly book-celebrating departments like English and history will notice if they see a critical mass of their colleagues from across the way making changes. If you encounter compelling and masterful specimens of nonmonograph projects, reference them when department chairs and deans ask for concrete examples. Like-minded faculty can set new standards by pursuing innovative research themselves. For instance, a candidate for promotion to associate professor whose file I recently read as an external reviewer had played it safe with the usual first monograph revised from a dissertation. For future research, though, they proposed and provided evidence of work underway for a large-scale digital humanities project in lieu of another book. Now tenured and in a position to inspire others, this scholar will be especially well suited to head these efforts at their own institution.

The takeaways I want my readers to have are, *first*, don't be intimidated by acquisitions editors at presses. As authors, we understand that getting their attention is a necessary first step in publishing a book, but we should also recognize that they are eyeing us as future collaborators, too, and equally invested in establishing connections with us. *Second*, consider pitching books for a broad audience. Realistically, most university press books won't have the reach of a true trade title, but packaging your work so it can speak to nonspecialists is one way to democratize access to our research. *Third*, if you are in a position to become part of the editorial process, consider giving voice to authors not normally prioritized in university press publishing. Accommodate crip time in setting and extending deadlines. *Fourth*, understand that, although the monograph still performs a valuable function, it is not the only way to showcase knowledge. If you have a role in deciding how your institution evaluates candidates for tenure and promotion, speak up in favor of innovative ways of disseminating research.

These suggestions won't remove every access barrier associated with the economies of professional capital linked to university press publishing. The primacy of the monograph will take a long time to abate, given how slowly change takes place in academia. The presence of one book series at one press that operates with the foregoing set of ethics will only scratch at the surface of academia's inequalities. However, I hope that making the work we do transparent will inspire others with power to act according to their capacities. As recent examples from other presses show, we are far from being the only ones working to democratize the creation and consumption of knowledge.

BIBLIOGRAPHY
Bell, Chris. 2006. "Introducing White Disability Studies: A Modest Proposal." In *The Disability Studies Reader*, 2nd ed., edited by Lennard J. Davis, 275–282. New York: Routledge.
Greenblatt, Stephen. 2002. "A Special Letter from Stephen Greenblatt." *Modern Language Association*, 28 May 2002. https://www.mla.org/Resources/Guidelines-and-Data/Reports -and-Professional-Guidelines/Publishing-and-Scholarship/Call-for-Action-on-Problems-in -Scholarly-Book-Publishing/A-Special-Letter-from-Stephen-Greenblatt.
Perry, David. 2015. "Why Write a Book?" *Chronicle of Higher Education*, March 3, 2015. https:// community.chronicle.com/news/925-why-write-a-book.
Samuels, Ellen. 2017. "Six Ways of Looking at Crip Time." *Disability Studies Quarterly* 37 (3): https://doi.org/10.18061/dsq.v37i3.5824.
Watkinson, Charles, and Melissa Pitts. 2021. "Re-envisioning Humanities Infrastructure." *Inside Higher Ed*, February 22, 2021. https://www.insidehighered.com/views/2021/02/22/institutions -and-funders-must-recognize-contributions-university-presses-humanities.

24

#DisabilityStudiesTooWhite

KRISTEN BOWEN, RACHEL KUO, AND MARA MILLS

Background: "Special Issues"

The title and impulse for this essay borrow from activist Vilissa Thompson, who created the hashtag #DisabilityTooWhite in 2016 to challenge the inadequate representation of disabled people of color in mainstream media and disability rights activism. The conversations sparked by #DisabilityTooWhite draw heavily on principles of disability justice, a term coined in 2005 by a group of queer disabled activists of color to levy intersectionality as a political challenge to whiteness in disability rights movements and ableism in racial justice movements (Sins Invalid 2019). In academic disability studies, which emerged in the United States in the 1980s–1990s (Garland-Thomson 2013), similar protests date at least to 2006, when Chris Bell published "Introducing White Disability Studies: A Modest Proposal" in the second edition of *The Disability Studies Reader*, calling out the dramatic exclusions and false universalizing of the field in its founding decades. Bell's edited volume *Blackness and Disability: Critical Examinations and Cultural Interventions*, published posthumously in 2012, further opened the door for disability theory and activism centering race, such as disability critical race theory (DisCrit), crip-of-color critique, Black disability studies, Black feminist disability studies, decolonial disability studies, LatDisCrit (see Padilla, this volume), and more.[1]

Given the burgeoning critique of "white disability studies" since 2005–2006, we set out to assess the state of the field today, examining both authorship and content related to race in key journals and anthologies from 2010 to 2020. We wanted to know if the field had changed in meaningful ways: Are there more articles about race in disability studies journals and in canon-making anthologies? More citations of DisCrit or Black feminist disability studies authors? More scholars of color, regardless of specialization, editing or writing for disability studies journals? Or, as Moya Bailey and Izetta Mobley have recently argued, do "disability scholars pay homage to Bell" while "citations of his work have not led to the fundamental shift that he desired Disability Studies to make" (Bailey and Mobley 2019, 12)? Mel Y. Chen, Alison Kafer, Eunjung Kim, and Julie Avril Minich further note that field transformation has been obfuscated by "reductive and extractive citation practices" as well as increases in author representation without "substantive engagement" in alternate theories and methods (Chen et al., 2023).

Authorship, citation, and representation matter in ways mundane and revolutionary. Beyond influencing the course of individual careers and livelihoods, they shape the historical record, laws and policies, and education. Publication and citation practices that continue to amplify white voices and present western work as the universal perspective demonstrate a "hierarchy of credibility" that devalues the intersectional experience of racial marginalization and disability (Becker 1967; Gibson, Bowen, and Hanson 2021). Our approach is informed by Rachel Kuo's previous work on "#CommunicationSoWhite," a 2018 study of authorship and citation in the field of communication, coauthored with Paula Chakravartty, Victoria Grubbs, and Charlton McIlwain. In that article, the authors depict the urgency of identifying and redressing racial disparities in academia:

> In the last decade we have seen the ongoing dismantling of affirmative action and other redistributive policies. Moreover, the growing "adjunctification of the professoriate" in the academic labor market (Sterne, 2011) has been disproportionately shouldered by women and people of color (Caruth & Caruth, 2013). These factors, in addition to institutionalized racism and academia's publish-or-perish mantra, perpetuate racial disparities (Gunning, 2000). New racial justice movements, from Black Lives Matter in the United States to Rhodes/Fees Must Fall in South Africa, have revived questions about representation within the academy and exposed ongoing inequities, including the prohibitive cost of higher education, insufficient attention to race and racial inequality in curricula, and racially hostile campus climates. (Chakravartty et al. 2018, 257)

In disability studies, racial disparities in authorship, content, citation, and editorship are particularly striking because people of color are disproportionately disabled (e.g., by substandard health care, environmental racism, or police violence) and tracked into special education (Minich 2016; Annamma 2018). Responding to these disparities requires not just "adding" elided perspectives into existing narratives but remaking disability studies models from different starting points. Scholars have mapped the complex historical and political relations between race and disability, which span coconstitution, analogy, intersectionality, shared social construction, and mutual exclusion (Erevelles and Minear 2010; Annamma, Connor, and Ferri 2013; Bailey and Mobley 2019; Tyler 2022). They have also argued for distinct social and historical sites, processes, and experiences of disablement (Puar 2017; Hinton 2021).

Although we borrow our method from "#CommunicationSoWhite," we acknowledge important differences between disability studies and communication, starting with institutional origins and power. Disability studies emerged out of disability activism, itself heavily influenced by feminist and civil rights activism. Early disability rights activism was often led by white men (Hinton 2021), but the activist relationship to university spaces was largely one of exclusion. The first journal in the field, *Disability Studies Quarterly* (*DSQ*), was launched in 1980 as a newsletter for the medical sociology group of the American Sociological Association. Edited by Irving Zola from 1982 to 1994, the journal adopted its current name in 1985 and became the journal of the Society for Disability Studies after that group became an independent scholarly organization in 1986, having initially been founded in 1982 as a section of the Western Social Science Association for the Study of Chronic Illness, Impairment, and Disability. Over the years, *DSQ* has shifted its publishing focus to the humanities, while *Disability and Society*, founded in the United Kingdom in 1986, is primarily anchored in the social sciences. Both of these journals formerly included rehabilitation perspectives, and we note that this legacy may have deterred humanities authors trained in cultural studies and critical theory from publishing with them at an earlier moment.

Even today, when disability studies has proliferated as a subfield of literature, history, anthropology, sociology, and media studies, the Society for Disability Studies is a comparatively small scholarly society that has struggled with funding. Unlike communication, disability studies has remained a field or subfield rather than a discipline, with few university departments or majors worldwide, which has implications regarding the kinds of institutional power (or lack thereof) with which it is associated. For many critical disability studies scholars and activists, this interdisciplinarity and lack of "discipline" is a strength. In the words of Julie Avril Minich (2016), "disability studies as a methodology rather than a subject" keeps the field committed "to its origins in social justice work." On the other hand, much publishing in the field takes place in established journals in the humanities and social sciences (e.g., *PMLA*, *American Quarterly*) with higher "impact factors" than the disability studies journals we investigate here. Especially before tenure, scholars may be more likely to publish within their disciplines of training and employment or to focus on producing monographs, which are not captured in this study. Until recently, pivotal special issues and fora exploring the relationship between race and disability have tended to come out in ethnic studies or cultural studies journals such as *MELUS* ("Race, Ethnicity, Disability, and Literature: Intersections and Interventions" [James and Wu 2006]); *Amerasia Journal* ("The State of Illness and Disability in Asian America" [Ho and Lee 2013]); *Lateral* ("Forum: Emerging Critical Analytics for Alternative Humanities: Critical Disability Studies" [Minich 2016]); and *African American Review* ("Blackness and Disability" [Pickens 2017]).

As we assessed authorship trends over the past decade in self-proclaimed journals of disability studies, as well as edited collections that draw from a wider author pool, we kept in mind the denigration—in terms of ranking and funding—of publishing in disability studies. The observation by Subini Annamma, David

Connor, and Beth Ferri (2013, 9–10) of a "professionally enforced line between special education and general education journals," which they attribute to ableism, holds true in disability studies publishing more broadly. Following Anna Hinton, we also acknowledge "alternative genealogies" that don't appear in our journal count, such as the deep archive of writing about "trauma, non-apparent disabilities, violence, illness, and disease" in Black Feminist Studies (Hinton 2021, 13, 17, drawing on the work of Sami Schalk and Akemi Nishida).

With this in mind, we offer our study as an audit of disability studies circa 2020. We appreciate criticisms of the false objectivity of censuses, and the potential for tokenization or essentialism in diversity, equity, and inclusion (DEI) "equity audits." We are also aware that we aren't coding for disability; a question mark hangs over the same decade regarding the inclusion of disabled authors in disability studies. But we believe even a rough tabulation of authorship and race-related content across a decade can reveal important trends—including stagnation—and spur accountability. We've witnessed the renewed, pragmatic and theoretical scholarly conversations that have followed similar studies in other fields. In addition to "#CommunicationSoWhite," we flag the Institute for Scientific Information report that revealed flat or decreased publishing rates for Black, Native American, and Hispanic authors in STEM fields between 2010 and 2020 (Beardsley and Halevi 2022). To move beyond counts and checklists, we point to Leah Lakshmi Piepzna-Samarasinha's *Disability Justice: An Audit Tool*, which asks organizations to assess the ways they are "centering disability justice politics, practices and leadership" (2022, 7).

Some of our findings, detailed shortly, are not unexpected: the diversification, if slow, of authorship in disability studies journals; the continuation of the issue, noted by Bell in 2006, of race often appearing in "special issues" of disability studies journals (and vice versa) rather than as a core analytic; and distinctions between the racial composition of authorship in the United States, United Kingdom, and Canada. Other findings took us by surprise: a stark underrepresentation of nonwhite authors (6.4 percent) and non-western sites of research (0.7 percent) in canon-making handbooks and anthologies, with the numbers being somewhat better in peer-reviewed journals (even though they rely on a smaller, submission-based pool); the fact that a third of the nonwhite scholars publishing in disability studies are non-western-based scholars; and a decrease in articles *about* race in certain journals (e.g., *Disability and Society*) over the past decade.

Methodology

Our methodology emerges from the 2018 study "#CommunicationSoWhite" (Chakravartty et al. 2018), which quantitatively assesses citational disparities in the study of communication by examining race and author names. In the present study, rather than look at disparities in citation counts—how frequently an author is cited and their racial background—we focus on authors' racial identity and whether race is used as a central analytic in research content at the levels of theory, methodology, and discussion and findings. We take these two factors—authorship and content—to be distinct but interrelated aspects of the "white disability studies" argument. In addition to approximating the representation of scholars of color in disability studies, we offer a starting point for assessing *how* racial scholarship is more broadly employed by both white and nonwhite authors in the field. Beyond the mere inclusion of scholars of color, our approach emphasizes race as a deliberate analytic that goes beyond relegating racialized people into populations for scientific or social scientific study.

Following the rationale in "#CommunicationSoWhite," we approach coding in a binary "white/nonwhite" or "yes/no" format, given the ways an antagonistic social order of white dominance is embedded in much historical and contemporary racism and imperialism (Wynter 2003; Hesse 2016). While we understand that the lack of data disaggregation collapses unique variables, we chose to aggregate statistical analysis given (a) the argument about a *lack of nonwhite authors* in the secondary literature that prompted this study and (b) the complexities of racial interpretation, coding, and categorization. The general nature of this binary also allows us to investigate claims about white disability studies while engaging critically—as opposed to strictly—with categorization practices found in the US Census.

Our corpus of data includes 4,693 total entries from the years 2010–2020 in the following Anglophone, peer-reviewed humanities and social science journals of disability studies: *Disability and Society, DSQ,* the *Review of Disability Studies: An International Journal,* the *Journal of Literary and Cultural Disability Studies,* and the *Canadian Journal of Disability Studies* (see table 24.1). We use Anglophone journals given the Euro-US-centricity in the field of study (Ng, White, and Saha 2020) and the longer-standing colonial legacies of western and English-speaking dominance in knowledge production. We excluded journals that simply have the word *disability* in the title—for instance, journals of nursing, education, rehabilitation, policy, and so on. We also excluded journals in Deaf Studies, which overlaps with but is not identical to disability studies. Lastly, although we acknowledge their field-building significance, we did not include journals that have been out of print for more than ten years (e.g., the *Disability Rag*); newsletters and "blog journals" (e.g., the Public Disability History blog, the Disability History Association newsletter); graduate student journals (e.g., *Critical Disability Discourses* at York University); recently launched journals (e.g., the *International Journal of Disability and Social Justice* and the *Indian Journal of Critical Disability Studies,* both founded in 2021); or book series.[2]

We additionally looked at edited collections—readers and handbooks—that curate what constitute "core" texts and themes in the field, including the

TABLE 24.1. Findings on disability studies journals and handbooks (2010–2020).

	Total entries	Content on race	Non-western site	Nonwhite authors
Disability Studies Quarterly	870	175 (20.1%)	73 (8.4%)	132 (15.2%)
Disability and Society	2,103	357 (17.0%)	179 (8.5%)	274 (13.0%)
Review of Disability Studies: An International Journal	552	156 (28.3%)	93 (16.8%)	146 (26.4%)
Journal of Literary and Cultural Disability Studies	277	48 (17.3%)	7 (2.5%)	32 (11.6%)
Canadian Review	438	48 (11.0%)	12 (2.7%)	58 (13.2%)
Handbooks and anthologies	453	57 (12.6%)	3 (0.7%)	29 (6.4%)
Total	4,693	841 (17.9%)	367 (7.8%)	671 (14.3%)

Disability Studies Reader, first through fifth editions (1997, 2006, 2010, 2013, and 2016); *Keywords for Disability Studies* (2015); *Routledge Handbook of Disability*, first and second editions (2012 and 2020); *Disability Studies: A Student's Guide* (2013); and *SAGE Handbook of Disability Studies* (2001). These collections draw from humanities and social science publishing at large, beyond disability studies–focused journals, and as such might be expected to reflect either broader trends in authorship or gatekeeping in the field.

We treated each combination of author and article as an individual entry regardless of the contribution of multiple authors to a single article, repeat authorship, or duplication of pieces in handbooks over time. Our study focuses on original peer-reviewed research articles and book chapters and excludes creative or multimedia works and book reviews that may be included in journals and anthologies. Our intention with this list of publications is not to make an argument about what does or doesn't "count" as disability studies scholarship or to participate in defining a canon. Instead, our goal was to locate publications that self-identify as contributing to the field of "disability studies" or resources that are frequently sought out and shared both by individuals wanting to learn more about the field and by those who are teaching within it. For this reason, we also chose not to include more specialized edited collections (e.g., on disability and digital media).

The data-collection component of our study was completed between March 2021 and December 2021 with two human coders (coauthors Kristen Bowen and Rachel Kuo) who manually interpreted authors' racial identities and the race-related content of articles or chapters. Given that Anglophone disability studies journals and anthologies are primarily published in the United States and United Kingdom (with one journal in Canada), we adopted a coding schematic from US Census categories as a starting point: white, Black, Latinx, Asian, and Native and Indigenous. We then expanded from this schematic, given its limitations, to account for Arab and Middle Eastern communities. In order to determine authors' racial identities, we primarily relied on publicly available material on the authors' faculty or staff pages hosted by their primary institution; personal websites; and social media accounts (e.g., LinkedIn, Twitter, and Facebook). Aware that studies like this can risk essentializing racial characteristics and traits, we examined a combination of headshots alongside biographical information, professional affiliations, and other published works. For example, authors may be visually misinterpreted as white by photo alone but may self-indicate racial, ethnic, or tribal backgrounds in their biographies or in position statements within scholarly articles.

This process surfaced many complicated questions about racial interpretation and, given the international dimensions of disability studies, many considerations about the geopolitics of race transnationally (Getsy and Gossett 2021). Again, our study is meant to provide baseline evidence for nearly two decades of qualitative claims about race and racial disparities in disability studies, rather than make objective claims about race per se. Following earlier studies and considerations of the racialization of geography (e.g., Chakravartty et al. 2018; Pulido 2002), we decided that both western and eastern European scholars would be counted as "white" unless they also identified as a person of color (e.g., being Black and German or South Asian and British). This slightly differs from other studies on geographic disparities in scholarship (e.g., Ekdale et al. 2022; Demeter 2020) that have taken a "Global North" and "Global South" distinction, where the Global North includes higher-income countries in Asia and Global South includes eastern Europe. Given our focus on Anglophone journals, we took into consideration historical and contemporary interpretations of whiteness, such as how East Asian scholars from Korea and Japan would be read as "nonwhite" within these sites of knowledge production. These are not easy distinctions. For example, we coded scholars from countries such as Portugal and Spain as "white" while scholars from Latin America were coded as nonwhite (which is an imperfect distinction given the ways that scholars from Latin America can also be white, depending on their relationship and positioning within historical systems of colonialism). Given the racialization of religion and global formations of Islamophobia, we coded Muslim scholars as nonwhite regardless of country of origin. Despite this, we could not adequately account for intragroup differences, such as caste and ethnic hierarchies (e.g., Han Chinese or Hindu Brahmins).

This process underscores the complexities of race, nation, and geography as a result of cross-cutting legacies of imperialism, empire, and migration. It requires attention to nuances and complexities in power relations that automated methods could not adequately account for. We emphasize these moments of tension and imperfect and messy decision-making to demonstrate the difficulties of categorizing mass quantities of data, even when only coding between two possible categories. The significant contributions of both critical race and disability studies as method and theory have long emphasized the trouble with categorical assumptions. We also want to highlight the qualitative aspects of quantitative research as well as the necessity of any research, regardless of field or method, to treat race as an analytic rather than a fixed object of study.

We assessed whether articles and chapters feature race as a key analytic by reviewing abstracts and keywords, since these are strong indicators of how significantly the authors identify race as a core part of their research. We also searched for terms including *race, racial, racism, whiteness,* and *colonialism* throughout the entire article as supplementary information. While we are specifically looking at race as a distinct category, we also aim to challenge the ways that social difference has been compartmentalized into individualized categories of identity; thus we did not include articles or chapters that only briefly mention race as a component part of a list of intersecting identities or a list of demographics as data points. We also did not include articles that generically discuss "diversity and inclusion" or "social justice" without explicitly engaging an analysis of race and power. However, an article on militarism and imperialism that does not explicitly discuss "racism" might still be coded as being "about race" if the authors engage legacies of those systems as structuring racial orders.

When we started the coding process, we also noted the inclusion of scholarship about non-US and especially non-western sites that emphasized *populations* of difference by authors in both western and non-western institutions, such as case studies of disability rights activism or medical and health policies in different geographic contexts. At first, we decided *not* to count these articles as scholarship about race, given the absence of an analysis of power as well as our own concerns about reproducing western-centric frameworks of "racial others" (e.g., treating case studies in Africa as peripheral or particular). However, we continued to observe that much of the disability studies scholarship that was not explicitly about white communities focused instead on non-western communities. Moreover, many of the authors of color represented were located in these same sites writing from the perspective of their current geolocation. Noticing this as a substantial pattern, we then went back to the beginning of our data set to recode, and we created an additional category for scholarship "about race" that was sited in non-western geographies. Here, similar to our note earlier about the slipperiness of Global North / Global South distinctions, we approach "non-western" primarily as referring to sites outside the United States, Canada, the United Kingdom, Australia, and Europe while also considering different transnational dimensions of local sites (e.g., studies on refugee communities in France). While we do not want to conflate race and nation, nor reify national boundaries, we made some coding decisions along these lines as a result of interpretations of race and racialization in the Anglophone sites where research is published.

At certain times, data about authors were simply not available. Some community-engaged researchers or other nonacademic authors, such as health and education practitioners, were harder to find and identify given factors such as searchability of public biographical material or transitions across organizations. For some social science articles with multiple authors, it was more difficult to find information about middle authors (e.g., the fourth, fifth, or sixth), such as coauthors who were graduate students at the time of publication but then did not remain in academia. While we did our best to locate all authors regardless of institutional and organizational affiliation, authors we could not identify—forty-three total—were left out of the final analysis.

Findings

We launched this empirical study to assess the widespread assumption that scholarship by people of color, as well as scholarship that explicitly addresses race, is underrepresented in disability studies. Not surprisingly, the numbers confirmed this intuition (table 24.1). More specifically, we wanted to understand the extent of these disparities after 2010, when the field was better established and the critique of "white disability studies" well known. In terms of author representation, we found that 14.3 percent of articles and chapters published between 2010 and 2020 in journals and handbooks combined were by nonwhite scholars. Here we would like to reemphasize that we treated each data entry as a unique individual entry, so this percentage may include the same nonwhite scholar more than once.

We found that 17.9 percent (841 out of 4,693) of total publications either used race as a deliberate analytic or centered scholarship beyond western contexts. Out of the total data set, 7.8 percent of entries focused on non-western sites of study, which means that nearly half (43.6 percent, or 367 out of 841) of the publications "about race" were actually sited within racialized, non-western geographies. Non-US and non-western scholars publishing articles from or about their specific location make up approximately one-third (32.9 percent) of the total number of nonwhite authors publishing in disability studies journals and anthologies. Notably, 8.5 percent of the total number of entries (400 out of 4,693) are articles by nonwhite scholars that also focus on race. This means two things. One, in the majority of cases (59.6 percent) of nonwhite authorship, race is a critical part of the work. Specifically, a majority of first authors who are scholars of color write about race; however, when scholars of color are included in multiauthored articles (but not as first authors), those articles are typically not about race.

Second, we observe that white and nonwhite authors contribute almost equally to the scant scholarship on race in the field; 50.6 percent of the articles about race are by white authors. While there are some similarities between our findings and the findings in "#CommunicationSoWhite" (Chakravartty et al. 2018), in the latter article the authors discovered that the inclusion of more nonwhite scholars does not necessarily improve disparities in scholarly recognition or distribution as measured through citations. Within disability studies, on the other hand, critical articles about race by nonwhite authors are sometimes highly cited.[3] For example, using Google Scholar metrics, Chris Bell's 2006 article "Introducing White Disability Studies: A Modest Proposal" has at least 307 citations as of November 2022; while not included in our data set, Subini Annamma, David Connor, and Beth Ferri's 2013 article "Dis/ability Critical Race Studies (DisCrit)," published in the journal *Race Ethnicity and Education*, has over 730 citations. As Moya Bailey and Izetta Mobley (2019) point out, citation is not the main problem in disability studies, but rather representation in terms of content and overall authorship.

Within the data set, several special issues on feminism and movement politics are notable in their inclusion of racial scholarship, suggesting that an explicit emphasis on the *collective politics* of disability necessitates critical engagement with race. A 2012 issue of *DSQ* on "movement politics" guest edited by Michael Ralph featured eight nonwhite authors and eleven articles (out of twelve total within the issue) centering race as a critical analytic, and a 2013 special issue on feminist theory and disability in *DSQ* had six articles engaging with race. New and forthcoming special issues on race and indigeneity in disability studies journals, such as *DSQ*'s January 2022 issue on indigeneity and disability, may further support transformations of the field. The goal, as Bell argued, is broad structural change, but special issues such as these have the potential to call in new authors and amplify underrepresented themes in the field.

Although disability studies is interdisciplinary, it is worth noting the similarities and differences between journals that are primarily located in the humanities and those that are primarily in the social sciences. For example, *Disability and Society* makes up 44.8 percent of our entries (2,103 total entries), given the more common practice of coauthorship in the social sciences. *DSQ*, a more humanities-focused journal, has only 870 entries. *Disability and Society* had 13 percent representation by nonwhite authors and 17 percent of articles centering race, while *DSQ* had 15.2 percent representation by nonwhite authors and 20.1 percent of articles centering race. The difference in content may be due to the longer legacy of humanities-oriented scholarship engaging fields such as postcolonial and decolonial theory, ethnic studies, and feminist studies.

The difference between representation in journal publications and edited volumes is even more notable. Within the edited anthologies and handbooks, which purport to represent the entire field at a given point in time, there were only three total entries (0.7 percent) in the ten-year period (across all anthologies) that emphasized non-western sites of study, which has implications for what knowledge is deemed canonical and generalizable. Only 6.4 percent of authors represented in the handbooks were nonwhite and 12.6 percent of scholarship engaged race. In the case of *Keywords for Disability Studies* (2015), we coded more generously for the inclusion of race, racism, colonialism, or imperialism given the brevity of each chapter. Additionally, aside from one chapter on feminist theory and disability studies and one chapter on Third World literatures, we observed no scholarship on race in the first edition of the *Disability Studies Reader* (published in the United States). After Bell's 2006 essay, which was subsequently included in later editions of the reader, there was a slight increase in scholarship on race. In both the 2013 and 2016 editions, there were eleven chapters that engaged substantively with race as an analytic and five nonwhite authors. However, neither edition included scholarship about non-western contexts. The *Routledge Handbook of Disability* (published in the United Kingdom) exhibited less change: two chapters on race and one nonwhite author in 2020, compared with one chapter on race and two nonwhite authors in 2012.

We also sought to see if there was any change over time across the entire data set. Using the two time periods of 2010–2015 and 2016–2020 as points of comparison, we found a slight increase in the inclusion of nonwhite scholars over time: 12.9 percent between 2010 and 2015 as compared with 16.1 percent between 2016 and 2020. There was also a minimal increase of scholarship about non-western sites, from 7.7 percent to 8.2 percent. However, we also noted a slight, but still surprising, *decrease* in scholarship *about* race between the two periods, from 18.7 percent to 17.9 percent. We looked more specifically at *DSQ* and *Disability and Society*, since these two journals make up the bulk of the data set and also represent one US-based publication and one UK-based publication. *DSQ* (based in the United States) saw a small increase in both nonwhite scholars (14 percent to 16.8 percent) and scholarship on race (19.4 percent to 20.8 percent), but a slight decrease in non-western-sited scholarship (8.5 percent to 7.5 percent). In comparison, *Disability and Society* (based in the United Kindom) saw an increase in nonwhite scholars (11.5 percent to 14.4 percent) but a decrease in both scholarship on race (18.5 percent to 15.5 percent) and non-western scholarship (8.8 percent to 8.3 percent). Because entries from *Disability and Society* make up almost half of the entire data set, their numbers influence the overall patterns in change over time. While the slight increase of nonwhite scholars publishing in disability studies journals can be heartening, the minimal scholarship in this area is still concerning.

Discussion

As noted, this study is offered as one way to assess the extent to which disability studies has shifted away from "white disability studies" over the past decade. We observe multiple reasons for the historical makeup of authorship in disability studies journals, from racial hierarchies in academia at large (disability studies scholars are mostly trained and employed in other fields), to the historical whiteness of the disability rights movement, to alternate genealogies that have not formally been recognized as "disability studies," to the impacts of interdisciplinarity on publishing patterns and ableism on journal rankings (e.g., the publication of many disability studies articles in non–disability studies journals).

Our study also offers a data point for comparison with future directions the field might take. A number of factors have contributed to a current expansion in discourse about the intersections of disability and race: the anticipated impact of the "ADA generation" (those who have experienced their entire education following the 1990 passage of the key legislation of the Americans with Disabilities Act) moving into senior positions in their institutions; the Black Lives Matter movement; the impact of the COVID-19 pandemic on conversations about care and accessibility in some academic contexts. The slowness of academic publishing in general and "crip time" in particular also means that scholarly disability studies work engaging race begun years ago may only just be coming out now (Samuels 2017). These factors, plus the small gains we documented regarding nonwhite authors and scholarship about race in humanities-based disability studies journals, and the growing presence of disability studies publishing in non–disability studies journals (including the excavation and creation of alternate genealogies), make us cautiously optimistic about more substantial changes in the coming years.

We urge social scientists working in disability studies to take up race as an analytic, given the surprising decrease in scholarship about race in disability studies journals in that subfield over the past decade. We also urge the field of disability studies as a whole to encourage more non-western scholarship in Anglophone journals, to incorporate decolonial and postcolonial perspectives across contributions, and to mark when understandings of disability have been developed from a US (or UK or Canadian) perspective so as not to falsely universalize. Following Bell, perhaps the time has come to note when a particular claim reflects "US disability studies" rather than a more global understanding of the field. As disability studies grows, we caution that non-western scholarship may be swamped by new research on the United States, United Kingdom, Europe, and Canada. Lastly, we point out the successes of certain peer-reviewed journals as compared with edited books in diversifying authorship, especially with regard to geographic region (e.g., the *Review of Disability Studies: An International Journal*). Publishers and book series editors should take into consideration the standpoints of editors for canon-making handbooks and encourage strategies like coeditorship and external review.

All of these factors contribute to the conversation about how we define a field, particularly one still as comparatively young as disability studies. "How might the who, the what, and the where of disability studies shift if the field searched for origin stories in unfamiliar places?" asks the call for papers for an upcoming special edition of *DSQ* titled "Origins, Objects, and Orientations: Towards a Racial History of Disability." These are vital questions for the ways we understand disability as inextricably intertwined with race. They are also vital to the concrete ways we shape and reshape our field. In the absence of analysis of race and racism as a structuring analytic, whiteness is reified. The editors of *Crip Genealogies*, another collection forthcoming (2023) at the time of our writing, similarly work to "provincialize" white disability studies as a step toward "expand[ing] our notions of what counts as disability studies" (n p). And journals such as *Disability and the Global South*, publishing scholarship that spans global health, international development, psychology, and anthropology as well as disability studies, "critique and challenge the Westerncentrism in dominant disciplines and practices"[4] in part by decentering rather than simply diversifying disability studies.

Ensuring that disability studies work engages in conversations about disability and race across disciplines requires us to go beyond an audit. Institutional, financial, and other structural support is necessary for more scholars of color and non-western scholars to publish in the field. So is increasing funding and status for disability studies and special education journals. What methods, developed out of disability ways of interacting, working, and sharing information, can help us achieve these goals?

NOTES

1 We note, however, a relative lack of conversation between theories of race and disability in education (e.g. DisCrit) and the humanities (e.g. crip-of-color critique).

2 This dataset was selected by Rebecca Sanchez and Mara Mills.

3 A separate study would be required to compare citation rates for white scholars and scholars of color in disability studies, including books as well as articles in the data set.

4 *Disability and the Global South*. https://dgsjournal.org/.

BIBLIOGRAPHY

Annamma, Subini. 2018. *The Pedagogy of Pathologization: Dis/abled Girls of Color in the School-Prison Nexus*. New York: Routledge.

Annamma, Subini, David Connor, and Beth Ferri. 2013. "Dis/ability Critical Race Studies (DisCrit): Theorizing at the Intersections of Race and Dis/ability." *Race Ethnicity and Education* 16 (1): 1–31.

Bailey, Moya, and Izetta Autumn Mobley. 2019. "Work in the Intersections: A Black Feminist Disability Framework." *Gender and Society* 33 (1): 19–40.

Beardsley, Ryan, and Gali Halevi. 2022. *Insights: Ethnic Diversity in STEM in the United States*. Philadelphia: Institute for Scientific Information.

Becker, Howard S. 1967. "Whose Side Are We On?" *Social Problems* 14 (3): 239–247.

Bell, Chris. 2006. "Introducing White Disability Studies: A Modest Proposal." In *The Disability Studies Reader*, 2nd ed., edited by Lennard Davis, 275–282. New York: Routledge.

Bell, Chris. 2012. *Blackness and Disability: Critical Examinations and Cultural Interventions*. East Lansing: Michigan State University Press.

Bolton, Sony Coráñez, Kelsey Henry, Leon J. Hilton, and Anna LaQuawn Hinton, editors. 2023. "Origins, Objects, and Orientations: Towards a Racial History of Disability." *Disability Studies Quarterly Special Issue*. https://networks.h-net.org/node/2606/discussions/7563116/disability-studies-quarterly-dsq-special-issue-cfp-towards-racial.

Chakravartty, Paula, Rachel Kuo, Victoria Grubbs, and Charlton McIlwain. 2018. "#Communica-tionSoWhite." *Journal of Communication* 68 (2): 254–266.

Chen, Mel Y., Alison Kafer, Eunjung Kim, and Julie Avril Minich. 2023. *Crip Genealogies.* Durham: Duke University Press.

Demeter, Márton. 2020. *Academic Knowledge Production and the Global South: Questioning Inequality and Under-representation.* New York: Palgrave Macmillan.

Ekdale, Brian, Abby Rinaldi, Mir Ashfaquzzaman, Mehrnaz Khanjani, Frankline Matanji, Ryan Stoldt, and Melissa Tully. 2022. "Geographic Disparities in Knowledge Production: A Big Data Analysis of Peer-Reviewed Communication Publications from 1990 to 2019." *International Journal of Communication* 16:2498–2525.

Eng, Chris A. and Amy K. King, eds. 2017. "Emergent Critical Analytics for Alternative Humani-ties." Forum, *Lateral: Journal of the Cultural Studies Association* 6 (1).

Erevelles, Nirmala, and Andrea Minear. 2010. "Unspeakable Offenses: Untangling Race and Dis-ability in Discourses of Intersectionality." *Journal of Literary and Cultural Disability Studies* 4 (2): 127–145.

Garland-Thomson, Rosemarie. 2013. "Disability Studies: A Field Emerged." *American Quarterly* 65 (4): 915–926.

Getsy, David J., and Che Gossett. 2021. "A Syllabus on Transgender and Nonbinary Methods for Art and Art History." *Art Journal* 80 (4): 100–115.

Gibson, Amelia, Kristen Bowen, and Dana Hanson. 2021. "We Need to Talk about How We Talk about Disability: A Critical Quasi-systematic Review." *In the Library with the Lead Pipe*, Feb-ruary 24, 2021. https://www.inthelibrarywiththeleadpipe.org/2021/disability/.

Hesse, Barnor. 2016. "Preface: Counter-racial Formation Theory." In *Conceptual Aphasia in Black: Displacing Racial Formation*, edited by P. Khalil Saucier and Tryon P. Woods, vii–x. Lanham, MD: Lexington Books.

Hinton, Anna. 2021. "On Fits, Starts, and Entry Points: The Rise of Black Disability Studies." *CLA Journal* 64 (1): 11–21.

Ho, Jennifer, and James Kyung-Jin Lee, eds. 2013. "The State of Illness and Disability in Asian America." Special issue, *Amerasia Journal* 39 (1).

James, Jennifer C., and Cynthia Wu, eds. 2006. "Race, Ethnicity, Disability, and Literature." Special issue, *MELUS* 31 (3).

James, Jennifer C., and Cynthia Wu. 2006. "Editors' Introduction: Race, Ethnicity, Disability, and Literature: Intersections and Interventions." *MELUS* 31 (3): 3–13.

Larkin-Gilmore, Ella Callow and Susan Burch, eds. 2021. "Indigeneity and Disability." Special issue, *Disability Studies Quarterly* 41 (4).

Minich, Julie Avril. 2016. "Enabling Whom? Critical Disability Studies Now." *Lateral* 5 (1). https://csalateral.org/issue/5-1/forum-alt-humanities-critical-disability-studies-now-minich/.

Ng, Eve, Khadijah Costley White, and Anamik Saha Saha. 2020. "#CommunicationSoWhite: Race and Power in the Academy and Beyond." *Communication, Culture and Critique* 13 (2): 143–151.

Pickens, Therí A., ed. 2017. "Blackness & Disability." Special Issue, *African American Review* 50 (2).

Pickens, Therí. 2017. "Blue Blackness, Black Blueness: Making Sense of Blackness and Disability." *African American Review* 50 (2): 93–103.

Piepzna-Samarasinha, Leah Lakshmi. 2022. *Disability Justice: An Audit Tool.* Portland, OR: Northwest Health Foundation. https://www.northwesthealth.org/djaudittool.

Puar, Jasbir. 2017. *The Right to Maim: Debility, Capacity, Disability.* Durham, NC: Duke University Press.

Pulido, L. 2002. "Reflections on a White Discipline." *Professional Geographer* 54 (1): 42–49.

Ralph, Michael, ed. 2012. "Movement Politics." Special Issue, *Disability Studies Quarterly* 32 (3).

Samuels, Ellen. 2017. "Six Ways of Looking at Crip Time." *Disability Studies Quarterly* 37 (3). https://doi.org/10.18061/dsq.v37i3.5824.

Sins Invalid. 2019. *Skin, Tooth, and Bone: The Basis of Movement Is Our People.* 2nd ed. Berkeley: Sins Invalid.

Tyler, Dennis. 2022. *Disabilities of the Color Line: Redressing Antiblackness from Slavery to the Present.* New York: New York University Press.

Wynter, Sylvia. 2003. "Unsettling the Coloniality of Being/Power/Truth/Freedom: Towards the Human, after Man, Its Overrepresentation—an Argument." *CR: The New Centennial Review* 3 (3): 257–337.

25

A Philosophical Analysis of ASL-English Bilingual Publishing

TERESA BLANKMEYER BURKE

Deaf academics whose work engages aspects of deaf community and populations are faced with the question of whether there is an ethical obligation to share their work with the relevant signing deaf communities in a more accessible format, such as their signed language. If so, this raises a host of complicated ethical issues around the hidden labor this obligation imposes in academic institutional structures that are not designed to support such work.

"Nothing about us without us" is a common slogan used in disability protests and advocacy movements.[1] It is not just a rallying cry but a normative judgment and prescriptive imperative. By normative, I mean it is a claim about what is the right thing to do ethically; by prescriptive, I mean it is a claim about what action one ought to take. For academics who use a signed language, a frequently occurring question is whether one has a moral obligation to share their work when the work features or concerns or otherwise affects signing Deaf people and their communities.

In this chapter, I begin by considering whether existing codes of ethics and professional expectations of conduct can provide guidance to signing academics. Following this, I ask whether such resources for the professoriate might satisfy the ethical obligations of signing academics, especially those working with deaf populations. This includes questions of what research findings should be shared, with whom, and how to share them. I then turn to the question of where to share one's academic work, offering a brief sketch of what might count as a signed language text. To illustrate this, I present two projects I worked on and highlight the ethical and epistemological issues raised in the course of these endeavors. Finally, I conclude with some suggestions of future directions for others thinking through the philosophical issues raised in ASL-English bilingual publishing.

Codes of Ethics and Professional Expectations

What does it mean to say that one has moral obligations as an academic researcher or scholar? One approach might be to consider what ethical expectations are at play in the creation of academic products such as conference presentations, journal articles, and books. A starting point for this could be codified ethical expectations, such as the American Association of University Professors'

(2009) "Statement on Professional Ethics"[2] or the "Core Practices" of the Committee on Publishing Ethics (n.d.)[3], which provide guidance for ethical scholarship and ethical publication standards.

Yet these guidelines are often written from a "god's-eye view" that presumes a universal white, middle-class, cis-gendered (but presumably male), straight, able-bodied, and Hearing perspective. Race, ethnicity, gender, and disability orientations are not even named. An implicit argument for this approach is that not naming various identity perspectives contributes to the universality of the expectations of the professoriate with no exceptions; another perspective is that ignoring identity perspectives contributes to the ethical concerns of hidden labor conferred by various positions within the academy. Just because such obligations are unnamed does not mean that they are not present.

The reader might push back on my assessment of the universal view, noting that the American Association of University Professors' "Statement on Professional Ethics" discusses scholarly obligations and other obligations of the professoriate, including the responsibilities to one's subject (noted in item 5 of the statement) and to one's institution (noted in item 4).[4] While the statement is heavily influenced by the concept of academic freedom, it also considers the weighing and balancing of competing obligations. Taking these one at a time, the first section includes the ethical responsibility of the advancement of knowledge, including "[exercising] critical self-discipline and judgment in using, extending, and transmitting knowledge" (American Association of University Professors 2009). While it does not designate who ought to be the recipient of such knowledge, judgment regarding the transmission of knowledge can also be found in other learned societies' codes of ethic or conduct.

For example, the American Anthropological Association's (2012) "Statement on Ethics"[5] takes particular care to note the importance of the relationship between the researcher scholar and the research participant, and to articulate the responsibilities that fall on the anthropological scholar, given the nature of their work and positionality within many different kinds of social structures and communities: "Anthropologists must be sensitive to the power differentials, constraints, interests and expectations characteristic of all relationships. In a field of such complex rights, responsibilities, and involvements, it is inevitable that misunderstandings, conflicts, and the need to make difficult choices will arise. Anthropologists are responsible for grappling with such difficulties and struggling to resolve them in ways compatible with the principles stated here."[6]

Signed language linguists are another group of scholars who have engaged substantially with signing deaf communities in their work. The Sign Language Linguistics Society (2016) has created an "Ethics Statement for Sign Language Research" that specifically takes up three issues: responsibility to deaf individuals, responsibility to deaf communities, and responsibility to scholarship and the public.[7] Although this ethics statement does not specifically call for

researchers to translate the results of their research into the relevant signed language, it does contain the exhortation, "Sign linguists must also strive to make
their research results available to the broader, non-specialized audience," which,
by extension, at least suggests the possibility that these results be made available
to the individuals and communities on whom such research has been conducted.[8]

A Sense of Duty: Reciprocity and Justice

Professional codes of ethics created by various learned societies are one structure
within the academy that can guide scholars. Such instrumental devices function
as a mechanism for keeping scholars compliant with minimal expectations of
ethical conduct. Accordingly, while it may be argued that scholars whose work
involves or engages with signing Deaf communities *ought* to disseminate their
research, it can also be argued that to call for this dissemination is to call for deaf
academics to engage in supererogatory behavior. In other words, knowledge dissemination of products in signed language designed to be distributed to signing
Deaf communities is a good thing in practice, but there is no duty to do this.
Such dissemination goes beyond the ethical duties of the researcher and should
only take place in certain narrowly defined contexts, such as those noted in the
Sign Language Linguistics Society's "Statement on Ethics," where the language is
the subject of the research.

An alternative approach might be not just to appeal to the statements on ethics of one's professional and learned societies but also to consider the ethics of
the other communities one belongs to. The scope of this chapter does not permit
the analysis of various theoretical ethical foundations. My work as an applied
ethicist has three influences: virtual theory, nonideal theory, and moral particu-
larism. I have argued elsewhere that virtue ethics is a helpful lens with which to
view the signing Deaf community, since the fine-grained aspects of identifying
virtues in a particular context can sharpen differences between a mainstream
hearing orientation and a Deaf-centric one.[9]

One behavior that is cherished within the signing Deaf spaces I have inhabited is information sharing. This is often the province of an educated deaf person
who has sophisticated English literacy skills. Such a person gets called up in the
signing Deaf community to share information that may be primarily available in
English text, such as local news stories. While mainstream news programs are
captioned, and there are now sources of news available in ASL (e.g., Daily Moth,
DPAN), the latter tend to either focus on big national news stories or feature
articles of particular interest to members of the signing Deaf community. Local
journalism is rarely made available in ASL, so it is frequently a topic of interest
that those in the Deaf community ask to be relayed and expanded on. This practice of information sharing is reciprocal and symmetrical between signed and
spoken languages. For example, a deaf person who has learned ASL later in life

as a second language may miss key parts of the conversation in ASL. An ASL-fluent Deaf person will then take on the information-sharing role by clarifying and expanding on culturally relevant content and using code-switching to add more English-like grammar and mouthing to get the message across.

This behavior of information sharing is associated with a cluster of related virtues. These include the virtues of transparency, reciprocity, inclusive justice, and respect. Given the shared deaf experience of exclusion from communication, it is not difficult to see why this has emerged as a cherished value. Even if one is a signing Deaf person who is also a speech reader or a signing Deaf person with voice privileges, this remains a universally shared deaf experience.[10] Setting is also important—the educational experiences of many deaf individuals frequently are framed as taking place in schools that are not portals to knowledge but rather places of partial inclusion and partial exclusion.[11]

If a signing Deaf academic takes up these virtues as part of their moral outlook, these not only buttress the guidance provided in the learned society's statements on ethics but provide a path to moral reasoning that is deaf-centric. This may not be the case for signing hearing academics, whose landscape of moral virtues may not be highlighted in the same way. That said, an instructive analogue might be to look at how hearing signed-language interpreters have considered the virtue of reciprocity.[12]

What to Share?

Suppose the researcher has convinced themselves that they do have a moral obligation to share her research products with the signing deaf community. This raises the question of audience. Who is the audience? Is it other deaf academics, most of whom are adept in a written language that may not be their first language? This can be assumed due to the gatekeeping function of the PhD dissertation requirement to enter the professoriate—it is quite uncommon for a PhD dissertation to be produced in a signed language. The benefit to rendering an academic article written in English into signed academic ASL is that it may be more accessible to deaf academics, and those possibly aspiring to be deaf academics. The disadvantage of narrowing one's work to an extremely small group of "readers" is that the work and time cost of this endeavor does not advantage the scholar in the current academic climate, where little recognition is bestowed for translation of one's own work. Translation of another's work can be regarded as a scholarly endeavor, particularly in translation studies and adjacent fields.[13]

But wait—the goal here is not to assess how to reward the signing deaf academic but to examine the ethical issues regarding the dissemination of their findings in an accessible format. Why should the deaf academic care about the lack of recognition for doing this work? Here is where it gets a little tricky. Deaf academics do not exist in a vacuum, or even in a system that is designed to support them. Instead, the system of academia reflects the experiences of those who initially had access to work within this system—namely, white hearing males. An especially pithy acknowledgment of this is the "coincidental" overlap of the tenure clock with the biological clock of those who can give birth. While adjustments have been made to the tenure clock system that allow for this, it should be noted that the system still permeates the academy. The analogy carries for the deaf academic, who exists within a system that has been established by hearing individuals (the vast majority of whom do not sign).

In general, translation of one's own work does not reap much reward in the academy. If one does opt to engage in this work as a moral imperative, the result is time and energy away from projects that would result in more reward, whether these are academic projects or personal projects. While academic, this work is more likely to be viewed as an act of service than scholarship in most US academic systems.

How to Share It?

Once a signing deaf academic has decided that they have a moral obligation to share their research with other signing deaf individuals, whether other deaf academics or members of the signing deaf community at large, the next question is how it ought to be shared. This raises ethical questions connected with copyright, production, and academic language modeling. In this section, I will address each of these in turn.

The typical copyright agreement for authors usually does not include a statement regarding the author's right to translate the work into a signed language as a matter of accessibility or disability accommodation. This emphasis on accessibility is distinct from the question of translation, which can be included in contractual language and may have constraints that have been developed with written versions of spoken languages in mind. If the audience is an academic one (or even if it is not), additional copyright issues arise regarding the logistics of housing: Where will such a document reside? Will it be open access? Will it be located on the publisher's website? The academic's institutional repository? Will the publisher or the academic be responsible for quality control and web maintenance?

Questions of production involve resource allocation issues of time and money. While it is possible to throw up a green screen backdrop and record oneself signing from a laptop or phone, an unedited or lightly edited video recording is more likely to be perceived as an information academic product (e.g., vlog) than as a research document summary. Additionally, not all academics have sophisticated or even sufficient video editing skills. Although deaf academics typically have more experience seeing themselves on video (especially before the pandemic) due to the wide use of videophones, this experience is helpful in giving one a sense of the parameters of the signing space, but it usually doesn't involve careful management of lighting for production purposes. Since the novel coronavirus pandemic's shift to virtual teaching, signing and nonsigning academics have acquired an increased sense of what is needed to make a streaming video more engaging, including strategic use of lighting. Case in point, my standing desk setup has nine sources of light, including two natural light sources that are managed throughout the day. Again, streaming video and vlogging are roughly equivalent to teaching (or giving a talk) and blogging. The production value requirements are low, and it is assumed that the person who is doing the speaking or unedited writing is doing this on their own without a production crew. While there are some academic blogs that provide editing and some peer feedback, this is not common practice. In order to produce polished and sophisticated published content in ASL, it is helpful to pull in others, just as is done with editorial support in written English academic publications.

Let me recount my experience of working with the *Deaf Studies Digital Journal (DSDJ)* to produce an (as yet unpublished) ASL article. *DSDJ* is one of very few peer-reviewed academic journals that publish bilingually in ASL and written English. Articles may appear in ASL, English, or both languages. The process of reviewing is done in both languages, with both ASL and English articles reviewed in shortened versions, rather than full length. This is in part due to a desire for equity—the production of ASL content is much more labor intensive, involving multiple individuals, and the current resource structure at Gallaudet University, where *DSDJ* is housed, is such that the production costs of accepted ASL articles come under the *DSDJ* budget, rather than being allocated to individual faculty members who are working on their own articles. This decision to treat submissions in different modalities differently is just one acknowledgment of the inequity experienced by signing deaf academics.

The economic and temporal costs of production are entwined with the issue of academic quality. Academic print publishing requires peer review, revision, copyediting, and proofreading. What might this look like for publishing in ASL? Is it necessary to require a similar means of production with checks and balances? As with most instances of translation, the issue is not whether the content of the scholarly argument passes muster, but whether the content of the translation sufficiently conveys the original.

If the goal is to produce an academic ASL article that is equivalent to the English version, it is possible that an ASL master (an individual who is fluent in ASL and can produce academic ASL and discuss editorial choices) may be needed. Who will do the translation is another matter—should the signer be the original author? This will depend on the ASL skills of the author. The bias of US academia toward mastery of written English can have the resultant effect of filtering out promising signing deaf academics from the pipeline if they are not English natives and need some support for their writing. Currently the structure of the academy does not provide (in general) such support for ASL or English. Even Gallaudet University, which has a mission statement proclaiming its commitment to two official languages of ASL and written English, is still building such infrastructure for its faculty.[14]

Additionally, there are other matters of quality control—if an ASL master is hired to focus on the academic ASL content, they may not have the background and training to assess the nuances of the disciplinary norms and how to adjudicate those with the requirements of the discipline. This is also a challenge for interpreters, which I have explained in a blog entry in *Disabled Philosophers* (Burke 2011), using the philosophical term *de re* as an illustration.[15] While these distinctions can be parsed through discussion between the original author and the ASL master, this becomes more challenging when neither has the sophistication of the other's domain. This is, of course, a problem of translation generally, but it can be more time consuming when it must be done in a language that does not have a widely accepted written version.

As a case in point, when I am working with translators who have rendered my work into German or Spanish, I often have discussions with them in written English about the choice of a given word or phrase—while my knowledge of German and Spanish is not that of a native, I have read enough philosophical texts in both languages to have a sense of how things are worded. My work is usually translated in Deaf studies publications, so the translator is not an expert in my academic discipline—setting up a situation somewhat analogous to the ASL master challenge. When such discussions about phrasing or word choice occur in ASL, the author and master often either must make videos and send them back and forth, which takes more time and advance notice to set up than typing on a keyboard, or make an appointment to have a conversation about the ASL choices in real time. Making a video requires that one has sufficient lighting conditions and perhaps privacy, depending on the setting and one's concerns about sharing research before it is published. This may be further complicated depending on where the language resides on the high-context-to-low-context continuum.[16]

Phonocentrism and Chirocentric Sign Language Publications

In 2018 I participated in a National Endowment for the Humanities Summer Institute titled "The Book: Material Histories and Digital Futures."[17] This institute brought together scholars from various humanities disciplines, including book arts, book history, literary criticism, and library sciences, and a smattering of other humanists, including ones from environmental studies, philosophy, and English. The research question I brought to this seminar was, "What does a book written in a signed language look like?" My lens for this question was metaphysical: In thinking about the *form* of a book, what would make a book a signed language book? This is a different sort of question from what makes a book have signed language *content*. My proposal suggested that there were four different forms of signed language books in ASL, the signed language I am most familiar with. These were the following: books that are written in one of the many sign writing systems developed to represent ASL, books written in English using ASL gloss, books written in ASL-friendly English, and books created in a hybrid of ASL and English, which may be electronic or made with more traditional materials.

The forms of ASL books that currently exist are an answer to a different question: What forms do currently existing signed language books take (in ASL)? To answer the question of possible forms for signed language books more generally requires a shift in focus from those books that feature signed language content to the existent and potentially existent metaphysical and ontological forms of said books.

My first attempt to consider what would make a book a signed language book was to look at the different forms of signed language books. The earliest versions included codex structured bilingual dictionaries, though usually these dictionaries had asymmetrical content and were severely abridged. These typically had alphabetized groupings of the dominant written language words accompanied by drawings of a corresponding sign, meaning that someone who knew the dominant language could use these as a dictionary, but the books lacked organization for people who were not literate in the dominant language. Sometimes these books provided a one-to-one correspondence with the manual alphabet and written alphabet. It should be noted that the manual alphabet is predicated on the written version of the spoken alphabet (i.e., a phonetic alphabet).

These books followed the material structure of books at the time—they used paper or similar material on which drawings of signed language words and written, spoken language text appeared. These pages were usually bound between covers that protected the pages—the first iteration of the form of a signed language book replicates the materiality of books written by spoken language users. This is not surprising, since a uniform system of writing signed languages had and has yet to emerge—they were phonocentric, not chirocentric.

The invention of film provides a way to record stories in signed languages. As Deaf studies scholars know, the National Association of the Deaf, in the early 1900s filmed several signers in a variety of contexts in response to their concerns that signed languages were potentially en route to becoming endangered.[18] Yet this raises a somewhat different metaphysical question: Is a filmed story in signed language a book? If so, are there relevant features that distinguish a filmed spoken language storytelling event and a filmed signed language storytelling event as a book? Is the difference in modality sufficient for such a claim? One criterion for a videobook to be a signed language book might be that it must contain a frozen (fixed) text similar to that of an audiobook. This is one example of this

stipulation, but the lack of a standard sign writing system raises the question of whether more than one modality is required.[19] With audiobooks, the original source book text is in the written modality of the English language, which is then transformed into spoken English when it is read. For videobooks, the original source text is often identical with the video product.

The innovation of digital recording and editing brings forth a few chirocentric examples of bilingual ASL-English books. Recently, three book models have broadened the idea of the signed language book. *The Baobab*, produced by the Gallaudet Visual Language and Visual Learning Center (Malzkuhn et al. 2013), is a bilingual ASL-English digital children's book with English text and watercolor pictures containing a central image of a signer who recounts the story on the page in ASL.[20] The book includes an English-to-ASL lexicon, which allows the budding reader to look up the English word and see (read) the word (sign) and definition in ASL. Yet, like so many ASL-English projects, this is an asymmetrical lexicon that does not allow the reader to look up the ASL word and find the English word and English definition.

The psychology textbook *Research and Evaluation in Education and Psychology* uses a different approach to making the written English text accessible in ASL with the development of an ASL companion volume.[21] The ASL companion volume is a separate video text that features summary vignettes by native ASL speakers with academic training in the field (see, e.g., Harris and Williams 2017). Authorship for each version, English and ASL, is separate. This partnership model is one that may be instructive for signing deaf academics wishing to make their work accessible in ASL.

Yet another approach is that used by the *DSDJ*, the ASL-English bilingual academic journal, which was founded by and first edited by H. L. Dirksen Baumann and is now edited by Patrick Boudreault.[22] While it is an academic journal and not a book, I believe its publishing model could easily be adapted to a book format. Each article is presented bilingually as one document in the table of contents, with ASL video and English text provided in separate translations.

Proof of Concept: *The Signed Language Book Metabook*

Where does a signed language book begin? Can a "pure" sign language book exist, and if so, what is the material form of such a book? In addition to writing about the philosophical aspects of ASL publishing, during the National Endowment for the Humanities Summer Institute I attended, I was also required to create a book for an exhibition that would take place at the end of the program at the Salt Lake City Main Library.[23] My book project was a proof-of-concept book—I wanted to explore the possibility of creating a book in ASL without using any English text. This would create a new category of ASL books in addition to the four I had listed earlier. This new category of signed language book would exist solely in the video format of ASL, with no English or spoken language text. While the material books published in written forms of signed language text also contain no English, the book form I attempted uses video clips as frozen text rather than a written system. One might liken this to an audiobook read by the author, with one critical difference—instead of the book being produced in one modality and converted to another modality, this book is produced in the same modality as the final form. I titled this proof of concept work *The Sign Language MetaBook*.

The first order of business was to choose a publishing platform that would (as much as possible) minimize the English content in the structure of the book. I opted to use Scalar, a free open-source online publishing program from the Alliance for Networking Visual Culture (n.d.) "designed to make it easy for authors to write long-form, born-digital scholarship online."[24] While there were certain English formatting constraints I could not get around, such as the table of contents, I was able to make the table of contents bilingual, adding video clips of the book sections in ASL to the English "skeleton" structure. These short video clips showed fingerspelling of each chapter's title. One challenge in producing bilingual content is the variability of translation. In part because I wanted to focus on philosophical concepts that had a rich history in English (more on this later), I opted to fingerspell the titles of these chapters.

In order to move toward what I have called Deaf philosophy,[25] each chapter's content was produced in ASL using iMovie and saved on Vimeo. My process for developing my thoughts and arguments in ASL paralleled my writing process in English. That is, I usually spend a lot of time thinking about what I want to produce before I ever start to capture it on a screen (written or signed). This includes sharpening the questions I want to ask, considering what the structure of my argument looks like (I often end up assigning parts of the argument in space as I think through it, whether that is in English or ASL), and thinking through objections and replies to various iterations of the arguments and subarguments. Although I did not consciously set out to follow my English language approach to thinking philosophically, I did set for myself the expectation that my philosophical thinking would include argumentation. Having taught philosophy in ASL for seventeen years at Gallaudet, I have developed a philosophical style in this language.[26]

The Scalar platform has its limitations, and I expected that the response of my colleagues and others viewing *The Signed Language Book Metabook* (all hearing, none fluent in ASL) might be to critique the structure of the design of the book, since we had spent a considerable amount of time talking about the metaphysics and ontology of book structure. The feedback I most often received was a request for a translation of *The Signed Language Book Metabook*, despite my initial description of my project as one that would not involve any English. This ironic response, given the context of my project, is worth mulling over in light of the ethical issues I raised earlier about access to research and scholarship on signing deaf communities. It not only positions academic English language access as an entitlement but also illuminates the question of whose labor will go into this access. It is not likely that a nonsigning academic will embark on a course of ASL study in order to access this work.

ASL Core Philosophical Lexicon Dictionary

Before my proof-of-concept signed language book experiment, I worked with a team to produce a more traditional kind of ASL digital book, a dictionary of philosophical signs in academic ASL. As with *The Signed Language Book Metabook*, this project was conceived through a deaf-centric frame, involving a signing subject matter expert (me); four ASL masters, including two who had previously studied philosophy at the college level; three hearing sign language interpreters who, combined, had several decades of experience interpreting philosophy courses taught in spoken English by nonsigning hearing professors at the Rochester Institute of Technology; a video camera crew to capture the discussions (there were three cameras in the room as we worked so that all conversations would be captured); and a website designer and editor. The labor for this project in the initial phase required ten people. Contrast this to the proof-of-concept book, in which I did the bulk of the work and only needed a cameraperson to assist with the video filming, which just needed to be sufficient to establish the concept and not done at the polished level required for academic publication.

The question of what counts as deaf-centric is complex and goes beyond the scope of this chapter. I will sketch out my reasons for why the originally titled "Philosophical Lexicon in ASL" project ought to count as a deaf-centric endeavor. This project was originally proposed by Miriam Lerner, an interpreter for the National Technical Institute for the Deaf at the Rochester Institute of Technology, using an in-house small grant fund from the Rochester Institute of Technology. Lerner and I corresponded for years before the project began, in part because she was so insistent that the project of generating an ASL lexicon for academic philosophy needed to have native and near-native signers at the center. I was initially hesitant to participate. Even though I have been teaching philosophy in ASL at Gallaudet University for nearly two decades, I am not an ASL-native signer and do not have the native language intuition that many of my colleagues do at Gallaudet. That said, I did come around to acknowledge Lerner's point that since there were no native ASL speakers with doctorates in academic philosophy, I was uniquely positioned to work on this project. Despite my L2 status, my knowledge of academic philosophy, including my experience teaching it in English and in ASL, when combined with the depth of knowledge of our ASL masters, would result in the needed expertise.

What made this project deaf-centric was not only the all-deaf team at the heart of generating content but our commitment to developing a process that prioritized the collaborative effort of the ASL masters, with their native language users' intuition, my expertise as the philosophy content expert, and the interpreters' collective experience interpreting philosophy classes. From the very first word we discussed a definition for (*aesthetics*), we were heavily engaged in being respectful of the history of language appropriation in deaf education, the oppressive nature of sign creation by nonnative users of the language, and the specific and narrow aim of this project, which was to provide ASL vocabulary for deaf students and their interpreters in undergraduate general education philosophy courses. If others found it useful and it received uptake in the deaf academic community, that would be a side benefit, but it was not the primary aim.

Two other observations about this project deserve attention. First, for deaf academics who wish to embark on a similar project, this kind of work typically does not count as scholarship but rather falls under service to the profession. In the US tenure track, academics are evaluated in three areas: research, teaching, and service to the profession. Service is the least prestigious category, and junior academics are cautioned to invest the bulk of their time in research and teaching rather than service—at least until they have obtained tenure. Despite the philosophical issues that emerged during the course of this project, including applied ethics and applied epistemology—both of which fall under my research agenda—there was little work-related incentive for me to pursue this project. The second observation is tied to the theme of hidden labor for deaf academics that I've woven throughout this chapter. If projects like this are needed (and I think that the need is indisputable), and ought to be carried out in a deaf-centric way in order to mitigate concern about cultural and language appropriation, then this is a task for deaf academics. At present, deaf academics who take on such specialized signed language lexicon projects are not rewarded for this labor under the current system of evaluating academics. This means that the system for how deaf (and disabled) academics are evaluated needs to be revised, and probably overhauled, in order to provide equity in the academy.

Future Directions

In this chapter I have identified several topics that could benefit from further analysis, beginning with the question of what the ethical obligations are for scholars who are bilingual in ASL and English to share our work as academics with the signing Deaf community. If the work of academics belongs to society, as I believe it does, the question of access and inclusion must be addressed. This will require the academy to evaluate its structural audism, including the impact of hidden labor and the absence of robust structures for evaluating the work of signing deaf academics in particular, who are called on to provide service through representation and as members of the signing deaf community who have unique access to information.

The COVID-19 pandemic brought an awareness of social inequity to the mainstream in a variety of ways, most notably in the areas of health care and education. The racial reckoning groundswell that captured the attention of the world in response to the murder of George Floyd raised awareness of the impact of race on this inequity. The social upheaval of the pandemic has provided an opportunity for all of us to evaluate current social structures, including those in the academy, and to develop law and policy that attempt to address these inequities, including those of ableism and audism. It is my hope that academics and educators will seize this moment to call for transformative change—carpe diem!

NOTES

1   James I. Charlton, *Nothing About Us Without Us: Disability Oppression and Empowerment,* (Berkeley, California: University of California Press, 2000), 3.

2   American Association of University Professors, "Statement on Professional Ethics", (Washington, DC: AAUP, 2009), https://www.aaup.org/report/statement-professional -ethics.

3   Committee On Publishing Ethics, "Core Practices", (Hampshire, United Kingdom, 2017), date accessed May 1, 2022. https://publicationethics.org/core-practices.

4   AAUP Statement on Professional Ethics.

5   American Anthropological Association, "Statement on Ethics", (Arlington, VA: AAA, 2012). https://ethics.americananthro.org/category/statement/.

6   AAA Statement on Ethics.

7   Sign Language Linguistics Society, "Ethics Statement for Sign Language Research", (SLLS, 2016), *https://slls.eu/slls-ethics-statement/.*

8   SLLS Ethics Statement, Section 3.

9   Teresa Blankmeyer Burke, "Regret: Considerations of Disability" in *The Moral Psychology of Regret,* Ed. Anna Gotlib, (London: Rowman & Littlefield, 2020), XX. Teresa Blankmeyer Burke, "DEAF-HEART: Virtue Ethics and Signed Language Interpreting", unpublished paper, (presented to Yale University Minorities and Philosophy, 2014), 2–3.

10 David R. Meek, "Dinner Table Syndrome: A Phenomenological Study of Deaf Individuals' Experiences with Inaccessible Communication," *Qualitative Report* 25(6) (June 2020):1676–1694.

11 Naomi Caselli, Wyatte C. Hall, and Jonathan Henner, "American Sign Language Interpreters in Public Schools: An Illusion of Inclusion that Perpetuates Language Deprivation", *Maternal and Child Health Journal* 24 (2020): 1323–1329.

12 Rico Peterson, "Deaf Interpreters and Repatriation," Street Leverage, accessed May 9, 2022, streetleverage.com. https://streetleverage.com/tag/reciprocity/.

13 Modern Language Association, "Evaluating Translations as Scholarship," accessed May 9, 2022, mla.org. https://www.mla.org /Resources/Advocacy/Executive-Council-Actions/2011 /Evaluating-Translations-as-Scholarship-Guidelines-for-Peer-Review.

14 Conversation with Dr. Patrick Boudreault, Editor of DSDJ, November 2, 2020.

15 Teresa Blankmeyer Burke, "Teresa Blankmeyer Burke" in *Disabled Philosophers,* September 13 2011, accessed May 9, 2022. https://disabledphilosophers.wordpress.com/2011/09/13/teresa -blankmeyer-burke/.

16 Naomi Sheneman, "Deaf Interpreters' Ethics: Reflections on Training and Decision-Making," *Journal of Interpretation* 25(1) (2016): Article 8, p. 7. https://digitalcommons.unf.edu/joi/vol25 /iss1/8.

17 National Endowment for the Humanities Summer Institute, "The Book: Material Histories and Digital Futures", accessed May 30, 2022. http://www.slcc.edu/neh/.

18 Sherman Wilcox and Corrine Occhino, "Historical Change in Sign Languages" in *Oxford Handbooks Online* (Linguistics, Sign Languages). Online publication date November 2016.

19 James Shokoff, "What is an Audiobook?", *Journal of Popular Culture* 34(4) (Spring 2001): 171–181.

20 Melissa Malzkuhn, Kristen Harmon, Benjamin Bahan, and Wanda Riddle. April Jackson-Woodward (storyteller) and Yiqiao Wang (conceptual artist), The Baobab (Washington, DC: Motion Light Lab, 2013), vl2storybookapps.com/the-baobab. Note: This work is the product of a collaborative team. While all of the individuals who participated in creating this work are listed on the website, I've opted to cite this by interpreting the "story by" section to be roughly equivalent to authors, and have noted others in parentheses.

21 Raychelle Harris and Felicia Williams, "Introducing the ASL Volume for Research and Evaluation in Education and Psychology Textbook" (Washington, DC: ASLized, April 5, 2017), https://www.youtube.com/watch?v=lLfaaraxvpw.

22 *Deaf Studies Digital Journal*, https://deafstudiesdigitaljournal.org/.

23 NEH Summer Institute Exhibition, "The Book: Material Histories and Digital Futures," July 2018, http://www.slcc.edu/neh/institute-exhibition.aspx.

24 Scalar, https://scalar.me/anvc/scalar/.

25 Teresa Blankmeyer Burke, "Doing Philosophy in American Sign Language: Creating a Philosophical Lexicon", in *Philosopher*, Ed. Meena Krishnamurty. https://political philosopher.net/2015/04/10/featured-philosop-her-teresa-blankmeyer-burke/.

26 Burke, "Doing Philosophy in American Sign Language."

BIBLIOGRAPHY

Alliance for Networking Visual Culture. n.d. Scalar. Accessed October 10, 2022. https://scalar.me /anvc/scalar/.

American Anthropological Association. 2012. "Statement on Ethics." AAA Ethics Forum, November 1, 2012. https://ethics.americananthro.org/category/statement/.

American Association of University Professors. 2009. "Statement on Professional Ethics." https:// www.aaup.org/report/statement-professional-ethics.

Burke, Teresa Blankmeyer. 2011. "Teresa Blankmeyer Burke." *Disabled Philosophers* (blog), September 13, 2011. https://disabledphilosophers.wordpress.com/2011/09/13/teresa-blankmeyer-burke/.

Burke, Teresa Blankmeyer. 2014. "DEAF-HEART: Virtue Ethics and Signed Language Interpreting." Unpublished paper presented to Yale University Minorities and Philosophy.

Burke, Teresa Blankmeyer. 2015. "Doing Philosophy in American Sign Language: Creating a Philosophical Lexicon." In "Featured Philosop-her: Teresa Blankmeyer Burke," in *Philosopher* (blog), edited by Meena Krishnamurty, April 10, 2015. https://politicalphilosopher.net/2015/04 /10/featured-philosop-her-teresa-blankmeyer-burke/.

Burke, Teresa Blankmeyer. 2018. *The Signed Language Book Metabook*. In "The Book: Material Histories and Digital Futures," National Endowment for the Humanities Summer Institute, June 17–July 13, 2018, Salt Lake Community College. https://www.slcc.edu/neh/institute -exhibition.aspx.

Burke, Teresa Blankmeyer. "Regret: Considerations of Disability." In *The Moral Psychology of Regret*, edited by Anna Gotlib, 203–220. London: Rowman and Littlefield.

Caselli, Naomi, Wyatte C. Hall, and Jonathan Henner. 2020. "American Sign Language Interpreters in Public Schools: An Illusion of Inclusion that Perpetuates Language Deprivation." *Maternal and Child Health Journal* 24:1323–1329.

Charlton, James I. 2000. *Nothing about Us without Us: Disability Oppression and Empowerment*. Berkeley: University of California Press.

Committee on Publishing Ethics. n.d. "Core Practices." Accessed October 10, 2022. https://publicationethics.org/core-practices.

Harris, Raychelle, and Felicia Williams. 2017. "Introducing the ASL Volume for Research and Evaluation in Education and Psychology Textbook." YouTube video, 3:25, posted by ASLized!, April 5, 2017. https://www.youtube.com/watch?v=lLfaaraxvpw.

Malzkuhn, Melissa, Kristen Harmon, Benjamin Bahan, and Wanda Riddle. 2013. *The Baobab*. Story told by April Jackson-Woodward. Concept art by Yiqiao Wang. Washington, DC: Motion Light Lab. https://vl2storybookapps.com/the-baobab.

Meek, David R. 2020. "Dinner Table Syndrome: A Phenomenological Study of Deaf Individuals' Experiences with Inaccessible Communication." *Qualitative Report* 25 (6): 1676–1694.

Modern Language Association. n.d. "Evaluating Translations as Scholarship: Guidelines for Peer Review." Accessed October 10, 2022. https://www.mla.org/Resources/Advocacy/Executive -Council-Actions/2011/Evaluating-Translations-as-Scholarship-Guidelines-for-Peer-Review.

Peterson, Rico. 2015. "Deaf Interpreters and Repatriation." Street Leverage, July 14, 2015. https://streetleverage.com/tag/reciprocity/.

Salt Lake Community College. 2018a. "The Book: Material Histories and Digital Futures." National Endowment for the Humanities Summer Institute, June 17–July 13, 2018. http://www .slcc.edu/neh/.

Salt Lake Community College. 2018b. "The Book: Material Histories and Digital Futures." Exhibition of the National Endowment for the Humanities Summer Institute, July 2018. http://www .slcc.edu/neh/institute-exhibition.aspx.

Sheneman, Naomi. 2016. "Deaf Interpreters' Ethics: Reflections on Training and Decision-Making." *Journal of Interpretation* 25 (1): article 8. http://digitalcommons.unf.edu/joi/vol25 /iss1/8.

Shokoff, James. 2001. "What Is an Audiobook?" *Journal of Popular Culture* 34 (4): 171–181.

Sign Language Linguistics Society. 2016. "Ethics Statement for Sign Language Research." https://slls.eu/slls-ethics-statement/.

Wilcox, Sherman, and Corrine Occhino. 2016. "Historical Change in Signed Languages." In *Oxford Handbook Topics in Linguistics*. Online publication date November 2016. https://doi.org/10.1093/oxfordhb/9780199935345.013.24.

26

Crip World-Making

ROBERT MCRUER

In March 2020, as the COVID-19 crisis escalated into a global emergency, I left the United States for Bogotá, to see my Colombian partner, who was at the time living there. The initial plan was to stay for ten days (spring break); I returned to the United States almost six months later, on a humanitarian flight. Among my circle of friends and colleagues, we had one of the strictest lockdowns, but the extension of my time in Colombia was in many ways not undesirable, as I was heading into a sabbatical and germinating a project (which I will continue to work on for the next few years) considering crip art, crip theory, and crip culture in Latin America. I write mostly in English but for some time have been very invested in critiquing the centrality of English in disability studies and considering whether or how that centrality short-circuits what I consider here as "crip world-making." The project I am germinating has put me into contact and conversation (in Spanish and English directly, and Portuguese in translation), over the past decade or more, with disability studies scholars and crip community from Mexico to Chile to Brazil and beyond. At the very least, during the strict lockdown in Colombia, I was able to extend, virtually, those connections.

Gabriel García Márquez, when asked about magical realism, once famously asserted that the mix of the fantastic and the real was not some anomaly, but just how life was in Latin America: "El surrealismo proviene de la realidad de América Latina" (Surrealism comes from the reality of Latin America) (as quoted in Tovar 2018). I've sometimes half-joked that *la teoría crip* (crip theory) in Latin America is something of an analogue. It seems to me that crip theory *as an analytic* is particularly useful for getting at what might *also* be called the mix of the fantastic and the real; that is, at the complexity of varied disabilities, impairments, bodies, minds, and behaviors in a range of Latin American locations. Although crip theory certainly does not oppose a positive disability rights and disability studies agenda that emphasizes, say, formal legal reform and substantive, recognizable identities (an agenda that has often developed most in North American locations above the Rio Grande), it is also always particularly interested in that which is in *excess* of an able-bodied/disabled binary (and this is perhaps especially important in locations where there is no exact translation for *able-bodiedness*). A crip analytic thus often works with and against identity simultaneously, affirming complex lived experiences of disability but getting at, nonetheless, what might exceed the analytic capacity of the signifier *disability*. This is useful for locations where, indeed, disability and impairment are widespread, even affecting at times the majority of people in a particular Latin American location. This certainly seemed to be the case during our 2020 lockdown in Bogotá, as daily COVID-19 cases were always noted with risk factors listed according to various disabilities (diabetes, hypertension, etc.), and as certain neighborhoods were hit particularly hard, even hanging red flags out the windows of apartment buildings to mark both hunger and suffering.

The double-edged move of affirming disability identity and culture *and* getting at what exceeds it marks *crip* as doing, in my mind, somewhat different work from an analytic such as *debility*. *Debility* has also been used by some scholars to describe a more generalized embodied or experiential state in a given location where many people experience chronic illness or impairment of some kind (and where, at times, no exact translation exists in a particular language for *disability*). It has sometimes been put forward as a replacement of sorts, as when Jasbir K. Puar advocates for "a move from disability to debility" (2009, 166). In multiple Latin American locations, however, colleagues and activists have told me over and over how important it is to mark disability, especially in contexts where it has so often been *unremarked* or actively dismissed or degraded (through, for instance, austerity regimes that directly target resources disabled people depend on for survival). Work in debility studies has sometimes been wary of such affirmations of identity, linking them to a limited disability identity politics "that is manifest through state, market, and institutional recognition" and even "overdetermined by 'white fragility'" (Puar 2017, xiv). This is, however, a neoliberal identity politics that has essentially had its greatest traction in the United States. As Lisa Duggan has suggested, at times some narrow critiques of identity politics "focus on the identities, and overlook politics, which is a way not to take any of it seriously" (2003, 86). Duggan's historical perspective advocates, instead, for noting carefully how identity politics work in particular times and places. When activists in Latin America are in fact advocating for naming and inhabiting a range of disabled identities, it seems to me important not to reduce their political efforts to neoliberal identity politics. A crip analytic can attend to that affirmation of identity while also attending to the ways in which Latin American crip politics is focused on intersections and coalitions that are in excess of disability identity per se.

A crip analytic also speaks to and about bodies, minds, behaviors, and experiences that get *invisibilized* in various locations and conversations but that should be absolutely central to those conversations. The conference "Cripping Development," in the Czech Republic in 2013, for example (a follow-up to a similar conference, "Cripping Neoliberalism," in 2010), focused on how disability should be at the center of critiquing dominant discourses of development; it was a conference also interested, notably, in finding (new) languages adequate for approaching disability and embodiment in postsocialist locations and the Global South.

And since crip perspectives have been widely shared across borders, crip theory is an analytic that seems particularly useful for Latin America, where "activismos *disca* latinoamericanos" (to use a phrase that has begun to circulate widely from Mexico to Colombia to Argentina) are regularly shared and discussed beyond any single national border.

Because it has spread so rapidly, the origins of the use of *disca* itself are unclear. Mexican anthropologist Jhonatthan Maldonado Ramírez tells me that to think with and through *disca* is a way of thinking of "una forma de vida enunciable y vivible" (a form of life that is articulable and livable). It is also a way of thinking intersectionally; both the Mexican activist group Femidiscas and Argentinian activists and journalists in the group Periodismo Femidisca, for example, link their anti-ableist work to a militant feminism focused on a wide range of issues, including sex education and the politics of abortion. Periodismo Femidisca asserts, "Reivindicar la discapacidad como una identidad política, nos otorga un lugar protagónico en la construcción de subjetividades. En esto radica nuestra existencia, en un abordaje transversal y comprometido acerca de los feminismos y la discapacidad" (Claiming disability as a political identity gives us a leading place in the construction of subjectivities. This is where our existence lies, in a cross-cutting and committed approach to feminisms and disability) (Periodismo Femidisca 2020). Regardless of its varied uses across the region, *disca* can provide in its very form a way of thinking about and living with *disability* without centralizing *ability* through the very word, since *disca* cuts short the *capacidad* part of the word *discapacidad* (it can be quite common to shorten words in Spanish, but for some users of *disca*, this is intentional). In Colombia and other locations, autistic activists have proclaimed #SoyDisca (I am Disca) or #OrgulloDisca (Disca pride) on Twitter, the latter partially speaking to the fact that the term has in some places been used pejoratively and is being reclaimed by activists. *Disca* is not exactly gendered (or could be seen as queerly gendered) as the words *discapacitado* and *discapacitada* are. *Disca* arguably, as well, circulates easily alongside *crip*, as in, for example, the virtual 2021 event "Teoría Crip y activismos *disca* latinoamericanos," which brought together groups from numerous countries, including the queer and Deaf group Colectivo de sordos LGBT de Guatemala, Edukdiversa from Colombia, Aneupi from Ecuador, and a selection of Argentinian activist groups (the event was organized by the Universidad Nacional de Córdoba, Argentina).

What's most important, of course, is not so much any one term (and I'll discuss a selection of others later), but the cultural work that an analytic performs (again, resignifying pejorative terms, working with and against identity simultaneously, focusing on processes of invisibilization, and so forth). Jhonatthan Maldonado Ramírez, writing about Down syndrome in a Mexican context and drawing on the work of Eve Kosofsky Sedgwick, uses crip theory and affect theory specifically to resist neoliberal modes of interpreting disability that would contain and domesticate it. He writes,

> Mi modo de interpretar esto es desde una crip-tica afectiva en la que discapacidad signifique una forma de vida siempre dispuesta a tocarnos, no como la advertencia de una desgracia o la búsqueda de la empatía inclusiva, sino como una experiencia que . . . nos estaría acariciando, conectando, alcanzando y abrazando a través del carácter relacional e interdependiente de nuestra vulnerabilidad.

> My way of interpreting this is from a crip-tic affect in which disability signifies a way of life always ready to touch us, not as the warning of a misfortune or the search for inclusive empathy, but as an experience that . . . would be caressing, connecting, reaching out and embracing us through the relational and interdependent nature of our vulnerability. (Maldonado Ramírez 2020; my translation)

Naomi Klein (2007) and others have analyzed at length how neoliberal capitalism was, essentially, test-run in Latin America. The unpopular ideas became more palatable globally in the years of Margaret Thatcher and Ronald Reagan after they had been (at times violently) imposed in Chile, Argentina, and other Latin American locations. In the wake of this now deeply sedimented history, what Maldonado Ramírez is reaching for as he imagines *una crip-tica afectiva* are embodied manners of relating ("acariciando, conectando, alcanzando y abrazando") that negate the utility of disability for neoliberalism. Like many countries, Mexico has celebrated (often for political photo ops) individual disabled people, such as, for instance, Paralympian Gustavo Sánchez Martínez, a disabled swimmer who won two gold medals, one silver, and one bronze at the 2012 London Paralympic Games. Former president Enrique Peña Nieto awarded the Premio Nacional de Deporte (National Award for Sport) to Sánchez Martínez, at a time when Peña Nieto was being protested by radical student movements calling out state violence and control of the media. Sánchez Martínez thus arguably functioned as a smokescreen for the embattled president, who asserted in the ceremony, "Este es el momento de México y vamos a hacerlo realidad. Quiero una nación sana, y fuerte, y ustedes, los deportistas son el mejor ejemplo a seguir" (This is Mexico's moment and we are going to make it reality. I want a nation healthy and strong and you, the athletes, are the best example to follow) (*Vanguardia* 2012, my translation; also see McRuer 2018, 159–161). Such neoliberal spectacularization is the opposite of what Maldonado Ramírez theorizes as he focuses on interdependence and on the vulnerability that can never be captured by a photo op. Ironically, such vulnerability could include Mexican Paralympians themselves, who have at times struggled to find accessible housing and have been forced to live in crumbling training facilities.

Maldonado Ramírez's and others' analyses should push us to question the hegemony of English in disability studies. The field has at times been faulted for the dominance of North American and European perspectives, but that easy critique should even more be directed, as I suggested at the outset, at the dominance of *English*. Indeed, some of the most exciting work in disability studies and crip theory, even in Europe, is being generated by scholars whose first language is not English and who write in other European languages (often in addition to English). And although (again) not the only keyword, *crip* has often been an important one for these scholars and activists: Melania Moscoso Pérez (2013, 170) has theorized "cripwashing" as a complex process of state control whereby the Spanish state uses the language of disability liberation to cover over neoliberal policies of control; Kateřina Kolářová (2014, 257) has examined a figure she calls "the inarticulate post-socialist crip" to get at perspectives in postsocialist locations that are erased by compulsory capitalist progress narratives (even when those narratives celebrate disability). Anticapitalist activists in Vienna periodically release, in German and English, *Crip Magazine*.

Of course, one could say that there is a danger of cultural imperialism when an English term such as *crip* enters other languages. The generative, world-making possibilities opened up as *crip* travels, however, exceed that danger, especially as it works *in tandem* with a range of other signs in a language such as Spanish. When my own book *Crip Theory* was translated into Spanish in 2021, I had a series of conversations not only with the translator (Javier Sáez de Álamo, based in Spain) but with colleagues and activists from Canada to Argentina and virtually every Spanish-speaking location in between. The conversations highlighted inventiveness and play with languages for disability in any and all Spanish-speaking locations. *Teoría tullida*, one of the first possibilities for a translation, has had some circulation as an alternative to *teoría crip*, but almost entirely in Spain itself (where in fact *tullido/a* can be adequately translated as "crip" or "cripple"). As with many Spanish concepts, however, *tullido/a* is used in a very different way in some locations. Although it's more common in Medellín than Bogotá, for example, in Colombia *tullido* is more common for talking about being cold, as in the expression *tullido del frío*. *Teoría coja* was another possibility (with *cojo* or *coja* roughly translating as "lame"). At least one colleague, from a Cuban perspective, was very much in favor of using *teoría coja*. He cited the Cuban double bassist Cachao López's performance of "Juana la coja" as evidence of the term's cultural generativity. The song is about a woman who has a wooden leg with termites in it; it plays with the Cuban tendency to use the term *coja/o* to refer to anyone in the neighborhood who walked in a way perceived to be "funny." The English translators of the Cuban song called it "Jane the Lame." In the end, however, *teoría coja* too seemed to other colleagues in different locations to be at least somewhat regionally specific. *Lisiada* as a term does have wide circulation, mainly because of a famous scene from a 1990s Mexican soap opera. A mother in the series enters a room where her daughter (who uses a wheelchair) is kissing an able-bodied boy: "Maldita lisiada!" (roughly, "wicked cripple" or "damn cripple"), the mother screams, and she continues to berate and hit her daughter and the boy, in a scene that has been shared millions of times on YouTube. *Lisiada*, too, has been reclaimed and resignified, as in Argentinian activist and poet Daiana Travesani's beautiful poem and performance "Lisiada":

> Me odié por largo rato,
> me negué infinidad de veces por ser disca ahora.
>
> En ese proceso de deconstrucción el odio calmó y clamó.
>
> He cambiado, mutado y transmutado,
> fui real e irreal.
>
> Mi piel a veces porosa y otras tantas una seda,
> a diferencia de mi lengua guerrillera.
>
> (I hated myself for a long time,
> I negated countless times that I am *disca* now.
>
> In this deconstruction process, hatred calmed and cried out.
>
> I have changed, mutated and transmuted,
> I was real and unreal.
>
> My skin is sometimes porous and sometimes a silk,
> unlike my militant language.) (Travesani 2020; my translation)

What struck me most about this extended conversation across the Americas, however, was how *crip, cojo, disca, lisiada*, and other terms were already in circulation and were functioning in a kind of world-making way, often repeating and reversing the negative, pejorative, or degrading terms by which disabled people have been kept in their place and imagining (and materializing) an elsewhen and elsewhere, "crip futures" and "crip horizons" as Kolářová describes them (2014, 259, 265). Queer world-making was first theorized by Lauren Berlant and Michael Warner (1998, 556); it has since been widely used to describe queer practices that are "creative, performative, intimate, public, disruptive, utopian, and more" (I draw this from the description used by the editors of the journal *QED: A Journal in LGBTQ Worldmaking* in their invitation for contributions) (QED 2013). *Crip* world-making, which activists, artists, and scholars are in the process of imagining and inventing, is arguably more concrete, at times focusing on the *literal* reshaping of spaces, always with an aim toward imagining more bodies, minds, and behaviors in those spaces. Aimi Hamraie's concept of "alter-livability" helps me to concretize crip world-making. Alterlivability is, Hamraie, writes, citing Anna Tsing, "a 'material-discursive' phenomenon" that "conjures visions of livability in spite of . . . 'capitalist ruins'" and encourages expanding "notions of lives worth living," pushing us "to theorize how livable worlds materialize" (Hamraie 2020, 407). "Lives worth living" (it should really go without saying) can and should be enunciated in any and all languages. The vibrancy of conversations across Spanish and (of course) other languages compels us to continually mark the fact that alter-livability and crip world-making *cannot exist* if they are not constantly critiquing the hegemony of English and pushing toward the multilingual.

García Márquez also famously said, "No tenemos otro mundo al que podernos mudar" (We don't have another world that we can move to) (as quoted in Andina 2013). We in fact live in a fantastic and real world of what crip activist and theorist Eli Clare calls "brilliant imperfection": "a way of knowing, understanding, and living with disability and chronic illness . . . rooted in the nonnegotiable value of body-mind difference" (2017, xvii). *Nonnegotiable value* is such a beautiful concept, a generatively *twisted* concept in the world of neoliberal capitalism that we inhabit (it is also, arguably, an ethic for valuing "body-mind difference" that permeates all of Clare's writing). *Nuestras lenguas guerrilleras*, to return to Travesani, *lenguas guerrilleras* in which crip worlds materialize, also have nonnegotiable value, and it should not only be those whose second language is English who apprehend that value. We don't have another world to move to, *pero otro mundo es posible* (but another world is possible), as counter-globalization activists have long insisted. Welcoming those crip ways of knowing differently, or at least discerning that crip horizon, requires patience, sharing across borders, and a deep appreciation for the worlds that translation across all our differences affords us.

BIBLIOGRAPHY

Andina: Agencia Peruana de Noticias. 2013. "10 frases para recorder a García Márquez." June 3, 2013. https://andina.pe/ingles/noticia-10-frases-para-recordar-a-garcia-marquez-su -cumpleanos=449948.aspx.

Berlant, Lauren, and Michael Warner. 1998. "Sex in Public." *Critical Inquiry* 24:547–566.

Clare, Eli. 2017. *Brilliant Imperfection: Grappling with Cure.* Durham, NC: Duke University Press.

Duggan, Lisa. 2003. *The Twilight of Equality? Neoliberalism, Cultural Politics, and the Attack on Democracy.* Boston: Beacon.

Hamraie, Aimi. 2020. "Alterlivability: Speculative Design Fiction and the Urban Good Life in Starhawk's *Fifth Sacred Thing* and *City of Refuge*." *Environmental Humanities* 12 (2): 407–430.

Klein, Naomi. 2007. *The Shock Doctrine: The Rise of Disaster Capitalism.* New York: Picador.

Kolářová, Kateřina. 2014. "The Inarticulate Post-socialist Crip: On the Cruel Optimism of Neoliberal Transformations in the Czech Republic." *Journal of Literary and Cultural Disability Studies* 8 (3): 257–274.

Maldonado Ramírez, Jhonatthan. 2020. "Sentir la discapacidad en tiempos neoliberales: Optimismo cruel y fracas." *Nómadas* 52 (January–June). http://nomadas.ucentral.edu.co/index.php/component/content/article/2592-estudios-criticos-latinoamericanos-en-discapacidad-nomadas-52/1054-sentir-la-discapacidad-en-tiempos-neoliberales-optimismo-cruel-y-fracaso.

McRuer, Robert. 2018. *Crip Times: Disability, Globalization, and Resistance*. New York: New York University Press.

Moscoso Pérez, Melania. 2013. "'De aquí no se ve nadie': Del uso del discapacitado para el aleccionamiento moral." *Constelaciones: Revista de Teoría Crítica* 5:170–183.

Periodismo Femidisca. 2020. "Somos Periodismo Femidisca." Periodismo Femidisca blog, November 24, 2020. https://periodismofemidisca.blogspot.com/2020/11/somos-periodismo-femidisca.html.

Puar, Jasbir K. 2009. "Prognosis Time." *Women and Performance: A Journal of Feminist Theory* 19 (2): 161–172.

Puar, Jasbir K. 2017. *The Right to Maim: Debility, Capacity, Disability*. Durham, NC: Duke University Press.

QED. 2013. "Description." *QED: A Journal of GLBTQ Worldmaking*. Michigan State University Press. https:msupress.org/journals/qed.

Tovar, Andres. 2018. "¿Por qué el realismo mágico de Gabriel García Márquez es eterno?" *Cambio16*, April 17, 2018. https://www.cambio16.com/gabriel-garcia-marquez-realismo-magico/.

Travesani, Daiana. 2020. "Lisiada." Periodismo Femidisca blog, August 15, 2020. https://periodismofemidisca.blogspot.com/2020/08/lisiada-por-daiana-travesani.html.

Vanguardia. 2012. "Entregan PND en Los Pinos." December 2, 2012. https://vanguardia.com.mx/deportes/2817627-entregan-pnd-en-los-pinos-EYVG2817627.

27

Disability in the Library and Librarianship

STEPHANIE S. ROSEN

Libraries and librarianship have a complex relation to disability and disabled people. On the one hand, modern professional librarianship is a nineteenth-century invention that developed alongside eugenic ideologies and charitable institutions. On the other, the profession has always had an explicit commitment to a principle of access and an ethic of care. In short, librarianship is linked to some of the very formations against which disability rights movements and disability studies developed (eugenics, charity), and it is also connected to some of the very principles that have emerged as central to recent waves of disability justice activism and critical disability studies (access, care). In recent decades, library and information science (LIS, the disciplinary field of library knowledge) has been explicitly influenced by disability studies and by the activism of disabled library patrons and workers. Those committed to librarianship and disability justice, working in both academic research libraries and public libraries, argue that the field of librarianship has a radical potential to remake knowledge systems, to advocate for collective access, and to cultivate spaces in which participation is not conditional on abled performance or capitalist productivity. At the same time, the field has to recognize its foundations in charity service models (Schlesselman-Tarango 2016) and eugenic logics (Adler, Huber, and Nix 2017), frameworks that have historically constrained the production and management of disability (Snyder and Mitchell 2006).

In recent years, critical librarianship informed by disability activism and theory has reckoned with the ways in which these frameworks still structure disability's presence within libraries and librarianship—in subject headings determined by medical models, in separate libraries for "specialized populations" with disabilities, and in a focus on patrons' but not workers' barriers to access. At the same time, recent scholarship and critical practice, led by disabled and other marginalized library workers, has been working to realize the promise at the intersection of library values and disability justice principles, to question and reframe the historical position of disability in the library.

Call Numbers, Classification, Description

In between the call numbers HV1551 and HV3024, books that treat the subject "people with disabilities" are located. These numbers come from the Library of

Congress Classification, a system for organizing publications according to subject, developed at the turn of the twentieth century and used by most academic libraries in the United States (Library of Congress, 2014). (The Dewey Decimal Classification, in turn, is used by most public libraries in the United States and is the most widely used system in the world; OCLC Online Computer Library Center 2003.) In many libraries, the classification system is not just a string of numbers attached to each book; it is the spatial logic that determines where and how each book is shelved. If you go looking for disability in the library, the shelves labeled HV1551 to HV3024 are one place you will find it.

Since the first publication of the Library of Congress Classification (1901–1911) and the Library of Congress Subject Headings (1909–1914), multiple waves of critique and correction have addressed the system's inadequate specificity and relationship among terms, the "currency or bias of the headings," and structural problems (Fischer 2005, 103; Berman 1971; Adler 2017; Roberto 2008). The bias of headings, in particular, has become a flash point around minoritized subjects, and for entire fields of study that critique the knowledge systems preserved in the catalog. Specific terms (such as "Illegal alien"), as well as larger hierarchies and juxtapositions (queer theory under "Homosexuality," next to "Sexual deviations"), have been contested and in some cases changed (American Libraries Magazine 2021). However, such controversies or changes generally leave untouched the consolidated power in the *unmarked* terms and categories: *citizen, white, male, heterosexual,* and so on. Furthermore, the slow and uneven process of updating subject terms, from the 1970s to the present, means that even today many subject terms do not reflect language used by communities to define themselves (Olson 2000), are not aligned with field-defining keywords (Howard and Knowlton 2018; Koford 2014), and can enact violence or retraumatize researchers at specific intersections (Loyer 2018; Brilmyer 2020).

With respect to disability in particular, critiques have shown that library classification systems are themselves part of the modern project to "classify and pathologize human differences" (Snyder and Mitchell 2006, 4–5) and use "medical and sociological frameworks" to reproduce normative assumptions about "people with disabilities as diseased and/or dependent" (Adler, Huber, and Nix 2017, 118). Critiques show that classification systems fail to represent the distinctions that matter to scholars in the critical interdisciplinary field of disability studies (Koford 2014). And they argue that archival description largely fails to expose the political-relational assemblages that produced archival materials about disabled subjects, including materials like "arrest records, asylum documentation, . . . legislation" (Brilmyer 2018, 107).

There has been successful activism to change subject headings related to disability, but changes have come shockingly late. "Monsters" became "Abnormalities" in the National Library of Medicine Subject Headings in 2009 (Adler, Huber, and Nix 2017, 127). "Mental retardation" became "Intellectual disability" in the Dewey Decimal Classification in 2020 (Fox 2020). Perhaps too late, these changes are also too little, since the hierarchical arrangement of classification systems continues to reflect the eugenic logic that informed their original development. For example, while "Defective" has been replaced with "People with disabilities," the term is still under "Special classes" of "Protection, assistance and relief," which is under "Social pathology / Social and public welfare / Criminology" (Library of Congress, n.d.). In short, the entire subject is still locked within its original eugenic framing as a problem for science and the state, even as specific terms evolve (Adler, Huber, and Nix 2017). Similarly, while some sections have been removed—for example, "HQ1036–1043 Marriage of degenerates and defectives"—they persist as silences and gaps. The current outline jumps from "HQ1001–1006 The state and marriage" directly to "HQ1051–1057 The church and marriage," leaving the sections in between unnamed but also unchanged (Adler, Huber, and Nix 2017; Library of Congress, n.d.). And where racialized terms have disappeared from spaces beside disability—for example, from the subsections of Dewey 379.1, "Education of Special Classes," that originally included "Blind; Deaf and Dumb; Feeble-minded; Freedmen. Negro; Indians; Orientals; Criminals. Reform Schools; Special Nationalities; and Co-education of Races"—their modern and seemingly race-neutral replacements—"Students with physical disabilities; Students with mental disabilities; Delinquent and problem students . . ." (quoted in Adler, Huber, and Nix 2017, 130)—only bury deeper the interlocking logics of racism and ableism.

Critical approaches to cataloging (represented in library literature and also in online spaces including #CritCat on Twitter and the Cataloging Lab website) (Fox 2018) are interested in these projects of correction, and also in the politics of correction itself. Some recognize correction's limits, encouraging instead a critical pedagogy that teaches the biased logics of knowledge organization systems, while also preparing researchers to use them (Adler 2017; Drabinski 2013; Loyer 2018). Beyond correction, some catalogers and archivists are supplementing existing disability classifications and descriptions with critical and community-generated keywords. For example, Sara White (2012) encourages archivists to draw on a disability theory of complex embodiment when appraising and describing materials about subjects with disabilities; Gracen Brilmyer advises an approach to archival description that would make more explicit the "complexity, power, and politicization" of that description, thereby "addressing—not redressing—contestable terms" (2018, 107, 95); and Meghan Rinn offers an approach that uses parts of the archival finding aid (a descriptive guide for a collection) to add relevant biographical information about disabled subjects in "sensitive writing that uses language preferred by the community" (2018, 14). And beyond libraries and archives, in the online social spheres that archive the present, disabled activists and other marginalized technology users are tagging work with hashtags of their own creation (Brock 2020). Hashtags such as #DisabilityTooWhite, started in 2016 by activist and social worker Vilissa Thompson, work to "acknowledge gaps" in mainstream retellings of disability rights history and to reorganize disability knowledge around new key terms (Thompson 2019, 3).

Specialized Services, Separate Collections, Universal Access

Modern professional library organizations name accessibility for individuals with disabilities as a core value. Both the International Federation of Library Associations and Institutions and the American Library Association claim a commitment to equitable information access "without regard to . . . disability" and "regardless of technology, format, or methods of delivery" (International Federation of Library Associations and Institutions 2019; American Library Association 2022). While these specific value statements were formalized at the turn of the twenty-first century (Johan Lor 2006; Jacobs and Berg 2011), professional library organizations have a much longer history of meeting the access needs of patrons with disabilities, often through specialized services and separate collections. There is, however, a tension between, on the one hand, attempts to situate disability access as integral to the profession and, on the other, the historical realities of achieving disability access by handling it separately (realities reinforced by, for example, specialized professional knowledge and practice, copyright law and its provisions for disability access, and the material properties of specific media formats). This tension between universal access and separate access (a familiar dialectic of accessible design and individual accommodations) persists into the present. Libraries may still redirect patrons with disabilities away from primary spaces, services, and collections to other, separate ones. And at the same time, there is ongoing work to embed accessibility in all library practice, such as movements to make new publications "born accessible," to design all services and spaces with disability in mind, and to recognize that workers as well as patrons have access needs.

This tension is played out, for example, in the long-twentieth-century history of professional librarianship, wherein the needs of segregated populations or separate collections lead to the emergence of professional specialization—which can address those needs but can also reinforce segregation and separation. For example, librarians within the International Federation of Library Associations and Institutions formed the Subcommittee on Hospital Libraries in 1931 to coordinate library services for hospitalized individuals (Panella 2009). In its first decades, the group became a site of emergent knowledge on assistive technologies (including microfilm, which allowed for increased text size and reading without holding a book) and accessibility policy (including copyright and customs exemptions for the reproduction and international exchange of accessible formats for use by disabled readers) (Panella 2009, 262). In the later twentieth century, it began both to expand into other sites of institutionalization (e.g., prisons) and to develop specialized guidance for all libraries (e.g., its Standards for Hospital Libraries, published as part of the 1973 Standards for Public Libraries) (Panella 2009).

Over time, what began as the subcommittee has gone through name changes, divisions, and mergers with adjacent specialist subgroups. Its current iteration is the IFLA Section on Library Services to People with Special Needs, and it focuses on library and information services to "people with . . . disabilities[,] . . . people experiencing homelessness, displaced populations, people in prisons, . . . people in hospitals and nursing homes" (Bolt 2021). In the development of this professional group (and its US equivalents in the American Library Association Interest Groups and Sections), there is an arc toward equitable, *integrated* library access for marginalized groups—in its creation of standards and guides for the profession—and also evidence of the repeated effects of the "institutional archipelago" (Chapman, Carey, and Ben-Moshe 2014). That is, institutionalization and its effects segregate people, creating barriers to access for specific populations. These barriers or "access problems" are often then treated as if they reside in the people themselves (Kumbier and Starkey 2016). And these access problems are addressed by emergent library specializations and then, only after some delay, incorporated into general professional practice.

In library collections, separation has come about through different processes. Print publications have historically been made accessible (to patrons with specific disabilities that prevent the use of print, often called "print disabilities") through processes of conversion that produced entire separate collections of alternate-format works: in Braille, recorded sound, and specialized digital formats. The development and distribution of those collections became regulated by copyright provisions that, while enabling access, also restrict it to specific users whose disabilities prevent the use of print. Today, the largest libraries of accessible-format publications in the United States are the National Library Service for the Blind and Print Disabled (n.d.; several hundred thousand popular books, magazines, and music scores in Braille, audio, and digital formats), BookShare (n.d.; over one million academic and educational titles in a range of digital formats), and HathiTrust (n.d.; seventeen million digitized scans of historical, academic, and government publications), according to the current estimates on their websites. Yet in accordance with copyright law, these services are only available to users who meet specific disability eligibility criteria. That is, users must be blind, or have a "visual impairment or perceptual or reading disability" that prevents reading "printed works to substantially the same degree as a person without an impairment or disability," or be "otherwise unable, through physical disability, to hold or manipulate a book or to focus or move the eyes to the extent that would be normally acceptable for reading" (United States Copyright Office 2018). In fact, this language is meant to apply to individuals with "*any* disability (including learning disabilities and mobility impairments) that affect the ability to read text in a standard format" (Butler, Adler, and Cox 2019). And additional disability legislation (the Americans with Disabilities Act) and copyright provisions (Section 107, or the Fair Use provision) allow the creation of accessible copies of works for individual disabled users, including users with disabilities not necessarily defined here and works not already in these libraries. Yet in practice, this eligibility requirement maintains a medicalized system of "proving disability" for those who do qualify (Samuels 2014, chap. 6), and it can result in patrons getting separated out or redirected—from their public library to the National Library Service, or from their academic library to campus disability services.

The history of separate collections and specialized services for individuals with disabilities, as well as the professional focus on *print disabilities* traditionally defined, continues to shape, as a recent review article puts it, "how we talk about disability" in LIS (Gibson, Bowen, and Hanson 2021). The review, of peer-reviewed articles on disability in LIS from 1978 to 2018, finds an over-reliance on external authority about disability, a focus on blindness and low vision, a tendency to use "single-axis definitions of disability" that ignore relevant intersections, and (after 1999) a focus on technology and digital access. Much of the research in this area, as surveyed by Amelia Gibson, Kristen Bowen, and Dana Hanson (2021), and previously by Heather Hill (2013), asks whether patrons with a (often specific) disability can access a particular service or collection, investigating the question through user surveys that ask disabled users about their experience or through accessibility testing procedures in which often nondisabled experts test a service against standards. This work is necessary—patrons with disabilities remain underserved, and barriers remain to both services and collections—but it has also occluded other questions, circled the same problems without exploring others, and failed to transform into more radical approaches to access. As such, it is symptomatic of what David James Hudson calls a profession-wide "imperative to be practical" that prevents much LIS literature from approaching critical theory or radical practice, leaving larger ableist and racist structures in place (2017, 207).

In response to historical legacies and professional imperatives that too often collapse *libraries and disability* into *library collection access for patrons with print disabilities*, various movements are working to expand the professional discourse of accessibility to include, for example, open and accessible publications for all, library services that center rather than segregate access needs, and an attention to library workers (not just patrons) with disabilities. In scholarly publishing, there is a movement away from separate collections of specialized formats, toward born-digital, born-accessible—and often open-access—publications, driven by scholars and consumers with disabilities as well as library and publishing organizations (Rosen 2018). The library profession's commitment to equitable information access for all library users, without barriers created by cost or format, is supported by a publishing model that is both accessible and open access—that is, digital publications that adhere to accessibility standards (and are therefore usable by readers with a range of technologies, disabilities, or access needs) and that are freely available online. Libraries, both as advocates and as publishers (many university presses are administratively part of academic libraries), have advanced this movement by making their own publications more accessible, by developing guidebooks for the production of accessible publications (Library Publishing Coalition Ethical Framework Task Force 2018; Seaman, Ober, and Kasdorf 2019), and by pressuring the vendors who sell access to scholarship via ebook and journal platforms to make those platforms and content more accessible (Pionke and Schroeder 2020). While libraries work to address access barriers created within the academic publishing ecosystem, disabled scholars have advanced this advocacy from their roles as authors, readers, and editors. For example, the Society for Disability Studies (2016) statement on publishing accessible books called for accessible publishing practices from academic presses, the "Disability Studies Reader 6 Collective Statement" (Clare et al. 2021) demanded ethical and consentful editorial practice in the creation of scholarly anthologies, and Cynthia Wu (this volume) has developed editorial practices that respect "crip time" by factoring in flexible deadlines for disabled writers and editors who "might need more time to accomplish something or to arrive somewhere" due to ableist barriers, unpredictable illness, or managing care (Kafer 2013, 26; Samuels 2017).

In the design of library services and spaces, there have long been efforts to broadly incorporate accessible practice and design. *Universal design*—the approach of designing spaces, services, and information to be readily accessible for a range of bodies, needs, and backgrounds—is a key term that has migrated from product design and pedagogy into LIS literature and is the subject of book-length studies on library service development (Spina 2021), online library instruction (Lund 2020), and the architecture of academic library spaces (Staines 2012), as well as hundreds of articles. Of course, the meaning of *universal design* may vary—from specific disability-centered designs, to "mere ergonomics," or to almost "any form of user-centered design"—and often leaves out the "politicized claims of disability rights advocates" in order to appeal to the mainstream desires of "normate" consumers (Hamraie 2017 211), or to the neoliberal demands of only the most privileged disabled consumer subjects (Puar 2017). At the same time, universal or accessible design approaches can be used strategically to center the needs of disabled and marginalized users and advance an intersectional political agenda that remakes spaces and services (Rosen 2017).

Just as universal design approaches shift from separate, "disability-specific" services toward an integrated, "disability-informed" approach, *trauma-informed* approaches in libraries shift from special treatment for trauma survivors, toward practices that reduce risk and foster resilience across individuals and groups with varying trauma histories (Carello and Butler 2015, 265). While trauma-informed approaches have arrived in librarianship and related fields by several avenues

(Gohr and Nova 2020; Mauldin, this volume), one is through direct partnerships between librarians and social workers (Zettervall and Nienow 2019; Tolley 2020). Certainly, both professions have common origins in an assimilationist discourse of moral uplift in which mostly white women tend to those marked as other to the healthy, national body (Schlesselman-Tarango 2016; Ettarh 2018). And both professions have been shown to at times police (or call the police on) those they serve, traumatizing or endangering marginalized, especially disabled and/ or Black, individuals (Robinson 2019; Roberts 2021). But library workers and their social work partners have also shown a commitment to social justice and community support—by empowering patrons with both information and connections to social services, by reducing unwanted patron interactions with the state and the police, and by training their own staff to de-escalate and use other informal techniques (Balzer 2020).

Finally, there is the push to recognize disability among library workers, not just library patrons, and to document the experiences of such workers (Brown and Sheidlower 2019). Autoethnographies, personal narratives, and scholarship from the perspective of library workers with disabilities emphasize that we are here, and highlight discriminatory working conditions that assume an able-bodied, flexible worker while viewing "disability as a problem in need of a solution" (Moeller 2019, 466). Discrimination and barriers facing librarians with disabilities are well documented (Oud 2019; Roulstone and Williams 2014), as are the professional discourses that can prevent critical action toward more sustaining and sustainable working conditions (Ettarh 2018). Recent counternarratives by library workers who claim disability function to "elevate . . . hidden voices" (Dube and Wade 2021, 316) and to critique the current practices of librarianship and think toward more liberatory ones (Lawrence 2013; Brilmyer 2018; Schomburg and Highby 2020; Dube and Wade 2021). Beyond the professional literature—which overrepresents white perspectives and underanalyzes race, just as in disability studies (Bowen, Kuo, and Mills, this volume)—this work happens in online spaces, events, and storytelling. For example, on Twitter, recurring #CripLib (n.d.) chats unpack topics at the intersection of disability and libraries; in an interview, Cyrée Jarelle Johnson (Brooklyn Public Library's inaugural poet-in-residence) speaks on ableism and racism in literary spaces (Bowen 2020); and online, the We Here (n.d.) platform provides a "safe and supportive community for Black and Indigenous folks, and People of Color (BIPOC) in library and information science professions and educational programs" to confront systemic social issues in the profession.

Disability Justice in the Library

In librarianship, a profession fundamentally concerned with questions of access, disability issues have long been part of the conversation. Only more recently have critical disability studies methods and the political demands of disability justice begun to influence libraries and librarianship. Disability studies as method "[employs] disability studies as a lens to analyze the intersecting systems of ableism, heteropatriarchy, white supremacy, and capitalist violence, particularly as they assign value or lack thereof to certain bodyminds" (Schalk and Kim 2020, 37–38). Disability justice is a twenty-first-century wave of disability activism that demands intersectional analysis, coalitional activism, and collective access, "led by disabled people of color, and disabled queer and gender non-conforming people" (Sins Invalid 2019, 21). Several examples of recent library scholarship and critical conversations—some of which explicitly address disability and some of which do not—resonate with the methods of disability studies and the politics of disability justice. This work can, in turn, form the foundation for future library practice committed to collective liberation. As Gibson, Bowen, and Hanson (2021) point out, we can imagine building toward future "co-liberatory information work" that would center the expertise of disabled individuals of color and ground information systems in disability justice, toward library cultures "built on care webs . . . and institutional responsibility," knowledge systems based in "wholeness . . . rather than clinical cure or rehabilitation," and decision making driven by disabled community needs in a neoliberal present.

Within LIS literature, the most well-known introduction of the concept of "disability justice" was in a 2016 *Library Trends* article by Alana Kumbier and Julia Starkey. Kumbier and Starkey argue that "access is not problem solving," critiquing approaches to library accessibility that treat access barriers as merely problems to solve, and that treat patrons as people who either have access or have access problems. Rather, they encourage an intersectional approach to creating access, dismantling ableism, and collaborating across disability—an approach explicitly informed by disability justice writings and the authors' own disability justice activism. Since this publication, new library work has continued to engage with disability justice.

Disability justice argues that understanding ableism requires "tracing its connections to heteropatriarchy, white supremacy, colonialism, and capitalism" (Sins Invalid 2019, 18). A good deal of library scholarship has worked to reckon with these interlocking systems—not always with an explicit disability lens, but rather with the critical race, decolonial, and other analytical lenses that are foundational for understanding disability. For example, some recent scholarship has critiqued the expectation that all library workers should embody culturally white (and implicitly able-bodied) social and professional performances to succeed in librarianship (Hathcock 2015; Galvan 2015; Andrews 2020). Others have worked to rearticulate the library's role in colonialist projects and in nationalist projects of assimilation (Honma 2005; de jesus 2014; Schlesselman-Tarango 2016, 2017). And others have critiqued the rhetoric of neutrality that libraries currently use to disavow political responsibility and, consequently, uphold a white supremacist status quo (Hudson 2017; Chiu, Ettarh, and Ferretti 2021).

The question of care is another site where libraries can think with disability justice. Collective care has always been a part of disability justice organizing, and it has received greater attention with the publication of *Care Work* (Piepzna-Samarasinha 2018), which has, in turn, influenced writing in disability studies (for example, Kim 2020). Care, for collections and for people, has likewise always been a part of librarianship and cultural heritage professions. And care in these professions has received renewed critical attention, following recent work in science and technology studies (Martin, Myers, and Viseu 2015), workers' insistence that care and maintenance are labor (Mattern 2018), and calls to reckon with the violent colonial foundations of care as performed by cultural institutions (Umolu 2020). There have been critical studies of the ways in which care in libraries is always shaped by raced, gendered embodiment and especially by histories of white saviorism (Ettarh 2018), and there have been offerings of alternatives. Anne Cong-Huyen and Kush Patel (2021) describe mutual support collectives as counterspaces that, by enacting care among marginalized academic workers, enable their survival in the neoliberal university and other hostile environments. Jessie Loyer (2018, 150) imagines library care practices as they could be, transformed not just by feminist critique but by Indigenous frameworks—based in "relational accountability between librarians and students" as students face the trauma of doing research within the violent structures of library classification, archival description, and educational institutions.

For many library workers and librarian scholars, including the specific examples just cited, the library remains a space of possibility—deserving of critique but also open for transformation. Celebrations of the library, as a key site that can sustain democratic possibility through access to information and support the lives of local communities through access to resources, can be problematic and are also based in truth. Certainly, such uncritical praise can be used to falsely position libraries as neutral or postpolitical (Seale 2016; Bourg 2015), and it can forestall critique of librarianship or gloss over the histories that have shaped it (Ettarh 2018). But the library really is an emancipatory space, even as it's also a hegemonic institution (Aptekar 2019). Under the pressures of neoliberalism (Bourg 2014), there is a real danger that libraries may lose the pro-privacy, anti-surveillance, noncommercial, access-oriented qualities that make them different from everywhere else—or that they might just be replaced by Amazon-funded simulacra (Johnson 2018). Maura Seale and Rafia Mirza (2020) argue that, given that libraries have to justify their existence in a context of neoliberal austerity, we can at least do so on our own terms by rejecting neoliberal regimes of value and claiming libraries' *political value*—as sites of care, mutual responsibility, and harm reduction. And if libraries can claim political value, they could also claim the specific political values of disability justice, including collective access, cross-movement solidarity, a recognition of wholeness, and sustainable transformation (Sins Invalid 2019, 22–27). Library spaces are already potential sites of cross-group solidarities. Public libraries in particular are spaces where individuals come to meet some of their needs, where resources are distributed "outside of capitalist market exchange," and where users make the "space their own through everyday practices" (Aptekar 2019, 1216). The principles of disability justice can steer the political work of and in libraries as the profession continues to reckon with the complex tensions and histories that shape it and its relationship to disability.

BIBLIOGRAPHY

Adler, Melissa. 2017. *Cruising the Library: Perversities in the Organization of Knowledge.* New York: Fordham University Press.

Adler, Melissa, Jeffrey T. Huber, and A. Tyler Nix. 2017. "Stigmatizing Disability: Library Classifications and the Marking and Marginalization of Books about People with Disabilities." *Library Quarterly* 87 (2): 117–135.

American Libraries Magazine. 2021. "Library of Congress Changes *Illegal Aliens* Subject Heading." *The Scoop* (blog). *American Libraries Magazine.* November 12, 2021. https://american librariesmagazine.org/blogs/the-scoop/library-of-congress-changes-illegal-aliens-subject -heading/.

American Library Association. 2022. "ALA Policy Manual Section B: Positions and Public Policy." https://www.ala.org/aboutala/governance/policymanual.

Andrews, Nicola. 2020. "It's Not Imposter Syndrome: Resisting Self-Doubt as Normal for Library Workers." *In the Library with the Lead Pipe*, June 10, 2020. https://www.inthelibrarywiththe leadpipe.org/2020/its-not-imposter-syndrome/.

Aptekar, Sofya. 2019. "The Public Library as Resistive Space in the Neoliberal City." *City and Community* 18 (4): 1203–1219.

Balzer, Cass. 2020. "Rethinking Police Presence: Libraries Consider Divesting from Law Enforcement." *American Libraries*, July 8, 2020. https://americanlibrariesmagazine.org/2020/07/08 /rethinking-police-presence/.

Berman, Sanford. 1971. *Prejudices and Antipathies: A Tract on the LC Subject Heads Concerning People.* Metuchen, NJ: Scarecrow.

Bolt, Nancy. 2021. "Annual Report Library Services to People with Special Needs (LSN) 2020–2021." *IFLA Library Services to People with Special Needs Newsletter*, July 2021.

Bookshare. n.d. Homepage. Accessed May 14, 2018. https://www.bookshare.org/cms/.

Bourg, Chris. 2014. "The Neoliberal Library: Resistance Is Not Futile." *Feral Librarian* (blog), January 16, 2014. https://chrisbourg.wordpress.com/2014/01/16/the-neoliberal-library-resistance -is-not-futile/.

Bourg, Chris. 2015. "Never Neutral: Libraries, Technology, and Inclusion." *Feral Librarian* (blog), January 28, 2015. https://chrisbourg.wordpress.com/2014/01/16/the-neoliberal-library-resistance -is-not-futile/.

Bowen, Liz. 2020. "'I Can't Make You See What I See': Talking with Cyree Jarelle Johnson and Jesse Rice-Evans." *Public Books*, April 27, 2020. https://www.publicbooks.org/i-cant-make-you -see-what-i-see-talking-with-cyree-jarelle-johnson-and-jesse-rice-evans/.

Brilmyer, Gracen M. 2018. "Archival Assemblages: Applying Disability Studies' Political/Relational Model to Archival Description." *Archival Science* 18 (2): 95–118.

Brilmyer, Gracen M. 2020. "'It Could Have Been Us in a Different Moment. It Still Is Us in Many Ways': Community Identification and the Violence of Archival Representation of Disability." In *Sustainable Digital Communities*, edited by Anneli Sundqvist, Gerd

Berget, Jan Nolin, and Kjell Ivar Skjerdingstad, 480–486. Cham, Switzerland: Springer International.

Brock, André. 2020. *Distributed Blackness: African American Cybercultures*. New York: New York University Press.

Brown, Robin, and Scott Sheidlower. 2019. "Claiming Our Space: A Quantitative and Qualitative Picture of Disabled Librarians." *Library Trends* 67 (3): 471–486.

Butler, Brandon, Prue Adler, and Krista Cox. 2019. "The Law and Accessible Texts: Reconciling Civil Rights and Copyrights." Association of Research Libraries. https://www.arl.org/resources/the-law-and-accessible-texts-reconciling-civil-rights-and-copyrights/.

Carello, Janice, and Lisa D. Butler. 2015. "Practicing What We Teach: Trauma-Informed Educational Practice." *Journal of Teaching in Social Work* 35 (3): 262–278.

Chapman, Chris, Allison C. Carey, and Liat Ben-Moshe. 2014. "Reconsidering Confinement: Interlocking Locations and Logics of Incarceration." In *Disability Incarcerated: Imprisonment and Disability in the United States and Canada*, edited by Liat Ben-Moshe and Allison C. Carey, 3–24. New York: Palgrave Macmillan.

Chiu, Anastasia, Fobazi M. Ettarh, and Jennifer A. Ferretti. 2021. "Not the Shark, but the Water: How Neutrality and Vocational Awe Intertwine to Uphold White Supremacy." In *Knowledge Justice: Disrupting Library and Information Studies through Critical Race Theory*, edited by Sofia Y. Leung and Jorge R. López-McKnight. Cambridge, MA: MIT Press. https://doi.org/10.7551/mitpress/11969.001.0001.

Clare, Eli, Aimi Hamraie, Lydia X. Z. Brown, Timotheus "T. J." Gordon Jr., and Ellen Samuels. 2021. "Disability Studies Reader 6 Collective Statement." March 22, 2021. https://docs.google.com/document/d/1L7Z7mLT00YeCzwOR2zx25DbwFFw99-fiHvlA5rHpY6k/edit.

Cong-Huyen, Anne, and Kush Patel. 2021. "Precarious Labor and Radical Care in Libraries and Digital Humanities." In *Knowledge Justice: Disrupting Library and Information Studies through Critical Race Theory*, edited by Sofia Y. Leung and Jorge R. López-McKnight. Cambridge, MA: MIT Press. https://doi.org/10.7551/mitpress/11969.001.0001.

#CripLib. n.d. Homepage. Accessed October 11, 2022. https://criplib.wordpress.com/.

de jesus, nina. 2014. "Locating the Library in Institutional Oppression." *In the Library with the Lead Pipe*, September 24, 2014. https://www.inthelibrarywiththeleadpipe.org/2014/locating-the-library-in-institutional-oppression/.

Drabinski, Emily. 2013. "Queering the Catalog: Queer Theory and the Politics of Correction." *Library Quarterly* 83 (2): 94–111.

Dube, Miranda, and Carrie Wade, eds. 2021. *LIS Interrupted: Intersections of Mental Illness and Library Work*. Sacramento, CA: Library Juice Press.

Ettarh, Fobazi. 2018. "Vocational Awe and Librarianship: The Lies We Tell Ourselves." *In the Library with the Lead Pipe*, January 10, 2018. http://www.inthelibrarywiththeleadpipe.org/2018/vocational-awe/.

Fischer, Karen S. 2005. "Critical Views of LCSH, 1990–2001: The Third Bibliographic Essay." *Cataloging and Classification Quarterly* 41 (1): 63–109.

Fox, Violet. 2018. "Creating Change in the Cataloging Lab: Peer to Peer Review." *Library Journal*, March 1, 2018. https://www.libraryjournal.com/story/creating-change-in-the-cataloging-lab-peer-to-peer-review.

Fox, Violet. 2020. "Making the Switch to Intellectual Disabilities." *The Dewey Blog*, January 22, 2020. https://ddc.typepad.com/025431/2020/01/making-the-switch-to-intellectual-disabilities.html.

Galvan, Angela. 2015. "Soliciting Performance, Hiding Bias: Whiteness and Librarianship." *In the Library with the Lead Pipe*, June 3, 2015. https://www.inthelibrarywiththeleadpipe.org/2015/soliciting-performance-hiding-bias-whiteness-and-librarianship/.

Gibson, Amelia, Kristen Bowen, and Dana Hanson. 2021. "We Need to Talk about How We Talk about Disability: A Critical Quasi-systematic Review." *In the Library with the Lead Pipe*, February 24, 2021. http://www.inthelibrarywiththeleadpipe.org/2021/disability/.

Gohr, Michelle, and Vitalina A. Nova. 2020. "Student Trauma Experiences, Library Instruction and Existence under the 45th." *Reference Services Review* 48 (1): 183–199.

Hamraie, Aimi. 2017. *Building Access: Universal Design and the Politics of Disability*. Minneapolis: University of Minnesota Press.

Hathcock, April. 2015. "White Librarianship in Blackface: Diversity Initiatives in LIS." *In the Library with the Lead Pipe*, October 7, 2015. https://www.inthelibrarywiththeleadpipe.org/2015/lis-diversity/.

HathiTrust Digital Library. n.d. "About." Accessed May 7, 2018. https://www.hathitrust.org/about.

Hill, Heather. 2013. "Disability and Accessibility in the Library and Information Science Literature: A Content Analysis." *Library and Information Science Research* 35 (2): 137–142.

Honma, Todd. 2005. "Trippin' over the Color Line: The Invisibility of Race in Library and Information Studies." *InterActions: UCLA Journal of Education and Information Studies* 1 (2). https://doi.org/10.5070/D412000540.

Howard, Sara A., and Steven A. Knowlton. 2018. "Browsing through Bias: The Library of Congress Classification and Subject Headings for African American Studies and LGBTQIA Studies." *Library Trends* 67 (1): 74–88.

Hudson, David James. 2017. "The Whiteness of Practicality." In *Topographies of Whiteness: Mapping Whiteness in Library and Information Science*, edited by Gina Schlesselman-Tarango, 203–234. Sacramento, CA: Library Juice Press.

International Federation of Library Associations and Institutions. 2019. "International Federation of Library Associations and Institutions Core Values." December 10, 2019. https://web.archive.org/web/20210624040447/https://cf5-www.ifla.org/about/more.

Jacobs, Heidi L. M., and Selinda Berg. 2011. "Reconnecting Information Literacy Policy with the Core Values of Librarianship." *Library Trends* 60 (2): 383–394.

Johan Lor, Peter. 2006. "IFLA: Looking to the Future." *Library Management* 27 (1/2): 38–47.

Johnson, Cyrée Jarelle. 2018. "Turning Libraries into Amazon Stores Is Class Warfare." *Vice*, July 24, 2018. https://www.vice.com/en/article/ne57jz/replacing-libraries-with-amazon-forbes-article.

Kafer, Alison. 2013. *Feminist, Queer, Crip*. Bloomington: Indiana University Press.

Kim, Jina B. 2019. "Love in the Time of Sickness: On Disability, Race, and Intimate Partner Violence." In "Open in Emergency: A Special Issue on Asian American Mental Health," edited by Mimi Khúc. *Asian American Literary Review* 10 (2) (Fall/Winter).

Koford, Amelia. 2014. "How Disability Studies Scholars Interact with Subject Headings." *Cataloging and Classification Quarterly* 52 (4): 388–411.

Kumbier, Alana, and Julia Starkey. 2016. "Access Is Not Problem Solving: Disability Justice and Libraries." *Library Trends* 64 (3): 468–491.

Lawrence, E. 2013. "Loud Hands in the Library: Neurodiversity in LIS Theory & Practice." *Progressive Librarians Guild*, no. 41 (Fall): 98–109.

Library of Congress. 2014. "Library of Congress Classification." Accessed October 13, 2021. https://www.loc.gov/catdir/cpso/lcc.html.

Library of Congress. n.d. "Library of Congress Classification Outline." Cataloging Distribution Service. Accessed October 13, 2021. https://www.loc.gov/catdir/cpso/lcco/.

Library Publishing Coalition Ethical Framework Task Force. 2018. *An Ethical Framework for Library Publishing, Version 1.0*. Atlanta: Educopia. http://dx.doi.org/10.5703/1288284316777.

Loyer, Jessie. 2018. "Indigenous Information Literacy: Nêhiyaw Kinship Enabling Self-Care in Research." In *The Politics of Theory and the Practice of Critical Librarianship*, edited by Karen P. Nicholson and Maura Seale, 145–157. Sacramento, CA: Litwin Books.

Lund, Brady. 2020. *Creating Accessible Online Instruction Using Universal Design Principles: A LITA Guide.* Lanham, MD: Rowman and Littlefield.

Martin, Aryn, Natasha Myers, and Ana Viseu. 2015. "The Politics of Care in Technoscience." *Social Studies of Science* 45 (5): 625–641.

Mattern, Shannon. 2018. "Maintenance and Care." *Places Journal*, November 2018. https://doi.org /10.22269/181120.

Moeller, Christine M. 2019. "Disability, Identity, and Professionalism: Precarity in Librarianship." *Library Trends* 67 (3): 455–470.

National Library Service for the Blind and Print Disabled. n.d. "Overview." Library of Congress. Accessed November 1, 2022. https://www.loc.gov/nls/about/overview/.

OCLC Online Computer Library Center. 2003. *Summaries: DDC Dewey Decimal Classification.* Dublin, OH: OCLC Online Computer Library Center. https://www.oclc.org/content/dam /oclc/dewey/resources/summaries/deweysummaries.pdf.

Olson, Hope A. 2000. "Difference, Culture and Change: The Untapped Potential of LCSH." *Cataloging and Classification Quarterly* 29 (1–2): 53–71.

Oud, Joanne. 2019. "Systemic Workplace Barriers for Academic Librarians with Disabilities." *College and Research Libraries* 80 (2): 169–194.

Panella, Nancy. 2009. "The Library Services to People with Special Needs Section of IFLA: An Historical Overview." *IFLA Journal* 35 (3): 258–271.

Piepzna-Samarasinha, Leah Lakshmi. 2018. *Care Work: Dreaming Disability Justice.* Vancouver, Canada: Arsenal Pulp.

Pionke, J. J., and Heidi M. Schroeder. 2020. "Working Together to Improve Accessibility: Consortial E-Resource Accessibility and Advocacy." *Serials Review* 46 (2): 137–142.

Puar, Jasbir K. 2017. *The Right to Maim: Debility, Capacity, Disability.* Durham, NC: Duke University Press.

Rinn, Meghan. 2018. "Nineteenth-Century Depictions of Disabilities and Modern Metadata: A Consideration of Material in the P. T. Barnum Digital Collection." *Journal of Contemporary Archival Studies* 5: article 1. https://elischolar.library.yale.edu/jcas/vol5/iss1/1.

Roberto, K. R., ed. 2008. *Radical Cataloging: Essays at the Front.* Jefferson, NC: McFarland.

Roberts, Dorothy. 2021. "Abolish Family Policing, Too." *Dissent Magazine*, Summer 2021. https:// www.dissentmagazine.org/article/abolish-family-policing-too.

Robinson, Ben. 2019. "No Holds Barred: Policing and Security in the Public Library." *In the Library with the Lead Pipe*, December 11, 2019. https://www.inthelibrarywiththeleadpipe.org /2019/no-holds-barred/.

Rosen, Stephanie. 2017. "Accessibility for Justice: Accessibility as a Tool for Promoting Justice in Librarianship." *In the Library with the Lead Pipe*, November 29, 2017. http://www.inthelibrary withtheleadpipe.org/2017/accessibility-for-justice/.

Rosen, Stephanie. 2018. *Accessibility & Publishing.* United States: Against the Grain. https://doi .org/10.3998/mpub.10212548.

Roulstone, Alan, and Jannine Williams. 2014. "Being Disabled, Being a Manager: 'Glass Partitions' and Conditional Identities in the Contemporary Workplace." *Disability and Society* 29 (1): 16–29.

Samuels, Ellen. 2014. *Fantasies of Identification: Disability, Gender, Race.* New York: New York University Press.

Samuels, Ellen. 2017. "Six Ways of Looking at Crip Time." *Disability Studies Quarterly* 37 (3). https://doi.org/10.18061/dsq.v37i3.5824.

Schalk, Sami, and Jina B. Kim. 2020. "Integrating Race, Transforming Feminist Disability Studies." *Signs: Journal of Women in Culture and Society* 46 (1): 31–55.

Schlesselman-Tarango, Gina. 2016. "The Legacy of Lady Bountiful: White Women in the Library." *Library Trends* 64 (4): 667–686.

Schlesselman-Tarango, Gina, ed. 2017. *Topographies of Whiteness: Mapping Whiteness in Library and Information Science.* Sacramento, CA: Library Juice Press.

Schomberg, Jessica J., and Wendy Highby. 2020. *Beyond Accommodation: Creating an Inclusive Workplace for Disabled Library Workers.* Sacramento, CA: Library Juice Press.

Seale, Maura. 2016. "Compliant Trust: The Public Good and Democracy in the ALA's 'Core Values of Librarianship.'" *Library Trends* 64 (3): 585–603.

Seale, Maura, and Rafia Mirza. 2020. "The Coin of Love and Virtue: Academic Libraries and Value in a Global Pandemic." *Canadian Journal of Academic Librarianship* 6 (December): 1–30.

Seaman, Robin, Elaine Ober, and Bill Kasdorf, eds. 2019. *BISG Guide to Accessible Publishing.* New York: Book Industry Study Group. https://docs.google.com/document/d/1eI10gbbt WgXnavuUnaGDz_iAKkzaw6R_1bDFq2kmJsA/edit.

Sins Invalid. 2019. *Skin, Tooth, and Bone: The Basis of Movement Is Our People: A Disability Justice Primer.* 2nd ed. Berkeley: Sins Invalid.

Snyder, Sharon L., and David T. Mitchell. 2006. *Cultural Locations of Disability.* Chicago: University of Chicago Press.

Society for Disability Studies. 2016. "Publishing Accessible Books." https://web.archive.org/web /20220122110807/http://disstudies.org/index.php/publications/publishing-accessible-books/.

Spina, Carli. 2021. *Creating Inclusive Libraries by Applying Universal Design: A Guide.* Lanham, MD: Rowman and Littlefield.

Staines, Gail M. 2012. *Universal Design: A Practical Guide to Creating and Recreating Interiors of Academic Libraries for Teaching, Learning and Research.* Oxford: Chandos.

Thompson, Vilissa. 2019. "How Technology Is Forcing the Disability Rights Movement into the 21st Century." *Catalyst: Feminism, Theory, Technoscience* 5 (1): 1–5. https://doi.org/10.28968 /cftt.v5i1.30420.

Tolley, Rebecca. 2020. *A Trauma-Informed Approach to Library Services.* Chicago: ALA Editions.

Umolu, Yesomi. 2020. "On the Limits of Care and Knowledge: 15 Points Museums Must Understand to Dismantle Structural Injustice." Artnet News, June 25, 2020. https://news.artnet.com /opinion/limits-of-care-and-knowledge-yesomi-umolu-op-ed-1889739.

United States Copyright Office. 2018. *Amendments to the Copyright Act as a Result of the Marrakesh Treaty Implementation Act.* Washington, DC: Library of Congress. https://www .copyright.gov/legislation/2018_marrakesh_amendments.pdf.

We Here. n.d. Homepage. Accessed October 15, 2021. https://www.wehere.space/.

White, Sara. 2012. "Crippling the Archives: Negotiating Notions of Disability in Appraisal and Arrangement and Description." *American Archivist* 75 (1): 109–124.

Zettervall, Sara K., and Mary C. Nienow. 2019. *Whole Person Librarianship: A Social Work Approach to Patron Services.* Santa Barbara, CA: Libraries Unlimited.

28

The Rebuttal

A Protactile Poem

JOHN LEE CLARK

Background

Protactile encompasses movement (a philosophy that emerges from the literal connection and touch centered in DeafBlind lives), practices (the application of those knowledges of touch and connection), and language. Distinct from visual ASL (and growing more so each day), Protactile has its own lexicon and grammatical features. The essence of *protactile* as an adjective is "dynamic, proprioceptive perception. . . . Not merely feeling something but both feeling it and feeling being felt by it" (Clark 2023).

"The Rebuttal" is a Protactile poem, with an English counterpart, that responds to an 1835 poem by Lydia Huntley Sigourney about a DeafBlind girl, Julia Brace. The publishing industry is set up to support English, but how best to publish and archive Protactile?

Description of the Protactile Poem "The Rebuttal"

The video shows me sitting in the classic Protactile three-way formation with Heather Holmes sitting to my left and Jelica Nuccio sitting to my right (figure 28.1). Our right knees are pressed against each other, and our left knees give warmth and presence by touching the next person's flank.

Throughout the performance, Heather's right hand is on my left hand and Jelica's left hand is on my right hand. My hands do the exact same things, in symmetry, so that they receive the same message. Their other hands rest together on my knee. From time to time, they react to my poem by squeezing my leg.

I note to them the title of the poem, "The Rebuttal." Before beginning, I draw their hands to my chest as I take a deep breath and blow on their hands.

The poem begins. I touch their upper bodies and settle both my closed hands on their chests near where their hearts would be. My knuckles begin to rhythmically press against their chests. It is a pumping cadence. I shift my hands, where each one now has two fingers extended. Those two fingers slide and press across their chests toward their arms, leading down to my knee.

Figure 28.1. Screenshot from John Lee Clark's "The Rebuttal."
Tactile description of Clark: Short hair of feline softness. Warm and smooth hands.
A scent of patchouli. Flutters betray his exhilaration.

Video available at DeafBlind Interpreting National Training and Resource Center,
"#PTSTOMPS: The Rebuttal," February 1, 2020, https://www.dbinterpreting.com/news/ptstomps
-the-rebuttal.

After a few slide presses, my hands scoot back to their hearts to do more closed-hand pumping. They fly back to where I left off the sliding presses. Back and forth, my hands pump their hearts and push the slide presses down their arms, down, down, down. Pressure builds up.

When the pumping has pushed the slide presses all the way down to their hands on my knee, my fingers hook between their fingers, fumbling.

The pumping force now pulls up along their arms. Back and forth, my hands pump their hearts and tug-press against their arms, up, up, up.

When the pumping has pulled the tugging all the way back to their chests, the pulling continues past their hearts, up, up, up. The tug presses wrap around behind their necks. There, my fingers spread over the backs of their heads and begin to vibrate.

The pumping is abandoned, and my vibrating hands roar back down their necks, across their chests, past their hearts, and down their arms to their hands on my knee. My vibrating hands clasp their hands, and all six hands are lifted up, vibrating, high above our heads. A pause; the vibrating ceases. I slowly bring all six hands back down to my knee. A pause. The poem is finished.

A Counterpart Poem in English

The Protactile poem has an English counterpart. This is not a translation but rather a parallel poem. The English parallel itself is an erasure of a problematic poem written in 1835 about Julia Brace. The erasure inspired the composition of the Protactile poem.

THE REBUTTAL

An erasure of Lydia Huntley Sigourney's "On Seeing the Deaf, Dumb, and Blind Girl, Sitting for Her Portrait"

Guide, passion, catch what
Hath no speech. Unknown
Joys, power, and meditation's
Unfolding sky. Feeling draws
Heart and wildering language
Still without speech to
Mind. Philosophy fails to
Sway this future child.

BIBLIOGRAPHY

Clark, John Lee. 2023. *Touch the Future: A Manifesto in Essays*. New York: W.W. Norton and Company.

Media

29

Crip Making

AIMI HAMRAIE

During the COVID-19 pandemic, many people turned to remote and digital forms of participation and communication, whether for work or social life. What many nondisabled people did not know was that disability communities had often developed (for themselves) the same technologies that many nondisabled people were using to survive the pandemic—despite often being denied the right to remote work and education. At the same time, Black, Indigenous, Latinx, and institutionalized disabled people have been at particularly high risk for severe COVID-19 complications, including death, and were deprioritized in medical triage and vaccination. Disability communities responded to these paradoxes of access in several ways. Some launched hashtag campaigns. For example, Alice Wong's #HighRiskCA pointed out that disabled people often had less access to vaccinations, while Kate McWilliams's #Accessibilityforableds offered examples of how remote access for nondisabled people was being prioritized during the pandemic. Others hosted online cultural events with ASL interpreters, live transcription, and image descriptions. Still others created digital networks for mutual aid and the distribution of items such as masks, hand sanitizer, and air filters. In the process, disability communities claimed expertise and design knowledge about remote forms of participation. Their practices illustrate the concept of "disability culture," comprising the norms, social relations, and technologies that form around collective experiences of disability (Barnes and Mercer 2001). Whether in the case of "homebound shut-ins" embracing radio technology in the 1920s (Kirkpatrick 2017), polio survivors sharing design hacks via newsletters in the 1960s (Williamson 2012), Autistic people finding community via email listservs in the 1990s (Sinclair 2012), chronically ill people organizing funerals and protests from their beds (Piepzna-Samarasinha 2018), or Black disabled feminists using "hashtag activism" for political advocacy (Thompson 2019; S. Jackson, Bailey, and Welles 2020), remote access has been central to the socio-technological life of disability in the twentieth and twenty-first centuries, highlighting the reaches of geographically dispersed and heterogeneous disability cultures.

Yet technology is not an easy fix. Disabled critics of technology highlight the role of "technoableism" (Shew 2020) in shaping the treatment of disability as a deficiency or problem to fix. Crip theorists note disabled peoples' "ambivalent relationships to technology" (Kafer 2013, 119), in which technological failures and conflicting accessibility needs create frictions. For example, remote learning that benefits some chronically ill people may cause "Zoom fatigue" or chronic migraines for the same people or for others. Telehealth and telework options during the pandemic are being rescinded in light of mass vaccinations, leaving chronically ill people without accommodations and sparking protests (Kovach 2011). Useful digital tools and electronics (including internet routers and ventilators) sometimes fail in locations facing power shortages due to heat, wildfires, or inadequate infrastructure. The many paradoxes of remote access illustrate that disabled people are makers and adapters, and not just passive users, of technology. Rather than eschewing technology, disability communities often turn to iterative design processes to address these apparent conflicts.

The politics of disability technology raise important theoretical and empirical questions about the epistemologies, methodologies, and societal implications of design *by*, rather than *for*, disabled people. In many cases, *making* is political in that it gathers networks of kinship and belonging around world-building practices that challenge mainstream cultural norms and values. Critical making theorist Jentery Sayers (2017) argues that making is a way of drawing boundaries: "Such boundaries mark how and where value is attributed and accrued. They also correspond with ideologies and environments for who gets to make, who can maintain, and who must source" (9). Consequently, *crip making* relies on and produces forms of knowledge and expertise that draw boundaries between assimilation and antiassimilation, able-bodied norms and disability culture. In this chapter, I explore the concept of crip making in three ways. First, I examine controversies surrounding the role of the maker (as author or progenitor) in debates about disability, design, and technology. Then, I examine political-relational and performance-based approaches to disability-led design, looking at the design politics of lived experience and complicating notions of "standpoint epistemology" and "situated knowledge." Finally, I draw on an example of crip making during the COVID-19 pandemic to highlight the complex politics of access friction and negotiation.

Users and Makers: Disability, Design, and Technology

Disability has been a present, but often unrecognized, force in user-centered design. Most often, disability has been treated as a problem to avoid or solve through technology. Nineteenth- and twentieth-century designers treated impairment as a confounding element in industrial systems and prescribed technological solutions focused on normalization and assimilation (Hamraie 2017; Serlin 2004). For example, artificial limbs combined functional and aesthetic considerations to make users appear typical. But disability also shapes contemporary and mainstream technologies (including remote-access technologies) in ways that are often latent or undocumented (Hendren 2020; Williamson

2012; Williamson and Guffey 2020). For example, Deaf people were historically viewed as testing sites for telephonic technologies and electronics that were then adapted into the mainstream (Mills 2011). Archivist and material culture historian Katherine Ott (2014) refers to this latency, and the broader circulation of disability-generated technologies, as "disability things," a concept that describes the material culture of disability as expanding beyond the body into built and social worlds.

Scholars document technological biases against disabled people. Critical scholarship has formed a consensus that technology (whether assistive, physical, or digital) is laden with assumptions about disability as an undesirable condition in need of normalization (Alper et al. 2015; Moser 2006; Gibson 2006). These assumptions undergird a type of inequality that disabled philosopher of technology Ashley Shew (2020) terms "technoableism." Corporate disability "hack-a-thons," for example, frequently treat disability as a problem in need of solving and enlist disabled people as user-experts, not designers (Wong 2015; Yergeau 2014). Critics reject technological saviorism, or the assumption that corporations and engineers—often nondisabled people—can liberate or enable disabled people through technology. For example, public historian and designer Liz Jackson (2019) describes "disability dongles" as well-intentioned technologies, such as stair-climbing wheelchairs or ASL gloves, that do not meet disabled users' actual needs or desires. In response, sociologists and philosophers of technology document disabled lived experiences as distinct from engineers' perceptions of disability (Shew 2020).

Disability studies scholars point out that technoableism and saviorism have not deterred disabled people from using technology, however. "Dismediation" theories of disability and digital media simultaneously engage with and trouble lived experiences of disability in order to "resist rehabilitation and standardization" (Mills and Sterne 2017, 365). Scholars propose instead that disabled people have "ambivalent relationships to technology" (Kafer 2011, 119), wherein users may adopt imperfect, uncomfortable, or less functional tools, even while critiquing them. This observation aligns with Lewis Mumford's classic assertion in the field of the philosophy of technology of the "ambivalence of the machine" (1934, 283), which simultaneously liberates and harms. Feminist science and technology studies (STS) scholars have likewise framed technology as "non-innocent," simultaneously produced by systems of oppression and in opposition to them (Haraway 1991). An understanding of technological ambivalence and non-innocence leads disability historians to point out that using imperfect technologies emboldens disabled users as design experts; likewise, disabled people have contributed to designing assistive technologies, in addition to using them (Virdi 2020; Ott, Serlin, and Mihm 2002; Williamson 2012; Hendren and Lynch, n.d.).

Disabled-led design is thus both an individual practice and a collective phenomenon illustrating disability culture. In contrast to technoableism, Alice

Sheppard (2019) argues that disability technology can emerge through a "body of knowledge . . . and a way of producing, developing, sharing, and accessing it . . . that are held both individually and in community." This communal, collective, and cultural understanding of disability rests on notions of aesthetic and relational community as emerging from disability culture.

Crip Making: Political-Relational, Disabled-Led Design

In their 1979 book, *Design for Independent Living*, nondisabled architects Raymond Lifchez and Barbara Winslow translate for other nondisabled architects the philosophies of the radical disability movement in Berkeley, California. Based on their close work with this movement in a design studio taught at UC Berkeley's College of Environmental Design, and further collaborations with the Center for Independent Living, Lifchez and Winslow transmit a sentiment that to most architects, rehabilitation professionals, and other nondisabled people would appear to be a bold assertion: that disabled people are not trying to be like everyone else, and in fact, they are changing the world by making things that refuse assimilation and conformity. In other words, disabled people are making things to make it in an inaccessible world.

In the book's epilogue, Lifchez and Winslow ask,

> Is the objective to assimilate the disabled person into the environment, or is it to accommodate the environment to the person? . . . Currently, the emphasis is on assimilation, for this seems to assure that the disabled person, once "broken-in," will be able to operate in a society as a "regular person" and that the environment will not undermine his natural agenda to "improve" himself. As we have shown, this assumption can be counter-productive when designing for accessibility. It may serve only to obscure the fact that the disabled person may have a point of view about the design that challenges what the designers would consider good design. (1979, 150)

The book documents this antiassimilationist worldview through photographs, design documentation, and narratives of the often-quotidian individual and collective tools that disabled people create. In doing so, it offers a snapshot of disability cultural approaches to technology. For example, in spaces shared by disabled people, where disabled people are not required to appear "normal," Lifchez and Winslow (1979, 51) write that there is "shared understanding" of access barriers and even "crip humor" regarding bodily differences and experiences. This early use of "crip" in relation to making and designing reveals the parallel and intersecting trajectories of antinormative disability philosophies and practices of making things (and thus "drawing boundaries," to return to Sayers) that disability introduces.

Movements of physically disabled people emerged in the 1960s and 1970s to challenge the primacy of physically nondisabled people in shaping the norms to which disabled people are held. Since that time, the word *crip* has expanded in its meanings, taken up as a philosophy of disability that agitates against compulsory normalcy of any kind, whether able-bodiedness or able-mindedness. Some have "claimed crip" in a similar manner to the term *feminist* (Schalk 2013). Many of these debates about the ontology of crip also address its epistemic status—who is an expert, who gets to claim to know—as determining its material and ethical stakes. Crip "onto-epistemology" (Barad 2007) can thus be understood as bound up in political questions of who gets to "know" disability and design in the name of disabled people. As in my broader work (Hamraie 2013; Hamraie 2017), I commit here to an additional step: that crip being and knowing are inseparable from crip ways of making and acting. In other words, crip "knowing-making" (Hamraie 2017) is a commitment to right action through changing existing material arrangements, not endorsing the nondisabled, assimilationist norm.

Since the early 2000s, crip theorists have addressed cultural, philosophical, and political dimensions of antiassimilation (Sandahl 2003; McRuer 2006; Kafer 2011). Crip making is implied within (but not often explicitly named in) these theories. That is, *crip* is not a synonym for *disability*, nor is it simply a political orientation. Rather, it is a specific commitment to shifting material arrangements, or what Robert McRuer names "the will to remake the world" (McRuer 2006, 35). Bess Williamson and Elizabeth Guffey's "design theory of disability" (2020) likewise stipulates that disability is a generative, world-changing phenomenon, not a deficit. Because most research on disability and technology presumes that disabled people are users, rather than makers and designers, new frameworks (such as crip technoscience) prioritize disabled-led design and making (Hamraie 2017; Hamraie and Fritsch 2019). Crip technoscience manifests in technological hacks, adaptations, or innovations emerging from what Leah Lakshmi Piepzna-Samarasinha (2018) terms "crip science," using the disability community's reclamation of the word *cripple* to define a locus of valuable expertise about navigating and adapting to inaccessible worlds. As the term *crip* has been reclaimed, it has grown into a field of scholarship (crip theory) and describes commitments to interdependence, collectivity, and anticapitalism, similar to the disability justice framework (Kafer 2011).

The emerging field of crip technoscience studies (Fritsch et al. 2019) addresses dimensions of disability technology that go beyond mechanical functionality or aesthetic assimilation to examine the cultural politics of technology, including how claims of expertise operate as forms of power that shape both knowing and designing. Thus, crip technoscience is not a "standpoint epistemology" (Harding 1992), a feminist and Marxist concept that positions the perspective of the oppressed as uniquely true or objective. Nor is crip technoscience a practice that derives solely from "disability expertise" (Hartblay 2020) or authorship. Not everything made by a disabled person is crip technoscience. Beyond knowledge itself, crip technoscience provides a framework for studying disability design with specific political commitments, specifically resistance to imperatives for normalization and assimilation (Hamraie and Fritsch 2019; Gotkin 2019; Sheppard 2019; Nelson et al. 2019; Wong 2019; Thompson 2019).

Crip technoscience theory speculates that disabled forms of creative ingenuity, resourcefulness, hacking, and trial and error are not only scientific or epistemic but *technoscientific*—a term that STS scholars use to describe the mutual reliance of knowledge production and technological innovation (Hottois 2018; Latour 2005; Haraway 1997). Justice-centered feminist and decolonial technoscience studies have taken up these latter meanings to examine the roles of race, gender, and the nation-state in framing technology (Murphy 2012; Subramaniam et al. 2016) and have accordingly offered both critiques and alternatives rooted in political frameworks devoted to unsettling science. A crip technoscience theoretical framework builds on feminist and decolonial technosciences to differentiate between technologies developed through models of disability-as-pathology (often in the name of rehabilitating injured soldiers) and those derived from disability culture communities, where technology supports embodied differences and interdependent socialities.

STS scholars in "user studies" have addressed the figure of the user and how it both configures and is configured by technology (Oudshoorn and Pinch 2003). Configuration names ontologies and epistemologies of use, or how design shapes the parameters of embodied interaction with technologies. Disability scholars and activists claim expert use as a form of design knowledge. For example, disability communities discuss disability-led design with frequency, with some declaring, "We are the original lifehackers" (L. Jackson 2018). In this context, studies of disability technology argue that disabled people are user-experts, who engage in "microactivist affordances" (Dokumaci 2016) and "disability hacktivism" (Yergeau 2014).

Since disability movements in the 1970s and 1980s made changes to the built environment their focus, philosophers of technology have shown interest in disabled peoples' critiques of inaccessible design as examples of the democratic politics of technology. Some philosophers have treated disability activists as prototypical user-experts, whose political advocacy stemming from lived experiences of disability shapes material arrangements (Winner 1980; Feenberg 2012). In all of these treatments of disabled people as makers, do-it-yourself capacities are largely taken for granted as radical and democratic. However, questions remain about *how* the lived experience of disability, as well as participation in disability culture, shapes design processes. What forms of knowledge matter, and how do they result in design decisions or material changes?

Crip making draws on STS approaches to expert knowledge and material practice, or "knowing-making" (Hamraie 2017), to inquire about how remote-access methodologies can inform understandings of community-generated "collective access" (Mingus 2010). It builds on disability studies approaches that treat disability as a "political-relational" (Kafer 2011) and interdependent (Berne et al. 2018) (rather than individual) phenomenon through which technologically mediated cultural collaborations yield new material arrangements. Drawing on elements of these literatures while following Black disabled scholar and wheelchair dancer Alice Sheppard's call to study the "cultural-aesthetic" dimensions of disability technology (Sheppard 2019), crip making examines the role of disability *community expertise* in shaping remote access.

Crip making highlights the central role of design frictions in shaping disabled relationships to technology. *Design friction* names the practices of tinkering and hacking that provide imperfect access or highlight conflicting access needs while simultaneously building sociality and interdependence (Hamraie and Fritsch 2019). For example, wheelchair users and blind people have historically had different needs regarding sidewalk construction because the same curb ramps that allow wheelchair users to move freely from sidewalk to street create dangerous situations for blind people who do not know a street is coming. However, activists in both communities approached conflicting access needs to develop "tactile paving," the raised yellow bumps that appear on sidewalk corners to announce the elevation change (Hamraie 2017). A material instance of friction thus came to exemplify the forms of conflict and negotiation that frame disability design.

Crip making also relates to the emerging frameworks of disability justice and design justice. Disability justice is a political framework that highlights the "leadership of the most impacted," "interdependence," and "collective access" (Berne et al. 2018). As discussed earlier, this movement is led by disabled people of color and collectives drawing on art and design to do political advocacy. Disability justice thus has a significant focus on the material manifestations of political values, in addition to creating a new theoretical framework for disability politics. However, there is not yet adequate empirical documentation of disabled designers of color and their contributions to shaping conceptions of disability and design justice. Similarly, design justice (Costanza-Chock 2020) is an emerging framework from within design discourse that challenges the charitable sensibilities of technology designed for users, and instead devises methods for prioritizing marginalized users. Crip making synthesizes the two frameworks into "disability design justice" (Hamraie 2020), naming and building on an existing field of protocols and theories.

Remote Access: Crip Making in Pandemic Times

If disability-led design does not seek quick fixes or technological saviorism, how does this phenomenon instead illustrate community knowledge and collaboration? To answer this question, we need to understand the meanings of *access* as related to making and design.

Access is often understood as a spatial phenomenon. Twentieth-century efforts to deinstitutionalize disabled people often focused on creating accessible public spaces in order to support integration into the community. As a result, the concept of accessibility is often contrasted with the isolation of institutionalization; consequently, disability scholars theorize "publicity as capacity," a type of power derived from being able to be present (Johnson 2020). Likewise, critical scholarship on accessibility has typically focused on technologies that enable physical presence in built environments (Guffey 2017; Hamraie 2017; Titchkosky 2011; Williamson 2019). Furthermore, rich ethnographic scholarship on digital accessibility practices and negotiations (Ellcessor 2006) and "digital activism" (e.g., McLean 2020; Thompson 2019) has interrogated notions of participation and use, but addresses digital spaces rather than technologies and design practices.

Yet many disabled people have required physical distancing for safety, accessibility, and well-being. This is particularly true for chronically ill, chemically sensitive, asthmatic, Deaf and hard of hearing, blind, and neurodivergent people. The widespread use of masks, social distancing, text-based internet communication, and video conferencing during the pandemic follows on practices that disabled communities have designed. Remote access, in turn, raises questions about how distance, rather than proximity, shapes disability culture. Remote access thus highlights how technological mediation creates or forecloses "cultural locations of disability" (Snyder and Mitchell 2010) through dispersed geographies of technoscience (Livingstone 2010). A crip making framework inquires about how physical distance—such as living in different cities or away from community, or being unable to share space without masking due to COVID-19—can also be an enabling condition for technological design and participation, while continually requiring adaptations toward more workable solutions.

Remote access is inherently frictioned and noninnocent in that the same conditions enabling access for some can create hierarchies of belonging for others. Distance can be a disenabling condition with important implications for disability world-making. For example, John Lee Clark offers a deafblind critique of "distantism," or "privileging of the distance senses of hearing and vision," which, unlike tactile senses, tend to operate across wider spaces (Clark 2017). Clark extends the critique of distantism to paternalistic attitudes and behaviors, such as assistants who presume to be experts about what deafblind people need. In one story, Clark recounts an assistant who accompanies him to the grocery store:

> She's confused when I do not give her a list and I take charge, directing us toward the places where we will find what I want. She is now more like a detector, or a device that I take out of my back pocket to consult. Only she is far more intelligent than any machine could be and there's a wonderful rapport—that is, if she is able to unlearn her distantism. It is my responsibility to learn and know the world around

me; it is part of her job to help me update that knowledge as we go along. But it is not her job to retain any of this knowledge herself. (Clark 2017)

In this example, Clark responds to distantist paternalism by asserting expertise and building communal rapport. Though not an explicit act of *making*, Clark's response configures the assistant as a kind of "device" who helps with shopping but within whom expertise is not expected to reside.

Clark's pivot and reconceptualization recall other practices of participatory access-making. Unlike assistive technologies focused on individual users, remote access frequently emphasizes mass technologies, in which communities participate in coproducing material norms and practices. Listservs and discussion groups emerged on the internet that were devoted to specific disability communities, such as chronically ill "spoonies" and neurodivergent people. In the 2010s, remote access became a norm within "cross-disability" spaces, which included people with more than one type of disability. Crip making illustrates remote access in disability culture, including activist meetings conducted from beds with phones during the Occupy at Home movement, live webstream performances with ASL and image description, Zoom parties, and text-only email courses and Twitter conferences. Emerging archival projects document these practices, building on earlier research regarding histories of disability and print media, such as letters, newsletters, telegrams, and phone trees (e.g., Burch 2021: Williamson 2012).

Digital and internet-enabled forms of accessibility have shifted the availability of access labor: whereas previously, ASL interpreters and captioners had to be available in person, new technologies such as video conferencing enable streaming access services. Artificial intelligence transcription services such as Otter. ai enable broader accessibility, but also displace paid labor for access providers and often display racial and gender bias (Hickman 2019). "Mobile technologies," such as the iPad, have promised access to language through assisted communication, but also produced inequalities of race, gender, and class (Alper 2017). Likewise, online digital communities enable disabled people to connect across long distances, but create inequalities within and among disability communities, such as when videos do not have closed captioning or websites are not built for screen readers, a technology used by blind people (Ellcessor 2016). Disability communities respond by exploring new design solutions. These points highlight considerations of how disability culture forms through "design friction" (Forlano and Mathew 2014), rather than consensus or heterogeneity.

The feminist STS concept of "protocol" (Murphy 2012) describes methodological practices that become both standardized and reiterated in pursuit of particular political goals. Crip making adopts protocol, alongside expert knowledge, as a site of inquiry into design methodologies more generally. Because disability communities comprise diverse individuals with different access needs, the design protocols for remote access are constantly being developed and rewritten. Emergent practices include developing protocols for rich textual descriptions of visual content (Finnegan and Coklyat, n.d.); hacking Zoom to integrate live captioning and audio description (Gotkin, Hickman, and Hamraie 2020); and developing apps that afford unique sensory, artistic, and even poetic experiences (Sheppard 2019). While these protocols purport to embody the disability justice principle of interdependence, questions remain about how lived and communal disability knowledge shaped them, and the technologies for which they create access. Remote access illustrates how such practices emerged, often in response to physical distance and technological mediation.

Protocols for Remote Access: Experiments in Crip Making

On a cold March afternoon in 2020, I turned on my laptop and clicked a URL to join a Zoom call. With my phone, I dialed into a different Zoom call, where I would be providing live audio description for the next hour. My computer screen revealed a grid of twenty faces, people seated before a screen. In the first image, a DJ sat at their table with mixing equipment and a speaker, backlit with pink light. In other boxes, partygoers wore outfits covered in glitter and sequins and swayed their bodies to slow tunes. A chatbox next to the images offered descriptions of the mood and speed of the music. Lyrics and spoken language were transcribed in on-screen captioning. An ASL interpreter signed the lyrics and other words. A team of volunteers worked as "access doulas" in the chat section, sparking conversation, describing sound, naming the songs, and making fun party banter.

The event was Remote Access: A Crip Nightlife Party, hosted by Critical Design Lab, a collaborative of disabled designers, artists, and researchers. Disability scholar and organizer (and lab member) Kevin Gotkin (aka DJ Who Girl) had been writing about histories of disability nightlife (Gotkin 2019). We started organizing the party as the COVID-19 pandemic took our teaching, organizing, and socializing online. We wanted to show what disabled communities were already doing with remote and digital forms of participation, as well as to create a space for our communities to share movement, celebration, and kinship in the midst of grief.

The party sought to bring elements of crip digital culture into a space of celebration and aesthetic exploration. Alongside the DJ set, Indigenous disabled artist moira williams's camera focused on natural materials—soil, rocks—in front of their screen. Taiwanese American disabled artist Yo-Yo Lin screen-shared work studying body movements and joints popping—a computerized image of a body moving in space, surrounded by orbs of neon light. The material, the elemental, the earthly, the embodied, and the digital married in an ecstatic jubilee of togetherness and belonging as DJ Who Girl mixed together popular dance music with slower vibes.

Muting my computer, I took my role as the live image describer by speaking into my phone. For the next hour, I described visual content while I danced along to the music and waved at my friends on the screen. When my shift was over, another participant took over. Many other participants did the same work via text in the chat box. On their own screens, participants danced and played. Sky Cubacub—a Filipinx queercrip fashion designer known for their neon spandex designs—danced in their studio with their mother. Cubacub wore a self-designed chainmail cap and a silver hologram outfit reminiscent of David Bowie, while their mother wore a long, flowing, neon skirt. In other screens, people danced with their hands, some voguing. Some wore costumes or masks, dressed as cats, or showed up in neon-pink furs. Others just sat and watched or listened to the music. Some showed their pets and other companions. Some sat outdoors.

Remote Access was not merely a celebratory event, however. It was also part of a series of research and design projects centered in the Critical Design Lab. By design, and due to access needs, physical distance, and living across many time zones, the lab already conducts all of our work remotely: we meet and host workshops using digital conferencing platforms with integrated captioning, and we create media (such as a podcast) and curate exhibitions using digital tools. But a Zoom party held for potentially hundreds of disabled people and allies also presented new challenges. The organizing team met to discuss what it would take to make an online party accessible. The graphics needed to be image-described and high contrast, legible for people with color-blindness. Though they were abstract and dynamic, the art visuals needed to have clear descriptions. The Zoom platform itself also had to be tweaked. Because Zoom only picks up on sound in the human voice range, the music did not sound very bass-heavy through the computer speakers. Also Zoom's chat box, if relied on for image descriptions, would mute out the sound for screen-reader users, meaning that blind people would not be able to hear the descriptions of the screen at the same time as the music.

The party thus became a site of design experimentation through crip making. We began by designing participation in the event with a protocol (Gotkin, Hickman, and Hamraie 2020), sharing it with many collaborators, incorporating feedback, and further designing the many ways of accessing information and aesthetics. In other words, the party itself (and the party-planning process) served as a design charette, an opportunity for real-time creative experimentation with the meanings of access. The "access doula" team (named by Gotkin), assembled from disabled artists and scholars we knew, formed a crucial piece of the technological puzzle. Working in shifts, we engaged with technology as a translational apparatus for also generating new poetics of crip culture and community. These descriptions and translations also appeared alongside party chatter, a digitally enabled form of sociality fostering collective belonging in the space.

Despite the pervasiveness of both social isolation and remote access in disability culture, many of our cultural spaces have been affected by the COVID-19 pandemic. Remote Access has been an ongoing party series, with the intention of further reiterating and making anew the social worlds that disability generates. But COVID-19 is also mobilizing disabled people to do what we have been doing: organizing mutual aid under difficult circumstances. Mutual aid is a central tenet of the disability justice movement, led by disabled people of color and queer disabled people, and enacted through principles of collective access and liberation, anticapitalist politics, and leadership of the most affected (Berne et al. 2018). As the pandemic continues, mutual aid can look like saving lives and reducing harm. But it can also take shape as creating crip joy, holding space for crip pain, and forging networks of solidarity to break isolation. Remote Access is thus more than a dance party. It is an enactment of crip making through disability culture as a political act of mutual aid.

BIBLIOGRAPHY

Alper, Meryl. 2017. Giving Voice: Mobile Communication, Disability, and Inequality. Cambridge, MA: MIT Press.

Alper, Meryl, Elizabeth Ellcessor, Katie Ellis, and Gerard Goggin. 2015. "Reimagining the Good Life with Disability: Communication, New Technology, and Humane Connections." In Communication and the "Good Life," edited by Hua Wang, 197–212. New York: Peter Lang.

Barad, Karen. 2007. Meeting the Universe Halfway: Quantum Physics and the Entanglement of Matter and Meaning. Durham, NC: Duke University Press, 2007.

Barnes, Colin, and Geoff Mercer. 2001. "Disability Culture: Assimilation or Inclusion." In Handbook of Disability Studies, edited by Gary L. Albrecht, Katherine D. Seelman, and Michael Bury, 515–534. Thousand Oaks, CA: Sage.

Berne, Patricia, Aurora Levins Morales, David Langstaff, and Sins Invalid. 2018. "Ten Principles of Disability Justice." WSQ: Women's Studies Quarterly 46 (1): 227–230.

Burch, Susan. 2021. Committed: Remembering Native Kinship in and beyond Institutions. Chapel Hill: University of North Carolina Press.

Clark, John Lee. 2017. "Distantism." Wordgathering 11 (3). https://wordgathering.com/past_issues/issue43/essays/clark.html.

Costanza-Chock, Sasha. 2020. Design Justice: Community-Led Practices to Build the Worlds We Need. Cambridge, MA: MIT Press.

Dokumaci, Arseli. 2016. "Micro-activist Affordances of Disability: Transformative Potential of Participation." In ReClaiming Participation, edited by Mathias Denecke, Anne Ganzert, Isabell Otto, and Robert Stock, 67–84. Bielefeld, Germany: Transcript Verlag.

Ellcessor, Elizabeth. 2016. Restricted Access: Media, Disability, and the Politics of Participation. New York: New York University Press.

Feenberg, Andrew. 2012. Questioning Technology. London: Routledge.

Finnegan, Shannon, and Bojanna Coklyat. n.d. Alt-Text as Poetry homepage. Accessed October 11, 2022. https://alt-text-as-poetry.net/.

Forlano, Laura, and Anijo Mathew. 2014. "From Design Fiction to Design Friction: Speculative and Participatory Design of Values-Embedded Urban Technology." Journal of Urban Technology 21 (4): 7–24.

Fritsch, Kelly, Aimi Hamraie, Mara Mills, and David Serlin. 2019. "Introduction to Special Section on Crip Technoscience." Catalyst: Feminism, Theory, Technoscience 5 (1). https://catalystjournal.org/index.php/catalyst/article/view/31998.

Gibson, Barbara E. 2006. "Disability, Connectivity and Transgressing the Autonomous Body." *Journal of Medical Humanities* 27 (3): 187–196.

Gotkin, Kevin. 2019. "Crip Club Vibes." *Catalyst: Feminism, Theory, Technoscience* 5 (1). https://catalystjournal.org/index.php/catalyst/article/view/30477.

Gotkin, Kevin, Louise Hickman, and Aimi Hamraie. 2020. "Remote Access: Crip Nightlife Participation Guide." With the Critical Design Lab. March 2020. https://docs.google.com/document/d/1vluVl73ZZLgMNX6qvXgjgbZnlO7yYoQUioJpvJ8Jh-Q/edit.

Guffey, Elizabeth. 2017. *Designing Disability: Symbols, Space, and Society*. London: Bloomsbury.

Hamraie, Aimi. 2013. "Designing Collective Access: A Feminist Disability Theory of Universal Design." *Disability Studies Quarterly* 33 (4). https://dsq-sds.org/article/view/3871/3411.

———. 2017. *Building Access: Universal Design and the Politics of Disability*. Minneapolis: University of Minnesota Press.

———. 2020. "From Exceptional Accommodations to Disability Justice Design: Ways of Thinking about Accessibility as Hospitality." In *Rehearsing Hospitalities Companion* 2, edited by Yvonne Billimore and Jussi Koitela, 113–126. Helsinki: Ministry of Education and Culture, Finland, and Archive Books.

Hamraie, Aimi, and Kelly Fritsch. 2019. "Crip Technoscience Manifesto." *Catalyst: Feminism, Theory, Technoscience* 5 (1). https://catalystjournal.org/index.php/catalyst/article/view/29607.

Haraway, Donna. 1987. "A Manifesto for Cyborgs: Science, Technology, and Socialist Feminism in the 1980s." *Australian Feminist Studies* 2 (4): 1–42.

Haraway, Donna. 1991. *Simians, Cyborgs, and Women: The Reinvention of Nature*. New York: Routledge.

Harding, Sandra. 1992. "Rethinking Standpoint Epistemology: What Is 'Strong Objectivity?'" *Centennial Review* 36 (3): 437–470.

Hartblay, Cassandra. 2020. "Disability Expertise: Claiming Disability Anthropology." *Current Anthropology* 61 (S21): S26–S36.

Hendren, Sara. 2020. *What Can a Body Do? How We Meet the Built World*. New York: Penguin.

Hendren, Sara, and Catrin Lynch. n.d. Engineering at Home homepage. Accessed October 11, 2022. http://engineeringathome.org/.

Hickman, Louise. 2019. "Transcription Work and the Practices of Crip Technoscience." *Catalyst: Feminism, Theory, Technoscience* 5 (1). https://catalystjournal.org/index.php/catalyst/article/view/32081.

Hottois, Gilbert. 2018. "Technoscience: From the Origin of the Word to Its Current Uses." In *French Philosophy of Technology: Classical Readings and Contemporary Approaches*, edited by Sacha Loeve, Xavier Guchet, and Bernadette Bensaude-Vincent, 121–138. Cham, Switzerland: Springer.

Jackson, Liz. 2018. "We Are the Original Lifehackers." *New York Times*, May 30, 2018.

———. 2019. "Disabled People Want Disability Design—Not Disability Dongles." CBC Radio, November 8, 2019.

Jackson, Sarah J., Moya Bailey, and Brooke Foucault Welles. 2020. *#HashtagActivism: Networks of Race and Gender Justice*. Cambridge, MA: MIT Press.

Johnson, Jenell. 2020. "Breaking Down: On Publicity as Capacity." *Rhetoric Society Quarterly* 50 (3): 175–183.

Kafer, Alison. 2013. *Feminist, Queer, Crip*. Bloomington: Indiana University Press.

Kirkpatrick, Bill. 2017. "A Blessed Boon." In *Disability Media Studies*, edited by Elizabeth Ellcessor and Bill Kirkpatrick, 330–356. New York: New York University Press.

Kovach, Sydney. 2011. "Disabled Student Union Hosts Hybrid Protest for COVID-19 Accommodations." *Daily Bruin*, October 11, 2011. https://dailybruin.com/2021/10/09/disabled-student-union-hosts-hybrid-protest-for-covid-19-accommodations.

Latour, Bruno. 2005. *Reassembling the Social: An Introduction to Actor-Network-Theory*. Oxford: Oxford University Press.

Lifchez, Raymond, and Barbara Winslow. 1979. *Design for Independent Living: The Environment and Physically Disabled People*. Berkeley: University of California Press.

Livingstone, David N. 2010. *Putting Science in Its Place*. Chicago: University of Chicago Press.

McLean, Jessica. 2020. "'It's Just Coding': Disability Activism In, and About, Digital Spaces." In *Changing Digital Geographies: Technologies, Environments and People*, 229–246. Cham, Switzerland: Palgrave Macmillan.

McRuer, Robert. 2006. *Crip Theory: Cultural Signs of Queerness and Disability*. New York: New York University Press.

Mills, Mara. 2011. "Deafening: Noise and the Engineering of Communication in the Telephone System." *Grey Room* 43:118–143.

Mills, Mara, and Jonathan Sterne. 2017. "Afterword II: Dismediation: Three Propositions and Six Tactics." In *Disability Media Studies: Media, Popular Culture, and the Meanings of Disability*, edited by Elizabeth Ellcessor and Bill Kirkpatrick, 365–378. New York: New York University Press.

Mingus, Mia. 2010. "Reflections from Detroit: Reflections on an Opening: Disability Justice and Creating Collective Access in Detroit." INCITE blog, August 23, 2010. https://incite-national .org/2010/08/23/reflections-from-detroit-reflections-on-an-opening-disability-justice-and -creating-collective-access-in-detroit/.

Moser, Ingunn. 2006. "Disability and the Promises of Technology: Technology, Subjectivity and Embodiment within an Order of the Normal." *Information, Communication and Society* 9 (3): 373–395.

Mumford, Lewis. 1934. *Technics and Civilization*. Chicago: University of Chicago Press.

Murphy, Michelle. 2012. *Seizing the Means of Reproduction*. Durham, NC: Duke University Press.

Nelson, Mallory Kay, Ashley Shew, and Bethany Stevens. 2019. "Transmobility: Possibilities in Cyborg (Cripborg) Bodies." *Catalyst: Feminism, Theory, Technoscience* 5 (1). https:// catalystjournal.org/index.php/catalyst/article/view/29617.

Ott, Katherine. 2014. "Disability Things: Material Culture and American Disability History, 1700–2010." In *Disability Histories*, edited by Susan Burch and Michael Rembis, 119–135. Urbana: University of Illinois Press.

Ott, Katherine, David Serlin, and Stephen Mihm, eds. 2002. *Artificial Parts, Practical Lives: Modern Histories of Prosthetics*. New York: New York University Press.

Oudshoorn, Nelly, and Trevor Pinch, eds. 2003. *How Users Matter: The Co-construction of Users and Technology*. Cambridge, MA: MIT Press.

Piepzna-Samarasinha, Leah Lakshmi. 2018. *Care Work: Dreaming Disability Justice*. Vancouver, Canada: Arsenal Pulp.

Sandahl, Carrie. 2003. "Queering the Crip or Cripping the Queer? Intersections of Queer and Crip Identities in Solo Autobiographical Performance." *GLQ: A Journal of Lesbian and Gay Studies* 9 (1): 25–56.

Sayers, Jentery. 2017. "Introduction: I Don't Know All the Circuitry." In *Making Things and Drawing Boundaries: Experiments in the Digital Humanities*, edited by Jentery Sayers, 1–17. Minneapolis: University of Minnesota Press.

Schalk, Sami. 2013. "Coming to Claim Crip: Disidentification with/in Disability Studies." *Disability Studies Quarterly* 33 (2). https://dsq-sds.org/article/view/3705/3240.

Serlin, David. 2004. *Replaceable You: Engineering the Body in Postwar America*. Chicago: University of Chicago Press.

Sheppard, Alice. 2019. "Staging Bodies, Performing Ramps." *Catalyst: Feminism, Theory, Technoscience* 5 (1). https://catalystjournal.org/index.php/catalyst/article/view/30459.

Shew, Ashley. 2020. "Ableism, Technoableism, and Future AI." *IEEE Technology and Society Magazine* 39 (1): 40–85.

Sinclair, Jim. 2012. "Don't Mourn for Us." *Autonomy, the Critical Journal of Interdisciplinary Autism Studies* 1 (1).

Snyder, Sharon L., and David T. Mitchell. 2010. *Cultural Locations of Disability*. Chicago: University of Chicago Press.

Subramaniam, Banu, Laura Foster, Sandra Harding, Deboleena Roy, and Kim TallBear. 2016. "Feminism, Postcolonialism, Technoscience." In *The Handbook of Science and Technology Studies*, 4th ed., edited by Ulrike Felt, Rayvon Fouché, Clark A. Miller, and Laurel Smith-Doerr, 407–434. Cambridge, MA: MIT Press.

Thompson, Vilissa. 2019. "How Technology Is Forcing the Disability Rights Movement into the 21st Century." *Catalyst: Feminism, Theory, Technoscience* 5 (1). https://catalystjournal.org/index.php/catalyst/article/view/30420.

Titchkosky, Tanya. 2011. *The Question of Access: Disability, Space, Meaning*. Toronto: University of Toronto Press.

Virdi, Jaipreet. 2020. *Hearing Happiness: Deafness Cures in History*. Chicago: University of Chicago Press.

Williamson, Bess. 2012. "Electric Moms and Quad Drivers: People with Disabilities Buying, Making, and Using Technology in Postwar America." *American Studies* 52 (1): 5–29.

———. 2019. *Accessible America*. New York: New York University Press.

Williamson, Bess, and Elizabeth Guffey, eds. 2020. *Making Disability Modern: Design Histories*. London: Bloomsbury.

Winner, Langdon. 1980. "Do Artifacts Have Politics?" *Daedalus* 109 (1): 121–136.

Wong, Alice. 2015. "Assistive Technology by People with Disabilities, Part I: Introducing Team Free to Pee." *Model View Culture*, November 4, 2015. https://modelviewculture.com/pieces/assistive-technology-by-people-with-disabilities-part-i-introducing-team-free-to-pee.

———. 2019. "The Rise and Fall of the Plastic Straw: Sucking in Crip Defiance." *Catalyst: Feminism, Theory, Technoscience* 5 (1). https://catalystjournal.org/index.php/catalyst/article/view/30435.

Yergeau, Melanie. 2014. "Disability Hacktivism." Computers and Composition Online. http://cconlinejournal.org/hacking/.

30

Fiction Podcasts Model Description by Design

GEORGINA KLEEGE

Let's say you want to produce a movie or video with access features such as captioning and audio description (AD). If this is the case, I applaud you. Clearly, you recognize that, as in architecture and product design, access always works better and is more in line with the original ideas of the producer when it is in the plan from the outset rather than added on later in postproduction. Also, there's some self-interest involved. You know that captioning has long been popular with people who are not deaf or hearing impaired. More recently, as more and more AD is available on streaming platforms such as Netflix and Amazon Prime, there is evidence that many people who are not blind or visually impaired also enjoy it for the way it allows them to consume visual media while doing something else with their eyes. AD can be helpful to people learning another language for the way it provides new vocabulary. And neurodiverse audiences appreciate how it can enhance comprehension by directing attention to specific aspects of a scene. So designing for access by taking charge of AD from the outset will mean that your project will reach a larger audience and allow consumers to choose how they will consume it.

Because I am blind and consume AD, and have written somewhat critically about current standards, you may come to me seeking my advice. I sense you there, with your fingers poised above your keyboard, waiting for a list of dos and don'ts, or perhaps a recommendation of a show or movie where the AD was especially good. I'm sorry to say that I will disappoint you. When I recommend the AD on something I've been watching as adequate or helpful, sighted friends often come back with criticism that the describer left out crucial visual details. Or else they may shrug and think, "I guess that's what the blind people want." As a blind person, I don't know what I'm missing and so tend to prefer AD that is not distracting. Other AD users have different preferences. Often I find AD simply perplexing, supplying odd bits and pieces of information I can't quite imagine needing to know. I am left to shrug and think, "So that's what sighted people find noteworthy." Keep in mind that I am of the generation that grew up listening to TV and movies without AD; I even studied film in college, and so I have a basic understanding of the conventions of visual storytelling. For the most part, without AD I can always follow the plot with only minimal additional information from sighted companions, whether in real time when screening at home or after the fact when screening in the movie theater. Usually I can derive meaning the same way I do in real life, from characters' words, ambient sounds, and the context of the plot.

There are now many sources of guidelines for AD I could direct you to with the caveat that you should read them critically. The Audio Description Project of the American Council of the Blind is a comprehensive clearing house for information about blind access to all genres of visual media, films, television, museum collections, live theater, and sporting events. It also provides information for people seeking training as a professional describer, technical specifications for the different equipment used, and numerous examples and lists of guidelines and best practices. There are now also books, such as Louise Fryer's *An Introduction to Audio Description*, which essentially offers a self-guided training course with both theory and practice in the form of exercises would-be describers can try out on their own. These instructions tend to assume that the art or media in question is already complete, and that description will be added on in postproduction and without the input of the creator.

But you want to do something different. Since it's part of your plan to have AD, you can write your script to allow space for description. You can also attend to the nonverbal aspects of your soundtrack that deliver meaning. Producers like you who wish to design for accessibility from the outset would do well to remember that since the advent of the talkies, film became both an audio and visual medium. The work of the soundtrack supports the visual content but also sets the mood and makes meaning. Actors' vocal performance enhances the meaning of the words spoken, while sound effects and music convey context and anticipate action. Audio describers are already enjoined to refrain from describing something that can be derived from an audible cue. For instance, if the phone rings, and the character can be heard picking it up and saying, "Hello," the describer does not need to mention that the character is answering the phone. Dialogue can also deliver descriptive information that the describer does not need to repeat. For example, if a character says, "What are you smiling at?" there's no need to describe the other character's expression.

As inspiration, you can find examples of media where some form of description is already built in—that is to say, description that is not necessarily directed at an exclusively blind audience. Take, for instance, baseball on the radio. Of course, radio has always been accessible to blind people. While news broadcasts deliver information primarily through speech, producers have always included ambient sound when recording in the field, and reporters and commentators may include visual details to help orient the audience. Although it is a complex visual spectacle, baseball is particularly well suited to audio broadcast, because it is comparatively slower than the back-and-forth sports like basketball and soccer. Long intervals of relative inaction are interrupted by sudden, dramatic events. During those long intervals, announcers fill the air with historical and biographical accounts of past games and players, recital of statistics, and bemused observations about the endearing antics of fans in the stands. And while the majority of play-by-play may simply be the counting of balls and strikes, the best broadcasters know how to paint a picture with both their words and voices. In fact, it is frequently the vocal performance that conveys the meaning. Imagine hearing this: "It's a line drive deep to right field." Even an unpracticed listener instantly recognizes from the way the announcer delivers those words whether the ball is likely to be caught or to clear the fence for a home run.

Radio broadcasts of baseball assume that the audience cannot see what the announcers do. There have been occasions when the announcers weren't seeing the action on the field either. When Ronald Reagan was a radio sportscaster in the 1930s, he narrated games from accounts he received via telegraph, and then added the play-by-play description with the embellishments of his imagination. More recently, during the pandemic seasons for 2020–2021, most baseball announcers did not travel with the teams and so delivered their commentary from watching the game on TV. Many complained that the camera angles and framing did not allow them to see certain plays, and so they had to resort to some speculation in order to describe them.

Baseball on the radio provides a century-old model of AD built into the medium. A more contemporary example is the narrative podcast. Long-form investigative journalism, as well as fictional dramas, tell their stories with both words and sounds. For example, in the many popular true-crime podcasts, the text may quote from missing persons reports or eyewitness accounts of crime scenes. In fiction podcasts, description may be subtly included in characters' speeches.

Fiction podcasts, like radio plays of the past, use ambient sounds to set the scene, sound effects to represent characters' movements and actions. And while the Foley artists of the past used physical objects and sometimes their own voices to duplicate footsteps, thunderstorms, and gunshots, the sound designers of today's fictional podcasts have a vast array of digital tools and techniques for sonic world-building.

The Truth podcast, produced by Jonathan Mitchell, is a collection of short radio dramas, described on its website as "movies for your ears," and features skillful sound design to convey setting and situation, typically without any kind of narrative voiceover. A private home, a lively dance club, and a lunar spacecraft are all rendered with recognizable sonic detail without characters needing to mention where they are. In "Visible," which first aired in February 2016, written by Louis Kornfeld with Diana McCorry, a newly blind man experiments with a new seeing-eye app. The app has a female voice with the slightly stilted delivery of smart speakers and Siri, though its speech rate is slower than the pace more experienced blind people tend to prefer. It provides enhanced navigation information, telling the blind man exactly how far he is from the elevator and announcing obstacles in the way. The man is able to venture forth from the medical facility where he is recovering from the accident that caused his sight loss, and cross a busy street without injury. These different environments are rendered with recognizable sonic detail. In the park across the street, the app counts and describes the song sparrows the man hears chirping. And then, as if to show the progress he's making at aural interpretation, he is the one who discerns their departure, from the collective fluttering of all their wings.

The man then asks the app to take him to an art gallery. There he asks the app to describe an abstract painting. The app does so, following the conventions of verbal description of art, mapping the composition and naming all the colors: "This picture is an abstract arrangement in a mosaic pattern composed of intersecting vertices of colored squares, alternating in hue from dark brown at the periphery to light orange in the center." The man is dissatisfied even while the app insists that it has provided an accurate description. A gallery employee offers to help. Her initial description also follows the conventions, with some art historical references thrown in: "It's an abstract mixed media in the style of Bauhaus, which captures some of the spirit of late Klee." The man interrupts her to ask how the painting makes her feel. She then provides a much more subjective and emotive description: "As I said, it's an abstract. It's warm and small and personal. I think it does a nice job of evoking a sense of memory. There's something bittersweet to it. When I look at this it makes me think of the feeling you have when you're just drifting off to sleep. Do you know the way one thought will become very vivid in your mind and then it vanishes and you can't remember what it was? There's that afterglow. That's what this picture feels like." The man thanks her, adding that her response is exactly what he was going for when he painted it, thus revealing that he is the artist.

The story somewhat self-consciously draws attention to a basic aspect of the podcast medium—that the audience derives all meaning from the combination of text, vocal performance, and sound design. Significant visual details must be communicated in words. The blind man's adaptation is presented as a reorientation to aurality and an assessment of the limits of assistive technology. When it comes to visual art, human interpretation is still preferable to artificial intelligence.

Depictions of blindness in fictional podcasts may be rare, but this kind of self-reflexive move to image description occurs elsewhere. *Within the Wires*, written by Jeffrey Cranor and Janina Matthewson, "is an immersive fiction podcast using found audio from an alternate universe," the website announces. The "found audio" includes relaxation tapes, black-box recordings from an airplane, and voicemail messages. Each season features a single character narrating the story in brief segments. Sound design is limited to a rendering of the sounds of sometimes obsolete audio recording and playback equipment—the click and whir of tape recorders and slight distortions of the speaker's voice. The ten episodes of the second season are formatted as audio guides to museum exhibits of fictional artist Claudia Atieno, narrated by her friend and fellow artist Roimata Mangakahia. From the biographical details and the narrator's increasingly emotional delivery, the listener pieces together a story about Atieno's life and mysterious disappearance and death, but the script includes lengthy descriptions of paintings that follow the standards for image description for blind and visually impaired museum visitors.

> Here are two humanoid forms, one holding the other. On first glance, the erect figure in the background appears to be cradling the limp figure in the fore.
>
> Look at their faces. Or at least the indentations that replicate human faces on each figure. The one being held has almost no countenance, perhaps a shadow for eyes, and the grayish blob to the left of that could be a distorted mouth, caught midway into a cry or a song. (Season 2, cassette 10)

While the imperative—"Look"—implies that the audio tour is intended for a general rather than blind audience, the speculation about what "perhaps . . . could be" represented would make the text equally informative for blind people. And of course, since the actual audience of the podcast, whether blind or sighted, cannot see the fictional paintings being described, as in the example from *The Truth*, the script self-consciously draws attention to the nonvisual nature of the medium.

In the *Everything Is Alive* podcast, produced by Jennifer Mills and Ian Chillag, each episode features a different putatively inanimate object—a can of soda, an elevator, a bar of soap, among many others—interviewed by the host, Chillag. The sound design duplicates that of a standard interview show. Occasionally the host calls on an outside expert whose remarks are recorded as if on the phone. On some occasions, the host asks the object to describe its visual appearance: "Do you just for . . . I guess for our listeners that can't see you . . . Do you just want to describe what you look like, for us?" But here description intertwines aspects of the object's lived experience and personality. For example, the episode titled "Connor" begins this way: "My name is Connor and I'm a painting, a portrait painting of President William Howard Taft. You see him from the waist up and he's wearing a double-breasted suit, sort of leaning back looking at the left foot, your left foot but my right. I'm a good painting, not a great painting, you know, I'd admit to that." When Chillag asks him how he distinguishes himself from President Taft, the subject of the painting, he explains, "No, I'm an image, it's an illusion, it's an optical illusion, it's an easy mistake made, I'm not him but I look like him, or I look like, part of me looks like him. . . . You know, a little bit of me looks like the wall behind him." The episode then goes on to explore the painting's inner life: its mild resentment that other portraits in the gallery are more popular, its sexual fantasies about the *Mona Lisa*, its trauma at once being touched by a toddler. Much is conveyed by the actor Connor Ratliff's voice, which is of medium and slightly nasal tenor. His tone is of someone who accepts his lot in life while still harboring longings for greater recognition.

Taken together, these three randomly selected examples could serve as models for image description of art, suggesting that description that attempts to be authoritative or to deploy art historical terms may be less effective than something more emotive. Why not ask the painting to describe itself? But these examples (particularly the first two) also provide models for would-be screenwriters of naturalistic situations where description occurs in the dialogue and so need not be added on separately as part of an AD track.

Although it is unlikely that mainstream podcast producers think about it this way, blind people are an ideal audience for the medium. Indeed, there are a number of informational podcasts produced for and by blind people, such as *Reid My Mind*, hosted by Thomas Reid, and *Be My Eyes* and *Say My Meme*, hosted by Will Butler, which treat topics of interest to blind people, including AD. In claiming that blind people are an ideal audience for podcasts in general, I am not subscribing to the myth that blind people are compensated for lost sight with augmentation of their other senses, especially hearing. Rather, people who have been blind for any length of time learn to attend to the sounds around them for general information, navigation, and so forth. Anyone, blind or sighted, interested in honing their listening skills should consider *The World according to Sound* by Chris Hoff and Sam Harnett (with support from the Lighthouse for the Blind and Visually Impaired in San Francisco).

Each ninety-second episode focuses on sounds in a given environment or situation. These may be the sounds of nature (mud pots or giraffes after dark) or they may be human-made sounds—the tinkle and hum of beer bottles on a conveyer belt in a brewery, the crunch and rustle of an artist cutting and crumpling heavy paper. The audience can listen to a horse walking, trotting, cantering, and galloping on a treadmill, or the sound of liquid flowing into a bottle through a funnel. The sounds are offered with little to no commentary, and the aftereffect is to heighten the listener's aural awareness and perhaps allow them to imagine scenarios where this sound would be prominent.

Fictional podcasts, movies for the ears, offer models for soundtracks that require little or no additional description. If AD turns Netflix videos into audiobooks, narrative podcasts offer models for soundtracks that describe themselves.

As delighted as I am, as a blind consumer of media, with the accessibility of these podcasts, I have to note that the medium is not accessible to people who are deaf and hearing impaired. Some podcasts provide transcripts, though it is not always easy to find them, and they are typically working scripts for the voice artists, without any rendering of nonverbal sound, music, or actors' tonal qualities. So these transcripts fall short as access tools for many of the same reasons that captions for film and TV do. The captions often don't mention nonverbal sounds or music, or else are inconsistent in supplying this information. And even when sounds are mentioned, they are merely named rather than described. So, as often happens in the world of media, something that is accessible to one group may be anything but accessible for another.

Alt Text as Poetry is a collaborative project from disabled artists Bojana Coklyat and Finnegan Shannon designed to raise awareness about accessibility in the online world. The main focus is on alt text, or the kind of short-form AD that can be added to a website or social media post to provide visual information to people who use screen readers. But the two founders of the site also commissioned disabled composer JJJJJerome Ellis to create music for the site, and in the interest of promoting access, they provide a verbal description of the music, in both one- and five-minute versions: "A melodic whirring begins slowly, with sounds akin to playful electronic bells dot [*sic*] the soundscape. Another beat, which feels like a very quick rushing back and forth is added to the mix. As the music warms up, a voice quickly joins in with a, 'Yo.' Fingers snap twice and add more texture to the layered composition." While a five-minute verbal description of music would be beyond the scope of real-time captioning, it suggests the possibility of a secondary source of information the consumer could consult asynchronously. Filmmakers who focus on sound design as a facet of nonvisual access would automatically be in a better position to describe significant sounds and include this as part of the captions.

Alt Text as Poetry goes beyond web accessibility compliance to model the ways that access can be an occasion for artistic innovation. As people both with and without sensory disabilities consume media in multiple modalities, producers like you who are interested in broadening their audience and making their creations more equitable would do well to explore new ways to present material. These new forms of media will probably not look or sound like older forms and will be produced with a heightened attention to both visual and aural aspects. What starts as an accommodation for people with sensory disabilities can become a new art form, with new possibilities of enjoyment for a much larger audience.

BIBLIOGRAPHY
Butler, Will. 2022. *Be My Eyes*. https://www.bemyeyes.com/.
Butler, Will. 2022. *Say My Meme*. Podcast. https://www.bemyeyes.com/podcasts-show/say-my-meme.
Coklyat, Bojana, and Shannon Finnegan. 2022. *Alt Text as Poetry*. https://alt-text-as-poetry.net.
Cranor, Jeffrey, and Janina Matthewson. 2017. *Within the Wires*. Podcast, second season. Presented by *Night Vale Presents*. http://www.nightvalepresents.com/withinthewires.
Fryer, Louise. 2016. *An Introduction to Audio Description*. Routledge Press.

Hoff, Chris, and Sam Harnett. 2022. *The World According to Sound*. Podcast. https://www
.theworldaccordingtosound.org/.

Kornfeld, Louis, and Diana McCorry. 2016. "Visible," In *The Truth*. Podcast, produced by Jonathan
Mitchell. http://www.thetruthpodcast.com/about.

Mills, Jennifer, and Ian Chillag. 2019. *Everything Is Alive*. Podcast. https://www.everythingisalive
.com/.

Reid, Thomas. 2022. *Reid My Mind*. Podcast. 2022. http://reidmymind.com/.

31

Podcasting for Disability Justice

BRI M.

For as long as I can remember, my life has been lived on the margins of society. As a Black disabled, neuroexpansive, trans, and queer person, I have always recognized the uniqueness of my experiences when compared with those of my more normative peers. I may not have had the language or the knowledge to articulate the reasons why I was so different, but it was these qualities that brought me to lead a life guided by social justice.

When I started *POWER NOT PITY* in 2017 after I became physically disabled, I knew I was on to something meaningful. I wanted not only to put my voice out there but to give the people in my community, disabled people of color, safe spaces to see themselves reflected in podcasting. In the beginning, I wasn't quite sure how the show would be received, but I knew I wouldn't be able to rest if it didn't exist. It was wondrous to see what came back to me as a result of the radical vulnerability found in each episode. Because of this, I want to extend my unending gratitude to each person who came onto the show. Thank you.

This chapter was transcribed from a talk I gave about cultivating a more accessible podcasting culture at the 2019 Werk It! Podcast Festival. I hope you receive it with an open heart.

This is Podcasting for Disability Justice: how you can make your podcast more accessible. Before I begin, I'd like to call in the fact that we are on unceded land. Land that belonged to the Tongva people going back centuries. Land that we now know as California. I want to call in all of the disabled people throughout history who have helped shape a more accessible world.

I'm Bri M., I'm the executive producer–host of *POWER NOT PITY*. It's a show all about the lived experiences of disabled people of color. I want to give you a chance to invite the stories of the disability community into your mind and your heart because . . . we deserve it.

So who am I? Why am I here to talk about disability justice and podcasting? Uh, I'll tell you a little bit about me. I'm a Black Jamaican American disabled, queer, nonbinary alien prince from the Bronx. That's right. That's right. B-X all day! (*Laughs.*) I did three years of music radio in college. I went around interviewing tattoo artists and piercers about gender, class, and race. I worked in the music industry for a little while until I received a surprise in the spring of 2014.

I was diagnosed with multiple sclerosis and it actually happened only four days after my birthday. So I came to podcasting while I was living in bed. I started to ask myself all of these different questions about who I was and where I was in life. And I realized that I found a safe getaway space in podcasts. Like *How to Survive the End of the World* and *LeVar Burton Reads*. And LeVar, if you're listening, I love you! (*Laughs.*)

But yeah. Podcasts had the power to expand my worldview and changed how I thought about all the different subjects [I was interested in], but they weren't without their shortcomings. Unfortunately, I started to realize that my safe space wasn't so safe after all. I was gaining more friends. I was learning about the disability justice community and then I realized that the voices of disabled people of color were missing from podcasting altogether. So I wanted to do something about it.

I started to ask myself all these different questions. Some of the questions I started to ask about what was missing were: Where are the voices of the people of my community? Where were the stories of Black and Brown disabled people? Or the voices of people of queer, trans, and nonbinary experience, or the stories that reflected the amazing breadth of a multiply marginalized life?

Within such an intimate medium, I just think there's so much change that's possible in podcasting. So why not try changing things up a bit? That's pretty much what I did. I created *POWER NOT PITY* in 2017 in the back of a Greyhound bus going back from Philly to New York. And I remember when I made the logo, I felt like I was stepping into something bigger than me.

I believe that podcasting can actually, it actually tweaked my perception of disability from a first-person issue, meaning the person and their individual condition. It tweaked my perception from that [a person-first issue] to a greater societal issue, meaning the systems at play that cause oppression. I think it's time to start thinking about those things and start thinking about the stories that we turn our minds away from, and why we do this.

What can we do to tell more authentic and inclusive stories? What can we do as women and nonbinary people to foster a more equitable world? *I think it comes down to tangible and intangible ideas.* When I start to think about what makes an accessible podcast, it takes a radical reframing of your mind.

Intangible Ideas

Can I offer you a quote? It says, "Disability is more than the deficit of diagnosis. It is an aesthetic, a series of intersecting cultures and a creative force" (Sheppard, n.d.). This was spoken by Alice Sheppard, the founder of Kinetic Light, a dance troupe that is so amazing, like two wheelchair dancers they flip and they twirl and they, like, balance off of each other. Alice and her dance partner literally hold each other up in the air while they are in wheelchairs. I saw them and it was absolutely amazing. So, if you get a chance to see Kinetic Light, please do.

Whenever I find a new podcast, I always assume that there won't be transcripts and I think that shouldn't be the norm. It should be the exception. Right? *So one thing I want to offer you is the idea of including every word in your transcripts that's said and edit for cultural competence.* That is something that is always missing from transcripts. It's always about like every standard language. So think about vernacular and different ways of, um, dialects, different ways of speaking. There are so many things that we could lose in translation.

I think, um, another tangible thing that you can do to make your podcast more accessible is to *include image descriptions.* Those of us who are unable to see deserve to visualize what's happening as well. So when you're doing image descriptions, make sure that every detail is described. I often find that creative image descriptions, like ones that really go deeply into what the image is portraying, it can really put me into a different state of mind.

All right. So can I drop some knowledge on you? All right. All right. I'm so glad you're ready. So one in four people in the US are disabled, so that means 25 percent of the population is overlooked and underserved, and made invisible. We fall victim to being invisibilized and we also fall victim to tropes of overcoming adversity and inspiration. Unfortunately, these stories are so common that people actually have a term for it. It's called inspiration trash. [This phrase is my reframing of "inspiration porn," defined by Alice Wong (2018) as "media coverage that finds ordinary activities by disabled people as extraordinary or inspirational to non-disabled audiences."]

Yeah. So I would challenge you to make more dynamic and authentic stories about disabled people, especially disabled people of color. *We're not inspiration trash made to make you feel better about your life.*

Another thing that you could do in terms of making your podcasts more accessible is to have an accessible workplace. Meaning not only your episodes, but where you work and where you basically produce your content. I want to challenge you to be an advocate of an accessible space to work. Disabled people are entitled to accommodations so that they can create the best content that they can.

This means advocating for good benefits. This means advocating for good health care. This means advocating for spaces where people are receiving adequate accommodations. I want to see the end of drug testing and background checks. It's too often that background checks and drug testing are part of the cycle that keeps disabled people, especially Black disabled people, underemployed. I was almost denied a job because I tested positive for marijuana. Even though I had a medical marijuana card and it's illegal to discriminate against a person from New York State, I had to go back and forth with HR and I had to really try to prove my case about why I deserved to be there. It was ridiculous.

Now that we've talked about that, I want to offer you an effective way of telling a story that centers a disabled person in your story.

Haben Girma is the first deafblind woman to graduate from Harvard Law School. You could say she's impactful. You could say she's inventive, you could say she's intersectional, but just don't call her an inspiration.

I want to offer you a couple of ways to tell an effective story about Haben, but let's talk about the wrong way first. Haben is often portrayed as a millennial Helen Keller, and this is just completely wrong because we're not monoliths. We're actually multiplicitous and a myriad of voices. Another way to think of creating a correct and more authentic version of an effective story is to try to use words that are more reflective of a genuine experience. You know, I want to dare you to not use the word *inspiration*. *I want to dare you to use words that are not one-dimensional to describe a [disabled] person. This is the best way to center a disabled person in your story.*

Uh, so like I said, the word *inspiration* has lost its impact because it's been so overused. I think when you want to talk about impact versus intent, when you're talking about your stories, I know that there are good intentions and well-intentioned people. But the words that you use, the ways that you portray disabled people, they actually have an impact. And good intentions don't always lead to positive impact, right?

So Haben also offers quotes and techniques on her website. One of the things that she says is, "We respect and admire disabled leaders just as we respect and admire our nondisabled leaders" (Girma 2016). It's just something to think about, you know?

So remember my show *POWER NOT PITY*? All right! So the last thing I usually ask people on the show is, "What's your disabled power? What is the thing that gives you the most power and agency in your disability?" And usually nine times out of ten people talk about adaptation. My [interviewees] and I, we want to see the end of injustice and systemic inequality.

Tangible Ideas

I'd like to offer you four tangible ways that you can, um, you can make your podcast more accessible. So here it goes, this is the acronym. It goes R-E-A-P. What does that spell? That's right. REAP. *R* is for Recognize, *E* is for Educate, *A* is for Amplify, and *P* is for Politicize.

R → RECOGNIZE

So let's start with *R*. Recognize.

I'll tell you that ableism is a systemic discrimination that keeps disabled people on the margins of society. It's time that we recognize that discrimination that happens. So I'd like to challenge you to begin to locate ableism and all its forms. Begin to recognize how ableism causes harm to disabled people of color.

E → EDUCATE

Here we go with *E*: educate to find ways to learn about the disability community. You know, there's articles and op-eds and like all these different ways [to connect]. It was Twitter and Instagram and you know, all the other platforms that exist. TikTok, I dunno, Snapchat, who knows (*chuckles*). Disabled people of color also organize for other social justice issues. So I would suggest becoming familiar with those as well and take time to get to know disabled people. It would actually really cause you to make fewer assumptions, I think.

A → AMPLIFY

A is for Amplify. Get out there and floss that knowledge that you have cultivated! Reach out to organizations and get involved with all the social media platforms that exist. Give disabled people more chances to reflect, to create reflections of themselves in mass media. Amplifying is all about passing the mic.

P → POLITICIZE

P for Politicize is my favorite. Organize and conquer, y'all. Get involved with organizations and groups that are doing the work. Find creative ways to financially support disabled people of color. That's really important. Feature disabled activists on your podcasts.

So now that I've talked about tangible things and intangible things that you can do to make your podcast more accessible, um, let's talk about, uh, what it means to actually do this and create culture. You know? Because we don't do this in a vacuum. And I think that all of our work, all of our content is so important that we can shape culture. So what's more possible in an accessible podcasting culture? I think one thing that I like to say is representation matters.

Say it with me. *Representation matters.*

Oh, you sound so good! So this, this means stories that show the community in a more authentic light, giving people the chance to feel seen and heard. Another thing that would be possible is intersectionality. We would cultivate a politic of realizing that all of our stories are tied up in one another. We don't live this life alone. So give everyone a chance to be liberated. Another thing that's possible is more listeners. We all love that, right? We would be catering to the 25 percent of the population that's looking for reflections of themselves in mass media. Disabled people are hungry for more media.

So I've talked about accessibility, right? This presentation is called Podcasting for Disability Justice. How to make your podcast more accessible, right? I've talked about the accessibility part, but what's disability justice? I would like to offer you another quote. This was written by Patty Berne: "Disability justice is a vision and practice of a yet to be. A map that we create with our ancestors and our great grandchildren onward in the width and depth of our multiplicities and histories. A movement towards a world in which every body and mind is known as beautiful" (Sins Invalid 2019, 26–27). Isn't that amazing? She's an amazing writer and she's a cofounder of Sins Invalid. It's a dance troupe of disabled people of color and it's also a creative collective and it's all about advocacy as well. She's an amazing person. Look her up, Patty Berne. So finally, I want to offer you my last thought. (*Shouts determinedly.*) Hire more disabled people of color! Thanks for listening!

BIBLIOGRAPHY

This chapter is adapted from the transcript for "Podcasting for Disability Justice," *Werk It: The Podcast*, WNYC Studios, December 17, 2019, https://www.wnycstudios.org/podcasts/werkit/articles/podcasting-disability-justice.

Girma, Haben. 2016. "Producing Positive Disability Stories: A Brief Guide." Haben Girma's website, October 12, 2016. https://habengirma.com/2016/10/12/producing-positive-disability-stories-a-brief-guide/.

Sheppard, Alice. n.d. "Intersectional Disability Arts Manifesto by Alice Sheppard." Alice Sheppard's website. Accessed October 12, 2022. https://alicesheppard.com/intersectional-disability-arts-manifesto/.

Sins Invalid. 2019. *Skin, Tooth, and Bone: The Basis of Movement Is Our People*. 2nd ed. Berkeley: Sins Invalid.

Wong, Alice (@SFdirewolf). 2018. "Inspiration porn: media coverage that finds ordinary activities by disabled people as extraordinary or inspirational to non-disabled audiences. It's tiresome, people." Twitter post, May 20, 2018. https://mobile.twitter.com/SFdirewolf/status/998383781995139072.

32

Willful Dictionaries and Crip Authorship in CART

LOUISE HICKMAN

Willfulness involves persistence in the face of having been brought down, where simply to "keep going" or to "keep coming up" is to be stubborn and obstinate. Mere persistence can be an act of disobedience.
—Sara Ahmed, *Willful Subjects* (2014, 2)

In the 1990s, the Museum of Modern Art in New York acquired an artwork by Jackson Pollock known as the *Stenographic Figure* (1942). The painting depicts two abstract figures seated at a table containing a grid-like object representing a stenographic machine. The suggestion of the midcentury writing machine grouped with the two figures elicits an interpretation that queries the boundaries of authorship. Pollock exploits this confusion by connecting the two figures with a backdrop of handwritten shorthand. Without training, the shorthand is unreadable. It is raw data. The museum curator Kirk Varnedoe described the acquisition of the *Stenographic Figure*: "The *willed confusion* of this eccentric, ugly-pretty picture introduces ways of visual thinking that will reappear, in different guises, for years to come." (Taylor 2003, 53–71) Of those guises, the socio-technological uncertainty that sits at the core of Pollock's work points to persistent anxiety around the practice of authorship. Historically, such anxieties appeared with the threat of women entering into the workplace and the ambiguity of transcriptions as intellectual property. These uncertainties raise the question is central to this chapter: Is crip authorship a problem of will? Here, I draw on my fieldwork to offer a fictive, speculative account of the precarious demands of coauthorship with speakers, d/Deaf and hard of hearing users, and Communication Access Realtime Translation (CART) captioners.

It is a hybrid conference at a university on the West Coast of the United States. There is a female CART captioner—a real-time writer—seated in front of her personal laptop at the front of the classroom. She sits at the margin of the room. Elsewhere, the same writer simultaneously appears behind a blank square on the familiar telecommunication platform, Zoom. Their hybrid Zoom name (a mix of their proper name and the name of the CART agency) identifies them as outside the rules governing online participation, an implicit gesture to define their neutral roles as observers to the unfolding conversation. Onsite, the stenographic equipment is set out before her on a table. On the table surface, there is a notepad ready to document the steno briefs (handwritten shorthand) spoken at the forthcoming panel. The room is still empty: this is the stenographer's prep time. Next to the notebook, the stenographer is underlining new vocab from the conference's description of events. She looks up individual speakers from the panel online, including the speakers' research interests and recent publications, mapping out their institutional affiliations and the description of the conference itself. If there is time, the speakers' names are added to the dictionary. The writer searches through her email to find two documents previously shared by two of the four speakers ahead of the conference; she skims through the two documents to find familiar topics while loading each of the documents into the CAT (computer-aided translation) software. A couple of people enter the room to take their spaces among the few chairs in the classroom. She pushes the stenographic keyboard under the desk in front to conceal her presence and her labor. The chair of the panel and two of the speakers enter the room. The writer nods to herself, pairing their presence with their online profiles and research interests listed online. The panel's chair is logging on to their personal computer. Sound check. The computer's camera is not working. Log out. Logging back in. The stenographer returns to her prep work before the panel discussion starts.

The writer searches for a suitable dictionary to work across each presentation and the final discussion in the remaining twenty minutes. Which of her job dictionaries will work for a debate focusing on emerging feminist technologies? The writer considers the dictionary of sociology for her client, who graduated two years ago, while looking for a more recent job dictionary. What categories do feminist technologies fit under? Computer science, visual arts, art practice, media and communication, philosophy, or is it engineering? The Zoom window is now populating with a mixture of blank squares and faces of people seated in their homes. The panelists introduce themselves to the other panelists online, and they enter into an exchange of small talk. The increasing workload of online teaching, travels to the conference, the effects of lockdown, new cats and new jobs and new research. The stenographer looks around the room onsite and at her chatbox for an indication to start writing. When is the right time to begin captioning? Is this a private conversation between the panelists? The writer looks around the room again for the client. Nobody identifies themselves online. Unsure when to start captioning, she places a stream text link into the chat. Nobody takes this as a prompt to introduce themselves. The stenographer is familiar with the practice of nondisclosure (Kafer 2016). In her training, she learns not all clients identify as d/Deaf or hard of hearing and must understand their wishes of privacy in shared spaces. The panel chair begins speaking, and the stenographer loads the sociology dictionary and begins captioning the panel discussion. The chair acknowledges that a CART captioner is providing their services today and refers to the difference between the captions created by a human stenographer and automated captions.

In a Facebook group the previous night, fellow stenographers trained as courtroom reporters noted that another transcription agency had been sold to a larger company. There are rumors of a digital restructure to phase out the use of human captioners altogether—the automation of their labor. It's not the first time. The courtroom is often the testing site of new technologies, which directly affect and devalue the work of stenographers themselves (Downey 2008). Another Facebook group pushed their campaign to sell personalized lanyards with "STENO-GRAPHER" inscribed on the ribbon in white letters. Members share images of themselves wearing lanyards in their home offices, courtrooms, and academic classrooms. The disembodied photographs are carefully staged to draw attention to their machine and the location of their jobs. The invisible cottage industry of captioners, often transcribing nightly news and academic discussion from their home offices, is made visible by the array of lanyards. There is talk of making a new lanyard with "Human Stenographer" to capture the not new but intensifying threat of automation on their horizon. Their response to this threat involves the collective practice of sharing stories and images, solidifying their connections to a hidden network of speech-to-text industries.

Crip authorship is not always visible. The first speaker begins their presentation, and the CART captioner realizes she has loaded the wrong job dictionary onto her software. The job dictionary designated for sociology classes would not match the speaker's background in engineering. Their technical jargon does not correspond with the sociology dictionary prepared and coded two years earlier. If we consider the coding of spoken speech as a type of data, we can then appreciate that the nonexistence of these data can cause real-time issues for the writers. In tech-driven spaces, the strategic move to conceal human labor backstage further contributes to the ongoing narrative of the magic of AI.[1] In other words, the training of data somehow occurs elsewhere. Demystifying the labor of dictionary work for the purpose of this chapter allows us to understand that the potential of *crip authorship is always happening elsewhere*. I repeat: crip authorship is not always visible. The coding of job dictionaries occurs in relation to other speeches, other disciplinary discourses, times, and places. It is a community of speakers that comes to populate a stenographer's dictionaries. On these terms, the crip authorship of access draws on the politics of crip futurity imagined by Alison Kafer to contend with the labor practices of captioning itself. (2013) It is the traces of previous speech captured by a community of speakers, readers, *and writers* that enable the coding of future meetings.

The stenographer waits for another lull in speech to load another job dictionary, but the break never arrives. The captions begin to lag in respect to the spoken content, parts of the sentence are dropped from real-time transcription, word conflicts appear on-screen for the readers. The pressure of real-time writing grows; more shortcuts are being made as more panelists engage with the discussion (further expanding the disciplinary backgrounds). The real-time writer moves between the speakers to capture their conversations in readable texts.

Crip authorship, as I use it here, is to be understood as a practical, ongoing assemblage always moving toward materializing the ephemeral, recapturing what tends to be lost at the margins. Enfolded into this practice is attention to precarity as it appears locally. I opened this chapter with the novel premise that crip authorship is a problem of will, which builds on Sara Ahmed's work *Willful Subjects*. Ahmed further writes, "To be identified as willful is to become a problem. If being willful is to become a problem, then willfulness can be understood as a problem of will" (2014, 3). Crip authorship is a necessarily incomplete project that focuses on the ephemerality of speech. Crip authorship appears in the discrete moments when a captioner catches the fleeting small talk between panel presentations and allows this to shape their growing dictionary. The willingness to capture these unremarkable moments is a willful turn away from treating captioning as a neutral process; rather, it gives authority to the speakers, readers, and writers to shape the outcome of the dictionaries they rely on. Working at this scale, the labor captioners do for their readers is localized and embedded in particular communities that give meaning to that work. If a mistake is made by a stenographer—most often speakers' names, places, local knowledge—they can and often do work in real time to repair this mistake. For automated captions, the system is not designed to recognize and understand a person's changing social context. Cloud captionings are trained to find patterns of speech, but have limited ability to grapple with or respond to local knowledge on the ground. Stenographers with local knowledge are more likely to recognize and *have already coded* distinctive landmarks in the area—for example, names of Indigenous lands occupied or nearby. The practice of captioning, as a form of documentation, can affirm the power of crip authorship as a situated ethics in particular times and places. Likewise, the will of captioners to build multiple job dictionaries that can reflect a range of speakers and experiences, rather than foreclose these through automation, is a reflection of the values embedded in particular communities. Crip authorship is an archive of values that are meaningful for speakers, readers, and writers.

Real-time captioning often gets enfolded into discussions of access and accessibility, rather than being understood as a potent cultural entity in its own right. With the automation of captioning ever present on the horizon, real-time writing is often scrutinized for human errors, which automated systems are built to improve on. By being more attentive to the assemblages of real-time captioning as a practice of crip authorship, the seeming binary of error versus verisimilitude is revealed as a practice that hides the diversity of those assembled in its standardization. Captioners are constantly working to mediate the potential harms of real-time writing. Is it possible to cultivate a feminist practice that allows for and forgives human-made mistakes in captioning, that privileges the will and persistence to improve dictionaries over the mandate to standardize? Perhaps this is an idealistic proposition when the stakes of access are necessary for d/Deaf readers. But yet, here is an opportunity to recognize that crip authorship is always in progress, focused on the ever-shifting margins, and assembling around the responsive dictionaries that mark the promiscuity of past interactions and the responsive diversity of crip futurities.

NOTE

1 Also see: Lilly, Irani, and Six, Silberman. 2013. "Turkopticon: Interrupting Worker Invisibility in Amazon Mechanical Turk." In *Proceedings of the SIGCHI Conference on Human Factors in Computing Systems*, pp. 611–620. Mary, Grey and Suri, Siddharth. 2019. *Ghost Work: How to Stop Silicon Valley from Building a New Global Underclass*. Eamon Dolan Books.

BIBLIOGRAPHY

Ahmed, Sara. 2014. *Willful Subjects*. Duke University Press. https://www.dukeupress.edu/willful -subjects.

Downey, Gregory J. 2008. *Closed captioning: Subtitling, stenography, and the digital convergence of text with television*. Baltimore: Johns Hopkins University Press.

Kafer, Alison. 2016. "Un/safe disclosures: Scenes of disability and trauma." *Journal of Literary & Cultural Disability Studies* 10, (1): 1–20.

Kafer, Alison. 2013. *Feminist, Queer, Crip*. Bloomington: Indiana University Press.

Taylor, Sue. 2003. "The Artist and the Analyst: Jackson Pollock's 'Stenographic Figure.'" *American Art*. 17 (3): 53–71.

33

How to Model AAC

LATEEF H. MCLEOD

In the last fifty years augmentative and alternative communication (AAC) technologies have become increasingly more accessible to people with complex communication needs (CCN). AAC is usually described as various icon-based or text-to-speech programs and devices that speak the words of a person with CCN. With the increased accessibility of AAC devices, individuals with CCN have gained the tools, independence, and confidence to express themselves more than previously possible. The passage of the Americans with Disabilities Act in 1990, which acknowledged the civil rights of people with disabilities, and the Olmstead Act in 1998, which granted individuals with developmental disabilities the right to live in the community, created new opportunities for disabled people to be engaged in the public sphere: making connections, sharing their perspectives, and contributing their talents. With these new opportunities for engagement and self-expression—the result of social as well as technological shifts—people who use AAC have been able to succeed in education, in their professions, and in building new relationships.

Despite the obvious advantages of AAC systems for enhancing the communication of people with CCN, there remain disparities in awareness, inclusion, and education that have hindered the technology's potential impact. AAC involves a blended approach of technology and supportive tools to enhance communication. There are multiple modalities that incorporate each individual's strengths and needs to achieve unique communication goals. However, this variability poses challenges when customizing AAC training plans and navigating additional hurdles of access, economics, and adaptability. An *AAC role model*, as a person who already uses AAC, helps bridge the divide by providing encouragement and advice on implementation strategies. Potential users may find it helpful to have AAC role models to emulate as they go through the challenges of daily life. These role models, or AAC mentors, exchange knowledge and experience with their mentees, promoting self-advocacy and leadership. The epistemologies cultivated in the AAC mentor-mentee connection can be applied to focus areas such as educational challenges, professional obstacles, friendship building, and romantic relationships. Harnessing the perceptiveness and discernment of an AAC mentor follows the tradition of epistemological innovation that originated in the disability community. As Cassandra Hartblay (2020) explains in the article

"Disability Expertise: Claiming Disability Anthropology," people with disabilities use their knowledge or disability expertise to navigate through a society where they encounter instances of ableism and marginalization. Disability expertise should come from people with disabilities themselves, developing a personalized approach to guide interactions in the world. AAC mentors draw from their life experiences to cultivate their disability expertise, and this knowledge not only benefits themselves, but it also assists their mentees and drives innovation that will affect future generations of people who use AAC.

Until recently most, if not all, individuals with CCN were victims of a long history of extreme marginalization. With the advent of capitalism, it was deemed inappropriate for people with impairments to live in regular society if they were not going to be economically productive. Because of this, disabled people were rounded up into almshouses and later institutions. Susan Schweik (2009) explains in her book *The Ugly Laws: Disability in Public* that nineteenth-century American cities passed laws barring people with disabilities from being seen in public. The police during this time harassed and arrested disabled street peddlers and threw them into almshouses—designated for the old, the maimed, and the distressed—which degenerated into abusive medical institutions. These institutions housed disabled people in horrible conditions, a situation also cataloged in *Disability Incarcerated: Imprisonment and Disability in the United States and Canada*. In a chapter entitled "Self-Advocacy: The Emancipation Movement Led by People with Intellectual and Developmental Disabilities," Mark Friedman and Ruthie Marie Beckwith (2014) discuss the way individuals with the most severe disabilities were relegated to the neglected corners of institutions, where there was little supervision and horrendous abuses occurred. It is in these shadows that many people with CCN lived, since they could not advocate for themselves for a different outcome. The innovation of AAC technology became instrumental in allowing people with CCN to advocate for themselves.

The introduction of AAC technology continues to revolutionize self-expression. The technology was developed in the late 1950s and 1960s, leading to some of the first AAC speech-generative devices. These devices became available to those who needed and could afford them in the 1970s (Wendt, Quist, and Lloyd 2011). AAC provided a reliable avenue for people with CCN to express themselves, sometimes for the first time. However, some people have always struggled in learning how to use their AAC adequately. I argue that people might find it easier if other people who have CCN, and are more adept at using their AAC devices, illustrate how these tools can be utilized more effectively. AAC mentors can be adviser figures to those who are experiencing a challenge with their devices by sharing knowledge and expertise with them. The AAC mentor and mentee develop a knowledge base together as they attempt to solve life challenges and obstacles.

One challenge AAC mentors can assist young people with is education. Many children with CCN struggle in using their AAC devices because they must learn to communicate with them while also trying to excel in their education. Those who feel overwhelmed by these extra challenges might find it helpful to see older people who use AAC proficiently. A few scholarly articles have pointed out the benefits of AAC mentoring in schools, although it is not yet common. In "Mentoring as a Communication Coach in a Public School Setting," Catherine George and Faye Warren (2012) focus on Warren's work as an adult who uses AAC and mentors students newer to the technology in the Orange County Public Schools in Orlando, Florida. Warren attends class with students who use AAC and encourages them to communicate more often with their devices. Students who use AAC see her accomplishments and are motivated to emulate some of the things she does. Warren's most productive sessions with the students occur when teachers give the students preplanned discussion topics or show-and-tell activities to complete before Warren arrives in the classroom. This engagement of the students assists with her primary goal as a mentor, which is to get them to use their AAC devices in conversation with her. Because of the benefits of mentoring, schools should provide funding for these programs, so that more students with AAC can gain knowledge and skills from the experience.

Mentors should also encourage young people who use AAC to excel in school, since education leads to more opportunities. With education, specifically a college education, AAC users gain the qualifications for occupational and organizational opportunities in the community. It is important for young students who use AAC to be engaged throughout their education careers. Young students need older mentors for advice not only on educational challenges but also on challenges they may have with their teachers, aides, or fellow students. A mentor can give a student advice on social issues such as how to make friends or how to navigate negative experiences such as bullying. These are just some of the ways a mentor can provide crucial information to a student who shares their AAC educational experience.

Another way mentors who use AAC assist their mentees is with professional challenges. Disabled people in general have a low employment rate, and for people who use AAC the employment situation is even more severe. When a young person who uses AAC completes their education, they may need guidance navigating the job market. They need advice on aspects of work such as searching for appropriate jobs, applying for those jobs, preparing for job interviews, and preparing for inaccessible work conditions or even an ableist work culture. The AAC mentors have experienced their own professional successes and challenges. With their advice and knowledge, young people who use AAC can avoid some of the professional mistakes the mentors themselves made.

When AAC users broaden their presence in the workforce, possibilities for others blossom. With people who use AAC occupying more career positions, it becomes more common for people who use AAC to be seen as professionals. And when this cultural shift happens, it will allow younger AAC users and their families to envision more for their professional futures. Rising expectations will also allow people who use AAC to demand more from their employers. They will advocate for accessible and anti-ableist work environments that are conducive to AAC communication, and to the flourishing of other disabled people.

Besides advice on professional relationships, people who use AAC need mentorship on how to navigate social and personal relationships. AAC users often have challenges building social relationships because of their unique mode of communication. Interacting with someone who communicates at a slower speed with an electronic speech-generative device is sometimes disconcerting for non-users of the technology, which makes them reluctant to engage with people who use AAC. This reluctance puts the onus on people who use AAC to make others comfortable talking with them. AAC users feel pressure to initiate communication with temporarily able-bodied people. Mentors who use AAC can prepare their young mentees on ways to store instant phrases on their AAC devices along with other strategies for being more responsive. They can advise their mentees in ways to be "approachable" and assertive when meeting new people and forming new relationships. Friends are important for everyone to have, and if people who use AAC learn how to form meaningful friendships early in life, it will serve them well.

People who use AAC also need more knowledge about maintaining their existing relationships. Some people who use AAC grow distant from family and friends due to their responses to disability. Because of the historical stigmatization of people with disabilities in society, people can be ashamed and embarrassed to have a disabled person in the family. It would be good for those family members to see people who use AAC handling their business proficiently and professionally, and contributing to society. A mentor who uses AAC serves not only as a role model for students and mentees but also as an example to family members of what those students are capable of.

Mentors who use AAC can also advise their younger mentees in navigating romantic relationships. Engaging in romance has always been challenging for people living with disabilities in modern Western society. This society has a long history of secluding disabled people in institutions or in their homes, rather than seeing and engaging with them in the community. Disabled people have historically had fewer opportunities to date and build romantic relationships. For people who use AAC to speak, it can be more difficult to navigate the social norms of dating, especially since they do not have many opportunities to practice these skills. In "Sexuality and Intimacy for People with Congenital Physical and Communication Disabilities: Barriers and Facilitators," Darryl Sellwood, Pammi Raghavendra, and Paul Jewell argue,

> Relationships and sexuality have been identified as two of the essential factors that contribute to quality of life for adolescents with cerebral palsy. Forming sexual

identities and learning the etiquette of relationship building usually occurs in youth through socializing with peers. However, people with physical and communication disabilities often lack adequate sexual and relationship education in their youth. Adolescents who use AAC often lack opportunities to discuss essential topics for their development such as sexuality, intimacy and relationships with peers and support workers. The participants in Collier et al. expressed strong feelings of being deprived of information about healthy relationships, opportunities for experiencing intimate relationships and being able to express their own sexuality. The participants perceived that support workers, parents and doctors saw them as asexual and as a result, not in need of such information. (2017, 237)

People who use AAC have many challenges regarding dating and sexuality as a result of the dominant culture thinking they are asexual and dismissing their sexualities. In an effort to alleviate these challenges, a mentor can advise about what worked and did not work regarding dating and expressing sexuality. A mentor might even describe the intricacies of navigating intimate scenarios with partners, whether they be disabled or able-bodied. This know-how can only come from another person who uses AAC. A person outside the AAC user community will not have the same insight or historical knowledge about such romantic situations. A temporarily able-bodied person or a disabled person outside the AAC community has limited knowledge about how to approach someone romantically using an AAC device. It is important for people who use AAC to discuss these issues with each other and expand the knowledge base for the community.

Mentors and mentees exchange knowledge about life challenges through their camaraderie as fellow AAC users. The path is still not clearly defined for what people who use AAC are supposed to do in society, or who they are supposed to become to contribute to their communities. With AAC mentorship relationships, mentors and mentees can collectively invent new ways to live and strive in an ever-changing society. There is no denying that AAC mentorship can improve the lives of young people who use the technology. AAC mentorship programs need to be widely known, encouraged, and funded by educational and community institutions so that more students have the chance to benefit.

BIBLIOGRAPHY

Friedman, Mark, and Ruthie Marie Beckwith. 2014. "Self-Advocacy: The Emancipation Movement Led by People with Intellectual and Developmental Disabilities." In *Disability Incarcerated: Imprisonment and Disability in the United States and Canada*, edited by Liat Ben-Moshe, Chris Chapman, and Allison C. Carey, 271–294. New York: Palgrave Macmillan.

George, Catherine, and Faye Warren. 2012. "Mentoring as a Communication Coach in a Public School Setting." *Perspectives of the ASHA Special Interest Group* 21 (3): 115–121.

Hartblay, Cassandra. 2020. "Disability Expertise: Claiming Disability Anthropology." *Current Anthropology* 61 (Supplement 21): S26–S36.

Schweik, Susan M. 2009. *The Ugly Laws: Disability in Public*. New York: New York University Press. Kindle edition.

Sellwood, Darryl, Pammi Raghavendra, and Paul Jewell. 2017. "Sexuality and Intimacy for People with Congenital Physical and Communication Disabilities: Barriers and Facilitators: A Systematic Review." *Sexuality and Disability* 32 (2): 227–244.

Wendt, Oliver, Raymond W. Quist, and Lyle L. Lloyd. 2011. *Assistive Technology: Principles and Applications for Communication Disorders and Special Education*. Bingley, UK: Emerald Group.

34

Digital Spaces and the Right to Information for Deaf People during the COVID-19 Pandemic in Zimbabwe

LOVEMORE CHIDEMO, AGNESS CHINDIMBA, AND ONAI HARA

Introduction

The COVID-19 pandemic and the subsequent lockdown and restrictions significantly disrupted life as we knew it. New ways of interacting had to be found to replace face-to-face interactions. Technologies had to be adapted, and new ones developed, to cope with the demands of what has been termed the "new normal." Unfortunately the rapidity of this transformation resulted in some sections of society being left behind. In this chapter we explore the impact of the migration of interactions to online spaces on the deaf community in Zimbabwe. We examine the challenges that the deaf community face in Zimbabwe in relation to access to information, as well as the ways some digital spaces have been inclusive of the needs of deaf people. We also discuss how the deaf community has leveraged digital spaces to drive forward the deaf agenda.

Background

The coronavirus disease (COVID-19), believed to have emerged in Wuhan, China, around October 2019, soon became a global pandemic resulting in lockdowns on an unprecedented scale in virtually all countries of the world by April 2020. Global travel ground to a halt and industries shut down as governments scrambled to contain the rapid spread of the virus. As a result, many people stayed indoors and human interactions as we knew them changed. New ways of doing business and interacting emerged in the new normal. Human interactions shifted online, resulting in explosive growth of virtual meeting platforms like Zoom, Teams, and Bluejeans. While most of these platforms were already popular, the pandemic allowed them to take off as demand for interactions that did not require face-to-face communication increased. However, there are segments of society that found it difficult to adapt to the new normal, either because of poverty and lack of access to the requisite infrastructure to participate effectively, or because the new platforms were not designed with them in mind. This particularly applies to deaf people all over the world who communicate through signed languages.

The "old normal" was characterized by face-to-face interactions, as there were no fears of spreading the coronavirus. Such interactions are particularly attractive for deaf people due to the visual nature of signed languages. Before the pandemic, deaf people could obtain information from television programs, such as those on Deaf TV Zimbabwe, that were produced for the deaf and in most cases by the deaf. Where there was a need for an interpreter, one could easily be found, as there were no movement restrictions in place. For example, if a deaf person wanted to access counseling services, an interpreter could be found to assist with the communication. Services were offered physically with fewer hindrances in the old normal. Unfortunately, in the new normal, most services migrated online.

In Zimbabwe deaf people found it hard to participate in the new digital meeting places due to a number of factors, including inaccessible platforms. Most of these platforms could not accommodate sign language interpretation, they were not optimized for interpretation, or service providers either intentionally or unintentionally chose not to include interpretation. This resulted in deaf people being unable to use these platforms to access critical services like counseling and other consultations with health-care professionals. In addition, deaf people could not access information on the fast-evolving pandemic situation, thus putting them at greater risk. Inaccessible online spaces also negatively affected remote education for learners and remote work for academics.

This situation in many respects violates the human rights of deaf people, which center on sign language, sign language interpretation, bilingual education, and accessibility in all spheres of life (Haualand and Allen 2009, 9)—factors that are missing in the new normal, although strides are being made to address these gaps, largely as a result of deaf people's advocacy. The situation of inaccessible services and digital spaces for the deaf in Zimbabwe obtains notwithstanding the fact that the government has an obligation to ensure that deaf people have access to information, even—and more so—in situations of humanitarian crisis like the COVID-19 pandemic.

Normative Framework for Access to Information in Zimbabwe

Zimbabwe is a signatory to a number of international human rights instruments that guarantee freedom of opinion and access to information. These instruments include, among others, the Covenant on Civil and Political Rights, which, in article 19(2), confers rights to access to information and freedom of thought. Of particular importance in the present context is the Convention on the Rights of Persons with Disabilities that Zimbabwe signed and ratified in September 2013. Article 21(b) of the convention specifically calls on state parties to accept and facilitate the use of signed languages, and state parties are implored to encourage mass media houses, including those that provide information through the internet, to make their services accessible to people with disabilities, including deaf people. It is important to highlight that most provisions of the convention have not been domesticated, as Zimbabwe has a dualist system that requires provisions of international instruments to be specifically enacted through an act of Parliament before they can be applicable.

The Constitution of Zimbabwe has a number of provisions dealing with access to information. Section 6 accords sign language official language status, together with fifteen other languages. Official languages are languages used in government business; however, declaring a language to be official does not necessarily mean that the language must be used, although it creates an expectation that this will be so. Section 6(3)(b) of the constitution specifically requires the government and its agencies to take into account the language requirements of people affected by governmental measures or communications. This creates an obligation for the government to ensure that information on the COVID-19 pandemic, for example, is provided in formats that include sign language, which is what deaf people understand. Further provisions in the Constitution of Zimbabwe that deal with access to information include section 61, which establishes the rights of people to freedom of expression, including the right to receive and communicate ideas and other information.

Challenges Faced by Deaf People in Zimbabwe during the Pandemic

We carried out a short survey of deaf people from across Zimbabwe to establish the challenges they faced in digital spaces during the time of the pandemic. We received nineteen responses to the survey via WhatsApp. The biggest life change that the lockdowns necessitated was staying at home. Unfortunately the deaf—most of whom live with nonsigning family members—became isolated, with limited to no interaction with other deaf people or family members with whom they lived. Digital spaces therefore became a requirement for deaf people in order for them to remain in touch with their communities.

For the deaf the biggest challenge is the cost of data and access to appropriate gadgets to participate fully in online spaces. Data charges in Zimbabwe are relatively high when compared with other regional countries, and this situation is exacerbated by frequent increases in data charges. For example, the mobile network operators increased data charges by almost 100 percent in June 2020, right in the middle of the pandemic, when WhatsApp and other online spaces were the major sources of information on the rapidly developing situation. Information about the pandemic itself has not always been provided in accessible formats, particularly at the beginning of the pandemic. The sole national broadcaster, Zimbabwe Television, failed to provide sign language interpretation during COVID-19 announcements and briefings, such that it had to be taken to court to be compelled to provide interpreters at briefings.

The pandemic and lockdown resulted in the closure of most social services, including schools. Schoolchildren lost a lot of valuable study time and, in order to ameliorate the situation, schools and the government introduced radio and TV lessons. Unfortunately radio is not accessible to deaf children, and TV was not a workable alternative because of the lack of sign language interpretation. As a result, deaf learners were closed off from such platforms. Viable alternatives were WhatsApp and Zoom. However, as most deaf children are from poor families, they could not afford the data charges needed to access lectures with video. Sign language delivery of lectures requires significant investment in not just internet bandwidth but associated gadgets as well. On top of that, qualified, paid interpreters would also be required.

While deaf people had previously campaigned for accessible public spaces and services, the advent of the pandemic and the disruptions it brought in communications about the lockdown and prevention protocols reversed many of these gains. For example, service providers had been providing sign language interpreters at meetings, but virtual spaces could not easily accommodate them; thus deaf learners could not easily participate in group discussions. Some online platforms do not enable deaf people and sign language interpreters to see each other optimally or to see the teacher for lipreading or watch signing. In Zimbabwe most online learning was restricted to the WhatsApp platform in the form of text messages without any interaction in signing with the teachers. Hence deaf learners were cut off and largely left behind even though these online platforms were hailed in many sectors as a boon during the pandemic.

The pandemic seems to have accentuated inequalities of access to information and services (Redfern and Baker 2020). The migration of services from physical spaces to virtual spaces has hit the deaf community particularly hard. Those with limited experience and access to smartphones have been especially disadvantaged. The deaf have also not been considered in the many services now being offered via telephone, or via websites and other forms of online access. An example is that of gender-based violence services like counseling and helplines, which were taken online. Unfortunately these helplines do not have facilities for sign language interpreters. Because of this inaccessibility, while many deaf women may have suffered domestic violence during the lockdown period, it was not always easy for them to report it or access the postviolence services they required.

Digital Spaces and the COVID-19 Pandemic

Online platforms, particularly social media, have been described as the new agora where people meet and where most human interactions now happen (Matende and Chidemo 2018). The pandemic and the associated lockdowns only helped to accelerate the migration of human interactions online. With the new media, interactions do not need to be physical, as they can be held virtually over long distances. In response to the lockdown and pandemic restrictions, there has been a boom in demand for services like Zoom, Microsoft Teams, and others that witnessed explosive growth, even while other industries declined. Before the pandemic, deaf people were already actively participating on social media, particularly on WhatsApp through groups, video calling (for those who could afford the data fees), and one-on-one interactions. The popularity of the WhatsApp platform is driven mainly by the discounted rates, through bundled pricing, offered by all the mobile network operators in Zimbabwe. The simplicity of the WhatsApp platform and its ubiquity make it particularly accessible to deaf people in Zimbabwe. Additionally, the platform can be easily accessed from readily available mobile phones. Social media has been particularly beneficial for deaf people all over the world, including in Zimbabwe, as it helps to democratize information flow, and deaf communities thrive on social media. Deaf people can access information in sign language posted by other deaf individuals or organizations specifically targeting deaf communities. The siloed nature of information flow within deaf communities, however, increases the risk of spreading misinformation among the community, especially as it relates to the COVID-19 pandemic. This is apparent in myths surrounding the origins of the virus and the current vaccination drive. For example, it is believed that one can become a zombie after taking the vaccine. Such information is widely circulated within the deaf network, thus severely affecting the uptake of vaccines within the deaf community.

Responses by Deaf Organizations

Deaf advocacy in Zimbabwe during the pandemic has been centered on making information about the pandemic accessible. As information is being shared through online spaces, the focus has been on making these accessible and inclusive of sign language. As a result, organizations like Deaf TV Zimbabwe and Deaf Women Included have been making videos and distributing them via services like Facebook and WhatsApp. The videos are usually repurposed for different platforms, with particular emphasis on video size, to take into account those with limited access to data. The lockdown saw an explosion in online content consumption as people were confined in their homes. The growth was curtailed, to an extent, by increases in the cost of data. However, a lot of deaf-friendly content made its way onto social media. The Zimbabwe Deaf Media Trust, the producers of Deaf TV Zimbabwe, produced a number of video clips in sign language that were mainly aimed at ensuring not only that deaf people have access to information on the pandemic but also that deaf people find their place in the new normal. The Zimbabwe Deaf Media Trust is a deaf-managed nonprofit organization whose main mandate is the promotion of Zimbabwean Sign Language and ensuring that deaf people in Zimbabwe have access to information in sign language.

Many deaf organizations and individuals have found a way to leverage the new agora to advance and promote Zimbabwean Sign Language by offering online training in sign language and posting content about Zimbabwean Sign Language on social media. With many people having free time to learn a new language, the lockdown period and new media provided an opportunity for the promotion of sign language. In response to the challenges with online learning for deaf learners, and in particular a lack of learning materials in sign language, organizations like the Zimbabwe Deaf Media Trust began to trial the translation of popular stories and content into sign language, a development that should hopefully encourage the production of more content for deaf learners in sign language for use in schools, particularly for the junior classes. These stories were distributed via social media, thus reaching a wide audience, not just the deaf.

Recommendations

There is a need to set up information clearinghouses for deaf people, particularly in the face of crises like the pandemic. In addition, minimum standards need to be set that guarantee access to information and services for deaf people; this applies to public and private organizations that provide information services. The provision of interpretation services should be prioritized by the government and public broadcasters. In addition, online platforms need to be made accessible through the provision of sign language interpreters so as to ensure that such spaces are not closed off to deaf people.

Conclusion

The COVID-19 pandemic has disrupted life as we know it, and the world has adapted to meet the demands of the new normal. With COVID-19 likely to be around for some time, it appears interactions will henceforth continue to happen mostly on digital platforms. Deaf people will continue to advocate to ensure that such spaces remain accessible to them. New technologies should continue to be adopted so as to ensure that new spaces are accessible to all, including the deaf. Deaf communities should also continue to advocate for accessible digital spaces, while governments should play a leading role in ensuring that both public enterprises and private entities offering digital services for public consumption make their products and services accessible to the deaf by including sign language on all platforms.

BIBLIOGRAPHY
Haualand, Hilde, and Colin Allen. 2009. *Deaf People and Human Rights*. Helsinki: World Federation of the Deaf.

Matende, Tawanda and Chidemo, Lovemore. 2018. "Social Media the New Agora," *Daily News*, December 30, 2018. https://dailynews.co.zw/social-media-the-new-agora/.

Redfern, Paul and Baker, Kevin. 2020. "Impact of Covid-19 on Deaf people with additional problems." *SW2020-21 Covid-19 Magazine*. July 14, 2020. https://sites.google.com/sheffield.ac.uk/sw2020-21-covid19/editions/5th-edition-14-july-2020/impact-of-covid-19-on-deaf-people-with-additional-problems.

35

Crip Indigenous Storytelling across the Digital Divide

JEN DEERINWATER

Digital Divides

As the COVID-19 pandemic has run rampant across the world, humanity has become more reliant on virtual access for survival, as well as cultural and community connections and storytelling.[1] Many disabled people in the so-called United States responded to the rise of remote work and distance learning as proof of ableism.[2] Deaf, disabled, and chronically ill people have been denied remote access needs in the past, effectively shutting us out of employment and education opportunities. Only when the able-bodied had a need for widespread virtual access was it made available.

Yet non-Native members of the disability community have neglected to raise awareness of the ways racism and colonialism intersect with digital access and disability accessibility. Many are still excluded from the new online reality through a lack of telecommunications access. In the United States, 141 million people, nearly 43 percent of the population, lack home internet access at the benchmark broadband speeds set by the Federal Communications Commission (FCC) of 25 Mbps down, 3 Mbps up. This digital divide only grows exponentially for Indigenous people.

American Indians and Alaska Natives have the highest rates of disability per capita in the United States. According to the National Congress of American Indians, 24 percent of American Indians and Alaska Natives have a disability, compared with the general population at 19 percent.[3] Disability rates are greater across all ages. They tend to be higher in older populations, but the rate of disability among Native youths is also the highest of any race, at 5.9 percent of the population.[4] These rates among Native people are due in large part to the long-standing impacts of colonialism and partially due to a lack of telecommunication access.

Left to Our Own Devices

The colonizer—that is, the US government—loves to pick and choose when our tribes are sovereign nations. When it comes to health care, or ensuring we have culturally appropriate housing, schools, roads, or telecoms infrastructure, we are "sovereign nations" and left to our own devices. But when pipelines, dams, or other extractive projects are proposed to cross our lands, we're no longer treated as sovereign nations. We are trapped in the hypocrisy and genocide that colonialism has brought to our doorsteps.

According to the written testimony of Geoffrey Blackwell, chief strategy officer and general counsel for AMERIND Risk Management Corporation, the deployment of fixed terrestrial internet at benchmark speeds deemed the acceptable standard for online streaming measures are significantly lower on tribal lands.[5] This makes it difficult—if not impossible—to connect to many websites or use phone service. In 2016, only 63.9 percent of total tribal lands had these services, but the numbers vary based on location, with rural areas suffering the worst. Only 36.2 percent of rural Alaskan villages, 43.5 percent of Native Hawaiian homelands, and 31.6 percent of rural tribal areas in the continental United States had telecommunication services at these speeds. Even telephone access is low, at only 68 percent on rural reservations versus 95.5 percent for the United States.[6]

Availability versus adoption of the internet is another common theme among Indigenous communities, as high rates of poverty create barriers to true digital access. In 2016, 26.2 percent of Native people were living in poverty, so even if the internet is available nearby, they often can't afford it or devices to connect to it.[7] These numbers vary across tribal nations. However, the Oglala Sioux Tribe on the Pine Ridge Reservation in South Dakota has significantly higher poverty rates than the rest of the United States. Ninety-seven percent of Pine Ridge residents live below the US federal poverty line. According to the organization Friends of Pine Ridge Reservation, the median household income on the reservation ranges between $2,600 and $3,500 per year, and there is a 90 percent unemployment rate. This poverty has real-life consequences for survival. Based on data before the COVID-19 pandemic, with the exception of Haiti, the Pine Ridge Reservation has the lowest life expectancy in the Western Hemisphere at forty-eight years for men and fifty-two years for women.[8] According to the Centers for Disease Control, between 2019–2021 the life expectancy for Native people has dropped 6.6 years in the United States.

The expense of up-to-date devices, such as smartphones and computers, to connect to the internet also presents challenges. Brian Howard, a research and policy analyst for the American Indian Policy Institute at Arizona State University, found in the 2019 study *The State of Internet Service on Tribal Lands* that researchers had to include flip phones as an option for phone access, as one elder they spoke with still used this older model of phone.[9]

Even when surrounded by wealth, tribal nations still suffer a digital divide. Vice Chairman Lance Gumbs of the Shinnecock Indian Nation states that 60 percent of his tribal members live in poverty while surrounded by one of the wealthiest areas in the United States: the Hamptons on Long Island, New

York.[10] There's only one internet provider for Shinnecock lands. "The fact that we're being serviced by only one entity—there's a premium that they're able to charge so it's a cost consideration," said Gumbs.

The digital divide doesn't end on our reservations for the Native community. Seventy-one percent of American Indian and Alaska Native people live in urban and suburban areas. According to Matthew Rantanen, director of technology for the Southern California Tribal Chairmen's Association, there are no reliable numbers for broadband access for urban Natives, and much of the data on access in general for the United States are self-reported by the telecommunication companies themselves.[11] The high rates of poverty for urban Native communities mean many have to use free resources at libraries and community centers—which were closed or had reduced hours during COVID-19—or access the internet at a friend or family member's home.

Native American Lifelines, a small organization in Baltimore and Boston, provides community resources and limited health care to urban Natives. During the COVID-19 shutdowns, Lifelines had to set up a telehealth room at their Baltimore location so that clients would have access to phones and internet for telehealth appointments.[12] While the shutdowns are currently over, Lifelines has decided to keep the telehealth room, as there's a clear need for it going forward.

As a partial solution to the digital divide, the FCC offered its first-ever free spectrum licenses to tribal nations on February 3, 2020. According to Rantanen, the process was mired in bureaucracy and it was incredibly difficult, if not impossible, for some nations to apply.[13] Given how COVID-19 spread like wildfire throughout Indian Country, leaving many ill or dead, tribes had their hands full, and the spectrum licenses may not have been a top priority. As a result, the FCC granted a thirty-day extension, beyond the original six-month application schedule, to September 2, 2020, for tribal nations to apply. Despite urgency expressed from legislators, tribal nations, and Native organizations that the priority window be extended again due to pandemic disruptions, the FCC closed the window to apply.[14] Under the Biden administration, new applications have been accepted.[15] As of September 21, 2021, the FCC reported 270 licenses were granted to tribes, with an additional 20 applications accepted.[16]

Storytelling across the Digital Divide

Beyond telehealth access, the COVID-19 shutdowns across the country and tribal lands left many with a strong need to connect to community and culture. Andrea Delgado-Olson (Ione Band of Miwok Indians), founder and chair of Native American Women in Computing and the program manager for Systers and GHC Communities at AnitaB.org, has a goal to "connect tradition with technology." According to Delgado-Olson, the internet is allowing Native people to practice traditions like talking circles.[17] Delgado-Olson was "longing for connection" when she created an online talking circle for Native women. It brought the women together to discuss their feelings and community issues. It became so popular that Delgado-Olson said participants were meeting four times a week, sometimes up to two hours. However, many in her tribal nation lack high-speed, reliable broadband and the devices to connect to the talking circle.

The Ione Band of Miwok Indians, located in Northern California, is small, with only 750 people. Delgado-Olson said that before the pandemic, students would search for places with the internet and do their homework in parking lots. With social distancing measures, though, this stopped. Not too far from the Miwok, "smartbuses" were providing the Sacramento area with internet by serving as Wi-Fi hotspots, yet these temporary solutions to internet access are often denied to tribes.[18] Diana Cournoyer, executive director of the National Indian Education Association, stated in a briefing led by the National Congress of American Indians that 37 percent of the students at the Bureau of Indian Education schools are without internet, making online distance learning impossible and "the school year a wash."[19] "Without internet access, it doesn't matter how hard they [students] work," she said.

With Native ingenuity, there are other ways to bridge this divide and tell our crip, Indigenous stories. On July 20, 2021, I, Tony Enos, and Marcy Angeles released an original song ("Others Like Me"), music video, and panel on the arts and access for disabled and ill Indigenous people. These works were made available for free download or view on Tony's website and on YouTube. Hard-copy CDs were also made available for free for Native-led organizations and tribes to distribute to their communities. This work joins the ranks of a growing crip Indigenous movement.

The song and music video were a gift to our communities, so we wanted to ensure that our work was accessible across disabilities, geographic locations, and the digital divide. Taking this a step further in my own work, I am now researching and creating opportunities to offer hard-copy newsletters, zines, books, art, and more to our relatives who are denied internet access.

While the internet may be relatively new to humanity, storytelling is a traditional Indigenous value and one that must be continued across the generations. This includes our crip stories. Only through the fight for our full rights and tribal sovereignty will the digital divide no longer affect our ability to share our lived experiences.

NOTES

1 This piece contains segments of the following: Disability Futures Festival, "A More Inclusive Community: The Power and Presence of Indigenous Disabled Stories" panel. Ford Foundation July 20, 2021. "Pandemic and Digital Divide Threaten Accurate Census Count of Native Populations" *Truthout*. "Historic Injustice Against Native People Put Them at Greater Risk of COVID-19." *Truthout*.

2 *So-called United States* is used here to denote that this land pre-dates the United States and is Indigenous land. What is known as North America is known as Turtle Island for many Indigenous people.

3 *Disabilities.* NCAI.org (n.d.). Retrieved April 25, 2022, from https://www.ncai.org/policy-issues/education-health-human-services/disabilities.

4 Bureau, U. S. C. (2021, October 8). *Childhood Disability in the United States: 2019.* Census.gov. Retrieved April 25, 2022, from https://www.census.gov/library/publications/2021/acs/acsbr-006.html.

5 Blackwell, Geoffrey C. "Oversight Hearing on GAO Reports Relating to Broadband Internet Availability on Tribal Lands," October 3, 2018, https://www.indian.senate.gov/.

6 Donnellan, Emily S. "No Connection: The Issue of Internet on the Reservation." *American Indian Law Journal* 5, no. 2 (July 1, 2017): 362.

7 "2016 ACS Shows Stubbornly High Native American Poverty and Different Degrees of Economic Well-Being for Asian Ethnic Groups." Working Economics Blog. Economic Policy Institute, September 15, 2017.

8 American Indian Life. Running Strong for American Indian Youth. Accessed April 7, 2020. https://indianyouth.org/american-indian-life/.

9 Deerinwater, Jen R. Interview with Brian Howard. Personal, December 4, 2019.

10 Deerinwater, Jen R. Interview with Lance Gumbs. Personal, May 6, 2020.

11 Deerinwater, Jen R. Interview with Matthew Rantenen. Personal, March 26, 2020.

12 Deerinwater, Jen R. Interview with Kerry Hawk Lessard. Personal, September 8, 2021.

13 Deerinwater, Jen R. Interview with Matthew Rantenen. Personal, March 26, 2020.

14 "FCC Closes Tribal Spectrum Priority Window Despite Objections." Native Business, September 4, 2020. https://www.nativebusinessmag.com.

15 "Wireless Telecommunications Bureau Announces Additional Rural Tribal Priority Window License Applications Accepted for Filing." Allnet, September 22, 2021. https://www.allnetinsights.com/blogs.

16 "Wireless Telecommunications Bureau Encourages 2.5 GHz Rural Tribal Priority Window Applicants to Resolve Mutual Exclusivity," September 22, 2021. Federal Communications Commission. https://docs.fcc.gov.

17 Deerinwater, Jen R. Interview with Andrea Delgado-Olson. Personal, May 19, 2020.

18 The WiFi Bus Pilot Comes to an End. Sacramento Regional Transit Authority, July 1, 2020. https://www.sacrt.com.

19 "Indian Country Addresses COVID-19," March 20, 2020. National Congress of American Indians. https://www.ncai.org/.

BIBLIOGRAPHY

Deerinwater, Jen. 2020a. "Historic Injustices against Native People Put Them at Greater Risk of COVID-19." *Truthout*, April 3, 2020. https://truthout.org/articles/historic-injustices-against-native-people-put-them-at-greater-risk-of-covid-19/.

Deerinwater, Jen. 2020b. "Pandemic and Digital Divide Threaten Accurate Census Count of Native Populations." *Truthout*, June 5, 2020. https://truthout.org/articles/pandemic-and-digital-divide-threaten-accurate-census-count-of-native-populations/.

Ford Foundation. 2021. "A More Inclusive Community: The Power and Presence of Indigenous Disabled Stories." Panel at the Disability Futures Virtual Festival, July 20, 2021.

ACKNOWLEDGMENTS

We thank the authors for taking on this project during a period of worry and many other demands—for meeting and composing and revising with us over three years. It has been sustaining to think and write together. For those who were not able to accept our invitation, your words and names appear across these pages.

Thank you to Emily Lim Rogers and Destiny Lopez for organizing many aspects of the collection with us. We are grateful to Alice Wong, Eunjung Kim, and Greta LaFleur for recommending authors at an early stage, to Nirmala Erevelles for feedback at an author workshop, and to Margaret Price for her generous comments on the manuscript. We'd also like to thank our anonymous reviewers for their time and suggestions, as well as Eric Zinner, Furqan Sayeed, and everyone at New York University Press who has supported this project and collaborated with us on aspects of publishing accessibility. Special gratitude goes to our meticulous copyeditor, Ashley Moore, and our insightful project manager, Christine Marra.

We thank the NYU Center for the Humanities for a working group grant that paid the authors to get together online for a series of workshops, and for a publication subvention grant to hire a Braille proofreader for the ebook version. The NYU Center for Disability Studies provided an incomparable home for this book.

We worked closely with Amari Sanchez, Emaline Kelso, and Juliet Kelso, whether they were in the same room or thousands of miles away. Thank you for your access intimacy and other forms of support.

ABOUT THE AUTHORS

KELSIE ACTON is an independent researcher in access and the performing arts and a member of the Critical Design Lab. She is the plain language translator of *McSweeney's* "The Audio Issue" and Alice Wong's *Year of the Tiger.*

CAMERON AWKWARD-RICH is assistant professor of women, gender, and sexuality studies at the University of Massachusetts Amherst and the author of *The Terrible We: Thinking with Trans Maladjustment* (2022).

SAM BARCLAY is a product designer based in London who has worked at Make architects, IDEO, and NB Studio. His design career started in graphic design where he sharpened his knowledge in type and typography. Since then he has become interested in the logic of designing for digital products, with typography and accessibility at the forefront of his thinking. He is the author of the book *I Wonder What it's Like to be Dyslexic*, featured in the Cooper Hewitt *Access+Ability* exhibition.

KRISTEN BOWEN is a Ph.D. graduate in information science from the University of North Carolina at Chapel Hill. She is a UX researcher who advocates for conducting user-centered investigations into the social media & technological experiences of various populations. Her other works include articles published in *JMIR Formative Research* and *In the Library with the Lead Pipe.*

LA MARR JURELLE BRUCE is associate professor of American studies at the University of Maryland, where he is also affiliate faculty in the Harriet Tubman Department of Women, Gender and Sexuality Studies and the Department of African American Studies. He is the author of *How to Go Mad without Losing Your Mind: Madness and Black Radical Creativity* (2021).

TERESA BLANKMEYER BURKE is professor of philosophy at Gallaudet University. She is the coeditor of the *Journal of Philosophy of Disability*, and her recent work in Deaf studies and philosophy has been published in the *American Journal of Bioethics* and *Kennedy Institute of Ethics Journal*, among others.

PAUL CONSTABLE CALCOTT is a recognized Australian Aboriginal artist and polio survivor from the Wiradjuri Nation, through his father. Paul is known for his storytelling through art, with artworks in collections internationally, including the Australian Embassy in Switzerland.

MEL Y. CHEN is Richard and Rhoda Goldman Distinguished Chair in Undergraduate and Interdisciplinary Studies, Associate Professor of Gender and Women's Studies, and Director of the Center for the Study of Sexual Culture at the University of California, Berkeley. They are the author of *Animacies: Biopolitics, Racial Mattering, and Queer Affect* (2012) and coeditor of *Crip Genealogies*.

LOVEMORE CHIDEMO is a deaf rights activist and founding executive director of the Zimbabwe Deaf Media Trust and Deaf TV Zimbabwe. Lovemore has an MPhil in disability rights from the University of Pretoria. His work involves, among other things, making information accessible to deaf communities in Zimbabwe and research into deaf issues in Zimbabwe.

AGNESS CHINDIMBA is founder and director of Deaf Women Included, a grassroots organization working with deaf women across Zimbabwe. She is a disability and women's rights activist and was the recipient of the Mandela Washington Fellowship for Young African Leaders in 2016.

JOHN LEE CLARK is a DeafBlind writer and Protactile educator based in Saint Paul, Minnesota. His writing includes *How to Communicate* (2022) and *Where I Stand: On the Signing Community and My DeafBlind Experience* (2014).

JEN DEERINWATER (Cherokee Nation) is founding executive director of Crushing Colonialism and a 2020 Disability Futures fellow. She is a contributor at *Truthout* and the coeditor of *Sacred and Subversive*.

FAYE GINSBURG (see Fanya Rappburg)

AIMI HAMRAIE is associate professor of medicine, health, and society and American studies at Vanderbilt University and the director of the Critical Design Lab. They are the author of *Building Access: Universal Design and the Politics of Disability* (2017). They are also the host of the *Contra** podcast on disability and design.

ONAI HARA is a qualified social worker and a sign language interpreter passionate about ensuring access to information for the deaf community in Zimbabwe. She has worked with numerous organizations, including the Zimbabwe Feminist Forum and the Zimbabwe Deaf Media Trust.

LOUISE HICKMAN is a research associate at the Minderoo Centre of Technology and Democracy, University of Cambridge. Her research draws on critical disability studies, feminist labor studies, and science and technology studies to examine the historical conditions of access work, and her most recent writing was published in the *Avery Review*.

MOHAIMINUL ISLAM is a current PhD student in the Department of English at Pondicherry University, India. His research interests include diaspora, disability, and translation studies. His recent coauthored paper "Text as a Cultural Archive: A Close Reading of Madan Vasishta's *Deaf in Delhi: A Memoir*" was published in the *Journal of Literary and Cultural Disability Studies*.

ISOLATION NATION was a project undertaken by a collective of neurodivergent and intellectually disabled artists in the northeastern United States during the first year of the COVID-19 pandemic. Its members spanned the spectrums of age, gender, socioeconomic status, race, and disability. Isolation Nation includes Alex Aerni, Arianna Priddle, Brad Goldman, Cathy James, EZ, JCW (Jordan), Johnny Mattei, Maria Zulic, Max Maven, MC, Michael Gluzman, Michael John Vecchio (Mike), Paris Victoria, Rayna, Uriel Levitt, and WS.

ASA ITO is director of the Future of Humanity Research Center at the Tokyo Institute of Technology's Institute of Innovative Research. She is the author of *Me no mienai hito wa sekai wo do miteiru no ka* (How do people without sight see the world?) and *Domoru karada* (The stuttering body).

UJJWAL JANA is a professor in the Department of English at Delhi University, India. His areas of interests are Indian poetics, translation studies, and digital humanities. He is the coeditor of *The Green Symphony: Essays in Ecocriticism* (2011), *Ecological Criticism for Our Times: Literature, Nature and Critical Inquiry* (2011), and *Subaltern Vision: A Study in Postcolonial Indian English Text* (2012). His recent coauthored paper "Text as a Cultural Archive: A Close Reading of Madan Vasishta's *Deaf in Delhi: A Memoir*" was published in the *Journal of Literary and Cultural Disability Studies*.

KEITH JONES is president and CEO of SoulTouchin' Experiences, an organization focusing on issues of access, inclusion, and empowerment. In addition to his policy and social justice work, Jones is a cofounder of Krip-Hop Nation, an international collective of artists with disabilities that was a 2021 Emmy recipient.

ALISON KAFER is Embrey Associate Professor of Women's and Gender Studies at the University of Texas–Austin and the coeditor of *Crip Genealogies*. She is the author of *Feminist, Queer, Crip* (2013), and her work has also appeared in *Disability Studies Quarterly* and *Feminist Disability Studies*, among others.

MIMI KHÚC is a writer, scholar, and teacher of things unwell, and an adjunct lecturer at Georgetown University. Her work includes *Open in Emergency,* a hybrid book-arts project decolonizing Asian American mental health; the Asian American Tarot, a reimagined deck of tarot cards; and the Open in Emergency Initiative, an ongoing national project developing mental health arts programming with universities and community spaces. Her forthcoming creative-critical book on mental health and a pedagogy of unwellness, *dear elia: Letters from the Asian American Abyss,* is a genre-bending deep dive into the depths of Asian American unwellness at the intersections of ableism, model minoritization, and the university, and an exploration of new approaches to collective care.

GEORGINA KLEEGE is emerita professor of English at the University of California, Berkeley. She is the author of *Sight Unseen* (1999), her collection of personal essays, and her most recent book is *More Than Meets the Eye: What Blindness Brings to Art* (2017).

RACHEL KUO is assistant professor of media and cinema studies at the University of Illinois Urbana-Champaign and the coeditor of the Critical Race and Digital Studies book series at New York University Press. She is also a cofounder of the Asian American Feminist Collective.

BRI M. is the creator and executive producer of *POWER NOT PITY,* a podcast about the lives of disabled people of color. Bri has contributed to many conversations about disability, race and gender within the podcasting industry and beyond. Zir work has also been featured in *Forbes Magazine, Colorlines,* and *Disability Visibility Project* to name a few.

LAURA MAULDIN is associate professor in women's, gender, and sexuality studies and human development and family sciences at the University of Connecticut. She is the author of *Made to Hear: Cochlear Implants and Raising Deaf Children* (2016). Her current research on caregiving was supported by the Social Science Research Council and a fellowship at the University of Connecticut Humanities Institute. She has a forthcoming book on the politics of disability and the US care crisis that will be published by Ecco in early 2025.

LATEEF H. MCLEOD is a graduate student in the Anthropology and Social Change doctoral program at the California Institute of Integral Studies in San Francisco. He is the author of *A Declaration of a Body of Love* (2010), and *Whispers of Krip Love, Shouts of Krip Revolution* (2020), and he is coauthor of *Studies in Brotherly Love* (2022). He is also a coauthor of a textbook entitled *Supporting Individuals Who Use Augmentative and Alternative Communication: Breaking Down Opportunity Barriers* (2023).

ROBERT MCRUER is professor of English at George Washington University. He is the author of *Crip Times: Disability, Globalization, and Resistance* (2018) and *Crip Theory: Cultural Signs of Queerness and Disability* (2006).

MARA MILLS is associate professor in the Department of Media, Culture, and Communication at New York University, where she cofounded and codirects the NYU Center for Disability Studies. She is also cofounder and editorial board member of the journal *Catalyst: Feminism, Theory, Technoscience*. She is the coeditor of *Testing Hearing: The Making of Modern Aurality* (2020) and (with Rebecca Sanchez) the republication of Pauline Leader's *And No Birds Sing* (2016).

LEROY F. MOORE JR. is founder of Krip-Hop Nation, which was a 2021 Emmy award recipient. Moore was also a founding member of the National Black Disability Coalition and an activist around police brutality against people with disabilities. His cultural work includes the film documentary *Where Is Hope: The Art of Murder*, the Krip-Hop graphic novel series, and the children's book *Black Disabled Art History 101* (2017). He is currently a PhD student in the Anthropology department at UCLA and an active member of the UCLA Hip Hop Studies Working Group.

XUAN THUY NGUYEN is associate professor in the Institute of Interdisciplinary Studies and the Feminist Institute for Social Transformation at Carleton University. She is the project director of the Partnership Development Project funded by the Social Sciences and Humanities Research Council of Canada. She is author of *The Journey to Inclusion* (2015), and her work has been published in journals including *Disability and Society* and the *Canadian Journal of Disability Studies*.

ALEXIS PADILLA is director of research at the Disability Policy Consortium and is an adjunct faculty member at Eastern Washington University's Department of Social Work, in the disability studies program. He is the author of *Disability, Intersectional Agency and Latinx Identity* (2021), as well as the coauthor of *Humanizing Disability in Mathematics Education* (2019).

LAURENCE RALPH is professor of anthropology at Princeton University and the director of the Center on Transnational Policing. He is the author of *Torture Letters: Reckoning with Police Violence* (2020) and *Renegade Dreams: Living through Injury in Gangland Chicago* (2014), the latter of which received the C. Wright Mills Award from the Society for the Study of Social Problems in 2015.

RAYNA RAPP (see Fanya Rappburg)

FANYA RAPPBURG is a collaborative identity of two New York University anthropologists and disability studies scholar-advocates, Faye Ginsburg and Rayna Rapp. They have coauthored numerous academic and popular articles, edited the award-winning collection *Conceiving the New World Order: The Global Politics of Reproduction*, and most recently edited "Disability/Anthropology," a special issue of the flagship journal *Current Anthropology*. Rappburg's current project is a book on the reshaping of public culture and everyday life since the Americans with Disabilities Act.

EMILY LIM ROGERS is a postdoctoral fellow in disability studies at the Cogut Institute for the Humanities, Brown University. Her work has been published in *Medical Anthropology Quarterly*, and she is currently working on a book project, *Biomedicine's Binds: ME/CFS, Patient Activism, and the Work of Debility*.

STEPHANIE S. ROSEN is director of accessibility and librarian for disability studies at the University of Michigan Library. She is the author of *Accessibility & Publishing* (2018), and her essays on disability, libraries, and access have been published in *In the Library with the Lead Pipe*, *The Scholarly Kitchen*, and elsewhere.

REBECCA SANCHEZ is professor of English and director of the Disability Studies Program at Fordham University. She is the author of *Deafening Modernism: Embodied Language and Visual Poetics in American Literature* (2015) and (with Mara Mills) the coeditor of the republication of Pauline Leader's *And No Birds Sing* (2016).

ELLEN SAMUELS is professor of gender and women's studies and English at the University of Wisconsin–Madison. Her most recent book is *Hypermobilities* (2021), and she is also the author of *Fantasies of Identification: Disability, Gender, Race* (2014).

HELEN SELSDON was the archivist for the American Foundation for the Blind from 2002–2021. During that time, she created online exhibits about *Helen Keller, Anne Sullivan Macy* and *Louis Braille*. She curated *Helen Keller: A Daring Adventure*, an exhibit located at AFB's former headquarters in NYC. Selsdon oversaw the Helen Keller Archive Digitization Project, creating a fully accessible digital archive. As an archival consultant Selsdon processed collections and created exhibits for a variety of organizations and a family archive including Pfizer Pharmaceutical company, the Whitney Museum of American Art, and the Mary Coolidge Rentschler manuscript collection.

FINNEGAN SHANNON is a project-based artist. Some of their recent work includes *Anti-Stairs Club Lounge,* an ongoing project that gathers people together who share an aversion to stairs; *Alt Text as Poetry,* a collaboration with Bojana Coklyat that explores the expressive potential of image description; and *Do You Want Us Here or Not,* a series of benches and cushions designed for exhibition spaces.

JAIPREET VIRDI is associate professor in the Department of History at the University of Delaware. She is the author of *Hearing Happiness: Deafness Cures in History* (2020) and the coeditor of *Disability and the Victorians: Attitudes, Interventions, Legacies* (2020).

LAURA J. WERNICK is associate professor at the Fordham University Graduate School of Social Service and a lifelong organizer and activist. Their work has been published in the *Journal of Community Psychology, Research on Social Work Practice,* and many other academic journals.

JEN WHITE-JOHNSON is an Afro-Latina, Disabled Parent, Design Activist, and Art Educator. Her design practice is rooted in the intersection of content and caregiving with an emphasis on redesigning ableist visual culture. Her design and photo work have been featured in the *New York Times,* CNN, the *Washington Post,* among other publications, and her client list includes Twitter, Target, Converse. In 2020 she was an honoree on the Diversability's D-30 Disability Impact List and in 2021 Jen was listed as one of today.com 20 Latina artists to watch. Jen has an MFA in Graphic Design from the Maryland Institute College of Art. She was born in Washington D.C. and currently lives in Baltimore with her husband and 10-year-old son.

ZOË H. WOOL is assistant professor in the Department of Anthropology at the University of Toronto, where she also directs the TWIG Research Kitchen. She is the author of *After War: The Weight of Life at Walter Reed* (2015), and her writing has been published in journals including *Medical Anthropology Quarterly, American Ethnologist, Catalyst: Feminism, Theory, Technoscience,* and *Cultural Anthropology.*

CYNTHIA WU is a professor of gender studies and Asian American studies and a faculty affiliate in American studies at Indiana University. She is the author or editor of three books, most recently *Sex, Identity, Aesthetics: The Work of Tobin Siebers and Disability Studies* (2021).

M. REMI YERGEAU is associate professor of digital studies and English at the University of Michigan. They are the author of *Authoring Autism: On Rhetoric and Neurological Queerness* (2017).

INDEX

Index entries were generated collectively by the authors.

Ingram Content Group UK Ltd.
Milton Keynes UK
UKHW032112290623
424295UK00006B/85